NINETEEN WEEKS

Books by Norman Moss

*Men Who Play God: The Story of the H-Bomb
and How the World Came to Live with It*

A British-American Dictionary

The Pleasures of Deception

The Politics of Uranium

*Klaus Fuchs: The Man Who Stole the
Atom Bomb*

*Managing the Planet: The Politics of the
New Millennium*

*Nineteen Weeks: America, Britain, and the
Fateful Summer of 1940*

NINETEEN WEEKS

AMERICA, BRITAIN, AND THE FATEFUL SUMMER OF 1940

NORMAN MOSS

HOUGHTON MIFFLIN COMPANY

BOSTON • NEW YORK

2003

For information about permission to reproduce selections from
this book, write to Permissions, Houghton Mifflin Company,
215 Park Avenue South, New York, New York 10003.

Visit our Web site: www.houghtonmifflinbooks.com.

Library of Congress Cataloging-in-Publication Data
Moss, Norman.
Nineteen weeks : America, Britain, and the fateful summer
of 1940 / Norman Moss.
p.   cm.
Includes bibliographical references and index.
ISBN 978-0-618-49220-6
1. World War, 1939–1945. 2. Great Britain—Military relations
—United States. 3. United States—Military relations—
Great Britain. I. Title: 19 weeks. II. Title.
D755.2.M67 2003
940.53—dc21   2002192159

Printed in the United States of America

Book design by Victoria Hartman

QUM 10 9 8 7 6 5 4 3 2 1

The lines from "Rum and Coca Cola" (music by Lord Invader, lyrics by Morey
Amsterdam) are reprinted by permission of International Music Publications.
The lines from "The Last Time I Saw Paris" (words and music by Jerome Kern,
Oscar Hammerstein) copyright © 1941 by Universal-Polygram International
Publishing, Inc. (ASCAP), international copyright secured, all rights reserved,
are reprinted by permission of Universal-Polygram International.

FOR TONY AND PAUL

CONTENTS

CONTENTS

ACKNOWLEDGMENTS

A NUMBER OF PEOPLE helped me during the writing of this book and deserve my thanks. My agent, Jill Grinberg, believed in the project when I first put it to her and helped get it going in the best possible way. At Houghton Mifflin my editor, Eric Chinski, handled my author's ego sensitively and made helpful suggestions, and copy editor Gary Hamel saved me from some embarrassing errors. I received help from the staffs of several libraries and research centers; in particular, the staff at the National Archives in College Park, Maryland, found some documents when I had only the vaguest idea what I was looking for. James Freund lent me a college thesis, Professor Frederick Rudolph of Williams College lent some papers on campus feeling in 1940, and Mrs. Hazel Hucker lent some family letters that proved useful. My friends Murray and Mary Drabkin provided hospitality and a base in Washington, D.C. And my wife, Hilary, provided unwavering support and encouragement.

We fight by ourselves alone. But we do not fight *for* ourselves alone.

— Winston Churchill to Parliament, July 14, 1940

What a wonderful thing it will be if these blokes do win the war. They will be bankrupt but entitled to almost unlimited respect.

— U.S. military attaché Raymond E. Lee, London, July 30, 1940

We are living as people lived during the French Revolution — every day is a document, every hour history.

— Sir Henry Channon, M.P., June 10, 1940

The American people mistook our sheltered position behind the British fleet and British continental diplomacy for the results of superior American wisdom and virtue in refraining from interfering with the sordid differences of the Old World.

— George F. Kennan, *American Diplomacy 1900–1950*

NINETEEN WEEKS

INTRODUCTION

The world changed forever during nineteen weeks in the spring and summer of 1940. Nazi Germany conquered France, Belgium, and Holland in one of the most astonishing military victories in history. Britain faced the possibility — some said the likelihood — of defeat. Americans felt for the first time since the birth of the republic that events in Europe threatened their own safety. In the last weeks of the summer the Royal Air Force and a determined British population turned back the most immediate threat of invasion, and the United States committed itself to Britain's defense. This commitment introduced a change in the policy the United States had pursued since George Washington's day and began the country's permanent involvement in the affairs of Europe.

The period can be dated precisely. On May 10, Germany launched its blitzkrieg and Winston Churchill became British prime minister. In the second and third week of September the tide was turned in the Battle of Britain, Germany called off its plan to invade Britain, and the United States supplied Britain with fifty destroyers and received bases in the British West Indies and Newfoundland.

In September of that year Hitler offered Britain a compromise peace, and Britain rejected it out of hand. Hitler was baffled. His deputy fuehrer, Rudolf Hess, took this up with a university lecturer in geography and occasional journalist named Albrecht Haushofer. The two men knew each other because Haushofer's father, Karl Haushofer, a military man and academic, had been Hess's mentor at university, and his ideas on geopolitics had influenced Nazi thinking. Albrecht Haushofer, he knew, had traveled widely and knew Britain well.

Hess pointed to the deal over the West Indies bases and said it seemed that Britain, instead of accepting a reasonable peace offer from Hitler that would have left its empire intact, was prepared to hand over its empire to the United States and bankrupt itself in order to continue the war. Why was this?

Haushofer recorded the conversation in his diary. He wrote: "My reply was: because Roosevelt is a man who represents a worldview and a way of life that the Englishman thinks he understands, and to which he can become accustomed, even where it does not seem to be to his liking. Perhaps he fools himself, but that at any rate is what he believes. A man like Churchill, himself half-American, is convinced of this. This feeling pervades the workers no less than the plutocrats. The Fuehrer, on the other hand, represents a point of view which is quite alien to the Englishman, and which he believes he detests." (Haushofer was executed by the Gestapo in the last days of the war.)

Haushofer offered an explanation not in terms of realpolitik but in terms of national sentiment. And he was right. Usually, when terms like "defending democracy" and "friendship" are used in international relations, they cloak motivations of national self-interest. But this was one of those rare occasions in which national feelings about such things were important. British and American attitudes to democracy, to dictatorship, and to each other, both among those in government and the general public, were crucial in determining their countries' policies.

But Hess was also right. By continuing the war, Britain was indeed ensuring that it would become something close to bankrupt and that its imperial power would pass to the United States. Britain ended the war greatly weakened, while America emerged as the strongest power, engaged with the entire world.

Churchill must have been aware that at the least this was a possibility. He knew what most British people did not know: Britain could not afford to continue the war for long, let alone win it, without American economic help. It followed that continuing to resist Germany would mean sacrificing its economic independence and therefore, in the long run, its position as a world power. Although he fought hard against American encroachments, his gut reaction was to accept this rather than a Europe ruled by Nazi Germany. He belonged to an aristocratic class that laid great store by the commonality of values and principles between Britain and America. But most British people would have agreed with his choice.

One does not have to believe in the "great man" theory of history to see that the events of that summer turned on the decisions, predilections, viewpoints, and even personalities of three men: Churchill, Roosevelt, and Hitler. Hitler ruled Germany as a dictator as few men have ruled in modern times, deciding alone the issues of war and peace. Churchill ensured that Britain would fight on when the odds against it were overwhelming. Roosevelt guided American policy and American opinion, although not alone and not without a push from events at home and abroad.

This was one of those rare periods in which the importance of what was happening was starkly apparent at the time. It was clear to the British public, suffering under bombing and watching air battles in the skies above their cities. It was clear to President Roosevelt and those who were trying to alert that part of the American public that was not yet convinced that what was happening across the Atlantic should concern them. And it was clear to Winston Churchill.

In August 1940, the king of Sweden suggested mediation between Britain and Nazi Germany. Foreign Office officials produced a carefully crafted reply, leaving options open, and sent it to Churchill for approval. Churchill's comment was a private memo to an official, not intended for publication. He said the contents of the proposed reply "appear to me to err in trying to be too clever, and to enter into refinements of policy unsuited to the tragic simplicity and grandeur of the times, and the issues at stake."

1

POSTWAR

World War One cast a long shadow over Europe in the 1920s and '30s. Some 615,000 British men and women died between 1914 and 1918, and many more returned wounded or maimed, constant reminders of the war. Every village green had its war memorial, and they are there still, usually a stone or granite cross or slab, bearing the names of the young men of the village who went away and did not return, often, heartbreakingly, two or three family names the same. Railroad stations, public buildings, even major corporations all had and still have on their walls granite plaques with the names of employees who, as it is said, gave their lives. The two-minute silence of remembrance was observed solemnly at 11 o'clock on November 11, the eleventh hour of the eleventh day of the eleventh month. Business stopped and people fell silent to remember the war dead.

The war changed Britain in many ways. Britain entered the war the world's biggest creditor nation; when the war ended, most of its overseas assets had been sold and it was in debt to the United States. It was no longer the world's economic powerhouse. Its empire was larger, for Britain took over some of the Arab world from the Ottoman Empire, but it was weakened economically.

Other nations suffered even more. France lost 1.3 million men, 27 percent of all men between the ages of eighteen and twenty-seven, and 7 percent of its territory was devastated. Nearly two million Germans were killed, and two million Russians before Russia quit the war in 1917.

Its effect on people's minds was all the greater because it came as a shock. No one knew there could be such a war. The century before 1914 had seen the greatest growth in wealth in history. Populations, resources, and machine power had all increased many times over. All were available to be poured into a war not just of armies but of whole nations, which went until one after another was exhausted.

Nothing had prepared people for the war. There was no contemporary literature of war to match the realistic memoirs, novels, and poems that were to come out of World War One. Most images of war were of patriotic adventure, of brave men in splendid uniforms, of charges and retreats, of gallant deeds and valiant deaths. When the war came in August 1914, crowds in Berlin and Paris cheered. In Britain, which unlike the Continental countries had never had conscription and had never maintained a large army, men rushed to enlist, eager to see action before it was over. The poet Rupert Brooke exulted at the opportunity for youth to prove itself. "Thank God that he has matched us to this hour," he wrote.

The war was fought on several fronts and at sea, and for the first three years the Germans were heavily engaged in Russia. But for the majority of British, French, Germans, and Americans who took part, the war was the Western front, two lines of trenches that separated the Allied and German armies, in which millions of men lived and died in mud and filth for four years. It was a uniquely static war fought over a small area of France and Belgium.

The battlefield was a symmetrical one. The trenches on the Allied side looked much like those on the German side, and the men in them lived the same lives exposed to the same dangers and the same horrors. This gave rise to a sense, particularly after the war, that there was another division besides that of the two armies, a division between those at the front, on both sides, linked by a common experience, and those back home who had sent them there, or cheered them on, ignorant of what they were enduring, either through naiveté or callous indifference.

One of the most widely read war novels was by a German, Erich Maria Remarque: *All Quiet on the Western Front*. It was a bestseller in many countries. British, French, and American veterans as well as Germans could identify with the protagonist's experiences in the trenches, and also with his disgust when he went home on leave and saw the patriotic bombast and glorified images with which schoolboys were being fed. Even Rudyard Kipling, that most patriotic of poets, whose only son was killed on his first day on the Western front, could write in 1919, in the persona of a dead soldier, "If any question why we died / Tell them 'Because our fathers lied.' "

Governments had lied to their publics, it was now clear. The Germans had not cut off the hands of Belgian children, as British newspapers reported, nor had they struck a medal to commemorate the sinking of the *Lusitania*. The British had schemed to get America into the war. While professing noble aims, the Allied powers had been concluding secret treaties carving up the territories to be wrested from the defeated. The war was widely regarded as either a fraud perpetrated on gullible publics to turn them into cannon fodder, or else a mistake, the inevitable result of the system of alliances which had dragged the nations in one after another like mountain climbers roped together. (This ignores the aggressive designs of the kaiser's Germany, some of which only came to light in documents uncovered in the 1950s.)

The war produced some fine literature — poetry, novels, and memoirs, written with a brutal realism. In the works of fiction particularly, the war was seen not as a dramatic struggle but as industrialized slaughter, a destructive and dehumanizing process that reduced men to a mass, "these unheroic dead who fed the guns," in the words of the poet Siegfried Sassoon. These spoke to a generation across national borders. They were a reaction against the values that had taken young men willingly to war.

The war shattered the belief in progress and rationality that had prevailed in European culture since the seventeenth century and the Enlightenment, and this was much more so in Europe than in the United States. The British scientist Freeman Dyson, when he first visited America in 1947, found that American students "lacked the tragic sense of life which was deeply ingrained in every European of my generation," and which stemmed, he said, not from the Second World War but the First.

To some, the answer to war lay in the League of Nations, created in 1920. This body would ensure that international life was regulated by laws much as civil life is, and that nations would band together to enforce the law and punish the transgressor. A public opinion poll in Britain in 1935 showed that 78 percent thought that supporting the League was the best way to preserve the peace. Others rejected war entirely. In Britain 130,000 people joined the Peace Pledge Union, promising never to fight another war.

In 1934 the Oxford Union, the university debating society that was and is a training ground of Britain's future leaders, voted for the proposition "That this house will never again fight for King and country." This sent shock waves through the country, and produced anxious editorials about the moral fiber of the nation's youth. But the students were rejecting, not all war, but the simple-minded patriotism that impelled young men to march off in 1914.

Most people in Britain supported the League of Nations and collective security, but they were reluctant to rearm. Armaments were deemed to be bad because they meant preparations for war, as well as spending money that could otherwise be used to improve people's lives. Socialists and Communists called for a stand against the fascism that was emerging in Europe, but they also voted against increasing armaments budgets. One slogan seen frequently on the Left was "Against Fascism and War." Soon, people would have to decide which they opposed more.

The American experience of World War One was different. Americans fought and died, but American losses were a fraction of those of the European countries, fifty-three thousand killed. It was a year after America entered the war in April 1917 before American troops went into combat. Two million American soldiers went to France, but fewer than a million saw combat, and most of those for only a few weeks. Many young Americans who did not get into combat felt, like F. Scott Fitzgerald, that they had missed a great adventure.

The United States entered the war for more noble reasons than selfish gain, or so President Woodrow Wilson insisted, and it maintained a lofty detachment from the war aims of Britain and France. It did not become one of the allies but a cobelligerent. Official communications referred to "the Allies and associated powers." American troops were not placed under the Allied command. Wilson enunciated America's war aims in the Fourteen Points, which called for a settlement that would not be a victors' peace but would establish a just international order. The United States had entered the arena, but it was going to change the game, to raise standards to a higher moral level.

The League of Nations was to be a cornerstone of this new order. But the U.S. Senate would not ratify American membership in the League. The senators were willing to go along with most aspects but were not willing to commit the United States to collective action, and Wilson, a stubborn, willful man, demanded an all-or-nothing response. Even so, a majority of senators voted for the treaty — something that is usually forgotten — but not enough to give it the two-thirds majority required. In the event, the nations that committed themselves to take collective action against an aggressor did not do so anyway.

If the war was widely seen to be a mistake, the peace certainly was. The Germans had asked for an armistice on the basis of Wilson's Fourteen Points, but the Allied powers had suffered as America had not, and they were in a mood to extract retribution.

The Versailles Treaty, which the Allies imposed on Germany, required Germany to accept sole responsibility for starting the war and to pay huge reparations to France and Britain. Germany had to give back Alsace and Lorraine, the two territories it had taken from France in 1871. It was made to disarm and to have only a small army and no air force. The Rhineland, the area bordering on France from which invading armies had come in 1870 and 1914, was to be demilitarized, for what France wanted above all else was security from its larger neighbor. Germany had to give up part of its eastern territory to the newly created Poland, and its few colonies in Africa and the Pacific were taken away. France, which had suffered most among its enemies and was the most vindictive, added to Germany's humiliation in 1923 by sending an occupation force into the Rhineland because Germany had not paid some of its reparations. Germany was acquiring victim status.

The reparations terms generated enormous resentment in Germany but most reparations were never paid. Nonetheless, Germans blamed their economic and other troubles on the Versailles Treaty. One German politician at least was frank in his intention to exploit the national resentment: "What a use could be made of the Treaty of Versailles . . . How each one of the points of that treaty could be branded in the hearts and minds of the German people until sixty million men and women find their souls aflame with a feeling of rage and shame, and a torrent of fire bursts forth as from a furnace, and a will of steel is forged from it," Hitler wrote in *Mein Kampf*.

At Versailles, the leaders of the victor nations invented new countries out of the pieces of the shattered Austro-Hungarian and Ottoman empires. Austria, no longer the head of an empire, was now a republic, a small country of 8 million people. The Versailles Treaty banned its union with Germany, which would have strengthened Germany. In the new countries, nationalities and ethnic groups were intermingled. Czechoslovakia, Yugoslavia, and the Balkan states all had ethnic and linguistic minorities, potential causes of discord for those who wanted to exploit them.

As America made war separately, so it also made peace separately. Since the Senate had rejected the Treaty of Versailles, America had to conclude its own peace with Germany. The treaty was signed by American and German representatives in 1921 almost furtively, in contrast to the ceremonial signing by the other powers in the Palace of Versailles. Ellis Loring Dressel, a diplomat who held the title of U.S. Commissioner for Germany, and four American officials signed the peace treaty at the German Foreign Ministry on August 25, along with the German foreign minister, Friedrich Rosen. No announcement was made in advance.

In 1920 the American people elected as president Warren Harding, who, unlike Woodrow Wilson, had no ambitious plans for America or for the world. In his inaugural address Harding said: "Our policy is non-involvement in Old World Affairs . . . This is not selfishness; it is sanctity. It is not suspicion of others; it is patriotic adherence to the things which made us what we are today." This was the feeling of most Americans. Isolation from the affairs of Europe was the natural state of things, part of what made America a special country. Harding promised the country normalcy, and normalcy meant distance from Europe's untidy politics.

One issue left over from the war was the question of war debts. The U.S. government had loaned money to the Allies. The Allies were slow in paying it back, partly because they counted on reparations from Germany to pay it. Britain had loaned money to the other allies and agreed to pay the United States when its own loans were repaid. Truth to tell, Europeans did not feel indebted to the United States, so great were their losses in lives and wealth sacrificed for the common cause compared to America's. Several schemes for debt repayment were floated, and then in 1932 the remaining debts were written off along with

German reparations. But the issue rankled with many Americans and was seen as one more reason not to get involved with those ungrateful Europeans.

To reduce competition in armaments, the United States, Britain, and Japan reached an agreement on naval disarmament in Washington in 1922. They agreed to maintain warship levels at a ratio of five-five-three, with the United States and Britain having five major warships to every three of Japan's. This showed how much Britain had been weakened by the war. Before 1914, no British government would have agreed that another country should have parity with the Royal Navy. Britannia ruling the waves was not only a part of every Briton's image of their country: it was also an essential part of maintaining Britain's worldwide empire.

Britain took another crucial decision at this conference. It had an alliance with Japan that had stood it in good stead during the war, protecting its Far East empire. The agreement expired in 1922. Now Japan's expansion in the Far East created a potential conflict with American interests. Britain had to make a choice, and it chose to let the alliance lapse in the interest of friendship with America, changing Japan from an ally into a potential enemy.

America's contribution to the postwar world was, characteristically, a collective promise of good intentions. Secretary of State James Kellogg drew up with French foreign minister Aristide Briand a treaty in which signatories promised to forsake war as an instrument of national policy. All the major nations of the world signed the Kellog-Briand Treaty in 1928, and its authors were awarded the Nobel Peace Prize.

• • •

The war ended with the overthrow of the kaiser in Germany, but the republic set up at Weimar in 1919 did not establish firm roots in German political life. Hyperinflation in 1923 shattered Germans' national confidence almost as much as the defeat in 1918 had. Right-wing extremists took up the myth of the "stab in the back," claiming that the German army was never defeated but was betrayed. Since there were no foreign troops on German territory when the war ended, this could be made to seem plausible. The republic was shaken by attempted coups by Left and Right. The army, small as it was because of the Versailles

Treaty limitations, operated as an independent force. It organized training in Russia in secret and backed favored political parties.

The worldwide depression triggered in 1929 hit Germany particularly hard as much of its industry relied on foreign investment. With widespread poverty and 6 million unemployed, the Nazi Party bounded from 810,000 votes in the election in 1928 to more than 6 million in 1930. The Nazis promised to end Germany's economic and political humiliation and make Germans a proud people again. They blamed the nation's troubles on Communists, Jews, and traitors. They were radicals, promising to sweep away the old institutions, such as parliamentary democracy, which seemed to be failing, and create a new nation. Hitler got financial backing from the industrialists by playing on their fear of Communism and political support from the army by promising to remove the restrictions imposed on it by the Versailles Treaty.

Under the Weimar constitution, the head of state was the president. He could appoint a chancellor, who was the chief executive. No one party got a majority in the 1932 election and there was an almost permanent political crisis, with one coalition government following another. The leaders of the conservative and Catholic parties decided that they might achieve stability with a coalition government in which Hitler was chancellor but the Nazis had only three seats in the cabinet, restricting their power to act. This was one of the bad ideas of history.

In 1933 the president was the eighty-four-year-old Field Marshal Paul von Hindenburg, a stout, upright figure with a walrus mustache, a symbol of German conservatism and patriotism. On the morning of January 30 in the *Kaiserhof,* the presidential palace, von Hindenburg, wearing full-dress military uniform, swore in Adolf Hitler as chancellor of the German republic. Hitler was the third chancellor in a year. That evening, thousands of brown-shirted Nazi Party storm troopers, braving bitter cold weather, marched through Berlin carrying flaring torches and swastika flags and singing Nazi anthems to celebrate the triumph of their movement, and Berliners got an inkling that this chancellor might be different.

Hitler's achievement was extraordinary. He did not, like Stalin, take over a revolutionary movement that was already in progress. He created the Nazi Party and Nazi Germany. He transformed the sick man of

Europe into a disciplined, powerful nation that would within ten years conquer Europe from the Volga to the Pyrenees.

Adolf Hitler was an Austrian from a village close to the German frontier, the son of a low-ranking customs official, self-educated. The family moved to Linz. Hitler tried to get into art school and failed. He went to Vienna and lived there in poverty, sleeping in flop houses; he earned a meager living doing odd jobs and by selling small water color paintings of city scenes. One of the surprising things in his book *Mein Kampf* is a sensitive account of the demoralizing effects of poverty on individuals and families.

He moved to Munich and joined the German army on the outbreak of war. He was a brave and highly motivated infantry soldier, earning an Iron Cross second class and a corporal's stripes. He was blinded by poison gas and was in the hospital with bandages on his eyes when Germany surrendered. After the war, in Munich, he moved into the shadowy world of extreme right-wing politics, joining and then taking over the tiny National Socialist Workers' Party, making it a power in Bavaria and then in the whole of Germany. He proved to be a natural leader and a spell-binding orator.

Hitler set out his philosophy in *Mein Kampf*, the book he wrote in 1924 when he was thirty-five years old and was in prison in Munich after leading a failed putsch, dictating much of it to Rudolf Hess. It is part autobiography, part exposition of a nationalist and racist ideology, and part prescription for Germany. Hitler never deviated either from the ideology he expounded in the book or the policies he prescribed.

Hitler saw all human life as a struggle. This is central to his thinking, and it comes out again and again in his book. "He who does not wish to fight in this world, where permanent struggle is the law of life, does not have the right to live." And "Nobody can doubt that this world will one day be the scene of dreadful struggles for existence on the part of Mankind . . . Before its consuming fire, this so-called humanitarianism, which connotes only a mixture of fatuous timidity and self-conceit, will melt away as under the March sunshine. Man has become great through permanent struggle. In permanent peace his greatness must decline."

He returned to this theme in an election speech in February 1928: "In the struggle, the stronger, the more able, win, while the less able, the weak, lose . . . It is not by the principles of humanity that Man lives or is able to preserve himself above the animal world but only by the most brutal struggle."

There were slaves and enslavers, and there was no doubt what he wanted his people to be. His people were the Germans, and he conceived of them as a race, with a history going back thousands of years. Inferior races deserved to be enslaved and forced to serve them. Another so-called race, the Jews, were malignant, vile beings, a permanent threat to all that was decent in the world. The Jews were behind Germany's defeat in 1918 and the rise of Bolshevism. Democracy was enfeebling because it substituted quantity for quality, the rule of numbers rather than the leadership of a man or men who are strong and enlightened.

Usually when one quotes a book that a political figure has written earlier in his career, it is to discomfort him by citing views that he left behind as he matured. But Hitler's views and his policies remained consistent. After this he wrote little, and even as chancellor he rarely put his policy aims down on paper. He expounded them sometimes at formal meetings, but more often in off-the-cuff conversations. Even important orders were often given verbally and passed on as "It is the Fuehrer's wish that . . ." This has left room for historians to argue about what he was intending at any given time; for David Irving, who has demonstrated a sympathy for Nazism, to say that Hitler did not order the Holocaust or even know about it; and for the distinguished British historian A. J. P. Taylor to argue, with less malign motives, that Hitler did not plan a campaign of aggression but simply took advantage of opportunities.

In *Mein Kampf* Hitler set out his aims for Germany. The German race should unite and then conquer more land, because a great nation must have a large territory. They must "acquire soil for the German plow by means of the German sword." That land was to be found in the Ukraine and Russia and was there for the taking. "No nation possesses a square yard of ground by decree of a higher Will and by virtue of a higher Right . . . The possession of such territory is a proof of the strength of the conqueror and the weakness of those who submit to him." Furthermore, "Destiny seems to point out the way for us here," because Bolshevism had corrupted the Russian state.

France had to be defeated because it would always be an enemy to Germany and would want Germany to be weak, for reasons which were quite understandable. Hitler seems to have seen this as an unfortunate necessity rather than a primary aim. Britain was a different matter. Hitler chided the kaiser's government for challenging Britain's naval supremacy and for seeking to emulate it as a colonial power. Britain should be sought as an ally, not challenged as a rival. Germany's destiny did not lie overseas but in Europe, in conquering lands to the east in the footsteps of the Teutonic knights of the twelfth century. He occasionally said that Germany should have its colonies taken away at Versailles returned, but he gave no sign of feeling strongly about this.

As a speaker he had an almost mesmerizing ability to focus the emotions of a crowd into one narrow, concentrated stream. He also had the ability to inspire devotion, not only in the crowds who listened to his speeches with rapt expressions and shining eyes but also in some of those who became his close followers. Hermann Göring, Prussian officer and war hero, said of the ex-corporal from the Vienna slums, "From the moment I saw him I was under his spell."

He was also adept in one-to-one meetings at creating the impression he wanted, even speaking through an interpreter. He could play the sober and responsible statesman, denying in his manner the extreme views and evil intent that were often imputed to him. Foreign politicians, newspaper publishers such as Colonel McCormick and William Randolph Hearst, businessmen, and even pacifists such as the British Labour Party leader George Lansbury would come away from a meeting with him reassured about his intentions. Anthony Eden, who would be an opponent of the British government's appeasement policies, told the foreign office after his one meeting with Hitler in 1933: "He is a surprise. In conversation quiet, almost shy, with a pleasant smile. Without doubt the man has charm."

There were mixed views abroad about Hitler's accession and a lot of let's-wait-and-see-ing. He was a revolutionary, as he had often said, but most people assumed that, like others who took a radical stance when they were not in power, he would shed some of his wilder ideas when he assumed the responsibilities of office. Britain's *Daily Telegraph* said in an editorial the day after he came to power: "Herr Hitler in office is very different from being the national and international peril that he has vowed himself to be given the chance . . . he is merely a party leader on a par with other party leaders." This attitude is understandable. Only a person with an excessively morbid mind could have imagined the extent to which the nightmarish fantasies of Hitler's ideology would be enacted.

While the Nazis' Brownshirts bullied and murdered their opponents, Hitler pushed through emergency legislation to establish a dictatorship. When Hindenburg died in 1934, the office of chancellor was combined with that of president. From then on the Nazi Party was for all practical purposes the state, and the party symbol, the swastika, became the German flag. The party took control of every area of German life. Schools, the press, the entertainment industry, youth clubs, sports, all were put at the service of the Nazi ideology. Germans would grow up on a diet of militaristic patriotism, hatred of Jews and other supposed enemies, and devotion to their leader. The British historian John Wheeler-Bennett visited Germany in the mid-1930s and wrote later: "Anyone but a half-blind idiot could see where this was leading."

All power was in Hitler's hands. The structure of government was loose and could be changed at his will. Ministers and generals were there to serve his purposes. The figure of Hitler became all-pervasive. He was the pinnacle of the gigantic pageants, the embodiment of the new Germany. In a custom not seen even when monarchs were said to be divinely anointed, a salute to the leader was made the official greeting, so that *"Heil Hitler"* was heard all over Germany a thousand times a day.

In 1935 the Nuremberg laws put the persecution of Jews on the statute books. Jews were placed under degrading restrictions and were barred from professions and from public life. Marriage and even sexual relations between Jews and non-Jews were barred. Aryan blood must not be polluted.

The government embarked on a series of public works programs, some linked to rearmament but civil projects as well. Hitler took over industry with dictatorial powers and brought Germany out of economic depression, ending unemployment, something no democratic leader was able to do. National income in 1937 was double the 1932 figure. Göring said famously that guns were better than butter, but the Germans were getting both. Hitler wanted Germany to be self-sufficient so that it could not again be crippled by a naval blockade as it had been in the First World War, and plants were set up to manufacture steel, petrochemicals, and synthetic rubber. The economy was being prepared for war. It needed war, because without it the growth could not be sustained.

. . .

Hitler soon set about tearing up the Versailles Treaty as he had promised to do. For foreign consumption, he said that all he wanted for Germany was equality with other nations. In March 1934 he announced that he was introducing conscription, breaching the restrictions on the size of the German army. He followed this a few days later with a speech in the Reichstag allaying fears that he was embarking on a path to war. "National Socialist Germany wants peace because of its fundamental convictions," he declared. It was a trick he was to pull again and again: an aggressive move accompanied by a declaration of peaceful intentions.

Most foreign diplomats in Berlin could see what was happening. The British ambassador, Sir Horace Rumbolt, told the Foreign Office a few weeks after the Nazis came to power that "hooligans" were now in power, "ruling Germany with a frivolous disregard for all decent feelings without precedent in history."

U.S. ambassador William Dodd arrived in Berlin a year after Hitler came to power. Dodd, a history professor who had gained his Ph.D. at Leipzig University, had edited the papers of Woodrow Wilson, and he embodied the Wilsonian concept of the American abroad as a missionary for democracy. His daughter Martha, who accompanied him to Berlin, said later that he had hoped to exercise a moderating influence on the German regime and thought there would be "a chance to bring them back to reason, to recall forcefully to them their democratic past." He was quickly disillusioned and wrote in a dispatch: "The Hitler regime is composed of three rather inexperienced and very dogmatic persons, all of whom have been connected with more or less murderous undertakings in the last eight or ten years ... In the back of [Hitler's] mind is the old German idea of dominating Europe through warfare."

Martha Dodd found a more active outlet for anti-Nazi feelings. She copied confidential embassy documents and gave them to her Russian lover, Boris Vinagradov, an agent of the KGB, the Soviet secret service, with diplomatic cover. Unwisely, they asked his superiors in Moscow for permission to marry. He was recalled and disappeared.

In 1935 German troops marched into the Rhineland, to be greeted by the cheers of a welcoming populace, violating the clause in the Versailles Treaty that said the Rhineland must remain demilitarized. Hitler assured foreign powers that this was purely symbolic and offered to sign a twenty-five-year nonaggression pact with France.

The British and French governments hastily conferred. Should they act? The French foreign minister, Paul Bonnet, thought Hitler would back down immediately if confronted by force, but France would have to order general mobilization, which would be unpopular. The British prime minister, Stanley Baldwin, told him, "Even if there was one chance in a hundred of war, I would not take that chance." There was a widespread view that, as one member of the cabinet put it, "Hitler was only walking into his own back yard."

Hitler was gambling. In poker terms, he was bluffing, betting high on a weak hand, hoping the other side would back down. It was something he was to do again and again. He did not have the forces yet to challenge Britain and France. He had promised his generals that if the move were opposed he would withdraw.

Hitler appointed Joachim Ribbentrop, one of his party confidants, as the Nazi Party's foreign affairs advisor. Ribbentrop had lived abroad as a child, and as a young man he had emigrated to Canada. He returned to Germany in 1914 to serve in the army and then joined his father-in-law's wine exporting firm. He was good-looking, a smart dresser, and spoke near-faultless English, with elegant manners that many found artificial. Ribbentrop negotiated successfully a naval treaty with Britain, which had the beneficial effect of making France annoyed at Britain for signing the treaty without consulting it.

Hitler appointed him ambassador to Britain to pursue his policy of gaining Britain's friendship. He wanted to detach Britain from its traditional link with France and make it an ally of Germany, the policy he thought the kaiser should have followed. Hitler wanted Europe. Britain could have the rest of the world. Within his own circle he said that he respected the British, who were of the same race as the Germans.

Ribbentrop set out to establish a strong presence. He rented Neville Chamberlain's house when Chamberlain was chancellor of the exchequer and lived in the chancellor's official residence, and he made headway in aristocratic circles and was a frequent guest in some country houses. But he also made blunders. He greeted King George VI with the Nazi salute. It was not the full outstretched-arm version but the one with the arm raised above the elbow; even so it caused offense. He got no response to his suggestions of an alliance. The British government did not want Hitler to have Europe.

Traditional British policy has always been to maintain a balance of power in Europe. It wanted to prevent a single power dominating the Continent, particularly the northwestern part, closest to Britain. This is why Britain gave a guarantee of Belgian independence and why it went to war in 1914 when Germany invaded Belgium. It did not see only Germany as the threatening power. In the 1920s, military planners envisaged France as a possible enemy. But a resurgent Germany was going to be the most powerful country on the Continent, and a Nazi Germany was particularly unwelcome.

Germany was not the only country to give cause for concern. In 1932 a militaristic fascist-style government came to power in Japan, and Japan moved to the Asian mainland and seized Manchuria. The League of Nations condemned this but its members would not take any further action. Japan quit the league.

Mussolini, who had invented the word *fascist* for the party he led in Italy, invaded Ethiopia. The League of Nations condemned the action and with Britain and France in the lead, initiated economic sanctions against Italy, but they would not extend the sanctions to cover oil, which would have made a difference. Only the Soviet Union called for full-scale action against the fascist aggressor. Britain and France earned Mussolini's antagonism without stopping his invasion.

In 1936 civil war broke out in Spain when, in a growing atmosphere of instability, General Franco led a military revolt against a democratically elected left-wing government. Italy immediately sent troops to help Franco, and Germany sent squadrons of its newly formed air force, rotating them to give the maximum number of airmen combat experience. The Soviet Union alone sent military advisors to the Spanish Republic, once again the only country to stand up to fascism. The war aroused passions in the democracies. Many people called for help for the republican cause. The governments did little, but forty thousand young men went as volunteers to fight.

In 1937 Japan invaded China, a country with which America had an almost avuncular relationship and with which Britain and America had close commercial links. Japan aimed to replace the Western "open-door" policy of maintaining China as an open market for all with its projected Greater East Asia Co-Prosperity Sphere. The European powers had empires in Asia. Japan also wanted its empire.

The aggressors were on the march and a line-up was forming. It stretched right around the world.

• • •

Five weeks after Hitler became German chancellor, on a blustery March day in Washington, D.C., Franklin Delano Roosevelt, leaning on two sticks and on the arm of his eldest son, walked slowly up the ramp outside the Capitol to be sworn in as thirty-fourth president, a look of strong determination on his face belying the feebleness of his body below the waist.

America's national trauma was not the war but the Depression. The images etched into the national psyche were not of barbed wire, muddy trenches, and death rolls but of banks with their doors padlocked, lines of unemployed men, and soup kitchens. The economic slump was worldwide, indeed it was the single event that characterized the 1930s, but nowhere else did it strike with such suddenness and nowhere else did it reverse a nation's fortunes so totally and so rapidly. The Depression shook the American people's faith in their system of government. It scarred a generation and shaped their attitudes. It was a time of hardship and anxiety for most American families, and disaster for many.

Roosevelt was elected in the depths of the Depression and foreign affairs played little part in the voters' thinking. "Our own troubles are so numerous and so difficult that we have neither the time nor the inclination to meddle in the affairs of others," said Massachusetts congresswoman Edith Nourse Rogers, and most people would have agreed with her.

Roosevelt set out to get the economy moving again. Acting with furious energy from his first day in office, he enacted emergency measures, created new federal agencies, put new legislation before Congress and enlarged the powers of the federal government. With his smile and the jaunty angle of his cigarette holder, he radiated confidence and a spirit that told Americans that they could solve the nation's problems. His "New deal for the American people" aimed not only to create more wealth but to spread wealth and power more evenly.

Roosevelt was the son of a wealthy patrician family from upper New York State, and had the education, at Groton School and Harvard, that exemplified his class. Like many with his background, he traveled and came to know Europe at an early age. From 1891, when he was nine, until 1900, he went every year with his parents to the German spa town of Bad Nauheim, because his father, James, was in poor health, and for a while he attended a local German school. Many years later, he told British officials that he had bicycled over a lot of southern Germany as a boy and gave them advice on bombing Germany. He went into politics very early on, becoming a New York state senator and then governor.

He had pronounced views on foreign policy, and they resembled those of his older cousin Theodore, who, in his youthful days, he admired and sought to emulate. Like Theodore Roosevelt he believed that America should be a world power and should be ready to project its power abroad. He was very much a navy man; as a boy he had wanted to go to Annapolis. He loved the sea and was a keen sailor in his younger days. He served as assistant secretary of the navy in World War One — Theodore Roosevelt had been navy secretary at the outbreak of the Spanish-American War — and like Theodore, he absorbed the teachings of Alfred Thayer Mahan, with his vision of the United States as a world power and his emphasis on sea power.

He was keen for America to enter World War One on the side of the Allies. When America did enter he wanted to see action, and extended his tour of naval installations in Europe to get close to the front-line trenches. His temperament as well as his viewpoint would lead him to seek an active role in world affairs.

He was still regarded by most who knew him as something of a rich playboy, likable but too light-weight to be presidential timber. Then, at the age of thirty-nine, he contracted polio and, an active and athletic man, he was transformed into an invalid. He was bed-ridden for two years, and the ordeal hardened his will. Some say the experience also gave him a new sympathy for those whose lot in life had not been as fortunate as his had been up to that point. With a struggle he gained movement in the upper part of his body and learned to move about and function, and he reentered political life.

Roosevelt was a consummate politician; he had to be to get through progressive legislation while heading a party that included in its natural constituency the rural South, conservative and racist, and labor unions and middle-class liberals in the Northern cities. As state legislator, governor, and president, he used persuasion, patronage, and pressure to push through his projects, sensing how far he could go, making compromises where he had to, working with anyone to achieve his ends. He was the first president to use the Internal Revenue Service as a weapon against opponents. But few doubted the sincerity of his ultimate purpose. When a southern senator complained that the appointment of an ambassador to the Vatican would offend many Protestants, Roosevelt wrote back saying, "If some of my good Baptist brethren in Georgia had done a little preaching from the pulpit against the KKK, I would have a little more genuine American respect for their Christianity."

He worked through people rather than institutions, bypassing established channels. He had charm, a winning informality, and great persuasive powers. Joseph Kennedy did not want to be chairman of the Maritime Commission but, explaining to a friend why he took the job when Roosevelt offered it to him, he said, "I can say no to that fellow on the telephone, but face to face he gets me." He had excessive confidence in his power to charm; later he tried to deal with the Soviet government in that way, saying, "I can handle Joe Stalin."

No president since Lincoln has been so loved and so hated. He inspired affection and loyalty in many who worked for him and in millions around the country. He was hated by most of the business community, who saw his New Deal program as a threat to their values and more than halfway to socialism, and was regarded with suspicion by others who worried about his arrogation of power for himself and the federal government. It says something about the respect accorded to the office of the presidency in those days that despite the hostility of many newspapers, none ever carried a photograph of him being lifted into or out of a wheelchair. Americans knew their president was crippled — he drew attention to the fact by sponsoring a charity for polio research — but they were not confronted with the indignities that accompany disability.

Despite his international viewpoint, his first act of foreign policy as president was an assertion of American unilateralism. Within a few weeks of taking office he torpedoed the London Economic Conference by declaring that America would not take part in any international system to regulate currencies.

Most Americans shared the widespread disillusionment with the war. A Gallup Poll in 1936 showed that a majority thought America's entry into World War One was a mistake. The Hollywood film version of *All Quiet on the Western Front* appeared in 1930 to wide acclaim. Americans responded to its depiction of the war as a pointless sacrifice.

In 1934 the Senate set up an investigations subcommittee headed by Senator Robert Nye, a North Dakota Republican, to look into the links between big financiers, weapons dealers, and America's entry into the war. In two years of wide-ranging investigations it failed to establish any cause-and-effect relationship. But it showed the extent to which the house of J. P. Morgan financed the British war effort and therefore was dependent on an Allied victory for repayment of its loans, and it uncovered some shadowy transatlantic trading by munitions firms. The constant airing of the subject affected public thinking.

The hearings were accompanied by magazine articles and books on the same theme. In 1934 *Merchants of Death* by Herbert C. Engelbrecht and Frank C. Hanigher, an exposé of the armament industry, was a Book of the Month Club selection and was serialized in *Reader's Digest*. Walter Millis's *The Road to War* was another bestseller. The dust jacket spelled out its message: "This book tells how a peace-loving democracy, muddled but excited, misinformed and whipped to frenzy, embarked on its greatest foreign war . . . Read it and blush! Read it and beware!"

Congress, looking at the stirrings in Europe, passed the Neutrality Acts in 1935 and 1936, with the most serious in 1937. These barred the transport of goods to belligerents on American ships, forbade American ships to sail in war zones, and forbade private credits or loans to belligerent nations. Since these were what brought the United States into the war in 1917, the Neutrality Acts were aptly described as laws designed to keep the United States out of World War One.

Most Americans approved. As they saw it, their forefathers had come to America to get away from Europe's quarrels and start a new life in a country that was different, and the emigrants were wiser and more enterprising than those who remained. The country had been tricked into entering World War One, but that was a deviation from the American way and a mistake.

Actually, America's supposed detachment from the affairs of Europe has always been something of a myth. It has never been totally detached. In the earliest days of the republic, the Federalist and Republican parties were divided over European affairs, Jefferson's Republicans supporting France in its war with England while Washington's Federalists argued for a strictly neutral stance. America continued to be involved, if only because three European nations possessed territory in North America contiguous to the United States.

America's geopolitical interests usually coincided with those of Britain. Despite Jefferson's early enthusiasm for the French Revolution, he said when Napoleon was conquering one country after another that America would be in danger if one power ruled Europe. "It cannot be to our interest that all Europe should be reduced to a single monarchy," he wrote. This has been the prevailing view of foreign policy specialists since then, partly because much of America's trade was still with Europe but also for strategic reasons. This was particularly true when the power was militaristic and aggressive, like the Germany of the kaiser or Hitler, or, later on, ideologically aggressive like the Soviet Union.

The Monroe Doctrine, warning European powers to keep out of the Western Hemisphere, was a tacit alliance with Britain. Indeed it had its origin in a suggestion by the British foreign secretary of the time, George Canning, of a *joint* declaration saying "Hands off the Americas" to the Continental powers. It was in Britain's interests to ensure that no European nation extended its power to the Americas, and President Monroe knew that the British navy, the most powerful in the world, would ensure that none did.

At the end of the nineteenth century, America went into its imperialist phase. It sought overseas markets for its products, and the nation felt newly powerful. Manifest destiny did not stop at the ocean shore. America extended its rule to Hawaii and then to the Far East, wresting the Philippines from Spain and suppressing its independence movement, and it joined the Europeans in imposing suitable economic and trading policies on China. This did not come into conflict with British imperialism but suited its interests. Britain would much rather America expanded into territories ripe for exploitation than its Continental rivals, France and Germany. British commentators urged the United States to annex Hawaii before others did. Rudyard Kipling's imperialist ode "The White Man's Burden" was written to urge America to take over the Philippines. It was in this period that the conjunction of interests and sympathies between the British and American ruling elites developed, to the point where, as was often said, "cultural factors" made war between them unthinkable.

Nonetheless, most Americans believed, as they always had, that physical and moral detachment from the world's quarrels was America's natural position. They did not know or want to know about British strategy or the British Navy. So far as they were concerned, a bounteous God had given America two oceans for its security and no further help from anyone else was required.

In the 1930s there were currents at work that mitigated against detachment. In China the Japanese capture of Nanking was accompanied by an orgy of massacre and rape, and photographs and newspaper accounts brought this home to Americans. Newsreels showed the Nazi book burnings, and tales of the Gestapo terror were recounted by correspondents and, increasingly as the decade went on, by refugees from Germany and Austria. There were horrors abroad in the world that were impinging more and more on the American consciousness. Some people were roused to anger. Others silently thanked their forefathers for having had the enterprise and good sense to come to the land that was far away from these horrors, and they determined to keep it that way.

The Anti-Nazi Council to Champion Human Rights was formed in 1934. It held rallies and urged a boycott of German goods. Some businessmen opposed the boycott, prominent among them the president of IBM, Thomas B. Watson, who was awarded the Order of Merit of the German Eagle for promoting trade with Germany. Trade with Germany fell off sharply, partly because of Hitler's policy of promoting self-sufficiency, although Germany's trade with Latin America increased. There was a move to boycott the Berlin Olympics in 1936 on the ground that Germany discriminated against Jewish athletes.

Roosevelt was far from indifferent to aggression abroad. As early as 1935, when Mussolini was poised to invade Ethiopia, he wrote to the chairman of the Senate Foreign Relations Committee, Nevada senator Key Pittman, asking for authorization to ban shipments to one or more of the belligerents. Pittman told him the committee was almost unanimous in refusing to distinguish between belligerents and so label one the aggressor. It would remain doggedly neutral. Pittman, who was named after Francis Scott Key, his ancestor, was best known in the Senate as a vigorous defender of Nevada's silver mining interests, and he pronounced himself an enemy of the dictators, but he would not ask senators to abandon their neutral stance.

Roosevelt sensed the mood of the American people, and he knew he could not go too far in involving the country in the affairs of Europe or Asia. But he wanted to show the dangers as he saw them and lead America to a more active role. He tempered his pace. As well as leading the American people, he also had to lead Congress, and Pittman's quick rejection of his request indicated that this was not going to be easy.

Cordell Hull, a tall, slender Tennessean who had served for twenty-four years in Congress, shared many of Roosevelt's concerns. Hull was a figure of rectitude and probity, a cautious man who believed in the decent proprieties of international relations and in free trade as a high moral principle and a guarantor of peace. In the autumn of 1937 Hull suggested that Roosevelt sound a warning to potential aggressors, particularly in the Far East.

Roosevelt chose a scheduled speech in Chicago on October 4, 1937, to warn the American people that no nation could isolate itself from economic and political upheavals. He suggested a "quarantine" of aggressor nations. "When an epidemic of physical disease starts to spread, the community approves and joins in a quarantine of the patients in order to protect the health of the community," he said. He seems to have had in mind an extreme form of collective sanctions directed against Japan, although the State Department said it had no plans.

The reaction to the speech was strong and largely negative. Pacifist organizations said the speech "points the American people down the road that led to the World War." Two congressmen threatened to have Roosevelt impeached. The *Boston Herald* said: "It may be true that the very foundations of civilization are threatened. But this time, Mr. President, Americans will not be stampeded into going 3,000 miles across the water to save them." In the ensuing weeks, magazines and newspapers featured articles with titles such as "We Don't Need to Go to War" in the *Saturday Evening Post,* circulation 3 million. Hull told Roosevelt he thought the speech had strengthened the isolationists.

In December, Japanese warplanes attacked the U.S. Navy gunboat *Panay* in the Yangtze River in China, sinking the ship and killing four American seamen. The Japanese government said it was a mistake and apologized and paid indemnities. Roosevelt told his cabinet he thought the attack was deliberate and was intended to make it more difficult for the Western powers to remain in China, but there was nothing he could do about it. However, he prepared a bill to put before Congress for a two-ocean navy.

2

PREWAR

In 1937 Neville Chamberlain succeeded Stanley Baldwin as prime minister. Chamberlain is often pictured today as a weak, vacillating figure bamboozled by Hitler, but this is wide of the mark. His contemporaries certainly did not see him as weak or vacillating. He dominated his cabinet with authority. He had great self-assurance, but this was a failing when it became rigidity and a determination to stick to his own policies whatever others said.

He was from a family prominent both in politics and business, the son and nephew of cabinet ministers, and he spent much of his career in city politics in Birmingham. He was a tall, spare figure, sixty-seven years old when he took office, with a sallow, gray complexion, prominent rabbit's teeth, and a long stringy neck that usually rose out of a stiff winged collar, the Victorian gentleman's dress. The rolled umbrella that he always carried became the defining characteristic that cartoonists picked on. Any lightheartedness in his nature he kept, like his love of classical music, for his private life. His speeches were well argued and logical but colorless. He had his critics, but no one doubted his high principles, his sincerity, or his determination.

He enjoyed the countryside. In London he rarely missed his morning walk in the park, and would occasionally write a letter to the *Times* noting an unusual bird he saw on his walk or the early arrival of a flower. His favorite country pursuit was not one of the social pursuits of the upper classes, fox-hunting or shooting, but, characteristically, the solitary sport of fly fishing. When he was called back to London from his country house one Sunday because Italy had invaded Albania, he managed to get in a couple of hours more fishing before leaving. He wrote to his sister Ida: "I fished in my London clothes and got two pulls but I got no satisfaction out of it. I couldn't concentrate on fishing and I was conscious of fishing carelessly and badly." A joke at the time went, "What's the difference between Chamberlain and Hitler? Chamberlain takes a weekend in the country, Hitler takes a country in a weekend."

He had firm views on foreign affairs and ignored those who disagreed with them. The head of the foreign office was Lord Vansittart, who had been warning of the danger of Germany with a hostility verging on the racist. Chamberlain pushed him out by creating for him the new post of diplomatic advisor to the cabinet and appointed Sir Alexander Cadogan in his place. His closest advisor was Sir Horace Wilson, who had been a civil servant at the Ministry of Labour, a man who had no experience of foreign affairs and had rarely traveled abroad. Chamberlain relied on Wilson's counsel over that of the foreign office professionals and gave him an office next to his own at 10 Downing Street, the prime minister's official residence. He replaced the ambassador to Berlin with Sir Neville Henderson, who believed that his mission was to prevent war between Britain and Germany at all costs. Henderson argued that Hitler's ambitions lay only in Eastern Europe and posed no threat to Britain.

Chamberlain's policy was appeasement, and this has become a dirty word. Today, to describe a policy as appeasement is to condemn it, and no one would admit to practicing appeasement. But the policy is best understood by recalling that the verb was rarely used with a person as its object. Advocates of the policy did not speak of appeasing dictators or anyone else; they spoke of "appeasement" of situations, meaning, in the dictionary definition, to make a situation calmer and reduce tension. Winston Churchill, when he was chancellor of the exchequer, said one of his aims was "the appeasement of class bitterness." In international affairs it meant seeking compromise rather than conflict, a peaceful solution rather than one achieved by force. This is not an ignoble aim, nor is it cowardly. But it is irrelevant in confrontation with a man who sees all life as struggle.

In the back of Chamberlain's mind, as in the back of everyone's mind in Europe, was the horror of 1914–18 and the possibility of another war. Sir Alexander Cadogan, who worked closely with him, wrote later: "He was not gullible. He was haunted day and night by the prospect that he saw clearly enough; he gave everything of his strength to try to avert it."

He disliked even preparation for war, and for decent reasons. "To me, the very idea that the hard-won savings of our people, which ought to be devoted to the alleviation of suffering, to the opening up of fresh institutes and recreations . . . should have been dissipated upon weapons of war is hateful and damnable," he said in a speech in 1938.

Lord Halifax, Chamberlain's foreign secretary, made the specifics of the appeasement policy clear to Hitler when he visited him in Berchtesgaden in November 1937. (The meeting almost got off to a disastrous start when Halifax, getting out of his car, mistook Hitler for a servant and started to hand him his coat. The foreign minister, Baron von Neurath, whispered to him urgently, *"Der Führer!"*) Halifax told Hitler he recognized that there were questions arising out of the Versailles Treaty that could cause difficulty, such as over Austria, Czechoslovakia, or Danzig. He said Britain would not stand in the way of a change in the status quo, providing it were reached peaceably.

Halifax was a tall, lean figure, soft-spoken, formal in his manner, a former viceroy of India. He was an aristocrat and a Conservative of the old school, a devout churchgoer, and a keen fox hunter. He was born with most of one hand missing but when the First World War broke out he used family influence to get a commission in an infantry regiment and fought in France. As a hereditary member of the House of Lords he never had to run for office. He disliked microphones, and when, on one occasion, he was filmed making a speech, he grumbled about the camera and lights, "These appurtenances of democracy are very distasteful." He shared Chamberlain's hopes for a policy of appeasement, although he shed these hopes sooner. In India he had established a working relationship with Mahatma Gandhi despite Gandhi's opposition to British rule, and he hoped similarly to establish a relationship with opponents in Europe.

Many in Britain shared Chamberlain's outlook. It was easy to believe Hitler when he said that all he wanted was equality for his country so that it could play its part in European affairs, and easy to sympathize with this desire. It was what all Germans wanted of every party, Left and Right. Besides, it strained credibility to believe that anyone who had lived through the 1914–18 war would risk another. The appeasers argued that the defeat of Germany in a war would open the way to Communism in Central Europe (which is what happened).

In their anxiety to avoid a war with Nazi Germany, some were ready to see the best in that society and ignore the worst. Nazi rule was brutal, but this could be explained as an inevitable accompaniment of radical change; the horrors that were to come later were not envisaged. It had, after all, transformed a nation wracked by economic distress and social and political instability into a stable, dynamic, and increasingly prosperous society and had banished the threat of a Communist Germany. Many were ready to admire this achievement and overlook the brutality that accompanied it, indeed that was essential to it, just as others with a different set of social values were ready to overlook or deny the cruelties in the Soviet system.

While some brought back from visits to Germany impressions of the militarism of the youth and the ever-present Gestapo, the British historian Arthur Bryant described thousands of children at a Nazi summer school camping out on a lake under the fir trees, "their faces gleaming with happiness and health and new-found knowledge of how to live." An American naval officer noted, in a confidential report that was passed on to the White House, the tremendous improvement: "such order, such discipline, such cleanliness." He remarked on the disappearance of prostitutes from hotel lobbies and the number of men in uniform, "the finest lot of men I have ever seen. Healthy, robust, erect posture and perfectly disciplined."

Arnold Wilson, a British member of Parliament and arch-appeaser, spoke for many when he told Parliament: "Behind Herr Hitler stands a united, virile and powerful nation which has given us all a lesson in the virtues and advantages of discipline and self-sacrifice." (Later, when appeasement turned out to have been a mistake, Wilson acted in the spirit of mea culpa. He resigned from Parliament and, although in his fifties, joined the Royal Air Force and became an air gunner, and was killed bombing the nation whose strength he had once admired.)

A left-wing journalist coined the phrase "the Cliveden set" for the group of appeasement-minded figures who met regularly at Cliveden, the country house of the American-born Lord and Lady Astor, conjuring up a picture of an upper-class cabal. In fact the Cliveden guest list was eclectic, but it is true that Halifax; Geoffrey Dawson, the editor of the *Times;* and other like-minded figures, sometimes accompanied by Ribbentrop, would talk as they strolled on the sloping lawns or sat around Lady Astor's elegant dinner table about how to soften the anti-Nazi tone of some of the press and avoid occasions for British-German friction.

Many of the appeasers would not even condemn too vigorously Hitler's persecution of the Jews. A degree of anti-Semitism was widespread and accepted at most levels of society in Britain and America, and even more in France. Mainly, this took the form of exclusion. It was normal for social organizations ranging from golf clubs to college fraternities and even holiday hotels to exclude Jews. Major schools and universities had quotas limiting the number of Jews. No president since Lincoln did more to advance the cause of ethnic minorities than Roosevelt, but some of the prejudices about Jews, Catholics, and African Americans that came naturally to his class rubbed off on him and occasionally emerged in private conversation. (His mother, Sarah, had them in abundance). Few in Britain or America would have approved of the Nuremberg Laws, but when the Nazis said Jews had too much power and something had to be done about it, this struck a sympathetic chord in many people.

Hitler himself continued to receive visitors and persuade them that, despite the violent tone of some of the speeches he made for domestic consumption, he was a statesman who wanted peace. Even David Lloyd George, the Liberal prime minister who had led Britain to victory in World War One and carried out radical social reforms, was impressed by Hitler when they met in 1936. Hitler told him, "You were Prime Minister, you don't know what the last war was like. I was a soldier in the trenches. I don't want a war," and Lloyd George believed him. Hitler flattered him, and he may have been sincere; in *Mein Kampf* he praised Lloyd George's oratory and his wartime leadership. Lloyd George wrote in the *Daily Express:* "He is a born leader, a magnetic, dynamic personality with a single-minded purpose . . . I am convinced that he has no desire to invade any other land."

Prominent among the opponents of appeasement was Winston Churchill. He argued constantly that Hitler was an aggressor and a threat and should be resisted. He had held cabinet offices since 1910 but was now out of office, although his party, the Conservatives, were in power. Again and again Churchill stood up in the House of Commons and uttered warnings about German rearmament.

The Left was outspoken in its condemnation of Nazism, as would be expected. But the Labour Party opposed rearmament and wanted to rely on the League of Nations to deter or halt aggression. The liberal tends to shrink from national self-assertion. The Labour Party drew back even from rearming to give bite to the League of Nations' bark. The Peace Ballot of 1935 in Britain got 11 million people favoring disarmament and membership in the League, but when it also asked whether nations should take military action to halt an aggressor, only 6.7 million answered in the affirmative, the others either voting no or abstaining.

There was much talk of world opinion as a force. Lord Cecil, the first British delegate to the League of Nations, explained: "By far the most powerful weapon at the command of the League of Nations is not the economic weapon or the military weapon or any other weapon of material force. By far the strongest weapon we have is the weapon of public opinion."

In retrospect, all this can be seen as wishful thinking. It is clear now that nothing but military force could have deterred the aggressors. But the horrors of 1914–18 were less than twenty years behind, and in the mindset of many people, only a moral degenerate could contemplate subjecting his country to another war. Planning and arming for one was morally repugnant. To adapt a phrase from the age of nuclear confrontation, it was thinking about the unthinkable.

There were even fresh horrors in store. In World War One the Germans had bombed British cities, and the bombing of cities had accompanied war in Spain and China. Now raids with high explosives and poison gas were expected, probably causing huge casualties and social breakdown. A program for civil defense was organized: the official name was air raid precautions, or ARP. There were few volunteers; many thought that even participating in this was militaristic.

Aircraft were the technical marvels of the century. People had dreamed of flying through the air since the beginning of civilization, and now this dream was being realized. For military men it added a third dimension to warfare; aircraft could attack an enemy from above. It was not only those who expected to be on the receiving end who saw aerial bombardment as the big new thing of the next war. Enthusiasts for air power saw attack from the air as the great technical fix that could win wars in the future. This was the thinking behind the creation of the Royal Air Force.

It followed a report in 1917 by the South African general Jan Smuts on the uses of military aircraft. Smuts recommended that the Royal Flying Corps become a separate service instead of a branch of the army. He wrote: "The day may not be far off when aerial operations with their devastation of enemy lands and destruction of industrial and population centers on a vast scale may become the principal operations of war, to which the older forms of military and naval operations may become secondary and subordinate." The Royal Air Force was created in April 1918, the world's first independent air force. The U.S. Army Air Corps did not become the United States Air Force until 1949.

The first RAF commander, Hugh Trenchard, believed that with air power a country could defeat an enemy nation without having to defeat its armed forces first. "Air power can dispense with this intermediary step, can pass over the enemy army and navies, and penetrate the air defense and attack directly the centers of production," he wrote in a memo in 1928. It seemed an attractive proposition because it meant that one could contemplate war without the nightmare of years of attrition as in 1914–18. The U.S. Air Force adopted the same doctrine and developed heavy bombers from its earliest days, although it said it would aim at specific targets.

Under Trenchard, the RAF set out to prove its worth in the 1920s in colonial fighting in Iraq and on the Indian northwest frontier, showing that it was cheaper and easier to bomb rebel tribesmen into submission than to send troops into the hills. When the RAF first bombed rebel villages in Iraq in 1921, Trenchard sent a triumphant account to Winston Churchill as colonial secretary. Churchill replied: "To fire willfully on women and children is a disgraceful act, and I am surprised you do not order the officers responsible to be tried by court martial." War erodes moral sensibilities. In World War Two Churchill favored all-out bombing raids on German cities.

It is a paradox that the two major democracies, Britain and the United States, prepared to wage air war on civilians, while the major dictatorships, Germany and the Soviet Union, kept their air forces primarily for use against military targets. One reason that suggests itself is that democracies are more sensitive to mounting casualties among their people and more anxious to avoid wholesale slaughter in the trenches. Another is that both America and Britain have a sea barrier between the homeland and an enemy, and thought in terms of fighting a war at sea, which translated naturally into fighting one in the air.

British governments accepted the RAF's view. Baldwin told Parliament in 1932: "I think it is well for the man in the street to realize that no power on earth can protect him from being bombed. Whatever people may tell him, the bomber will always get through. The only defense is offense, which means that you have to kill more women and children more quickly than the enemy if you want to save yourselves." In other words, Britain would be defended by deterrence.

In the 1930s the RAF was getting the lion's share of defense spending, with the navy second and the army a poor third. It was concentrating on its bomber force. The British government, like the American, did not envisage sending a large expeditionary force overseas. The army's role was to be limited to colonial policing. In 1934 the RAF had twice as many fighters as bombers. But in December 1937, with rearmament under way, the minister for coordination of defense, Sir Thomas Inskip, decided to build more fighters than bombers. RAF chiefs cried foul and said the change was only because the government had promised to build more planes and fighters were cheaper than bombers. The accusation was probably true, but as things turned out, the decision probably saved the British nation.

• • •

Roosevelt felt that the United States might have a part to play as mediator. He and his undersecretary of state, Sumner Welles, hatched a plan for an international conference to discuss all outstanding issues, with a view to satisfying every country's needs on access to raw materials, security, and territory. Secretary of State Cordell Hull was cool to the idea, dismissing it as "Welles' pyrotechnics." He also did not like Roosevelt's practice of ignoring the State Department machinery and making policy with his friends, of whom Welles was one. Welles, a stately figure who even as a young man always wore a three-piece suit and sported a Molucca cane, shared Roosevelt's Groton-Harvard background and had been a page boy at his wedding.

Hull gave his reluctant consent to the plan but said Roosevelt should try it out on Britain first. Roosevelt put it to the British government in

January 1938. Chamberlain turned it down. He explained that he was at that point negotiating with Mussolini. Mussolini was sounding aggressive, laying claim to territories around the Mediterranean, part of the French Riviera, Corsica, even British-owned Gibraltar and Malta. He also had Italian troops fighting in Spain. Chamberlain was offering to recognize the conquest of Ethiopia in return for Italian promises of good behavior.

Chamberlain sent the reply to Roosevelt without consulting his foreign secretary, Anthony Eden, who was on holiday in the south of France. Eden was furious; like Hull, he felt he was being bypassed, and he was against the idea of appeasing Mussolini.

Hull also did not like the idea of appeasing Mussolini. He told the British ambassador that recognizing the Italian conquest of Ethiopia would encourage "desperado nations" in aggression in the future.

Appeasing Mussolini may have been distasteful but for Britain it made sense. The service chiefs reported to the cabinet in 1937 that they did not have the forces to oppose attacks on Britain and the empire from Germany, Italy, and Japan simultaneously. Their report went on: "We cannot, therefore, exaggerate the importance from the point of view of imperial defense of any political action that can be taken to reduce the number of our potential enemies and gain the support of political allies."

Britain then was the only nation with interests and influence on every continent. In modern terminology, it was a superpower. Japanese aggression could threaten Britain's Asian possessions. Even in China it had more investments than the United States. Italian attempts to control the Mediterranean threatened Britain's supply routes to its Far East empire. Britain had given guarantees to France and Czechoslovakia, but it had also promised Australia that if Japanese aggression became a threat it would send a fleet to Singapore. Germany, Italy, and Japan were now joined in the anti-Comintern Pact, the Comintern being the Communist International run from Moscow.

In the spring of 1938 Chamberlain told Roosevelt he would like to reconsider the proposal for a conference, but then Hitler began his campaign against Austria, and Roosevelt said the time had passed. Soon after this, Eden resigned from the government to join Churchill in the antiappeasement camp. Young and handsome, Eden was popular and was regarded as the glamour boy of the Conservative Party. His resignation was a blow to Chamberlain.

Hitler now began his first thrust outside Germany's borders, against Austria. In 1938 Austria was a quasi-fascist dictatorship on friendly terms with Mussolini's Italy. Hitler made use of the Austrian Nazi Party to engineer a series of crises in German-Austrian relations. Austrian chancellor Kurt von Schuschnigg cracked down on the Austrian Nazis. German radio ranted about the persecution of Germans and said Austria was German territory. To head off German claims, Schuschnigg announced that he would call a plebiscite on union with Germany. Hitler preempted this by sending his troops across the border. They went in unopposed.

Hitler went with them. He stopped at the village of Leonding, his birthplace, where he laid a wreath on his parents' grave, and then at Linz where he had gone to school, and where most of the 120,000 inhabitants turned out to give their hometown boy a rapturous reception. He then went on to Vienna. He was retracing at the head of his army the route he had traveled as a child and a young man.

Once again, as in his move into the Rhineland, Hitler was gambling. The German army was in no condition to stand up to Britain and France if they opposed this breach of the Versailles Treaty. More than half the German tanks and armored cars that set out for the Austrian border broke down before they got there. Hitler asked Mussolini not to oppose the move, and when Mussolini agreed, he promised him his undying gratitude, cementing the new Berlin-Rome Axis.

Hitler incorporated Austria into his Third Reich. The term used for the process was *anschluss,* which means not "annexation" but "connection," a joining together. This implied that the Austrians were joining their people, the Germans. In fact Austrians, although German speaking, had never been a part of a German nation. Nevertheless, crowds cheered the German troops when they marched into Vienna, and Austrians launched a reign of terror against the country's half-million Jewish citizens with an enthusiasm that surprised their German masters. Not everyone cheered when the German soldiers marched in; Austria, and particularly Vienna, had a long and strong socialist tradition.

One Austrian who was worried about the *anschluss* was a young policeman in the small town of Wels. As a detective in the antisubversion branch, he had been decorated for his part in rounding up and jailing local Nazis. Now he feared for his job and even his life. He joined the Nazi Party and sought a transfer out of Wels to a place where he would not be known. When the Austrian police force merged with the German, he got a transfer to Berlin, and through hard work and diligence he rose in the ranks and was given more responsible posts, until in 1943 Franz Stangl was appointed commandant of the concentration camp at Treblinka, where a million people were killed by gas as part of the Nazi extermination program. As the Nazis took over the organs of the state, they also took over the channels along which energies and ambitions flow.

It became clear that Ribbentrop as ambassador was not going to be able to give Hitler the alliance with Britain that he wanted, so Hitler recalled him from London and made him foreign minister, Nazifying the Foreign Ministry. Two years later, when Sumner Welles talked to Ribbentrop in Berlin, he found him, he wrote, "saturated with hate for England to the exclusion of any other dominating mental influence." It sounds like a spurned suitor.

In February 1938, Joseph P. Kennedy arrived in London to take up the post of American ambassador. The post was a reward for contributions to Roosevelt's election campaign and for helping Roosevelt get the Democratic nomination in 1932. It was an unusual choice. American ambassadors to the Court of St. James have usually been WASPs. Kennedy was a Boston Irish Catholic, two generations away from tenant farming in County Wexford, with his nine children accompanying him to London, one of them the future President Kennedy.

Although a Harvard graduate, Joseph Kennedy was the son of a saloon keeper and political ward captain in Boston, and he made his fortune in finance without the help of family connections. He was regarded by the Wall Street old guard as a pirate. He also prospered in Hollywood, creating the conglomerate that was RKO, and in anticipation of the ending of Prohibition, he acquired the agency for several Scotch whiskeys. He turned his wealth into political clout and he was considered presidential timber. Roosevelt appointed him chairman of the Securities and Exchange Commission to watch over Wall Street, the poacher turned gamekeeper.

In London Kennedy approved of Chamberlain's appeasement policy and became close to him. He hated and feared war above all else and once told a friend, "I don't want a war. I have four sons and I don't want to see them go to war." (His anxiety was prophetic: the war was to take the life of his oldest son, Joseph Jr., as well as that of his British son-in-law.) He believed that trade and sound finance were the answer to the world's problems and that Communism was a greater danger than Nazism.

Reprimanded by the State Department for speaking out undiplomatically in favor of appeasement, he cabled Roosevelt and Hull: "On my way to Edinburgh with speech. All international affairs omitted, talking about flowers, birds, trees. The only thing I am afraid of is that instead of giving me the freedom of the city they will make me queen of the May."

Another American in Europe was urging appeasement, and he influenced Kennedy's views. Charles Lindbergh, the aviator hero, was now living in a village in Kent. He and his wife left America after the tragedy of the kidnap and murder of their baby and the press attention that amounted to harassment. Lindbergh was a friendly visitor to Germany and had received a decoration from Field Marshal Göring. He had access to people in high places in Paris and London, and he warned anyone who would listen that the German air force was stronger than the British and French air forces together and could lay waste any city in Europe.

His view had influence. Tom Jones, former secretary to the British cabinet, wrote in his diary in 1938: "Since my talk with Lindbergh on Monday I've sided with those working for peace at any cost in humiliation, because of the picture of our relative unpreparedness in the air and on the ground which Lindbergh painted, and because of his belief that the democracies would be crushed."

With Germany expanding, France stepped up construction of its Maginot line. This was a technological version of the trenches of 1914–18, a chain of forts connected by underground tunnels.

Before 1914 the French army had been imbued with the spirit of attack. Dash, boldness, aggressiveness, and élan were the virtues cultivated. But the slaughter of hundreds of thousands of men hurled against barbed wire and entrenched machine guns changed that. Now the prevailing view was that the defender had the advantage. The Maginot line was a long defensive trench. It had antitank traps in front, barely visible above ground; the tunnels and the forts were shellproof and gasproof and had their own generators to supply electricity and water. Germany started constructing its own fortified techno-trench, the Siegfried line, and the two faced each other.

The British Lieutenant General Alan Brooke visited the Maginot line and wrote a perceptive comment in his diary: "An astonishing engineering feat, but I am not convinced that it is a marvelous military accomplishment . . . The most dangerous aspect is the psychological one; a sense of false security is engendered, a feeling of sitting behind an impregnable iron fence; and should the fence perchance be broken, the French fighting spirit might well be brought crumbling with it."

Behind the Maginot line, France was a divided society. In response to the threat of a fascist coup in 1934, the left-wing parties, including the Communists, had combined to create a Popular Front,* and in 1936 it formed a government under the premiership of the Socialist Léon Blum. So hated was he by the Right, all the more so because he was Jewish, that many declared, "Better Hitler than Blum." A series of political scandals brought governments into low esteem, and, with a number of parties forming and reforming alliances, they changed frequently. Between 1933 and 1940 there were nineteen governments and eleven prime ministers.

• • •

As spring became summer in that eventful year 1938, Hitler turned his attention to Czechoslovakia, one of the countries created at Versailles out of the pieces of the shattered Austro-Hungarian Empire. It had resources that made it a prize for the Third Reich: agriculture and minerals and a technically advanced armaments industry that took 10 percent of the world's arms export market. The eastern part of the country, Sudetenland, was largely German speaking and had grievances against the central government in Prague. It contained 2.5 million of the country's 13 million inhabitants, and also its frontier fortifications. Hitler exploited Sudeten grievances to draw a picture of ethnic Germans suffering oppression, once again getting help from a local Nazi Party, and insisted that they must be liberated.

The crisis over Sudetenland culminated in the conference at Munich

---

* This is what it is usually called in English, but this is actually a too-literal translation of *Front Populaire*. A more accurate translation would be "People's Front."

in September, which is seen as the zenith, or perhaps the nadir, of the appeasement policy. The German government said Sudetenland should be detached from Czechoslovakia. France had a treaty of mutual assistance with Czechoslovakia, and Britain was committed to go to war alongside France. The Soviet Union was also committed to defend Czechoslovakia and it promised to do so. The French cabinet was divided. The British government told the French that since they could do little to help the Czechs militarily, the Czechs should be pushed into making concessions.

Roosevelt intervened covertly, evidently with the aim of stiffening opposition to Hitler. On September 20 he called the British ambassador, Sir Ronald Lindsay, to the White House. He told him that their meeting must be kept secret. What he then proposed was a de facto alliance against Germany. He said that if the major powers called a conference he would attend, providing it were not held in Europe. He suggested the Azores or another Atlantic island. If Germany attacked Czechoslovakia the powers could blockade Germany. They would not call it a war but nations would simply refuse to trade with Germany and cut off Germany's trade with others. He implied that the United States would participate. America could even continue to send weapons to Britain despite the Neutrality Acts, providing Britain did not declare war.

In his cabled report to Halifax, Lindsay said: "Several times in the conversation, he showed himself quite alive to the possibility that somehow or other, in indefinable circumstances, the United States might again find themselves involved in a European war. In that case he regarded it as almost inconceivable that it would be possible for him to send any American troops across the Atlantic . . . But it was just possible that if Germany were to invade Great Britain with a considerable force, such a wave of emotion might arise that an American army might be sent overseas." Halifax did not respond to this surprising offer but simply told Roosevelt that they were still trying to satisfy Germany's grievances.

Roosevelt did not explain how a blockade could be imposed without war. In his New Deal Roosevelt created new institutions to deal with new problems. It seems that in foreign affairs also, here as in his "quarantine" speech in Chicago, he was seeking to create some new institution, something that was not *quite* a war but that would allow America to damage an enemy country. Two months later Lindsay told Halifax in another cable, "Mr. Roosevelt is of course notoriously inaccurate as to detail, especially where the detail hampers his progress of his own pet schemes," words which would have evoked hearty agreement from many in Roosevelt's administration.

When the situation reached crisis point, Chamberlain, in a dramatic and unprecedented gesture, went to Germany to see Hitler, traveling by air for the first time, and taking Sir Horace Wilson with him as his advisor. After he met Hitler, he decided that he could trust him. He wrote in his diary: "In spite of the hardness and ruthlessness I saw in his face, I got the impression that here was a man who could be relied upon when he had given his word."

Hitler raised his demands and also the emotional volume, making ranting speeches and insisting that his patience was at an end. He demanded the immediate annexation of Sudetenland and moved troops up to the border, and the formidable Czech army mobilized. British opinion was now hardening against Hitler. Even the *Times,* which had pushed appeasement policies even further than Chamberlain, said his latest demands were "the language of the bully."

Britain prepared for war. Families that could were urged to send their children out of London to escape the bombing, and some private schools moved to the countryside. Civil defense volunteers had already been enlisted, and they learned to deal with wounded, put out fires, and identify poison gas. Trenches were dug in public parks to be used as shelters. The unthinkable seemed possible. Moyra Charlton, a novelist living with a husband, children, servants, and dog in a village near London, spoke for many when she wrote despairingly in her diary, "Thousands, millions of young lives to be lost only twenty years after last time. It can't be! God can't let it happen!"

The service chiefs presented a report to the cabinet on the military situation. It made grim reading. Halifax called it "an extremely melancholy document." It said German forces outnumbered the British and French on the ground. The British army could field only two divisions, and they would be deficient in equipment. The expansion of the RAF ordered the year before had not yet begun to show results. It had only four fighter squadrons, and two of these were Gloster Gladiators, open-cockpit biplanes that would not have looked out of place over a World War One battlefield. (Some of these Gladiators saw action in the war in the Mediterranean theater.) On the plus side, it said the Czechoslovak army, with twenty-one divisions behind strong fortifications, was a force to be reckoned with, as was the French army. Britain was in a weak position.

Mussolini proposed a meeting in Munich with Britain, France, and Germany. The Soviet Union, which had promised to defend Czechoslovakia, was excluded. The four powers signed an agreement that amounted to surrender, thinly disguised. Germany occupied the Sudeten areas and expelled non-German speakers. The Czechs bowed to an agreement imposed upon them by their allies. Hitler encouraged Poland to join in the carve-up, and it demanded from a now-helpless Czechoslovakia the frontier city of Teschen, which had a partly Polish population.

The truncated state of Czechoslovakia lost its fortified defense line, and Germany gained rich resources and the Skoda works, the second-largest armaments plant in Europe, which immediately began producing tanks and guns for the German army. The four powers guaranteed the new frontiers of Czechoslovakia. Hitler promised that he had no more territorial demands to make.

Chamberlain flew back to announce "peace in our time" to a tumultuous welcome which expressed a nation's relief. He went straight from the airport to Buckingham Palace, where he was accorded the rare privilege of appearing on the palace balcony beside the king to receive the acclamation of the crowd. In inviting him to the palace, King George was exceeding his constitutional powers. A British monarch is supposed to have no political views, but the king was giving the Munich agreement royal approval before it had been accepted or even discussed by Parliament. King George and Queen Elizabeth were known in political circles to approve of the appeasement policy. But no one objected. Chamberlain was hailed as a savior.

In the House of Commons, Winston Churchill was one of a small minority in the Conservative Party who condemned the agreement. "We have sustained a defeat without a war, the consequences of which will travel with us far along our road," he warned. An honest reaction came from Léon Blum in Paris: "I felt relieved and ashamed."

The following Sunday this message was read out in churches in Czechoslovakia:

The land of St. Wencelas has just been invaded by foreign armies, and the thousand-year frontier has been violated. This sacrifice has been imposed upon us by our ally, France, and our friend, Britain. The Primate of the ancient Kingdom of Bohemia is praying to God Almighty that the peace efforts prompting this terrible sacrifice will be crowned with permanent success, and should they not, he is praying to the Almighty to forgive all those who imposed this injustice on the people of Czechoslovakia.

Hitler was strengthened. The Hungarian-born historian John Lukacs recalls that Germans were transformed by their country's expansion. "From Podolian villages to the avenues of great cities such as Budapest or Trieste or Prague, Germans, whether tourist visitors or white-stockinged youth, walked or marched with an arrogance and self-confidence that had never been theirs before."

Another Roosevelt appointee in a diplomatic post was William Bullitt, the ambassador to France. Unlike Joseph Kennedy, he had wide experience of foreign affairs. As a young man he had been in the U.S. delegation to the Versailles Conference, and he was the first American ambassador to the Soviet Union. He was not a career professional in the foreign service and he spent the 1920s as an international playboy, as well as writing a successful novel. He had a considerable fortune, which he found useful both as a playboy and as a diplomat, for in his Paris post he was known for his lavish entertaining and his cellar was the envy of connoisseurs. Bullitt was soon on intimate terms with French political leaders. He had Roosevelt's ear, and reported and counseled constantly on the affairs, not only of France, but of all Europe. He supported the appeasement policy at first because he feared Soviet ambitions more than German, but changed his view after Munich.

A few days after the Munich agreement, Bullitt lunched with French prime minister Edouard Daladier. Daladier said that unlike others in the cabinet, he thought the Munich agreement was a disaster and he expected Hitler to make more territorial demands soon. He said that if France had three or four thousand military aircraft he would not have signed the agreement. Bullitt was so impressed that he went back to Washington and told Roosevelt during a long evening at the White House that he thought war would break out soon and America should arm the Allies, particularly France and particularly with aircraft.

Roosevelt told reporters the next day that he wanted $500 million more in the defense budget, to be spent on aircraft, and that America could produce up to twenty thousand planes a year. Military men in discussion with him said they found it hard to get him to accept that if planes were to be built, money had to be spent on pilots, training, hangars, and airfields. Clearly, in Roosevelt's mind, many of the planes were destined not for American airfields but for France.

Roosevelt's secretary for war, Henry Woodring, was opposed to any moves to sell warplanes to France or Britain — the air force was then part of the army, the Army Air Corps. Woodring was an isolationist. He had impressed Roosevelt by winning the governorship of Kansas, traditionally a Republican stronghold, as a Democrat, and Roosevelt had appointed him assistant secretary for war in 1933. Roosevelt bypassed him on the matter of arms sales and gave the responsibility for overseas sales to the treasury secretary, Henry Morgenthau.

Morgenthau, a tall, balding figure who usually had a worried look, was a neighbor of Roosevelt's in Dutchess County, and a member of a wealthy family with a long involvement in public affairs. The publisher of an agricultural magazine, he shared with Roosevelt a strong attachment to the Hudson Valley countryside. He was one of Roosevelt's oldest political friends and a person Roosevelt turned to for difficult or sensitive tasks. Morgenthau was also a fervent antifascist, and had wanted America to help the Republican cause in Spain.

Jean Monnet, a French banker much involved in governmental activity, headed a purchasing mission to America. He wanted to buy the latest American aircraft. Morgenthau told Roosevelt, "If your theory is that Britain and France are our first line of defense, then if you want them to be the first line, either you give them the good stuff or tell them to go home."

The French team were allowed to inspect in secret the latest twin-engine Douglas bomber, which was not even ready for the U.S. Air Force yet. The aircraft crashed in California and one of the men pulled out of the wreckage, listed as a Douglas Aircraft mechanic, turned out to be an official of the French Ministry of Aviation, and that cat was out of the bag.

Chamberlain told British reporters that he foresaw new disarmament agreements with Germany and Italy and years of peace and prosperity ahead. But he was never starry-eyed enough to believe that appeasement could remove all threats, and rearmament was stepped up.

Defense expenditure was increased from 8 percent of GNP to 21 percent. Germany's was 23 percent. Military talks began with the French, and it was agreed that a British expeditionary force would go to France in the event of war.

The rearmament program changed direction. The government set about expanding the army so that it could fight on the Continent. But it still put the biggest effort into the RAF, which was now permitted to buy aircraft in America. It bought Lockheed Hudson bombers and North American Harvard trainers.

In America the New York World's Fair opened in April 1939. Ignoring the menacing war clouds in Europe, it had as its theme "The World of Tomorrow," depicting a future world of good living and leisure brought about by the marvels of technology. Twenty-five million Americans went to the fair and were given a taste of the future that seemed to await them. In the General Motors pavilion they saw cities with elevated avenues along which futuristic cars glided, and in the Bell Telephone pavilion the marvels of high-fidelity stereophonic sound. However, the world of peace and plenty was to be delayed for a while.

When Germany seized Czechoslovakia, the *New York Daily News* wrote: "This to Americans should be an interesting show to watch, not a fight to mix into." But Americans were coming to feel that the show was a drama and it had a villain. Correspondents in Europe were reporting the brutalities of the Nazi regime. Radio journalism was coming into its own and bringing the affairs of Europe closer. The voices of men such as Edward R. Murrow, Eric Sevareid, and William Shirer reporting over the air waves from Europe were becoming familiar. The marvel of radio also brought other voices into American living rooms for the first time: Chamberlain and Masaryk during the Munich crisis, and the frenzied *Sieg Heils* rising above the *Sportspalatz* in Berlin.

Soon after the Munich meeting came *kristallnacht*. In response to the shooting of a German diplomat in Paris by a young Polish Jew, gangs of Nazis, encouraged by the government, rampaged through the streets beating up and murdering Jews and wrecking synagogues and Jewish-owned stores. Wealthy Jews were singled out and hauled off to concentration camps, to be released only on surrender of their wealth. This was a pogrom, carried out, not in some backward part of Czarist Russia but in the cities of a civilized nation in the center of Europe. It shocked even many of those prepared to give Nazi Germany the benefit of the doubt. Roosevelt told a press conference: "It is amazing that this could happen in Twentieth Century civilization." He recalled his ambassador from Berlin for consultations, and the ambassador never went back.

Powerful voices now were saying that the existence of such a regime was itself a threat to American values and even American interests. Hamilton Fish Armstrong, the editor of the prestigious journal *Foreign Affairs,* published a book called *We or They,* arguing that democracy and totalitarianism were necessarily in conflict and that America should mobilize against the dictators. Max Lerner's book about the Nazi threat contained its warning in the title, *It Is Later Than You Think,* and this became a slogan of the anti-isolationists. Quincy Howe responded with a tract with another self-explanatory title, *England Expects Every American to Do His Duty,* for there was still a great deal of suspicion of Britain.

Adolf A. Berle, the assistant secretary of state for economic affairs, a former Columbia University economics professor who had been a member of Roosevelt's "brain trust" in the early days of the New Deal, worried that anti-Nazi sentiment might be distorting perceptions of America's true interests. He wrote in a memo to the president:

> Our emotion is obscuring the fact that were the actor anyone but Hitler, with his cruelty and anti-Semitic feeling, we should regard this as merely reconstituting the old system, undoing the obviously unsound work of Versailles, and generally following the line of historic logic. American emotion ought to be reserved to combat the atrocities rather than by entering a general war to try to maintain a situation which was always untenable from the time it was created . . . The generous emotions of American liberals are likely to be abused now as they were in 1914. We have yet to encounter the full weight of British propaganda.

Roosevelt made no move to admit Jewish refugees from Nazism, although some close to him urged him to do so. These included his wife, Eleanor, who was coming to be seen as his liberal conscience, and his treasury secretary, Henry Morgenthau. In 1938 there were 150,000 visa applications from Germany and 27,370 places on the immigration quota. Roosevelt said privately that Congress would not support him if he tried to alter the immigration quotas, and opinion polls indicated that he was right. Instead he tried to set up a scheme whereby other countries would accept Jewish refugees, but this did not come to anything.

Britain had no body of immigration laws but it limited immigration; refugees were admitted if they had jobs or sponsors. Funds were set up to provide sponsorship. The *Times* carried advertisements such as these in its "Situations Wanted" columns: "German girl, Jewess (18) still in Germany, able to do housework, good dressmaker, very fond of children. Turiner Strasse 5, Berlin." "Viennese doctor of philosophy, Jewish . . . seeks position as tutor." The government allowed a *kindertransport*, bringing in 9,800 children, who were found homes. Some 80,000 German and Austrian Jews came to Britain.

In May 1939 the British government, with its troops in Palestine battling an Arab revolt, put a quota on Jewish immigration to that country to appease the Arabs. The government was worried about the looming prospect of war in Europe and it made sense to reduce the demands on its armed forces. But it was half closing the door of a haven for Jews fleeing persecution and murder, and this angered Jewish communities around the world.

Hitler scored a point when he scoffed: "The whole democratic world is oozing sympathy for the poor tormented Jewish people, but remains hard-hearted and obdurate when it comes to helping them."

Six months after Munich, Hitler shattered whatever hopes anyone still harbored about his intentions. He exploited Slovak separatism in the truncated Czechoslovakia to seize the entire country. When the aging and ailing President Hacha, faced with Slovak demands, went to Berlin to ask him to help preserve the nation as one of the guarantors of its frontiers, Hitler shouted at him and threatened to raze Prague to the ground. Cowed and on the point of collapse, Hacha agreed to surrender. The next day, German troop carriers rolled into the rain-drenched streets of Prague past glum crowds while bombers circled low overhead. Hitler spent the night in Hradny Castle, the presidential palace. Once again he had achieved a bloodless victory.

Hitler seems to have underestimated the outrage this would provoke. Curiously, Chamberlain did also. In Parliament the next day he said he regretted what had happened but added: "Do not let us on that account be deflected from our course . . . It would be very wrong to exchange angry words about Germany and Herr Hitler. I have so often heard charges of breach of faith bandied about that I do not want to associate myself with charges of that character." Members were astonished, and that evening some talked about replacing Chamberlain.

Halifax had always worried that the Munich agreement might have been a mistake. Now he told Chamberlain firmly that his response to this latest bloodless conquest by Germany would not do. Chamberlain was due to make a speech in Birmingham two days later. It was to be about domestic affairs, but at Halifax's urging he threw away his prepared speech and spoke about Germany and Czechoslovakia, adopting a new tone. He cited one after the other the promises that Hitler had broken, and asked, "Is this the end of an old adventure, or is it the beginning of a new? Is this the last attack on a small state, or is it to be followed by others? Is this, in fact, a step in the direction of an attempt to dominate the world by force?"

British opinion swung around. Press comment was universal in condemning this latest seizure of territory. There could be no pretense that this was simply bringing other ethnic Germans into the German nation. The *Daily Telegraph,* which had supported Chamberlain's appeasement policy, declared: "The 'spirit of Munich' is dead and buried, for who can hope to appease a boa constrictor." The *News Chronicle* was clear about what must be done now: "Hitler must be told flatly . . . 'Thus far and no farther.' If he attempts to commit any further acts of aggression, it will be regarded as an act of war against all."

In that same month, the exhausted defenders of Madrid surrendered to General Franco's troops, and the drawn-out death throes of the Spanish Republic came to an end. Democracy was in retreat everywhere.

■   ■   ■

Roosevelt was coming to believe, as he told intimates, that Nazi Germany was America's enemy, and that if Britain and France did not stop Germany, America would have to do so. On January 31, 1939, he met the members of the Senate Military Affairs Committee and told them that Germany, Italy, and Japan were bent on world domination. He described Hitler as a wild man, somebody "we would call a nut." He said that if Germany moved westward and Britain and France fought, it was a fifty-fifty chance that Hitler and Mussolini would win, and then the next step would be Central and South America.

He was more cautious in his public statements. He had to be cautious, for 1938 had not been a good year for him. After a steady recovery from the depths of 1932, the economy had slid back and unemployment had risen again. America's national income was still 14 percent below the 1929 level. Labor battles racked the nation. Roosevelt's attempt to enlarge the Supreme Court after the Court declared much of his National Recovery Program illegal had been blocked by Congress, a major defeat in a major battle. The Republicans and some of his Democratic opponents had gained ground in the 1938 congressional election.

He made it clear in his 1939 New Year's message that he regretted signing the Neutrality Act. "We have learned," he said, "that when we deliberately try to legislate neutrality, our neutrality laws may operate unevenly and unfairly, may actually give aid to the aggressor and deny it to the victim." Britain, an island nation, would benefit from wartime trade with America and from being able to purchase armaments much more than Germany. In any case no one envisaged selling armaments to Germany.

The armed forces had a low priority in the years of isolation and the Depression. In military strength on the ground America ranked twentieth in the world, below Holland. Now, in 1939, Roosevelt asked Congress for almost two billion dollars for defense. He stressed in his message to Congress that this was for national and hemisphere defense.

Roosevelt tried to get the Senate to revise the Neutrality Act. On the evening of July 18 he convened leading senators from both parties in the White House, along with Vice President John Vance Garner and Cordell Hull. He received them in his shirtsleeves, but his informality was not intended to denote any lack of seriousness. While a butler served them drinks and sandwiches, he launched into an alarming exposition of the international scene. "We base our need for changing the present law on the ground that war may come at any time," he told them. He said he wanted to be able to help countries deter aggression and deter war. Hull followed, supporting his view.

Senator William Borah of Idaho, a tall, imposing, white-maned figure, a senator since 1907 and the dean of the Senate, had been a passionate opponent of any involvement with Europe from the League of Nations onward. He challenged Roosevelt's view and said there would be no war in Europe. "All this hysteria is manufactured and artificial," he said.

Hull said, almost through clenched teeth, "I wish the Senator from Idaho would come down to the State Department and read the dispatches that come in from all over Europe from day to day, and I am sure he would change his opinion."

"I have my own sources of information and on several occasions I have found them more reliable than the State Department. I can say to you there is not going to be any war!" Borah insisted. Hull was so outraged at this dismissal of the State Department that he could barely contain himself.

The meeting went on until midnight, and at the end Garner turned to Roosevelt and said in his perky Texan voice, "Well, Captain, let's face it. It looks like you just don't have the votes."

On the floor of the Senate, the vote went against revision. This was a matter of domestic as well as foreign politics. Congress was asserting itself in the face of Roosevelt's unprecedented use of executive power. Senator Nye put the position plainly: "It is a question of presidential power, presidential discretion, presidential chance to commit the country in a way that makes staying out of war exceedingly difficult . . . We need the neutrality law. We need restraints upon the President."

Roosevelt thought the hands-off attitude encouraged Hitler. The next day he wrote in confidence to New York congresswoman Caroline O'Day: "I honestly believe that the vote last night was a stimulus to war."

Given the international atmosphere in the summer of 1939, it was inevitable that when King George VI and Queen Elizabeth visited the United States for four days on their way back from Canada, the first-ever visit by a British monarch, it should have political significance. Indeed, it was intended to have. As Eleanor Roosevelt wrote later: "My husband invited them to Washington because, believing that we all may be involved in a life or death struggle, in which Great Britain would be our first line of defense, he hoped that the visit would create a bond of friendship between the two countries."

Roosevelt could count the visit a success. He personally supervised every detail. He could not control the weather, and the ninety-four-degree temperature in Washington made the ceremonials an ordeal long remembered, but King George and Queen Elizabeth concealed their discomfort. They toured the New York World's Fair, and the king ate a hot dog to show that he was a regular guy. The king and queen proved to be a draw. A crowd estimated at 3.5 million lined New York City streets to see them. Isolationist newspapers worried that the king might put something over on honest Uncle Sam. Senator Borah warned against "giving to George the Sixth what we took away from George the Third." In fact, it was Britain that was being asked for something, not America.

After visiting New York the royal couple went upstate to Roosevelt's home in Hyde Park for an overnight stay. The president was at his most charming. "He is easy to get to know and never makes one feel shy," the king wrote later. The conversation went far beyond goodwill platitudes. They discussed the prospects of war. Roosevelt said that if war broke out he would like the American navy to be able to patrol the Atlantic from bases in the British-owned islands of Bermuda and Trinidad. He said he thought the Neutrality Act could be modified. King George's notes of the conversation say he also said that "if London was bombed USA would come in."

The conversation went on until 1:30 in the morning, when Roosevelt tapped the forty-seven-year-old monarch on the knee and said, "Young man, it's time you went to bed."

Roosevelt sent appeals. At the time of Munich he appealed for conciliation. He appealed to Mussolini, through the new Italian ambassador, to throw his weight against war. He appealed to Hitler to promise nonaggression against a list of thirty-two countries in Europe and the Middle East. Hitler responded with derision, pointing out that these countries had not asked for American protection and that some of them were British and French colonies.

In Britain people now saw that war was, if not inevitable, at any rate likely. Life was taking on a temporary character; if people made plans for more than a few months ahead, they were tentative. Volunteers swelled the ranks of the Territorial Army, the part-time reserve, many of them men who thought there would be a war and they would be conscripted anyway and there was some advantage in getting in early. More than two million people now enrolled in one branch or another of civil defense. The Oxford Union, which seven years earlier had shocked the country with a majority vote saying its members would never again fight for king and country, voted for conscription.

The British government decided to defend anyone who looked like being Germany's next potential victim. As Chamberlain told the cabinet, if it came to war, "We should attack Germany, not in order to save a particular victim, but to bring down a bully." The language was significant. "Bully" is not a word in the vocabulary of international politics. Running through the deliberations of the British government was a current of morality, as well as the geostrategic considerations that govern the interaction of states.

This current emerged into open expression only occasionally. Alfred Duff Cooper, resigning from a junior post in the government over the Munich agreement, said: "So far as we were concerned, the soul and honor of England were at stake." Sir Alexander Cadogan wrote in his diary after the occupation of Prague: "We must have a moral position, and we shall lose it if we don't do something now."

Behind these words lay a simple, old-fashioned set of moral principles, never spelled out, that applied to national and occasionally to international life. A person in public office should not put his own career ahead of the welfare of his country. Promises should be kept. A ruler should not be wantonly cruel. He should not deliberately incite war or aggression. These principles are, perhaps, of limited value in making society more equal and more just, but they had relevance to international affairs in the Europe of that time. They colored the views of the men ruling Britain, and influenced their responses.

*

Chamberlain announced in April that he would bring in a very limited form of conscription, the first time this had ever been done in peace time: men aged twenty and twenty-one would be called up for three months' military training. The opposition Labour Party, like left-wing parties in other countries, had by now stopped voting against rearmament measures. The British government was determined to draw a line in the sand which Germany must not be allowed to cross. Hitler demanded a revision of the sections of the Versailles Treaty that fixed the German-Polish borders. It was clear that Poland would be the next target of German aggression, and Chamberlain announced that if Poland was attacked, Britain would come to its defense, joined by France. Having given in to Germany the previous year, Britain was now standing up to a much stronger Germany. Having refused to defend democratic Czechoslovakia, or being unable to do so, it was now promising to defend a dictatorship that had helped to dismember it.

Yet the German offer implicit in *Mein Kampf* and in many exchanges in the past four years was still there, and the British knew it. A message came through an intermediary from a highly placed Nazi official, Walter Hawel, saying Germany only wanted "her rightful place, in partnership with Britain, as a world power." Chamberlain noted in the margin: "This only means a free hand in E and SE Europe." Neville Henderson continued to argue in dispatches from the Berlin embassy that Germany's ambitions in the East did not affect Britain's interests.

In fact, Germany's claims on Poland had much more justification than its claims on Czechoslovakia. Danzig, which had been placed under international control to give Poland a port, had been a German city and had a German population. Germany wanted a readjustment of the "Polish corridor" which separated East Prussia from the rest of Germany, an arrangement that no country would willingly accept. But now the rights and wrongs of a specific issue did not matter. Britain and France were making a stand.

This policy had its critics. It seemed to place the issue of war or peace for Britain in the hands of the government of Poland, a country with which Britain had had no close connection up to now. The terms of the guarantee to Poland were unclear. Chamberlain seemed to think he was guaranteeing Poland's independence but not necessarily its present frontiers. Ambassador Kennedy, seeing the appeasement policy crumbling, wrote despairingly: "The futility is frightful. They can't save the Poles, they can only carry out a war of revenge, and that will mean the destruction of Europe."

Once again Britain prepared for war. The Munich crisis had been a dress rehearsal. Evacuation plans were prepared. Civil defense was readied, more volunteer air raid wardens recruited. The government, anticipating gas attacks, distributed gas masks to the entire population, and everyone became familiar with their pig-snout appearance and the rubbery smell inside one — the children's gas mask had a Mickey Mouse face. Britain began building air raid shelters. It designated some buildings as shelters, and it distributed advice on how to build an air raid shelter in the back yard and made the materials available. These were the so-called Anderson shelters, named after Sir John Anderson, the head of the Imperial Defence Committee that had designed them. They were cheap, and a householder could make one himself. Two curved sections of corrugated iron were sunk into the ground, and a shallow pit was dug underneath, like a miniature Quonset hut. Soon millions of suburban homes would have them in back yards.

A blackout was instituted so that cities would not be visible from the air. Antiaircraft guns were emplaced around London, and barrage balloons floated above the city; these trailed wires, and, at 5,000 feet, were designed to keep bombers above them.

Britain was seeking allies urgently. It wanted to deter Germany by ringing it with states all agreed to defend one another. It signed mutual defense agreements with Romania and Turkey. But the big one was Russia. The Soviet Union had called consistently for collective resistance to fascism. Chamberlain resisted for a long time the urging of many in Britain that he seek an alliance with Russia. He had a visceral dislike of Communism and a suspicion of Soviet intentions. But he finally agreed with those who said Britain needed the Soviet Union as an ally against Germany, and sent a mission to Moscow.

The Russians wanted a defensive arrangement to include Poland, the Baltic states, and Finland, but these feared Soviet protection as much as German aggression and would not take part. Stalin, still smarting from his exclusion from the Munich conference, found the British mission halfhearted in its bid for an alliance. Meanwhile, Germany began negotiations for an agreement with Russia, in secret. The Soviet government now had two suitors.

Roosevelt knew about these secret talks. The German ambassador in Moscow, Werner von Schulenburg, was one of many German officials who thought Hitler's policies were disastrous for his country, and he told the American embassy about the Soviet-German negotiations. The information was sent directly to the president.

Roosevelt wanted the Soviet Union on Britain's side rather than in alliance with Germany. When the Soviet ambassador to Washington, Constantine Oumansky, left for Moscow, Roosevelt told him to tell Stalin that if his government joined up with Hitler and Hitler conquered France, Hitler would surely turn on Russia next. He followed this up with a message to the new U.S. ambassador in Moscow to give to the Soviet government, recounting what he had told Oumansky in more circumspect language. The urgency of the message was underlined by its extreme secrecy. It was cabled to Paris and taken to Moscow by special courier, and the ambassador was told not to refer to it in any message delivered through normal State Department channels.

Roosevelt could not tell the British that he was getting secret information from the German ambassador in Moscow, but in August he finally told them that a German-Soviet agreement was imminent. The British government had already received a warning from Eric Kordt, the head of Ribbentrop's secretariat and a secret anti-Nazi, who had urged the British government to stand firm at the time of Munich. He delivered the message in person at some risk. But it was too late for Britain to come up with a counteroffer.

Ribbentrop flew to Moscow to sign a nonaggression pact on August 17. In addition to promises of nonaggression, there was a plan for increased trade and secret clauses laying out the division of Poland.

The cynicism was breathtaking. This was realpolitik at its harshest. The Soviet Union was supposed to be the ally of workers the world over, the bastion from which Communism would spread to liberate the oppressed, and the opponent of fascism. This was its justification for demanding the unstinting support of Communists everywhere. One result of the pact was that when war broke out Communist parties around the world, in obedience to the line laid down by Moscow, reversed their earlier stand for a united front against Hitler and said the war was an imperialist war and the workers should not support it.

Some individual Communists rebelled. The secretary of the British Communist Party, Harry Pollitt, was one of these, and he was removed from his post by the party's governing council (to be reinstalled later after Germany invaded Russia and things were in their proper place again). The head of the American Communist Party, Earl Browder, went along with the Soviet line, although he had said a few weeks earlier that a Nazi-Soviet pact was "about as likely as my being elected President of the Chamber of Commerce." Like many other Communists, he felt it was his duty to support whatever the Soviet Union found it necessary to do to secure its safety. Several Communist members of the French National Assembly broke ranks and said they would continue to oppose Nazi Germany.

Germany, secure now in the east, stepped up its demands on Poland. Britain did not rule out a revision of frontiers achieved by negotiation, and to most people Germany's claim on Danzig seemed legitimate. Chamberlain asked the Polish government to negotiate over Danzig, but Poland, emboldened by the British guarantee, refused to consider a compromise. In any case it seems that Hitler was not interested in a compromise. Not content with claiming that the frontier arrangement was unjust, he said a German minority was being persecuted in Poland and faked the murder of Germans by Polish police.

Roosevelt made one more appeal for a peaceful solution, this time to the German and Polish leaders and to King Victor Emmanuel of Italy. Adolf Berle wrote in his diary: "My private opinion is that these messages will have about the same effect as a valentine sent to somebody's mother-in-law out of season, and they have all that quality of naiveté which is the prerogative alone of the United States. Nevertheless, they ought to be sent. The one certain thing in this business is that no one will be blamed for making any attempt, however desperate, to preserve peace."

The U.S. War and Navy Departments passed the word to aircraft and weapon manufacturers with orders from Britain and France that they should get everything they could across the border to Canada immediately because once war broke out the Neutrality Act would prevent them from sending them.

On September 1, as the first light of dawn touched a cobalt Baltic sky, the German battleship *Schleswig-Holstein* opened fire on the Polish shore defenses at Danzig, and the German army rolled across the Polish frontier from East Prussia and Czechoslovakia. William Bullitt in Paris got the news from the American embassy in Warsaw and telephoned Roosevelt to tell him, at 2:30 A.M. Washington time. "Well, Bill, it's come at last. God help us all," Roosevelt said.

The British and French governments issued their ultimatums, and they were ignored. There was a flurry of diplomatic activity with a Swedish intermediary passing messages. Germany made offers of negotiation which seemed to be aimed only at causing confusion and delay. The one piece of good news was that Italy was not going to join alongside Germany.

Early in the morning on September 3, Joseph Kennedy called in at 10 Downing Street. Chamberlain showed him the speech he was about to make, announcing a declaration of war. Kennedy telephoned Roosevelt, although it was four o'clock in the morning Washington time, and once again Roosevelt was awoken with news of war. "It's the end of the world, the end of everything," Kennedy said in a choked voice.

At eleven o'clock, Neville Chamberlain told the British people in a broadcast that he had asked Germany for an assurance that it would withdraw its forces from Poland. Then he said: "No such assurance having been received, I have to declare that this country is now at war with Germany." His BBC producer thought he looked "crumbled, despondent and old." It was a sad speech said in a sad voice, not a call to arms but an announcement that peace was at an end.

War was seen as a necessity, not welcomed joyously, as it had been in 1914. Nella Last was the wife of a tax inspector living in the shipbuilding town of Barrow, and she kept a diary throughout the war. She knew nothing about the last-minute diplomacy, but after hearing Chamberlain's broadcast she wrote, "I could tell by the dazed look on many faces that I had not been alone in my belief that 'something would turn up' to prevent war."

Moyra Charlton, who had written despairingly in her diary at the time of Munich, was now reconciled to war. She wrote that evening: "The declaration of war made me feel so sad, but now we must finish Hitlerism and win this."

France declared war on the same day, and as expected, Britain's Commonwealth partners, Canada, Australia, New Zealand, and South Africa, followed suit. It is often forgotten now that Eire, as Ireland was called, was also a member of the Commonwealth then. Eire was not expected to declare war on Germany and did not do so.

3

PHONY WAR

The Britain that went to war in 1939 was a stable society. Unlike in most countries on the Continent, there was little support for extremist political parties. Political differences were argued out passionately, but by and large the political system, including the royal family, was accepted. The British Union of Fascists and the Communist Party were both small, although the Communists had considerable influence and support in the labor movement and in intellectual circles.

British people assumed that their country was the world's top dog. If anyone doubted this they had only to look at their atlases. In those used in British schools, nearly a quarter of the world was colored red, meaning that it was either ruled by Britain, like most of Africa and all the Indian subcontinent, or was a British dominion, tied to the mother country in the Commonwealth and by bonds of sentiment and history.

For a country that had conquered nearly a quarter of the world Britain was a remarkably peaceable society. The crime rate was low. Policemen did not carry guns. In 1926 the labor unions staged a general strike and volunteers, mostly from the middle classes, drove buses and trucks to keep essential services going. This took place without any serious outbreak of violence. There are not many countries where this could have happened. It was a socially disciplined society. Crowds were orderly, the rules of social behavior were observed. Sportsmanship and fair play were taken as cardinal virtues.

Modesty was assumed to be a virtue, self-advertisement frowned upon. No British politician would boast of his war record. The Board of Deputies of British Jews, in a leaflet with advice for Jewish refugees from the Continent, said: "Do not make yourself conspicuous by speaking loudly, nor by your manner or dress. The Englishman greatly dislikes ostentation."

Britain had a firmly established class structure. At the top of the social hierarchy there was a ruling class of landed aristocracy and gentry which was almost a separate caste. Most were wealthy, their wealth coming from their estates, on which tenant farmers paid rent and treated the owner with an almost feudal deference, or else from the coal fields underneath. They went to the same schools, usually Eton and Harrow, where top hat and tails were part of the school uniform, and the men belonged to the same clubs. Their most common form of coming together was at weekend country house parties. Large numbers of servants catered to all their wants; nannies took care of their children. If a member of this class went to university — and it was normally Oxford or Cambridge — a "scout" would take care of his daily needs. If he went into the army, and it would be as an officer, a batman would act as his personal servant. He need have no direct contact with the lower orders. At home a butler would deal with the other servants; in the army a sergeant would be the go-between with the lower ranks.

Chamberlain was not a member of this class, although he was wealthy; his family background was in business. Winston Churchill was a member, and so was Lord Halifax, the foreign secretary; the king gave Halifax the keys to the garden of Buckingham Palace so that he could take a short cut through the garden on his way to his office. So was Sir Alexander Cadogan, the head of the Foreign Office; his ancestor, the first earl of Cadogan, was chief of staff to Churchill's ancestor, the duke of Marlborough, when the duke commanded the British army in the 1700s. Field Marshal Lord Gort, who was to command British troops in France, was a member of this class, and so was Anthony Eden.

This class had a strong sense of social obligation. Most members carried out some public functions, even if only at a local level. In wartime they led from the front. Every family of the aristocracy lost sons in the First World War; most did in the Second. Of the eight members of the 1939 Eton rowing team, four were killed in action in the next six years.

Below this was an upper-middle class which adopted the values of the aristocracy, particularly the sense of duty. They were educated at private schools, and it was from these that most of the administrators of the empire were drawn. In wartime they formed a natural officer class. Below this level the middle class expanded in the 1920s and '30s; the suburbs spread and ownership of homes and cars multiplied several-fold.

The working class, industrial and agricultural, was immediately identifiable by clothes, leisure pursuits, and particularly by speech — regional working-class dialects were often barely comprehensible to speakers of standard English. Their homes were small and outdoor plumbing was the norm. Among the worse-off in towns, particularly the unemployed, whole families often lived in a single room, with the accompanying evils of tuberculosis and incest. Many were politically class-conscious and militant, acting through the Labour or Communist Party and the labor unions.

The gulf between the classes was illustrated unwittingly by a magistrate who pronounced, when the war was well under way, "This is a people's war, as well as ours."

Class divisions carried over into the services. Officers were expected to be gentlemen, enlisted men not. A memo on living arrangements would refer to "officers and their ladies" and "other ranks and their wives." Leslie Hore-Belisha, appointed secretary for war in 1937, was unpopular with the top brass because he tried to make the army more democratic, improving conditions for enlisted men and opening up Sandhurst, the army's officer training academy, to boys from state schools as well as private schools. He was a social outsider in the Conservative Party and Jewish as well, which made his task all the more difficult. When he was moved to another post four months after war broke out, this was seen as a victory for the top brass.

British inventiveness and enterprise spearheaded the Industrial Revolution. In the nineteenth century Britain was the world's leading manufacturing country and London was its financial and commercial center. But in the twentieth century Britain lagged behind its principal economic rivals. Inventiveness was not matched by efficiency in manufacture. Productivity was poor. Aircraft designers were creating some of the best aircraft in the world, but factories were slow at producing them. Britain relied on imports for high-grade steel, machine tools, and many precision instruments, such as altimeters for aircraft and fuses for shells, and this became very important when war began.

British people by and large were pleased with their country. They fully acknowledged that it was not efficient industrially; they saw themselves as a nation of amateurs and were content to be so. "Muddling through" was sometimes contrasted happily with the furiously energetic Americans or the comically overorganized Germans.

A prototypical example of the British pride in amateurism is seen in a passage in the book *Falling Through Space* by Richard Hillary, the deeply serious autobiography of a fighter pilot, written in 1941. As an Oxford undergraduate in the 1930s, he and some fellow students found that a cheap way of touring Europe was to present themselves at universities on the Continent as an Oxford rowing team. At Bad Ems, a German told them England was clearly a decadent nation, since they obviously had not trained hard and were vague about arrangements. They had not even brought their own boat. He says, "We were quite untrained, lacked any form of organization, and were really quite hopelessly casual. We even arrived late for the start, where all five German crews were lined up eager to go." They were trailing until halfway through, when a German on a bridge spat on them. "A tactical error," Hillary comments. Spurred on by this, they pulled ahead with heroic effort and won by a hair's breadth. He concludes, "Looking back, the race was really a surprisingly accurate pointer to the course of the war."

Most British people's images of America came from the movie screens, which meant a world of glamour, gangsters, and cowboys. Ambassador Kennedy noted that even in wartime Al Capone's release from prison made the front pages of British newspapers. The cultural Right tended to view America as the source of a new barbarism, swamping civilization with a degraded popular culture. Many on the Left were excited by the New Deal and looked to it for ideas. But for most British people, serious knowledge of America had not progressed much since Alfred Duff Cooper, in World War One, came upon two officers discussing the American Civil War, uncertain about which side George Washington was on.

British people tended to regard America as a younger brother that had grown faster than he had matured, big and strong but clumsy and undereducated, often goodhearted but naive, and lacking the finesse and subtlety for diplomatic skills. This was a creature requiring guidance from older, wiser minds.

But it was a brother who was very useful to have around when trouble was brewing. As Europe moved into a crisis, British governments were more and more concerned to get American support. In records of discussions at government level, one finds time and time again ministers and officials considering how something will be received in America, both in Washington and by public opinion. When Britain and America signed a treaty reducing import tariffs in 1938, Chamberlain wrote to his sister: "The reason why I have been prepared to go a long way to get this treaty is precisely because I thought it would help to educate American opinion to act more and more with us, and because I feel sure it would frighten the totalitarians." Discussing bombing policy on the outbreak of war, his secretary for air, Sir Kingsley Wood, said in the cabinet that it was important for American public opinion that the first civilians killed should be British and not German. "How will it play in Peoria?" was a constant preoccupation.

• • •

When war broke out in Europe in 1914, President Wilson urged Americans to be "neutral in thought and deed." President Roosevelt spoke differently on September 3, 1939. "This nation will remain a neutral nation. But I cannot ask that every American will remain neutral in thought as well. Even a neutral must take account of facts. He cannot be asked to close his mind or his conscience," he said.

He made it clear that he believed that American interests were involved as well as American sympathies: "Passionately though we desire detachment, we are forced to realize that every word that comes through the air, every ship that sails the sea, every battle that is fought, does affect the American future." However, he also said: "I hope the United States will stay out of this war. I believe that it will. And I give you assurance and reassurance that every effort of your government will be directed to that end."

He also issued an appeal to the belligerents to refrain from bombing civilian targets, and all said they would.

Convinced though most Americans were of the evil of Nazism, they saw no need to line up with its European opponents. In December, the *Atlanta Constitution* said that judging by the excitement over the premiere in that city of the movie *Gone with the Wind,* most people were more interested in the Civil War than in the war in Europe.

For most Americans, the Atlantic Ocean represented a moral as well as a geographical distance from Europe. It was axiomatic that their country's conduct was morally superior to that of other countries. Their forefathers had crossed an ocean and struggled to build a life in a new country, away from the quarrels of the old continent, in order to give their children something better. To get embroiled in the affairs of Europe would be to throw this gift back in the faces of their forebears and to go back into a pit from which these forebears had escaped, a place of sordid quarrels unworthy of free Americans. As the commentator Oswald Garrison Villard wrote on the eve of the war: "The lesson for us Americans is clearer than ever: to keep out of this ungodly, revolting mess in Europe, in which one can have respect for neither side in the power-politics struggle."

Back then before America was a superpower, Americans thought more than now of their country in terms of what its founders had wanted it to be. Unlike most countries which evolved into nation-states, the United States was created for a purpose. It was to be a country living by certain principles, contained in the Declaration of Independence, the Constitution, and in elements in its history, a country different from the ones that its citizens or their fathers had left behind.

These principles have always been reference points for national conduct. They are so much a part of the American identity that America has always had something of the character of a secular faith. Its most extreme followers sometimes speak of "Americanism." Like most faiths, it has always had two impulses which pull in different directions. One is to evangelize, to spread the beliefs and practices which have brought its adherents happiness so that others may share in this good fortune. The other impulse is to hold tight to the faith, to keep oneself apart, and avoid dilution of one's distinctiveness and corruption of one's practices by too-close association with others.

In the 1840s these two impulses emerged in an argument between some who wanted to help European peoples struggling for national independence, such as the Poles and Hungarians, seeing in their situation an echo of America's own fight for independence, and others who thought that America had no business involving itself in European quarrels. These latter were labeled "isolationist" by their opponents, and the word entered the political vocabulary, although it did not gain wide currency until the twentieth century.

Lajos Kossuth, who led the Hungarians' struggle for freedom from the Austro-Hungarian Empire, received a rapturous welcome in the United States, but when he sought American help for his struggle, Henry Clay disabused him. Clay said the cause of liberty would be better served by "keeping our lamp burning brightly on this side of the Western shore as a light to all nations."

John Adams spoke similarly: "America goes not abroad in search of monsters to destroy. She is the well-wisher to the freedom and independence of all. She is the champion and vindicator only of her own."

In the twentieth century these two tendencies were exemplified in competing calls to help fight the monsters who threatened democracy and to concentrate on keeping the lamp burning at home.

Historically, the Midwest and the West were most suspicious of embroilment in European affairs. The West has been seen as the repository of native American virtues since Andrew Jackson's day. The majority of people in these areas still lived outside big cities, and life for most of them was bounded by hometown and county. Washington, D.C. was a place visited with a high school class once in a lifetime. The countries of Europe were the subject of geography or history lessons at school. Their affairs might occasionally be interesting but were not of immediate concern, and certainly would not provide a reason for sending their sons into danger. The standing of the local high school football team was more likely to be the subject of conversation and concern than the war in Europe.

As Senator Robert La Follette Jr. of Wisconsin said, echoing Henry Clay's sentiment: "Our patriotic course is clear. It is to stay out of Europe and the Far East, which would drain our blood, our manhood and our wealth forever. It is to concentrate on making democracy function in the last great industrial nation which has a chance of making it function in the modern machine world."

Their political leaders were not, like most of the leading appeasers in Europe, representatives of a conservative business or aristocratic class that could be accused of some sympathy with Nazism. Most of them were prairie radicals who fought for their constituents against Wall Street and the eastern bankers, what they called the "money interests."

Many of them, such as Senators La Follette and George Norris of Nebraska, were associated with the Progressive Republicans, the dissident wing of the Republican Party which rallied behind Theodore Roosevelt. Senators Robert Nye of North Dakota and Burton Wheeler of

Montana supported the Non-Partisan Farmers' League, which had a quasi-Socialist program. Senator Hiram Johnson was elected governor of California in 1912 after campaigning against the depredations of the Southern Pacific Railroad (of which his father was counsel) and was the Progressive Party candidate for president in 1916. As governor he introduced prison reforms and the most liberal workmen's compensation law in the country.

Senator Borah of Idaho, the most prominent among them, objected to the term "isolationist," and with some justification, because, he said, he and those who thought like him did not seek to isolate America from the affairs of the world. Borah was instrumental in convening the 1922 Washington naval disarmament conference and fought hard for the Kellogg-Briand Treaty. He and his allies wanted America to work for peace, he said, but independently, without any commitments.

This was the widely accepted picture of isolationist sentiment, but ethnic background was another factor, which commentators were slow to acknowledge. Most midwestern states had a large German-American population. In the time of Nazism there was much less outright pro-German feeling among German-Americans than there had been in World War One, but German-Americans tended to be less willing to identify with the Allies. Surveys of voting in congressional elections showed isolationist opinion strongest in counties with a German-American population. Arthur Miller recalled that in those days one knew in New York that Hitler was evil, but: "The further into the country one moved, the more human Hitler seemed to look, simply another German leader who was out to avenge his country's defeat of 1918, a not entirely dishonorable ideal, come to think of it."

A minority of German-Americans joined the pro-Nazi German-American Bund, which drew what strength it had from the cities in the East. At its peak the Bund had 20,000 signed-up members but more followers. It ran sinister summer camps and staged rallies festooned with swastikas at Madison Square Garden in New York. It distributed literature and films from Göbbels's propaganda department. The Bund was unfortunate in its choice of fuehrers (the title their leader took). Its first, Fritz Kuhn, was sent to prison for embezzling Bund funds; his successor, William Kunze, fled to Mexico when he was questioned by police about his management; and *his* successor, George Froboese, committed suicide. After that the Bund dwindled, to disappear after Pearl Harbor.

Charles Lindbergh was back in America now to join in the argument. The Lindbergh family represented a passage from left-wing to right-wing isolationism. Grandfather Ola Lindbergh was a radical member of the *Riksdag,* the Swedish Parliament, until he became disillusioned with politics in his country and emigrated to Minnesota. His son, Charles Lindbergh Sr., sat in Congress for ten years as a Progressive Republican in a German-American constituency and argued against entry into World War One, which he said was brought about by the "money interests." When he ran for governor in 1918 on the Farmers' League ticket, his son, Charles Lindbergh Jr., then a teenager, drove him to meetings, and saw his father denounced as a traitor and a "gopher Bolshevik" and threatened by mobs, threats which Lindbergh senior met with steely disdain.

The younger Lindbergh, the aviator hero, opposed American involvement in World War Two, but he was coming from somewhere different. Lindbergh was impressed by the philosophical views of Alexis Carrell, a French medical scientist and Nobel laureate, which were racist and antidemocratic. Although he and his wife made their home in England when they left America, he displayed some sympathy with Nazi Germany. He was not concerned to isolate America from war — he was ready to engage in war against an Asiatic menace, he said — but would not support a war against Germany. There were isolationists on the Right as well as the Left.

American labor was worried about getting involved in the war. Working men would be doing the fighting and the unions feared that, as AFL President William Green warned, if America went to war, labor would be regimented and would lose the gains they had made under the New Deal.

The argument was creating some strange bedfellows. The International Ladies' Garment Workers' Union was more concerned than most of labor with the consequences of the war, being based mostly in East Coast cities with a largely Jewish membership. A speaker at their annual conference in late 1939 was Dean Acheson, former assistant secretary of the treasury, a Groton-Harvard-educated lawyer, socially a million miles away from ILGWU leader David Dubinsky but politically an ally. Acheson pointed to a banner reading "Dictatorship Dooms Labor. Labor Dooms Dictatorship" and drew a dramatic picture of the consequences for labor of a Nazi victory. "I have already mentioned the admiring echoes of Nazi conduct and efficiency which we have heard. These in the event of a German victory would increase. We would hear again from those who reported with admiration that Mussolini made the trains run on time, and that Hitler solved the problem of Jewish encroachment . . . The very framework of labor legislation could be turned against the labor movement."

Walter Millis, who had given a boost to isolationism with his best-selling 1936 book arguing that America was suckered into joining in World War One, now opposed the isolationists with an article in *Life* magazine titled, "1939 Is Not 1914." The debate cut across party lines and across traditional lines of Left and Right. The journal *Christian Century* said the war was simply one of rival imperialisms. But thirty-three senior Protestant clergy signed a statement saying the war was a moral issue and Christians could not remain neutral.

• • •

Roosevelt set about once again to get Congress to amend the Neutrality Law, and convened a special session for September 21. The Senate had refused to consider this earlier in the year, but now war was not merely threatening, it had arrived, and the mood was different. Ambassador Kennedy told him that for the British, the repeal of the act would be "the greatest psychological lift they could have at this time." The importance was much more than psychological. In Paris Prime Minister Daladier told William Bullitt: "If we are to win this war, we shall have to win it with supplies of every kind from the United States."

At first Roosevelt wanted to repeal the whole act, but when he met with leading senators from both parties on the eve of the special session they persuaded him that this would not get through. "The trouble is," Republican senator Charles McNary explained to him, "people would think if we repealed the Neutrality Act that we were repealing our neutrality." So he settled for calling for repeal of the arms embargo part of it, a compromise thrashed out in the Senate Foreign Relations Committee. Belligerent nations would be able to buy war material in America on a cash-and-carry basis. They would have to transport the material themselves. American ships would be banned from entering combat zones, which was a blow to American shipping.

France and Britain had been making large purchases of armaments in the United States, but under the existing Neutrality Law these could not be sent in time of war. Orders worth $79 million had to be canceled, most of them French, the rest British. A billion dollars' worth of orders were expected if the Neutrality Act were amended to allow them.

Roosevelt pointed to the advantage for industry of repealing the arms embargo, and he said the embargo was "dangerous for American security and American peace." Cordell Hull said in his memoirs that he and the president believed that repeal would help keep the war away from America. "If Britain and France won the war we could remain at peace, whereas if Germany won there was every likelihood that we should soon have to fight," he wrote.

Citizens' groups sent their representatives tens of thousands of telegrams and letters opposing any revision, including the League of Nations Association (because conflict should be settled by peaceful means) and the General Federation of Women's Clubs.

Lindbergh argued against revision in a broadcast that was relayed over all three networks. "I speak tonight to those people in the United States of America who feel that the destiny of the country does not call for our involvement in European wars," he said. He also revealed his racist view: "This is not a matter of banding together to defend the white race against foreign invasion. This is simply one more of those age-old struggles within our own family of nations, a quarrel arising from the errors of the last war." The networks said the broadcast drew more mail than any other they had ever aired, nearly all of it favorable.

In the Senate, the Republican leadership led the fight against repeal. The leading figure in the debate was Republican senator Arthur Vandenberg of Michigan. A bulky, jowly figure, he was a former newspaper publisher and the author of two hagiographic books on Alexander Hamilton, a thoughtful man on his way to being the elder statesman of the Republican Party. On the Senate floor he warned, "Consciously or otherwise, we are asked to depart from this policy of strict neutrality on behalf of one belligerent, whom our personal sympathies largely favor, and against another belligerent whom our personal sympathies largely condemn. In my opinion, this is the road that may lead us to war."

Hiram Johnson summoned up the familiar specter of devious, sophisticated Europeans putting one over on straight-talking Uncle Sam. If the embargo were repealed, he warned, "we will be pushed about by those wily men who play the game of power politics in which some of our people, some of those who are snobbish, imagine they can play better than the diplomats of Europe."

Congress passed the amended act, called the Neutrality Act of 1939, and Roosevelt signed it into law on November 4, at the beginning of the Thanksgiving recess. Vandenberg wrote in his diary: "We are beaten 63–30. But we won a great moral victory . . . It is going to be much more difficult for FDR to lead this country into war."

As soon as the bill became law, the tarpaulins were pulled off several hundred aircraft that were stored in a free-trade zone on Staten Island, and they were loaded on to ships bound for France. More orders flowed in. Britain and France said they wanted to buy up to 10,000 air frames and 10,000 engines. When the War Department objected Roosevelt overruled them. He told two aides, "These foreign orders mean prosperity, and we can't elect a Democratic Government unless we get prosperity."

Investment and purchases by the Allies gave a much-needed boost to the American aircraft industry and put it in a position later on to provide for America's defense needs. The Allies not only bought aircraft and aircraft engines, but also set up production lines with $180 million worth of machine tools, which they paid for. As the official history of Britain's war economy says: "The British and French Governments had to spend most of their dollars, not on combat aeroplanes and weapons — they were not ready — but on developing America's capacity to produce them." At the end of the year, two-thirds of the aircraft industry's $600 million worth of orders were from overseas. The British Admiralty ordered sixty ships from the Todd-Kaiser shipyards in California and got the shipyards going again. These orders provided jobs at a time when there were nearly ten million unemployed.

Eighteen months later, when the United States was embarking on a crash program of rearmament, Secretary of War Henry L. Stimson told a senator: "Without the head start given to industry by these foreign orders, we would at the present time be in a very grave situation as to the plants and facilities we need for the pending emergency."

Roosevelt went on reassuring the American people. He said on the radio on October 26: "In and out of Congress, we have heard orators and commentators and others beating their breasts and proclaiming against sending the boys of American mothers to fight on the battlefields of Europe. That I do not hesitate to label as one of the worst fakes in current history. The simple truth is that no person in any responsible place in the national Administration has ever suggested in any shape or form the remotest possibility of sending the boys of American mothers to fight on the battlefields of Europe."

The administration's immediate concerns centered on Latin America. Roosevelt had thought for a long time that this might be the next area of German expansion. In January he told a cabinet meeting that 80 percent of Argentina's exports were to Europe, and if Hitler dominated Europe, he could demand that Argentina accept his principles and then turn other countries in the area against America.

Nazi influence in South America was causing anxiety to the State Department. The Nazi Party had an *auslander* office dealing with overseas German communities, and its representatives were active among the 1.5 million ethnic Germans in Latin America. In some embassies Nazi Party representatives outnumbered the professional diplomats. Pro-Nazi parties were well established in Chile and Uruguay, and Brazil had a fascist-style government that contained Nazi sympathizers. The Uruguayan authorities were worried about an invasion from southern Brazil, where more than a million ethnic Germans lived.

German language news services were being set up in Latin America. Germans controlled the commercial airlines in Brazil and Colombia, and German military missions were entrenched in Argentina and Brazil. Germany had large trading arrangements with several South American countries. The Scadta Airline in Colombia was under Nazi control and its pilots were all German. It was operating within 300 miles of the Panama Canal, and it had extensive photographic survey facilities. The State Department took action on this. The American airline Panair also had a stake in Scadta, and the State Department pressed Panair to extend its holding. Eventually the airline came under Panair's control.

The War and Navy Departments' war plans were designated by color, each dealing with war with a particular country or group of countries; the navy's plan for war with Japan was Orange Plan. In 1939 the Joint Planning Board drew up the first of what were called Rainbow Plans, for the defense of the Western Hemisphere in an array of situations. This looked to the possibility of Axis intervention in South America, in particular in Brazil, and said that in the event of war the navy should interdict all Axis traffic with South America.

The annual fleet exercise in 1939 also showed the administration's concern. In the annual exercise, the navy was given an imaginary crisis situation to deal with. Most years this was a crisis in the Pacific, where most of the fleet was located. The situation presented to the navy in 1939 was a revolt in Brazil aided by a European country with military advisors and weapons. Ships were moved from the Pacific to take part.

Immediately after the outbreak of war, the United States convened a conference of all twenty-one American republics in Panama under the chairmanship of Cordell Hull. The conference passed a motion barring all belligerent activities over a wide area ranging from 300 to 1,000 miles from the coast of the Americas, a motion which, as Hull admitted privately, had no standing in international law. All the governments felt threatened by the Axis powers, and all of them willingly joined America in trying to keep the war away, even countries like Argentina, which usually resisted American leadership. The United States backed this up with a Neutrality Patrol of cruisers and destroyers in the waters off the east coast of the Americas.

The American government did not know it at the time but Hitler, trying to avoid an incident with the United States, was observing the strictures of the Declaration of Panama. He ordered Admiral Karl Doenitz, the commander of Germany's submarine fleet, to keep his U-boats away from the coasts of the Americas. Doenitz wanted to attack British convoys as they set out from American shores.

* * *

The outbreak of war changed everyone's life in Britain immediately. It was expected that the war would begin with massive air raids on Britain, quite likely with poison gas. All places of public entertainment were closed so as to avoid a crowd of people collecting in one building. Radio weather forecasts were banned because they might be of help to enemy raiders. Police leave was canceled. Hospital wards were cleared of all but the most urgent cases. Works of art were taken down from the walls of the National Gallery and removed to a cave in Wales. The London Zoo's poisonous snakes and insects were killed with chloroform in case a bomb should free them. Television went off the air. The BBC had started a television service in 1936, the second such service in the world, three years before the first commercial TV broadcast in America, albeit broadcasting to only 20,000 viewers in the London area. BBC TV closed down with a Mickey Mouse cartoon on September 1, not to re-open until after the war. (The world's *first* TV service was in Germany; it began in 1935 and continued broadcasting until 1944.) Restrictions on travel and financial dealings were imposed. People, apart from children and the elderly, could not travel abroad or send money or assets abroad without permission.

To slow the flow of money overseas, the government established tight control over imports. This cut into American exports, particularly of farm goods. Cordell Hull pointed out to the new British ambassador the difficulties this was causing, and when the import of American tobacco was cut he reminded him of the congressmen from tobacco-growing states who sat on the Foreign Relations and Finance committees. In London, Ambassador Kennedy, as a onetime Hollywood studio boss, argued over the restrictions on the import of American films and got the level raised.

The Air Ministry, overestimating the size of the German air force, thought German bombers might drop 700 tons of bombs a day on British cities for the first two weeks of the war. The Air Raid Precautions Department of the Home Office studied the effects of the bombing of British cities in World War One and the bombing raids on Barcelona in the Spanish Civil War. Extrapolating from these, and using an overestimation of the size of the German air force, officials concluded that 600,000 people could be killed in the first two months of the war and 1.2 million injured. (Deaths from air raids in five years of war were just over a tenth of that figure.) The Ministry of Health issued local authorities with a million burial forms and envisaged burying bodies in lime because there would not be enough wood for coffins. The War Office was told to be ready to supply troops to handle panic-stricken mobs fleeing London.

This erroneous expectation of the effects of aerial bombardment was widespread and had serious long-term consequences. Official thinking overestimated the effect of bombing on the enemy as well as Britain, and this determined offensive as well as defensive policy. The RAF, like the U.S. Air Force, exaggerated the contribution that strategic bombing could make to winning the war and planned a bomber offensive accordingly.

People carried their gas masks at all times, in their cardboard boxes with shoulder straps. Two million people were now enlisted in volunteer civil defense work of one kind or another. Sandbags were piled around government buildings. Big stores and hotels prepared their basements as shelters for customers. The *Brewers' Journal* advised: "Where public houses [pubs] are to be used as shelters, it is highly desirable that stocks should be partitioned off so as to be inaccessible."

Cities were blacked out at night to ensure that no lights guided enemy bombers. Householders had to seal in the light, on pain of a fine if they slipped up, a daily routine carried out at sundown. Curtains were taped to windows; black masking tape covered gaps. Volunteer air raid wardens patrolled the streets bawling a warning where a chink of light was spotted. Street lighting was banned and so were car headlights. The streets after sundown were in pitch darkness unless there was a moon to provide some thin illumination, and anyone who went out risked bruises from colliding with a lamppost, not to mention another pedestrian. They were like no cities had been since the Middle Ages.

The writer Malcolm Muggeridge wrote in his diary a few days after war broke out: "London left dark, childless, cinemaless, at night scarcely existing at all, obliterated."

The evacuation was the biggest disruption. Women and children were urged to leave the cities and some 3.5 million did so, half on their own initiative, the others under government-run schemes. The government set up evacuation centers where families brought their children to be transported, the smaller ones to be accompanied by their mothers. One helper at an evacuation center in a working-class district of London described a scene repeated in many cities: "The mothers were trying to hold back their tears as they marched these little boys and girls with their gas masks into the center . . . The children were wild with excitement but most mums were pale and drawn, no doubt wondering when they would see their children again."

The children were shepherded away and herded on to trains. At their destinations, in small towns and villages across the country, newly appointed billeting officers told householders how many children they were to receive. They were paid a small sum for the children's keep. For many children as well as parents it was a wrenching, unhappy experience. Some children were welcomed, some received unwillingly. But the aim was to get the children away from danger in a hurry, so any mismatch of evacuees and refuge was assumed to be an acceptable price. Two million homesick children cried themselves to sleep.

An entire generation went through the evacuation experience as children, and for many this was the most intense experience of the war. Many had never been away from home. Some city children learned the pleasures of the countryside, of games in the fields, climbing trees, searching for birds' eggs. Some were evacuated up the social scale and lived in a manner they had never known before. The nine-year-old Michael Caine, who lived in a tenement in London, arrived at a country railroad station and was driven to his new home in a Rolls Royce, an experience he was not to have for another thirty years. Others moved from middle-class suburbia to a farm worker's cottage. One little girl was sent from a comfortable apartment in London to a coal miner's home in a Welsh village. It was a warm, welcoming family and community, but her mother blanched at learning that she was bathed in a tin tub in front of a coal fire.

Some children were exploited and abused. Some developed lasting friendships with their surrogate parents. Some had the humiliating experience of being taken by a billeting officer from door to door and turned away, for not everyone was welcoming. Some families evaded their obligation to take in evacuees. In one town, a suspicious billeting officer found that working-class homes were full while twenty-three town councilors had among them room for seventy-six more people.

There were bruising meetings between the cultures of urban slums and the village middle class. Some villagers were horrified to find children with head lice, who did not know about toilets or fresh fruit and vegetables or knives and forks. Often the children had no nightwear and their underwear consisted of father's old shirts stitched up, and some had no shoes. Two children from Glasgow refused to sleep on white sheets, saying, "That's a bed for dead folk."

Rationing of food and gasoline was introduced, although the restrictions were mild compared to what was to come. Many things became scarce in the shops, from stockings to whiskey. Nella Last wrote in her diary: "We have been in luck this weekend, for a friend who could not go out lent us a three-gallon coupon, which means we could go off to Windermere Lake this afternoon." A black market soon grew up; there were people who could get you anything for a price.

When the air raid alarms sounded an hour after the declaration of war, people rushed to the shelters and waited for the worst. But it was a false alarm. Britain braced itself for the worst, and it did not happen. There were no air raids. Movie houses and theaters reopened, evacuees drifted back to their homes. Air raid wardens were regarded as a nuisance. Weeds grew in the Anderson shelters. Gas masks found their way to the bottom of the closet and remained there. Blackout restrictions were eased slightly; cars could have dim headlights and pedestrians were allowed to carry a low-voltage flashlight.

On the outbreak of war, Prime Minister Chamberlain wanted an all-party government but the Labour and Liberal Parties refused. He brought in some new figures, notably Winston Churchill, who became first lord of the Admiralty, the post he occupied in the First World War. Although it was not one of the top government posts, he was brought into the War Cabinet and, with a wealth of both political and military experience behind him, he played an active part in it, sometimes more active than his colleagues liked.

Britain would have to finance the war, as it financed its daily life, by spending money overseas. The Treasury estimated that overseas reserves amounted to £500 million in gold — $2 billion; the pound dropped from five dollars to four on the outbreak of war — plus £200 million in securities that could be requisitioned and sold. It said that at the present rate of expenditure overseas, reserves would be spent in two years. It said it was unlikely that Britain could finance a three-year war without loans from the United States.

. . .

German forces overran Poland more quickly than expected. The German air force struck at airfields and knocked out most of the Polish air force on the ground on the first day. The Polish forces fought back fiercely, but they were outgunned. The Germans bombed Warsaw and other cities when Polish forces defended them, violating the promise the German government made to Roosevelt that it would not bomb civilian targets. Soviet forces invaded from the east on September 17, to divide up Poland under the secret terms of the Ribbentrop-Molotov Pact, and the Polish government surrendered after just three weeks. (Strictly speaking, Britain should have declared war on the Soviet Union since it had promised to defend Poland against any aggressor, but no one was speaking or even thinking that strictly.) Those Poles who could went on fighting. Troops escaped through Romania and made their way to

France, and pilots also, and Polish warships sailed to Britain, all to play their part in the war.

The Polish people became victims of the racial ideology of Nazism. As Slavs they were *untermenschen,* a lower order of humanity. The policy toward Poland was stated by Hitler at a dinner with Hans Franck, the governor of occupied Poland, and others in October. "It is necessary to keep the standard of life low in Poland, and it must not be permitted to rise," he said. "There should be only one master for the Poles — the Germans. Therefore, all representatives of the Polish intelligentsia are to be exterminated."

The Germans expelled people from their land to make way for German settlers — eventually 1.2 million of them. (In the eastern part of the country the Russians displaced another million.) They imposed brutal discipline. In the town of Torun the authorities announced that Poles must give way to Germans on the street because "the street belongs to the conquerors." After two German soldiers were killed in a brawl in the town of Wawer, 170 men and boys, the youngest ten years old, were shot. The chief of staff of the First Army, Major General Friedrich Mieth, told his officers that the behavior of the SS in Poland had "besmirched the honor of the German Army." Shortly afterward he was relieved of his command.

Lord Halifax had told the cabinet when the guarantee to Poland was signed that it would confront Hitler with war on two fronts. In fact Hitler had war on one front for three weeks and on no fronts after that. The Poles expected the Allies to attack in the West to relieve the pressure on them, but French and British forces did nothing apart from a brief incursion into the Saar. The invasion of Poland was another Hitler gamble. He drew forces away from the western front so that only 23 German divisions manned the Siegfried line facing 110 French divisions.

A British expeditionary force went over to France and manned the northern sector of the front, facing Belgium. It soon numbered 350,000, but this was only a tenth the size of the French army. British bombers made a few sporadic raids on German military targets and learned the limitations on bombing accuracy. On the day after war broke out ten bombers attacked German warships in harbor at Wilhelmshaven. Five of the bombers were shot down; no German warship was hit. Both sides refrained from bombing one another's cities. A situation of mutual deterrence prevailed.

At sea the war was a continuation of World War One. The Germans tried to blockade Britain with submarines and surface raiders. An island nation, Britain imports many of its needs, particularly food and raw materials, and it has always been vulnerable to blockade. The war at sea began on the first day when, despite a German promise that they would not attack passenger ships without warning, a submarine torpedoed and sank the British liner *Athenia* off the Scottish coast, killing 112 people including 28 American passengers. The Germans claimed that a British submarine had sunk the liner to try to bring America into the war. Evidence turned up after the war showed that the German government had intended to keep its promise about passenger ships at least for the time being and the U-boat captain had acted without orders. German policy on sinkings changed after a few months.

The German blockade would have been more effective if Germany had more submarines. Hitler's strategic thinking was continental in military as in political affairs. He had given little thought to war with Britain. He did not build a large fleet of U-boats, the weapon that had almost starved Britain out of the war in World War One. On the outbreak of war Germany had only forty-three submarines, and twenty-five of these were small 250-tonners with limited range. After war began, production was stepped up from four a month to twenty a month. Germany built 1,000 submarines in the course of the war. The commander of the German submarine fleet, Admiral Karl Doenitz, said later that if he had had half of these submarines at the outbreak of war they could have brought Britain to its knees.

British merchant ships sailed in convoys, escorted by destroyers. U-boats sank twenty-three British merchant ships in the first month of the war, a German surface ship sank one, and two were sunk by mines. Losses went down after this as British warships got the better of the U-boats, but the new magnetic mines took a toll until the British developed "de-gaussing," which created an electric current around the ship that neutralizes magnetism. There were a few battles at sea, notably the destruction of the German battleship *Graf Spee* outside Montevideo.

Britain, meanwhile, was doing its best to stop any supplies reaching Germany by sea, stopping ships bound for German ports or ships carrying goods intended for Germany wherever they were bound. Since this included ships on their way to neutral countries, American ships were stopped and searched. The United States protested but officials did not press the point. Britain developed rules for blockading Germany. A neutral ship might ask for a certificate from the British government saying it had complied with blockade rules, and this ensured that the British navy would not interfere with it. America acquiesced in these rules. The minister for economic warfare, Hugh Dalton, wrote: "This was a vital condition of success and a most friendly neutral act."

After two months of war, the army had no men killed by enemy action, the RAF 79, and the navy 586. Civilian deaths in accidents caused by the blackout were said to be 1,130. More than two thousand merchant seamen were killed.

In one small area connected with the war there was parallel activity in Britain and America. A few days after war broke out, two Hungarian-born physicists in America drafted a letter to President Roosevelt alerting the administration to the possibility opened up by recent experiments in nuclear physics of an entirely new type of explosive, that would work by the splitting of the uranium atom. They got Albert Einstein to sign it, to lend it the prestige of his name, which ensured that it got attention. The result was the setting up of a Uranium Advisory Committee under the Bureau of Standards to look into the possibilities.

Otto Frisch, the Austrian physicist who, along with Lise Meitner, had worked out what happens when a uranium atom divides, was now in Britain, at Birmingham University. He was living as a lodger in the home of an old friend also on the faculty, the German physicist Rudolf Peierls. Together they decided that a bomb could be made to explode through atomic fission — the term Frisch coined for the process — and wrote a paper suggesting how this could be done, the first plan for an atomic bomb. They took it to the authorities, and in April 1940 a committee was set up to work on the project.

The Anglo-French strategy at the start of the war was a holding one. Germany was stronger on the ground and in the air but not at sea. The Allied plan was to hold off German attacks and take action against Italy in the Mediterranean if Italy entered the war. Britain and France would build up their forces until they were ready for the big offensive against Germany, in 1941. In the meantime the British navy would blockade Germany. The newly established Ministry of Economic Warfare assured the Chiefs of Staff that by 1941 Germany would be suffering acute shortages of food and industrial supplies. This was overly optimistic. The German economy was not fully stretched and had spare capacity.

The Soviet Union and Poland were supplying Germany with most of its needs, the former willingly, the latter unwillingly.

The British government also had hopes of a popular movement in Germany to overthrow Hitler and end the war once economic restrictions started to bite. Aircraft flew over Germany showering the cities with anti-Nazi leaflets, with no noticeable effect. As an official history says: "Their chief value was probably the practice they gave to Bomber Command in navigating over Germany at night."

The war was to become an all-out war to crush Nazi Germany, but it did not begin as one. Chamberlain wrote to Roosevelt a month after war broke out, in a letter emphasizing the importance of lifting the arms embargo: "My own belief is that we shall win, not by a complete and spectacular victory, which is unlikely under modern conditions, but by convincing the Germans that they cannot win."

Officially, the aim was to "rid Europe of the menace of Hitlerism," as Chamberlain put it in Parliament, but this was unclear. Cadogan asked in his diary, "What if the Germans replaced Hitler with Göring?" Göring was thought to be a more moderate Nazi and had been the point man for peace feelers. It was generally agreed that Germany would have to leave the territory it had conquered and desist from aggression. The French, invaded by Germany twice before, were more ambitious. The phrase was: *"Il faut en finir"* — "We have to finish with it," meaning end the threat from Germany once and for all.

The war was not total for Britain either in its aims or its commitments. British industry was not fully mobilized. Mobilization and arms production moved ahead slowly. Much of industry was still producing luxury goods. Six months after the outbreak of war there were still more than a million unemployed. Not surprisingly, the government's lack of wholehearted commitment was matched among the public. A survey by the Ministry of Information kept secret at the time estimated that 10 percent of the population were opposed to the war.

In October Hitler offered peace to Britain and France. "Why should this war in the West be fought?" he asked in a speech. "For the restoration of Poland? The Poland of the Versailles Treaty will never rise again . . . What otherwise, then, could be the reason for the war? Has Germany made any demands on England which threaten the British Empire in any way?" He proposed a conference on security and settlement of national questions, but made it clear that Germany would continue to rule Poland. Lloyd George and a few others said Britain should take it seriously, and at least make a counteroffer, but Chamberlain would not countenance even this.

The option for Britain was essentially the same as it had been before the war when Ribbentrop went to London to seek Britain's friendship. As Chamberlain wrote to his cousin Arthur Chamberlain on October 25: "One thought has been constantly present to him [Hitler] and one sees it coming back again and again in his speeches: 'If England will only leave me a free hand to do what I like in Europe which doesn't concern her, I would be ready to leave her a free hand to do what she likes in the rest of the world.'"

Ambassador Kennedy still preached the virtues of a negotiated peace and the hopelessness of the war to anyone who would listen. He told Roosevelt in a cable: "Democracy as we now conceive it in the U.S. will not exist in France or England after the war regardless of which side wins or loses. In fact, it hardly does now."

Not surprisingly, this kind of thing was making him increasingly unpopular in government circles. A Foreign Office official suggested in a memo that Kennedy should no longer be treated as "a kind of honorary member of the cabinet." Halifax commented in a note in the margin — and one can almost hear his icy tone in the words — "I should think this is a diminishing temptation."

Others in the American embassy were still admitted into officials' confidence, one of them First Secretary Walton Butterworth. When someone in the Foreign Office complained that Butterworth was learning things that perhaps should be kept hidden, the deputy head, J. V. Perowne, wrote in a memo that is a fine example of Foreign Office prose: "I quite agree that the skeletons in our cupboard have been far too freely exposed to the kindly but searching glance of Mr. Butterworth. But I don't know how we are to stop high officials from indulging in the delights of the Confessional with so engaging an interlocutor."

• • •

This was the period that was labeled the "phony war." In France, in the fields between the Maginot line and the Siegfried line, the leaves turned brown and dropped off the trees, and the winter snows came and then melted away with the coming of spring, all undisturbed by the mark of any military boots or tank treads. U.S. ambassador William Bullitt reported to Roosevelt: "It is the opinion of the General Staff that whichever army attacks first the line of fortifications that now divide France and Germany will be defeated."

The Maginot line was a shield that covered only half the body. It stopped short near the Belgian border. The gap was political as well as military. Until 1936 Belgium and France had a military alliance. But when France failed to take action in response to Germany rearming and occupying the Rhineland, the Belgian government decided that this was not an ally to be counted on and switched to a position of neutrality.

The gap did not seem to worry the French. In February 1940, Walter Lippmann asked the French commander, General Maurice Gamelin what would happen where the Maginot line stopped. "The Maginot Line will narrow the gap through which the German Army can come, and thus enable us to destroy it more easily," Gamelin said. The plan was that if Germany invaded Belgium the British and some French divisions would move forward into Belgium to meet them.

French army morale was weakening. The appalling losses in 1914–18 had sapped French martial spirit. There were already a substantial number of Frenchmen who had expressed sympathy with Nazism. German radio was broadcasting in French saying that Frenchmen had been dragged into the war by Britain and Britain was going to let Frenchmen do all the fighting. The French Communist Party was the largest in the Western world; of sixty-five Communist members of the National Assembly, fifty-two followed the official party line and opposed the war. Communists were telling soldiers that they were fighting the bosses' war. Paul Reynaud, who succeeded Daladier as prime minister in November, confided to Churchill that German propaganda was having a worrying effect.

In December, another war broke out. The Soviet Union demanded naval bases and territorial rights from Finland, which were important for the defense of Leningrad (now St. Petersburg), and when these were refused it invaded Finland. What happened next surprised the world. The Finns, although outnumbered, fought heroically and drove the Russians back, surrounding Soviet units in the snow-covered forests and cutting them to pieces. Finnish soldiers manufactured simple incendiary grenades to hurl at tanks by filling bottles with gasoline. They named the improvised weapon after the Soviet foreign minister, introducing the term "Molotov cocktail" into the language.

Stalin had executed many of the Soviet Army's commanders in the purges in the 1930s, and the Finns' success seemed to confirm the widespread view that this had emasculated the army. Churchill said, "The Finns have exposed for all the world to see the military incapacity of the Red Army and the Red Air Force," making the mistake that others made, including Hitler.

There was enormous sympathy for Finland in Britain and France, as in America. Despite their own shortages both countries sent aircraft and weapons to Finland; France sent 125 planes and 500 artillery pieces; Britain sent 100 planes and 200 guns.

With the French government leading the way, they developed a plan which was one of those projects occasionally taken by governments which in retrospect seem so foolish that one wonders how intelligent people could have come up with it. They decided to attack Russia. The plan was to land troops at the northern Norwegian port of Narvik, violating Norwegian neutrality, which would have the double aim of seizing iron ore bound for Germany and opening a supply route to Finland. They would then send troops through Narvik to fight alongside the Finns. They even had plans to bomb the Soviet oilfields at Baku, at the other end of Europe, which were supplying oil to Germany. They did not seem to think ahead to how Russia might respond, or that the result might be that Britain and France would be fighting the two largest armies in Europe instead of just one of them. Russia reinforced its forces fighting in the north and overwhelmed the Finns, and Finland sued for peace in March, saving Britain and France from this folly.

In February Roosevelt sent Undersecretary of State Sumner Welles on a mission to the main European capitals to ascertain the possibilities of ending the war. Walton Butterworth of the U.S. embassy in London spelled out one version of his aim to a Foreign Office official, who reported it in a memo: "He [Butterworth] said Roosevelt believes the Allies can't win, the U.S. can't afford to have them lose, so he wants to make peace, which would make him popular at home."

Welles, a fluent German speaker with no need of an interpreter, reported that he found Hitler impressive, "dignified in both speech and movement." Churchill he found a nonstop talker the worse for drink.

Welles asked Chamberlain whether he would be willing to negotiate if Hitler withdrew from Czechoslovakia and Poland. Chamberlain said he would not because Hitler personified "a system with which the British Government has learned from bitter experience it is impossible to make terms." In any case there was no suggestion of any withdrawal.

The British government was nervous about American intervention. Chamberlain wrote to his sister Ida, his principal confidante, on January 27, 1940: "Heaven knows, I don't want the Americans to fight for us — we should have to pay too dearly for that if they had a right to be in on the peace terms."

He had some reason for his anxiety. The State Department wanted to take advantage of the situation and use any influence it had to acquire some input into the organization of the postwar world. For one thing, Cordell Hull wanted a world with fewer tariff barriers, and that meant a reduction or abolition of the set of trade rules by which members of the British Commonwealth gave preference to one another's goods.

Hull issued a statement in January saying: "If peace should come, we shall be confronted, in our own best interests, with the vital need of throwing the weight of our moral and material influence in the direction of creating a stable and enduring world order under law." He quoted this in his memoirs and, in case it was not clear, he spelled out the message: "In other words, while trying to keep out of the war, we would insist on being in on the peace."

In the week that the war began, a new British ambassador arrived in Washington, Lord Lothian, the eleventh marquess, the inheritor of a 400-year-old title and a vast estate in Norfolk. A tall, athletic figure, a keen golfer, gregarious, he was not a professional diplomat but he was an establishment figure experienced in public affairs. He had been Lloyd George's private secretary and a senior official in South Africa, and he was president of the Rhodes Scholarship Trust, which gave him many contacts in America. He had also been an ardent supporter of appeasement; he had told Roosevelt on a previous visit to Washington that Hitler should be allowed to repair "the crime of Versailles." He was a frequent guest at Cliveden and a close friend of Lady Astor, who brought him to Christian Science.*

---

* And thus probably foreshortened his service to his country. In December 1940 Lord Lothian suffered kidney pains and refused to see a doctor, relying on Christian Science practitioners. He died within weeks of what doctors believe was uremia.

A confidential assessment prepared for Roosevelt described him accurately as a representative of the liberal imperialists, and "an appeaser who failed to understand the nature of Nazi Germany." But it also predicted that he would be popular in Washington, saying: "He is very good company, likes a drink and can tell a good story."

In February Lothian cabled home: "There is the rising feeling here that the U.S. is playing an unworthy role in one of the great dramas of history, and is in danger of losing her soul unless she shoulders her share of the burden . . . I think that essentially the same process is going on in the United States today that went on in Britain and France in the past few years, the process which gradually led from the retreats and paralysis of the pre-Munich era to the violent action of today."

Throughout this time, official Washington was occupied with conflict in Asia as well as Europe. Japan was continuing its efforts to drive the Western powers out of China. Immediately after the outbreak of war in Europe, it "suggested" that all foreign forces leave China; the United States and Britain, which had small garrisons in some ports, rejected this. Then it set about establishing a puppet regime based in the Japanese-occupied area. Britain, with its hands full in Europe, suggested to the U.S. administration what amounted to a policy of appeasement, trying to get a Chinese-Japanese agreement with compromises on both sides. But Sumner Welles told the British ambassador that America would not be intimidated and would not agree to any arrangement that gave Japan a special position in China.

The United States had one weapon it could use. An important U.S.-Japanese trade agreement was due to expire in January 1940. Japan wanted to renew it. There were calls in Congress and elsewhere for the United States to refuse to renew the treaty and to go further and impose a trade embargo on Japan. The administration took a midway course; it did not renew the treaty, but it did not impose a trade embargo. Japan's war machine was dependent on American oil and scrap iron. If the sale of these was blocked, Japan would be faced with a choice of either abandoning its plans for an East Asian empire, or going to war. The administration was reluctant to provoke Japan.

As it happens, an event occurred in May 1940 that had as powerful an effect on Japan's trade in the long run as any government measure could have. The first nylon stockings went on sale. The previous year, American women alone had bought 580 million pairs of silk stockings, most made with Japanese silk. Now the great era of silk was coming to an end.

• • •

Soon after war broke out, Roosevelt took an extraordinary step. He wrote a private letter to Winston Churchill asking to be kept informed personally of the progress of the war. This was the beginning of a correspondence that went on until Roosevelt's death, and that eventually totaled some 1,700 letters. This correspondence was kept secret at the time. If word of it leaked out, Roosevelt's opponents would have leaped on it as confirmation of all their fears that he was making America a partner of one of the belligerents.

In retrospect, it may seem natural that two great war leaders should carry on a personal correspondence, but in fact it was unprecedented; there is no other instance of such a correspondence between two heads of government. When it began, they were not two war leaders. Roosevelt was the leader of a neutral country, and Churchill was not a leader at all but only a cabinet minister.

Roosevelt did not know Churchill. They had met only once, at an official dinner when Roosevelt visited London in 1917 as assistant secretary of the navy, and Churchill had barely bothered to speak to Roosevelt. In fact Churchill had forgotten about the meeting, as he revealed embarrassingly when they met in 1941, but Roosevelt remembered it. He told Kennedy on one occasion: "I always disliked him since the time I went to England in 1917 or 1918. At a dinner I attended he acted like a stinker." But he added: "I'm giving him attention now because of the possibility of his being PM, and wanting to keep my hand in." Whatever Roosevelt said to Kennedy, who had never liked Churchill, he may also have been attracted by their common interest in naval affairs, and perhaps by Churchill's spirited attitude of resistance to Hitler.

Roosevelt's first letter read:

> It is because you and I occupied similar positions in the World War that I want you to know how glad I am that you are back again in the Admiralty. Your problems are, I realize, complicated by new factors, but the essential is not very different. What I want you and the Prime Minister to know is that I shall at all times welcome it, if you will keep me in touch personally with anything you

want to know about. You can always send sealed letters through your pouch or my pouch.

I am glad you did the Marlborough volumes* before this thing started, and I much enjoyed reading them.

Churchill replied immediately, signing himself "Naval Person," after first obtaining the permission of his prime minister. He sent twelve messages in the next eight months, and Roosevelt sent three. It would have been improper for him to take on some of the role of either prime minister or foreign secretary, so he confined himself to reporting on the naval aspects of the war.

President Roosevelt was always proud of his Hudson Valley heritage, and he did not hold the Anglophile sentiments common to his class. Nor did he feel any great affection for British institutions and the English countryside. On honeymoon in Britain in 1905, he wrote to his mother: "I cannot tell you how delighted we shall both be to get back home again, we speak of it every day." He did not go along with the view of most State Department professionals that the maintenance of the British Empire was a force for stability and was in the interests of the United States. When a columnist in the *Washington Post* said Roosevelt's background inclined him to be pro-British, he refuted this vigorously in a letter to his press secretary, Steve Early, pointing to generations of Roosevelts and Delanos who had battled with British commercial interests in the West Indies and China.

However, his conception of world affairs, which was Alfred Thayer Mahan's and Theodore Roosevelt's, allied America's global concerns with those of Britain. Mahan, the strategic theorist of America's world role, saw the British navy as an ally of the United States through circumstance, its domination of the Atlantic an assurance for America. This was the prevailing view of the foreign policy establishment. The removal of Britain and France from the scene, abandoning the continent and opening the Atlantic to another dominant power, would leave America exposed.

This view harks back to the presidency of Roosevelt's cousin, Theodore Roosevelt, the first president to proclaim American expansion overseas as a philosophy (his predecessor, McKinley, only practiced it).

---

* This was Churchill's three-volume biography of the Duke of Marlborough, his ancestor.

Some of the earlier Roosevelt's concerns were prophetic of the anxieties that were to trouble F.D.R.'s administration. He warned his secretary of state, Elihu Root, in 1900: "If disaster came to the British Empire, America might in a few years' time face abandoning the Monroe Doctrine and submitting to the acquisition of American territory by some great European power, or going to war." He even had the same concerns about Germany and Latin America. Writing to his navy captain brother-in-law about the need for a bigger navy he said, "If Germany seizes South Brazil and puts in a couple of hundred thousand men there, we of course could not touch her at all unless we whipped her fleet."

Theodore Roosevelt also was aware that his feeling for Britain was not shared by much of the populace or their representatives in Congress. When King Edward VII sent him a miniature as a present, he told one of his cabinet members that he would say nothing about it to Congress. "They would talk about it for a month," he said, "insult the King and myself and then decide by a vote of 15 to 9 that I should not have it."

This strategic alignment in the early years of the twentieth century coincided with the growth of a new sense of an affinity among the upper classes of the two nations. The most obvious development was a spate of marriages between the daughters of wealthy American families and the sons of the British aristocracy. In the years before 1914, 130 young American women married into the British peerage. Among the most notable unions of British breeding and American money were those of Winston Churchill's parents; the marriage of Churchill's uncle, the duke of Marlborough, to Consuelo Vanderbilt, which brought the duke a hefty block of shares in the New York Central Railroad; and that of Mary Leiter, the daughter of a department store magnate, to Lord Curzon, future foreign secretary.

There was also among the wealthy classes a swelling tide of sentiment that linked Britain and America, sometimes racial in its evocation of the Anglo-Saxon virtues. In a peroration typical of this feeling in 1910, the American ambassador in London, Whitelaw Reid, hailed "the undivided and indivisible English-speaking race, that race which is united in its history, in its language, in its pride in the past, in its hopes and aspirations for the future, whose kindred flags girdle the world."

Institutions were set up to express and channel these sentiments: the Rhodes scholarships to Oxford University, the Pilgrim Society, the English-Speaking Union. Gentlemen's clubs on the two sides of the Atlantic set up exchange agreements. A member of the Cosmos Club in Washington has entrée to the Travellers' Club in London; a member of the Oxford and Cambridge Club in London may dine and entertain at the Harvard Club or the Yale Club, and he (or, nowadays, she) would feel at home there. The American upper class, of which the kernel was east coast WASP, tended to be Europe orientated and Anglophile in sentiments.

Many non-WASP Americans who did not belong to a gentlemen's club and whose relatives did not marry English aristocrats were highly suspicious of this kind of hands-across-the-sea sentiment and of any ties to a foreign power that they implied. Anglophile WASPs seemed to them to be effete snobs of dubious patriotism. The British still had a monarch and lords and ladies while Americans had gotten rid of these a long time ago. And Britain had an empire and ruled over other countries, which was not the way Americans thought things should be. Many, particularly those of Irish ancestry, still saw the British as haughty oppressors, the redcoats the early Americans had driven off, George Sanders with a curled lip confronting the rough frontiersman John Wayne in the 1939 movie *Allegheny Uprising*. Chicago Mayor Bill Thompson spoke for these when he promised that if King George came to Chicago, he would punch him on the nose.

Hostility to Britain was not limited to the kind of people who would conduct international relations with punches on the nose. A number of people in the State Department and the services were suspicious of British intentions. Assistant Secretary of State Adolf Berle wrote in his diary: "We have no necessary interest in maintaining the British Empire, aside from the fact that we prefer the British as against the German method of running an empire." Jay Pierrepont Moffat, the State Department's head of European Affairs, said once that two or three years at Oxford or Cambridge was enough to ruin most Americans.

America in 1940 was more Atlantic-focused than it is today. It was also much less urbanized; nearly half of Americans lived in small towns. There was no large ethnic group of non-European origin apart from African Americans. English was the only language spoken in most of the country. The Pacific coast was less important, California's population a quarter of what it is today; there had never been a president from west of the Rocky Mountains.

Among most Americans there was the sense of a common culture with Britain, most obviously a common language. In school, while they learned about the War of Independence and mad King George III, they learned also about English literature and read English poems about English landscapes. British people, while foreign, were not as much so as other foreigners. Many Americans of all classes looked to them as a model of good manners and behavior.* When Gallup pollsters asked Americans in 1937 which European country they liked best, 55 percent opted for Britain, against 11 percent for France and 8 percent for Germany.

• • •

The Allies went to war in Scandinavia. Sweden was supplying iron ore that was vital to German industry, and it was being brought by sea down the Norwegian coast. Churchill, looking for ways to get at the enemy, devised a plan to mine the waters off Norway. On April 8 British destroyers started laying mines off Narvik, in Norwegian coastal waters, drawing a protest from Norway at this violation of its neutrality. They were prepared to go further and seize Norwegian ports. Leo Amery, a member of the cabinet, wrote, "We salved our consciences by telling ourselves that the Germans would react first to our mining the leads." German freighters were already approaching Norway with troops concealed on board and a German naval force was at sea.

German troops crossed the frontier into Denmark in the early hours of April 9 and occupied Copenhagen with almost no resistance. At the same time German warships and troopships sailed into Narvik and Oslo. The Norwegian armed forces had not been in action since Napoleon's day, but the shore battery in Oslo fjord and the three small warships there opened fire immediately. They sank the cruiser *Blücher*, killing the Gestapo officers who were to have headed the German administration of occupied Norway. But at Narvik in the north, German ships sank two Norwegian destroyers in the harbor and captured the city.

German aircraft landed troops at Oslo airport and they seized the

---

* When, fresh from England, I arrived at P.S. 6 in New York City, my teacher told my mother that since I was English she hoped I would set an example of good behavior and decorum. She was disappointed to find that, like any eleven-year-old, my aim was to be as rough and uncouth as the others in my class.

capital. Young Norwegians flocked to the hills to join the army. Germany installed a puppet government under one Vidkun Quisling, a Norwegian politician who had been prepared for the role in Berlin, introducing another word into the English language.

British, French, and Polish warships attacked the Germans right away and scored victories. British warships sank ten German destroyers at Narvik in the next four days. Royal Navy dive bombers based in the Orkney Islands, off Scotland, sank the German cruiser *Königsberg*, the first time aircraft ever sank a warship in wartime, a milestone in the history of naval warfare that is rarely recalled. But a U-boat sank a British aircraft carrier.

British and French troopships set sail. The government in London ordered a bombardment of Narvik followed by a landing. The commander on the spot, General Edward Mackesy, objected in terms that deserve to be remembered: "There is not one officer or man under my command who will not feel shame for himself and his country if thousands of Norwegian men, women and children at Narvik are subjected to the bombardment proposed," he said. The government rescinded the order.

On the ground the Allied intervention was characterized by poor planning and muddle. The French had Alpine units, some of them ski troops trained to fight in the mountains in the winter conditions they would find there; but the troops' skis and snowshoes could not be landed because the ship carrying them was too big to get into Namsos harbor. The British troops were neither trained nor equipped for winter weather and most had never even seen deep snow before. They often lacked even proper maps. In scattered engagements, the British and French came out worst.

British forces finally wrested Narvik from the Germans on May 28, but by that time the Germans were in control of most of the country, and the battle was raging in France; the British abandoned Narvik soon afterward.

The debacle in Norway produced profound discontent at home. There was a feeling that a straight line led from the political mistakes of appeasement to the military muddle in Norway, that the government in power was not the one to wage war. As a leader Chamberlain had tried desperately to avoid war, and now he seemed a reluctant warrior. He was not the man to sound a trumpet blast. The opposition put down a motion in Parliament directed against Chamberlain and his government, and members knew that this would be a historic debate. Attacks on the government were mounted, not only by the opposition, but by members of Chamberlain's own Conservative Party.

The seventy-seven-year-old Lloyd George, who had led the country to victory in World War One, was scathing: "The Prime Minister has appealed for sacrifice . . . I say solemnly that the Prime Minister should give an example of sacrifice, because there is nothing which can contribute more to victory in this war than that he should sacrifice the seals of office."

The final blow came from a senior member of his own party, Leo Amery, in what became one of the most famous political speeches of the century in Britain. He ended his peroration by saying: "This is what Oliver Cromwell said to the Long Parliament when he thought it no longer fit to conduct the affairs of the nation: 'You have sat here too long for any good you may be doing. Depart, I say, and let us have done with you! In the name of God, go!'"

When the vote came the government had a majority of eighty-one, but thirty Conservatives voted against and sixty abstained. Although technically a victory, it was a political and moral defeat, and Chamberlain decided that he must resign. Under the system then prevailing, a prime minister could choose his successor (theoretically, he was advising the king on whom to appoint). It must be someone who would gain the approval of a majority in the House of Commons, and this usually dictated his choice.

The two obvious candidates were Lord Halifax, who had been foreign secretary for the past four years, and Winston Churchill. Chamberlain's own preference was for Halifax, and this was shared by many others including the king. Halifax was intelligent, respected, experienced, and a lifelong insider. But he was associated with the prewar appeasement policy. Churchill was popular with the country now because of his panache and his prewar stand against Nazism. But he was mistrusted by the establishment and by many in his own Conservative Party as someone given to rash ventures and poor judgment. He had been the principal instigator of the disastrous Norwegian campaign.

Chamberlain summoned Halifax, Churchill, and D. R. Margesson, the Conservative chief whip, and asked them who should succeed him. Margesson said he favored Halifax. If Halifax had simply been ambitious for high office, the premiership might have been his. But he demurred and said that at this juncture it would not be right to have a prime minister sitting in the House of Lords, as he did; the real political action was in the Commons. But this difficulty had already been discussed, and it could have been overcome. Halifax refused the highest office because he thought Churchill might be a better war leader, better able to rally the country. As he said later, Churchill had "important qualities compared with my own at this particular juncture."

The next day, May 10, brought momentous news. As dawn broke, German troops invaded Belgium, Holland, and Luxembourg and attacked across the French frontier.

Chamberlain at first thought that now he should stay on, that Britain should not change government at such a crucial moment. But cabinet colleagues told him that, on the contrary, the situation now required more than ever a broad-based national government to include members of the Labour and Liberal Parties. Chamberlain consulted the leaders of the Labour Party, who were then at the party conference in the seaside town of Bournemouth. They said they would not serve under him but would serve under another Conservative prime minister.

So at twilight that day, in a light drizzle, the sixty-five-year-old Winston Churchill, in his familiar dark suit and floppy bow tie, was driven through London to Buckingham Palace, where King George, eighteen years his junior, went through the formality of asking him to become prime minister. Churchill knew full well that the king would have preferred Halifax. The king had agreed with the appeasers, and Halifax was a family friend. Furthermore, Churchill had backed the king's brother, Edward VIII, in the abdication crisis four years earlier.

Driving back from the palace, Churchill's bodyguard, Inspector William Thompson, congratulated him on his appointment. He was astonished at Churchill's response. "I hope it is not too late," Churchill said to him, and tears came into his eyes. "I am very much afraid that it is. We can only do our best."

. . .

Churchill is today an iconic figure, one of the giants of modern history, his round pudgy face, hunched figure, and cigar almost as familiar to anyone who knows anything about the history of the twentieth century as they were to wartime Britain. But he was not an obvious choice as prime minister in 1940 and he was far from universally admired. Other politicians mistrusted his judgment and used terms such as "impetuous," "verbose," and "restless." John Colville, a civil servant who was to become his private secretary for the next two years, wrote later: "The country had fallen into the hands of an adventurer, brilliant no doubt and an inspiring orator, but a man whose friends and supporters were unfit to be entrusted with the conduct of affairs in a supreme emergency. Seldom can a Prime Minister have taken office with the 'Establishment,' as it would now be called, so dubious of the choice and so prepared to find its doubts justified." He added, "The mere thought of Churchill as Prime Minister sent a cold chill down the spines of the staff at Ten Downing Street."

A reaction more in keeping with the public mood came from Norman Brook (later Lord Normanbrook), a senior civil servant. He recalled listening to Churchill on the radio back in October, and hearing Churchill say in his powerful, measured voice: "The Royal Navy has immediately attacked the U-boats and is hunting them night and day — I will not say without mercy, because God forbid that we should ever part company with that — but at any rate with zeal, and not altogether without *relish*." Normanbrook wrote later: "It was these last words, and the tone of voice in which they were spoken, which made me realize that this was the man to give us the leadership that we now needed."

Churchill is often represented as being the essence of Britain, the "bulldog breed," yet he was in many ways the antithesis of the traditional British character, flamboyant, loquacious, frankly ambitious, and openly emotional. British people are supposed to be phlegmatic; he was emotionally volatile, swinging between gloom and ebullience.

Winston Spencer Churchill, to give him his full name, was the product of one of those marriages between American wealth and British nobility. His father, Lord Randolph Churchill, was a prominent Conservative politician. His mother was Jenny Jerome, the daughter of an American financier, born in Brooklyn but raised partly in Paris, a pretty, vivacious woman whom he adored. Lord Randolph, a distant father like many members of the British aristocracy, died when Churchill was twenty-one. Jenny remarried, divorced her husband, and married a third time, a man younger than Winston.

All his life Churchill liked excitement. He joined the army as an officer in a fashionable cavalry regiment, but on his first long leave in

1896 he went in search of a war. He traveled to Cuba, where insurgents were fighting the Spanish army, and managed to come under fire. Later he fought in the empire's battles on the Indian northwest frontier and in Sudan, and he was in South Africa as a war correspondent in the Boer War, where, famously, he was captured and escaped.

He seems even to have enjoyed combat. With the cavalry in Sudan, facing the army of dervishes, he wrote to his mother: "I have a keen aboriginal desire to kill several of these odious dervishes . . . and I anticipate enjoying the exercise very much." After he met the dervishes at the Battle of Omdurman he wrote to a friend: "We emerged into a region of scattered men and personal combats. The troop broke up and disappeared. I pulled into a trot and rode up to individuals firing my pistol in their faces and killing several — 3 for certain — 2 doubtful — one very doubtful."

He was not a cruel man, and he understood the contradictions in his nature. On the eve of World War One, when he was first lord of the Admiralty, he wrote to his wife, Clementine: "Everything tends towards catastrophe & collapse and I am interested, geared up and happy. Is it not horrible to be built like this? The preparations have a hideous fascination for me. I pray to God to forgive me for such fearful moods of levity." (In Washington, Roosevelt, a busy assistant secretary of the navy and another man who liked excitement, wrote to his friend Livingston Davis at just this time: "I have had the most interesting ten days of my life.")

Churchill was a patriot and an imperialist. He never ceased to believe what he said in the House of Commons as a young member in 1901: "In spite of every lie uttered or printed, the truth comes to the top, and it is known alike by peoples and rulers, that on the whole British influence is healthy and kindly, and makes for the general happiness and welfare of Mankind." He quarreled with the Conservative leadership over their granting a measure of self-government to India.

He was unashamedly ambitious. He decided early on that soldiering was not going to be his career but politics was and he set out to acquire a reputation. He wrote to his mother about a firefight on the northwest frontier: "I rode on my grey pony all along the skirmish line where everyone else was lying down in cover. Foolish perhaps but I play for high stakes and given an audience there is no act too daring or too noble."

He became a Conservative member of Parliament in 1900 and held senior cabinet offices over the years. In the First World War when he was first lord of the Admiralty, characteristically frustrated by the stalemate on the western front, he pressed the idea of a seaborne attack on Turkey, an ally of Germany, at Gallipoli. He was held responsible for the disaster that followed and would always be associated with it in British minds. He resigned and joined his regiment, to experience trench warfare at firsthand.

He was humane, and sensitive to suffering where no threat to his country was involved. He made himself unpopular with officers in Sudan by criticizing in print the army's treatment of enemy prisoners. As home secretary he created more decent conditions in prisons. He broke with his party over its rejection of welfare measures and crossed the floor of the Commons to join the Liberal Party for a while. A political opponent sneered, "Winston is full of the poor, who he has just discovered." In one ministerial post after another he intervened in situations where he thought someone was being treated unjustly: a sailor dismissed from the service without a fair hearing, Jewish refugees from Nazism who were being denied asylum.

He was a natural conservative, opposed to radical change. When labor unions challenged the government in the general strike he was for vigorous countermeasures. He supported Mussolini at one point because he saw the Italian dictator as an alternative to Communism. It was not without reason that some people looked on his warnings about Germany as typical Churchillian warmongering, and that the Left regarded him as a reactionary.

Like most members of his class, he never identified with the mass of people, nor did he pretend to. His private income did not support his lifestyle. He had to earn his living for most of his life, and at one time was faced with selling his country estate until he was saved by a gift from a political supporter. But he never lived without servants, nor did he drop his living standards below the level of luxury. His well-known fondness for alcohol was for champagne, whiskey, and brandy. His wife once said to his doctor, "You probably don't realize, Charles, that he knows nothing of the life of ordinary people. He's never been on a bus and only once on the underground [subway]."

He was a man of words. He was not a politician who wrote; he was a writer as much as a politician or a man of action. With Churchill words *were* action, his figures of speech powerful, his judgments severe. He wrote dispatches for a British newspaper when he was on the Indian northwest frontier and turned these into a book which was published when he was twenty-three. He earned his living by his pen for most of his life, pouring out articles for newspapers and magazines on both sides of the Atlantic. His books include major works of history: his four-volume *Marlborough: His Life and Times;* and his five-volume history of the period 1912–1920, *The World Crisis.* His style was characteristic of the late Victorian age in which he grew up. It was the style of the classic English historians, of Macauley and Gibbon, epigrammatic, sometimes witty, grandiloquent, judgmental, the choice of words sometimes archaic but resonant, with long elaborate sentences interspersed occasionally with short pithy ones.

It was the style of his speeches, which he always wrote himself, as well as his written work. He would spend hours on his wartime speeches, often dictating to a secretary as he walked around the room, honing the phrases until they achieved the impact he wanted, refusing to be interrupted by other business. His speeches rallied and inspired Britain, the phrases stirring the blood when all else spelled discouragement. He created phrases and sentences that live on in history. Even socially, it was said of him that he was a good talker rather than a good conversationalist.

From the day Churchill took office a stream of messages went out to all departments and to the armed services, the polite Victorian phraseology clothing an urgent tone. "Pray let me have, by this evening . . ." figures on tank production, the location of antiaircraft units, the stockpiles of meat, the criteria for draft deferral. His energy coursed through the veins of Whitehall, the home of the civil service, immediately. One Whitehall figure said he knew things had changed when he saw a senior civil servant *running* down a corridor. Colville, so full of anxiety when Churchill took over, said later, "I doubt if there has ever been such a rapid transformation of opinion in Whitehall and of the tempo at which business is conducted."

He knew how much hung on the events that would come in the next months, how desperate was the situation, and how grave would be his responsibility. But this responsibility was what he had always wanted. Years later, when he was in retirement, he was asked what year of his life he would like to live again, and he said, "Nineteen-forty, every time."

4

BLITZKRIEG

The Luftwaffe struck soon after sunrise. Bombers attacked Holland, flying out over the North Sea and curving in across the coast to achieve greater surprise. They flew low over acres of tulip fields in bloom, where girls working there in the early morning waved to them, not noticing the markings on their wings. Then they bombed Dutch army bases and all the country's airports, and destroyed half the Dutch air force.

More than seventeen hundred German bombers roamed through the clear blue skies over northern Europe on that Friday morning, May 10. The largest number attacked northern France, bombing road and rail junctions and headquarters buildings, disrupting French efforts to organize troops and get them moving. They also bombed forty airfields, knocking out all eighteen British bombers on the ground at one field near Rheims. Some bombed the Belgian frontier defenses and rail junctions in Brussels. The State Department's first news of the attack came from the American ambassador in Brussels, John Cudahy, who said he heard bombs falling near the American embassy.

Other aircraft introduced a new kind of warfare. Transport planes dropped four battalions of paratroops, some 3,000 men, over Holland. These seized key bridges and also canal locks, to forestall the Dutch plan to flood the border areas, which was a part of the Dutch defense strategy. In some cases paratroops were led by Germans in Dutch uniforms to confuse the defenders. At several points Dutch troops fought off the paratroops and blew up the bridges, but German army engineers rushed up with the attacking troops to repair them. This was the first large-scale use of parachute troops in warfare (a small number had landed at Oslo Airport in the Norwegian campaign). Among other nations, only the Soviet Union even had paratroops.

The Allies had some warning. On April 30, the French military attaché in Bern learned from a reliable source that the Germans would attack between May 8 and 10 with their main thrust at Sedan, and this was passed to the French general staff. An anti-Nazi officer in Berlin, Colonel Hans Oster, told the Dutch military attaché on May 3 that Holland would be attacked soon, and Dutch forces were put on alert.* On May 7, the U.S. ambassador in the Hague reported that the Foreign Ministry believed an invasion of Belgium was imminent.

Facing the armies of four countries, the Germans did not have the advantage of numbers. They had 2.7 million troops engaged, compared with more than 3 million French, British, Belgians, and Dutch. They had about 2,700 tanks, slightly fewer than the Allies, although more of them were new. But the newest French tank, the thirty-three-ton Hotchkiss B, had a more powerful gun and thicker armor than any German tank. The Germans relied on horse-drawn transport for most of their supplies and even to move much of their artillery, as the French army did. But they had the advantage of choosing the time and place of the attack. The place they chose was where the Maginot line stopped, along 150 miles of front, through Belgium, Holland, Luxembourg, and northwest France.

Hitler masterminded German strategy, and he was a radical in military matters as he was in politics. He supported the new kind of mobile warfare that General Heinz Guderian and some other panzer leaders were pressing for, and he favored unconventional warfare, special operations of the kind that preceded the main attack.

The special forces in the operation against the tiny principality of Luxembourg were German "tourists" who had come across in the past few days on bicycles and motorcycles, and suddenly donned uniforms and seized key road junctions. Others landed by light aircraft nearby and neutralized Luxembourg's tank traps so that German tanks could

---

* Oster later took part in the July 1944 plot to assassinate Hitler and was executed.

roll through without interference to the Belgian frontier. In Belgium, airborne troops landed in light planes to capture two villages that commanded a vital road.

The most important success of the special forces was the capture of the Belgian fort of Eben Emael, a brilliantly planned and executed operation. Eben Emael was the linchpin of the Belgian defense system. It was a half-mile-long, heavily fortified structure atop a sheer cliff overlooking the Albert Canal on three sides, in a position to pour fire down on anyone trying to cross the canal. The Belgian army believed it could hold off any attacking force for at least five days, giving time for Allied troops to arrive. Eighty-five German troops landed by glider on the roof of the fort; the gliders were released from behind the German frontier thirteen miles away and came in silently, achieving complete surprise. From the roof the Germans demolished the fort's guns with specially prepared explosive charges. They held on until early the next morning when reinforcements joined them, and soon after the 1,100 defenders surrendered.

The British Expeditionary Force, regular soldiers and Territorials who had been called up on the outbreak of war, immediately advanced into Belgium as planned, marching along Belgian roads to meet the Germans as their fathers had in 1914. Drew Middleton of the Associated Press watched them and wrote: "It was almost as if they were retracing steps taken in a dream. They saw again faces of friends long dead and heard the half-remembered names of towns and villages."

The spearhead of the German attack was the panzers, the armored divisions consisting of tanks and armored vehicles. Rivers and canals were the natural obstacles. Where the Dutch fought off paratroops and blew up bridges, the Germans repaired them quickly. British and Belgian aircraft flew in low to attack bridges and armored columns — the French air force was slower to respond — and they were met with a hail of antiaircraft fire. They were encountering the German army's new light AA guns, which were moved up with the troops.

Some eighteen hundred tanks came through the Ardennes, where France, Belgium, and Germany meet. The French had decided that the Ardennes, with its thick forests and deep ravines, presented such great difficulties to an army that an attack there was very unlikely, so this sector was only lightly defended. (This was a mistake the U.S. Army was to make in December 1944, when the Germans staged their last counterattack in what came to be known as the Battle of the Bulge.) In fact it had roads, and there were tracks even through the thick forests along which armor could pass. Facing the Ardennes was the French Ninth Army; many of its troops were elderly reservists, and it was the last in line for new equipment and woefully short of antitank guns.

The Dutch army fought fiercely although it was heavily outnumbered. Frustrated, the Germans set out to crush resistance by bombing Rotterdam. The raid was a tragedy. The Dutch asked for a cease-fire, and the Luftwaffe ground control sent out an order calling off the attack, but the planes were already in the air and only a few understood the signal and turned back. Sixty Heinkel 111s bombed the city for twenty minutes, razing a square mile in the center. The Dutch foreign minister, overwrought, said 30,000 people were killed. It was found later that the actual figure was 980. But the figure of 30,000 was accepted, and Rotterdam became, like Guernica, Madrid, and Warsaw, another symbol of Nazi terror from the air. The Dutch government surrendered that evening, May 14, and Queen Wilhelmina sought refuge in Britain.

The Germans went through the Ardennes, and in two days they reached the Meuse River near Sedan, as the French attaché in Bern had predicted. This was a place of historic significance for both France and Germany as the scene of the surrender of Emperor Napoleon III and his army to the Prussians in 1870. The French blew up the bridges, but a group of German troops found a weir still standing and clambered across it at night to establish a bridgehead on the other bank of the Meuse; more Germans crossed in rubber boats under heavy fire. German engineers built pontoon bridges and RAF bombers attacked them, flying low. These planes were Fairey Battles, produced in the early 1930s and soon to be replaced, slower and more vulnerable than newer bombers. Antiaircraft guns and German fighters shot down forty of the seventy-one bombers, the RAF's highest rate of loss of the entire war. The pontoon bridges remained intact. French aircraft followed with no more success.

The next day, outside Sedan, the largest concentration of bombers ever seen over a battlefield pounded French defenders. An observer gave an account of the effect. "Quickly, the rearward artillery command posts emptied: telephones to the front went dead; forward gunners — still manning their guns against the advancing Germans in the Sedan pocket

— found themselves stranded. Without communications or firing instructions, these also decamped. The panic spread in widening circles."

No one on the Allied side had any idea yet of the speed with which events would unfold. In London, the chief of the Imperial General Staff, Field Marshal Edmund Ironside, wrote in his diary: "On the whole, the advantage is with us. A really hard fight all this summer." He could not imagine that the war in France would be over before the summer had properly begun.

This was a new kind of warfare, *blitzkrieg*, or lightning war. Its defining element was speed. The spearhead of the blitzkrieg was the tank. The tank was invented in Britain in 1916 and was used to great effect on the western front to break through barbed wire and clear a way for the infantry. In 1940 the British and French tank regiments were still deployed to operate with infantry, not concentrated as they were in the panzer divisions. After the war the French general Charles Delestraint exaggerated only slightly when he said, "We had 3,000 tanks which we used in a hundred packets of 30. The Germans had 3,000 tanks which they used in three packets of 1,000."

The panzer divisions were designed to operate independently, to forge ahead into enemy territory, bringing along with them motorized infantry and their supplies in other armored vehicles and their own antiaircraft guns. Where the panzers came up against strong resistance, as they did on the Meuse, they needed more fire power. This was supplied, not by heavy artillery, which could not be moved up quickly enough, but by the Luftwaffe.

The German air force had never accepted the doctrine of winning a war by destroying an enemy's cities. It was designed to operate in support of forces on the ground. Aircraft were to be used, as in these first days of the battle in the west, to attack the enemy forces and disrupt communications. This was an essential element of the blitzkrieg. The attacks on Warsaw and Rotterdam were limited and were intended to clear the way for advancing troops.

The Germans built a plane designed for close support of advancing troops, the Stuka* dive bomber, or JU87, easily identifiable by its V-shaped wings. The Stuka was the brainchild of Ernst Udet, the pilot-

---

* The word is an abbreviation of the mouthful *sturzkampfflugzeug*, which means diving war plane.

adventurer who became one of the chiefs of the Luftwaffe. Visiting the United States as a civilian in 1933, he saw the Curtis Hawk dive bomber at the Cleveland air races and piloted one. He persuaded Luftwaffe chief Hermann Göring to buy two for evaluation, and the program to build a dive bomber was set in motion. Close support tactics in cooperation with ground forces were developed in Spain. The abiding image of air power in the Spanish Civil War is Guernica, the Basque town destroyed by German planes, but the lesson for the Luftwaffe was the effectiveness of air attacks in support of troops. Plunging earthward at an angle twenty degrees from the vertical, the Stukas would drop their two 500-pound bombs on enemy positions directly in front of the troops with formidable accuracy. It proved to be a terrifying weapon, and the Luftwaffe made it more terrifying still by attaching whistles to the wings so that it shrieked as it plummeted down.

The Stuka acquired notoriety. A British officer attached to French headquarters wrote: "I soon became accustomed to hearing it described as a nerve-shattering irresistible weapon, attacking vulnerable points with uncanny pertinacity. Guns were helpless against it; so was infantry." Time and time again French officers referred to German armor-air coordination in accounting for their defeat.

To counter a blitzkrieg, a defender needed flexibility, rapid decision making, and good communications and coordination. These were all areas in which the French army was deficient. The commanders still operated at a World War One tempo. Communication was by telephone or motorcycle courier, which was slow and unreliable. Unable either to coordinate their forces or reach decisions quickly, the French were overwhelmed by the rapidity of the attack. One officer, Captain Marc Bloch, found General Paul Blanchard, the commander in the north, where all the fighting was, "sitting for an hour in tragic immobility, staring at a map as if seeking an answer there."

* * *

In London during these days, Churchill was preoccupied with choosing the members of his government. It seemed that there was no immediate action to take over the German attack. The plans for the response were in place, an advance into Belgium to meet the attacking force, and they were being executed.

Churchill made himself minister of defense since conducting the war was clearly going to be the major task of this government and he felt himself well qualified to fill the post. Because it was to be an all-party government he named as his deputy, with the official title lord privy seal, Clement Attlee, the quiet, colorless, but deceptively strong-minded leader of the Labour Party (who was to become prime minister in 1945). Aware that many in the Conservative Party had strong reservations about his leadership and that he was not secure in his position, he asked Chamberlain, who was still the leader of the party, to be in his cabinet as lord president of the council, a powerful position, and he kept Lord Halifax as foreign secretary. He made Anthony Eden, who had quit the Chamberlain government because of his opposition to appeasement, minister of war. He created an inner, five-man war cabinet of senior ministers which in these weeks met almost daily and sometimes twice a day. As a courtesy to Chamberlain, whom he respected, he told him he could remain in the prime minister's official residence, 10 Downing Street, for the time being, while he lived in his old official apartments at the Admiralty.

Some critics complained that the architects of the appeasement policy were still in office; Lloyd George, the former Liberal prime minister who had earlier wanted a negotiated peace, refused an invitation to join the cabinet while these were members. The *Daily Mirror* called them "the old blunderers." But Churchill told *Daily Mirror* publisher Cecil King that if he were dependent on people who had been right in the past few years, it would be a very small group. "I will not run a government of revenge," he said. Besides, he knew that men like Chamberlain and Halifax had a lot of support in the Conservative Party while his own was uncertain.

Two appointments were unexpected. Churchill made Ernest Bevin minister of labor. Bevin, who left school at twelve to drive a dray cart, was the head of Britain's largest labor union, the Transport and General Workers' Union, which he had welded together from several unions of unskilled workers. Bulky, slow-moving, and aggressive, he was a man of the people in speech and manner, a leading figure in the Labour Party, of which the unions were constituent members. His appointment was designed to get labor behind the war effort and keep industrial strife to a minimum; it was vital when it became necessary to exercise dictatorial powers over industry and direct workers to places where they were most needed.

The other surprising appointment was also concerned with industry. Churchill created a new ministry, the Ministry of Aircraft Production, and put Lord Beaverbrook in charge of it. Beaverbrook was a Canadian-born newspaper publisher, a dynamic figure who Churchill hoped would energize this most vital of industries. He had been a power broker at the highest levels of British politics and was a close political friend of Churchill, and so was going to be an important cabinet figure.

On May 13 Churchill addressed the House of Commons as prime minister for the first time. He talked in measured tones about the formation of the government, and ended on a peroration with the first of his many wartime phrases that became famous:

"I have nothing to offer but blood, toil, tears and sweat. You ask what is our policy? I will say: It is to wage war, by sea, land and air, with all our might and with all the strength that God has given us, to wage war against a monstrous tyranny, never surpassed in the dark, lamentable catalog of human crime. You ask what is our aim? I can answer in one word. Victory, victory at all costs; victory in spite of all terror; victory however long and hard the road may be." This was as different from the speeches of Neville Chamberlain as the battle developing on the Continent was from the phony war.

The news from France was bad, and the cabinet also had to consider the likelihood that Germany's ally Italy would now enter the war, to be in at the kill and reap some of the spoils. The speed of the German advance was staggering. They were crossing in days territory over which armies had struggled for years in World War One.

Late on the night of May 14, four days after the German attack began, Churchill sat with Ambassador Joseph Kennedy and gave him a gloomy assessment. He said that if Italy entered the war then the chance of Allied victory would be slim. He said he expected an attack on Britain within a month, and help from America was badly needed. But, as Kennedy reported the conversation in his cable to Washington, "He said that regardless of what Germany does to England and France, England* will never give up as long as he remains a power in public life, even if England is burned to the ground. Why, he said, the Government would move to Canada and take the fleet and fight on." On several oc-

---

* He probably said "Britain." Americans and others often say "England" when they mean "Britain." Apologies to the Scots and Welsh.

casions during this period, Churchill spoke in private in pessimistic tones that were far from the unquenchable confidence that he always expressed in public.

In his cable, Kennedy added his own opinion. He could not see that America could do much to help the Allies at this stage. "It seems to me," he said, "that if we had to fight to protect our lives, we would do better fighting in our own back yard." Roosevelt wanted to keep the fighting *away* from America's back yard.

Roosevelt was trying to help the Allies. At the request of French ministers, passed on through U.S. ambassador Bullitt, he appealed to Mussolini in a cable not to enter the war, dropping a none-too-subtle hint that if he did America might also get involved. "A further extension of the area of hostilities, which would bring into the war still other nations which have been seeking to maintain their neutrality, would necessarily have unpredictable and far-reaching consequences, not only in Europe but also in the Near and Far East, in Africa and in the Americas," he wrote.

Early in the morning of May 15, five days after the attack began, Churchill received a telephone call from French prime minister Paul Reynaud. He was appalled to hear Reynaud say, in English, "We are beaten. We have lost the battle." Churchill said this surely could not have happened so soon, but Reynaud told him the front had been broken at Sedan, and the enemy were pouring through. Churchill tried to encourage Reynaud, telling him that the offensive would have to come to an end after a while, as they had learned from the German offensive in 1918. He said he would fly over to Paris to see him. A second desperate message from Reynaud came that evening: "The way to Paris lies open. Send all the troops and planes you can."

Reynaud, a small man with narrow eyes and an erect strutting manner, was called in France "the fighting cock" for his pugnacity. He had opposed the appeasement policy and had wanted to stand up to Germany over Czechoslovakia. He could be fierce in argument, but during these weeks he seems to have been wavering. Sometimes he was grimly determined, at other times he yielded to the pressure from others in his cabinet who were in a defeatist frame of mind.

Actually, his pessimism was premature. While many of the French troops were fleeing in panic or surrendering, others had rushed up to counterattack. French Hotchkiss tanks were taking a toll on the German armor. But the weaknesses of the French army at every level were telling. There was poor coordination and planning, and by the end of the day the Germans had pushed ahead and extended the Sedan bridgehead into a huge salient.

Before going to Paris Churchill dictated a letter to Roosevelt, his first as prime minister. Retaining the informality of their correspondence, he signed it, not "Naval Person" but "Former Naval Person." This letter was quite different from anything he had written before. Up to now he had given only accounts of the progress of the war, and had not tried to make policy by conducting relations with America. Now he was the head of the government.

His message was, more than anything else, an appeal for help. When Churchill first entered Parliament forty years earlier, Britain was the most powerful country in the world and the head of the largest empire the world had ever known. Now Britain was still the head of the empire, but as its prime minister he was having to ask for help to fight a war.

He pointed to the early German success, said Britain expected to be attacked, and then raised the possibility of Allied defeat. He would never acknowledge this in public, but to Roosevelt he set it out as a warning.

> I trust you realize, Mr. President, that the voice and force of the United States may count for nothing if they are withheld too long. You may have a completely subjugated, Nazified Europe established with astonishing swiftness, and the weight may be more than we can bear.
>
> All I ask now is that you should proclaim non-belligerency, which would mean that you could help us with everything short of actually engaging armed forces. Immediate needs are, first of all the loan of forty or fifty of your older destroyers to bridge the gap between what we have now and the large new construction we put in hand at the beginning of the war. This time next year we shall have plenty. But if in the interval Italy comes in against us with several hundred submarines we may be strained to breaking point. Secondly we want several hundred of the latest types of aircraft, of which you are now getting delivery. These can be repaid by those now being constructed in the United States for us. Thirdly, anti-aircraft equipment and ammunition, of which again there will be plenty next year, if we are alive to see it . . . We shall go on paying dollars for as long as we can, but I should like to feel

reasonably sure that when we can pay no more you will give us the stuff all the same.

America had the destroyers. Some 170 four-stack destroyers were built in World War One primarily for convoy duty. Many of them had been out of service and in dry dock since 1919. Some of these were now being reconditioned.

Roosevelt replied the following day. He adopted an encouraging tone but said the transfer of the destroyers would need the authorization of Congress, "and I am not certain that it would be wise for the suggestion to be made to the Congress at this moment." He went on, "Furthermore, it seems to be doubtful, from the point of view of our own defense requirements . . . whether we could dispose even temporarily of these destroyers." Regarding other military supplies, he said the request was being considered favorably. He said nothing about what would happen when Britain could not pay any more.

Churchill also associated Roosevelt with Britain's war effort by arranging for him to receive the daily summaries on the war prepared for the British cabinet. Every day they were sent over to the White House from the British embassy on Massachusetts Avenue, three or four pages of gray foolscap paper with brief reports: "Yesterday enemy aircraft bombed shipping off Petershead but without effect . . . Our fighter aircraft operating over France yesterday shot down six Messerschmitt 109s . . . Four British ships were torpedoed off the Western coast of Europe, two of which sank."

When Churchill arrived in Paris and met the French government and military chiefs, he found that they all shared Reynaud's gloom. Gamelin explained the situation with the aid of a map. The Germans had broken through at Sedan on a fifty-mile front and eight or ten motorized divisions were pushing ahead, driving a wedge between two French armies, what he was now calling the Sedan bulge. Churchill asked, "Where is the strategic reserve?" and then repeated the question in French. Gamelin shook his head and said, *"Aucune"* — None. Churchill was dumbfounded. He had assumed that the point of the Maginot line was to have a static defense line behind which reserves could be rushed up to meet an attack at any point.

Reynaud assured Churchill that Paris would be defended at all costs. But looking out of the window into the courtyard, he saw men bringing up state documents in wheelbarrows to a bonfire where they were being burned so that the Germans would not get them. The newspapers gave Parisians no idea of the German successes, but to some the black smoke from the bonfire in the Foreign Ministry courtyard and the tiny bits of paper drifting over the streets like charred confetti gave a clue as to what was happening.

It was at this meeting that the question was first raised that was to be a contentious issue between the two Allies. General Gamelin told Churchill the French were handicapped by their inferiority in the air, and asked Churchill to send over more planes. He wanted bombers but principally fighters, in addition to the four squadrons that the British had already agreed to send over. He said the fighters were needed to provide air cover and also to stop the tanks. Churchill argued that it was the task of the artillery to stop tanks. But he said that aircraft would provide cover over the Sedan bulge.

Britain had not been attacked from the air but it was expected that it would be, and the question of whether to take more fighters from the home defense force and send them to France was a grave one. Churchill was not willing to make the decision alone. He cabled the cabinet recommending sending six more fighter squadrons to France. The meeting ended and Churchill went to the British embassy. There he received a cable from London saying the cabinet had agreed to send the extra fighters.

It was now late in the evening but Churchill decided that he must tell Reynaud this right away. He telephoned Reynaud and went over to his apartment. Reynaud hastily summoned Daladier, now secretary for defense, and Paul Baudouin, the secretary of the War Cabinet, and received his guests in a dressing gown. Churchill gave him the good news about the ten fighter squadrons coming over to France. Daladier, evidently moved, came over and shook his hand silently. Then Churchill started talking about the likely course of the war, and swung into the same mood in which he had spoken to Kennedy.

Paul Baudouin describes Churchill at that meeting as "remarkable for his energy and vehemence, crowned like a volcano by the smoke of his cigars." Churchill said that even if France were defeated Britain would go on fighting until the United States came to her aid, which it surely would. He said they would starve Germany out, destroy its towns and burn its crops and forests. Baudouin says, "He saw himself in the heart of Canada, directing, over an England razed to the ground by high explosive bombs and over France whose ruins were already cold, the air war of the New World against the Old dominated by Germany." Strangely, given the apocalyptic nature of this vision, Baudouin then says: "He made a great impression on Paul Reynaud and gave him confidence."

When Churchill got back to London, the cabinet had changed its mind on the question of fighters for France. Air Chief Marshal Sir Hugh Dowding, the head of Fighter Command, had presented a paper to the cabinet that swung opinion around. Dowding's mission was the defense of the home islands, and he harbored his fighter planes for this purpose zealously. He refused to allow any Spitfires, the most advanced fighter, to go to France. He pointed out in his paper that the home-based fighter force was already below the minimum requirements, and said: "If the Home Defense Force is drained away in desperate attempts to remedy the situation in France, defeat in France will involve the final, complete and irremediable defeat of this country." Cabinet ministers could not argue with this kind of statement.

The German advance provided another argument in favor of keeping the aircraft at home. Three RAF bases had to be moved before the oncoming panzers, and the chief of air operations in France said the new bases could not accommodate more than three squadrons of Hurricanes. The cabinet decided that these planes would operate over France but from airfields in southern England, although this would limit their range.

Dowding continued to struggle doggedly to keep his fighter planes in Britain. The official historian of the RAF said of him: "However many calls there might be on our resources, Dowding was convinced that one call — the safety of the base — was primary and absolute, and till that was met he proposed neither to understand other arguments nor to compromise nor even to accept with good grace the decisions that went against him." Whatever his temperamental limitations, history has justified his stand. No number of RAF fighter planes could have changed the outcome in the Battle of France. The lack of them might have changed the outcome of the Battle of Britain.

The War Cabinet took another decision regarding the RAF that day. It decided to authorize the nighttime bombing of Germany; railroad marshaling yards, oil refineries, and a few specified industrial plants were to be the targets. At first their success was extremely limited. On the first night seventy-eight bombers were sent against oil targets and only twenty-four found them and attacked them. These raids were the first moves toward putting into practice the RAF philosophy of the knockout blow against an enemy's homeland.

• • •

The Germans continued to advance. Gamelin warned Reynaud that they could be in Paris within a day. The government made plans to leave the capital and armed the Paris police with rifles in case of civil disorder. There was no time to remedy the deficiencies of the French forces in morale, in plans, in coordination. While Reynaud was asking Churchill for more planes, French aircraft were standing in fields useless because they were unarmed, while their armaments were in depots a few miles away.

Gamelin asked a staff officer for a report on the Ninth Army, which, with its underequipped and undertrained troops, had borne the brunt of the attack through the Ardennes. The officer reported: "The disorder of this army is beyond description. Its troops are falling back on all sides. The Army General Staff has lost its head. It no longer knows even where its divisions are. The situation is worse than anything we could have imagined."

The Allies were outnumbered in the air. Most of the French aircraft were old and outmatched by the Luftwaffe, and even many of its modern bombers were not combat-ready. The RAF had 220 bombers and 130 fighters in France, reinforced by more fighters in the first days of the battle, and their pilots were hard-pressed. The commander of RAF forces in France, Air Marshal Sir Arthur Barratt, reported to London on May 16: "Our fighter pilots were very tired. They had to deal all the previous day with waves of 40 bombers every hour, heavily escorted by fighters. Squadrons of fighters were the proper counter to this form of attack, but they had to operate with flights of three or five, always in great numerical inferiority. Every pilot was carrying out four or five sorties a day."

The Belgian army was fighting fiercely, reinforced now by some elements of the British and French armies, but they were outgunned. When they mounted an artillery barrage as a prelude to a major counterattack, Stukas destroyed every gun within half an hour. The British advanced as planned to the Dyle Canal, which they believed was fortified to create a formidable obstacle, but they found no fortifications there, and came under heavy attack. They fought back and held the Germans for a time.

They fought in the streets of the ancient Belgian university town of Louvain. The historic library there, a national treasure, had been destroyed in the First World War and rebuilt with the help of a nationwide American charity appeal. It was burned down again in the fighting. Other place names coming into the news now were familiar to British people from the First World War, Ypres, Cambrai, and Menin.

People fled from the advancing Germans, abandoning their homes in towns and villages. Soon the battle for France was accompanied by a mass movement of people. Millions were on the roads. Most were short of food and drink and clamored for both in every village they passed through, often clearing out stores. They would have been safer where they were. On the roads, German aircraft bombed and machine-gunned them, sometimes because they were mingled with troops, sometimes just wantonly, for no reason that anyone could see.

There were cars with French, Belgian, and Dutch license plates, with mattresses strapped to the roof and whole families inside, horse-drawn wagons, and many people pushing wheelbarrows containing the family's belongings, some of them near to collapse from fatigue. Here and there were incongruous vehicles such as a hearse, an ice cream van, or a fire truck. Major General Sir Alan Brooke wrote in his journal: "They were all haggard-looking, and many women were in the last stages of exhaustion, many of them with their feet tied up with string and brown paper where their shoes had given out. They were covered with mud from throwing themselves into ditches every time a plane flew over. There were old men trundling their old wives in wheelbarrows, women pushing prams piled high with all their belongings, and all their faces distorted by fear, a heart-breaking and desperate sight." Pierre Mendès-France, a French army officer (later, in 1966, to be prime minister), saw "strings of these wagons stretching for a kilometer or more representing the combined evacuation of an entire village, with its mayor, its priest, the old schoolmaster, the policeman."

All the fighting was still in the northwest corner of France, in the Belgian border area. The French government realized that the Germans were not advancing on Paris. But relief was followed by another kind of alarm. The Germans were not directing their main thrust against Paris but were swinging around toward the sea. The troops that had advanced into Belgium had gone into a trap.

German tanks broke out of the Sedan bulge and streaked ahead, covering thirty miles in a day. They were a spearhead with hardly any shaft behind them, ahead of the rest of their army, getting their gasoline from French stores. Demoralized French troops surrendered at the first sight of them or allowed the Germans to bypass them. On the evening of May 20, the panzers reached the coast at Abbeville, at the mouth of the River Somme. As exhausted but exhilarated German soldiers washed off dirt and grime in the water of the English Channel, the Allied commanders knew that the trap was closed. Now the million French, British, and Belgian troops would have to either break through the ring or escape by sea, or else be captured.

In this atmosphere of retreat and bewilderment, rumors of fifth column activities abounded. A waitress had been heard whispering in German down a telephone. A field was ploughed so as to show from the air the direction of a French gun position. A villager was seen flashing lights as a signal to enemy airplanes. People were arrested because they had a foreign accent or were out at night without an explanation, and some were shot after the minimum of interrogation.

There were episodes of heroism. Near Sedan, two French tanks with defective motors took it in turns to tow one another until both finally broke down. Called upon to surrender they refused, fought on, and destroyed two German armored vehicles. Then the two tank commanders told their crews to escape on foot taking with them the tanks' machine guns. The commanders remained, manning their cannon through the day, and knocked out three German light tanks and two other vehicles. When they ran out of ammunition they destroyed their tanks, hid in a ditch while a panzer column rolled by, and made their way back to the French lines.

And there were episodes of horror. Back in England after being evacuated from France, Lieutenant Peter Vaux looked up a dispatch rider in his tank regiment who was now in a psychiatric hospital. As Vaux recalled later:

> He said, "Shall I tell you what happened in France, sir?" And I said, please do. "Well," he said, "I was on my motorcycle doing a job for the colonel and I was at a crossroads in a village and there

were masses of refugees there, and there was quite a traffic jam. And the Germans came over and they bombed it, and it was a dreadful scene and I was blown off my motorcycle and I found myself next to a little boy of about five and he'd had his legs blown off. And he was blinded in one eye and he was in terrible pain and I took him in my arms and I could see he was dying and I took out my revolver and I shot him, sir. I did do right, didn't I?" I said, "Yes, you did right, I would have done the same." And we talked of other things and he said, "Shall I tell you what happened in France, sir?" and he did it again all the way through."

A nurse told Vaux that he never stopped telling the story, repeating it again and again.

■ ■ ■

Reynaud tried to halt the demoralization of the army by sacking Gamelin — he had been on the point of doing so when the Germans attacked — and bringing in as his replacement General Maxime Weygand, from the French colony of Syria. A small, dapper figure who wore a cavalry officer's uniform down to the spurs, he conveyed an impression of vigor despite his seventy-three years. He had a good reputation from World War One, and Reynaud wanted to summon up just this patriotic tradition. For this same reason he brought into his cabinet as vice premier the aging Marshal Philippe Pétain, the hero of Verdun, the very embodiment of resistance to *les Boches,* now ambassador to Madrid.

Bad feeling was developing between the British and French. The French accused the British of limited commitment and refusing to cooperate; the British felt the French were not fighting with sufficient vigor. The commander of the British Expeditionary Force, Lord Gort, thought little of the French commanders and complained to the War Office, "It is no uncommon occurrence to agree with the French to retire at, say, 9 P.M. and find that the French troops had in fact started to pull back at 4."

On May 19, Churchill spoke to the British people. He said, "It would be foolish to deny the gravity of the hour. It would be still more foolish to lose heart or courage, or to suppose that well-trained and well-equipped armies numbering millions of men can be overcome in the space of a few weeks or even a few months by a swoop or raid of mechanized vehicles, however formidable." Evidently, Churchill still could not imagine that an advance this rapid could be anything more than a "swoop" or "raid."

He was dismayed to see, on the same day, the message that Gort had sent to the War Office suggesting that evacuation was a possible course. However, it was prudent to make contingency arrangements, and Vice Admiral Bertram Ramsay, naval commander of the channel port of Dover, was charged with drawing up plans to evacuate the BEF if this should prove necessary.

Churchill sent over Field Marshal Lord Ironside to disabuse Gort of the idea of evacuation. Ironside found that the situation was just as bad as Gort had indicated. He was a towering figure of six-foot-four, inevitably, given the British proclivity for ironic nicknames, known as "Tiny." He had an aggressive temperament, and had earned the Victoria Cross, Britain's highest medal for bravery, in World War One. He was appalled by his meeting with Generals Blanchard and Billotte. He found them both, he wrote in his diary, "in a state of complete depression. No plan, no thought of a plan. Ready to be slaughtered. Defeated at the end without casualties."

Well if they had no plan, he would give them one. In a rage at one point in their exchange he grabbed hold of Bilotte by his jacket and shook him. Together they devised a scheme for a British-French attack south toward Arras. The attack proved to be an Allied success. Seventy-four British heavy tanks plus infantry inflicted heavy losses on a German panzer unit under Major General Erwin Rommel and an elite SS division, and took four hundred prisoners. But the Germans brought up reinforcements, and after two days fighting the British had to withdraw to avoid being encircled. As so often the case, the attack was not coordinated. The French attacked again the next day, but there was insufficient follow-up. The lack of coordination was made worse when Bilotte was killed in a car accident.

On May 23, panzers reached the channel port of Boulogne, to find it defended by Irish and Welsh Guards who had arrived from England two days before. With French garrison troops they fought off the Germans from behind the port's thick stone ramparts, which served the town as they had when they were built in the seventeenth century. Eventually the Germans blasted a hole in the wall with heavy artillery and the Guards fell back, and most were taken off by British destroyers under heavy fire. The French troops were left behind still fighting, an episode that added to the bad feeling that was developing between the Allies.

As BEF troops withdrew, they were put on half-rations. To survive they pillaged abandoned farms and stores. One soldier recalls taking turnips from the fields and scavenging in villages. "In their cellars they used to cure meat and we were able to help ourselves to an extent to that. The only water we had to drink was water out of ditches which we were able to boil," he said. Major General Bernard Montgomery's Third Division drove cattle with them, meat and milk on the hoof. One British soldier separated from his unit was fortunate to stumble on a group of French soldiers making a meal over a campfire of baked beans and champagne, and they invited him to join them.

Ironside, so full of aggressive spirit when he was talking to the French generals, was now thinking of defeat. He wrote in his diary: "The final debacle cannot be long delayed and it is difficult to see how we can help. It cannot mean the evacuation of more than a minute portion of the BEF and the abandonment of all the equipment of which we are so short in this country. Horrible days we have to live through . . . We shall have lost practically all our trained soldiers by the next few days unless a miracle appears to help us."

Gort despaired of his French commanders and of Weygand's plan for a counteroffensive and began to act independently. The government in London was of a similar mind. On May 26 Anthony Eden, as war minister, sent a message telling him that if, as it seemed, the planned French offensive was too weak to succeed, "you will be faced with a situation in which the safety of the B.E.F. will predominate." The message went on: "In such a situation, the only course open to you may be to fight your way back to West where all beaches and ports east of Gravelines will be used for embarkation . . ." The message made clear that this was still only a hypothetical situation, but it gave some substance to French accusations of bad faith by adding, "In the meantime it is obvious that you should not discuss the possibility of the move with the French or Belgians."

On May 27 the Belgian King Leopold said his army could fight no longer and surrendered, exposing the British and French flank. His cabinet ministers sought refuge in Britain, but Leopold refused their appeals to go with them. Churchill told his cabinet that this might sting the French to anger, in which case they would be "more formidable opponents than in their present stunned, bewildered state."*

It certainly stung Reynaud to anger. In a broadcast to the nation, he said Leopold had surrendered without warning the British or French who had gone to his aid, and called this a betrayal "without precedent in history." Churchill spoke in Parliament in more measured tones, refusing to pass judgment. Reynaud protested at this high-mindedness, and a few days later Churchill, evidently to appease him, spoke about it again and this time condemned the surrender as Reynaud did.

Most British people did not know how bad the situation was. Those who did were appalled. Halifax wrote in his diary on May 25: "The one firm rock on which everyone was willing to build for the last two years was the French Army, and the Germans walked through it like they did the Poles."

Weygand could not retrieve the situation. He devised a plan for a counteroffensive but the different elements were not coordinated. Churchill flew over for another meeting and he was impressed by Weygand's vigor, and even accepted some of his criticisms of the BEF. Weygand devised a plan to attack the encircling German ring from both sides. Churchill ordered Gort to attack the next day with eight divisions in accordance with the plan. The order infuriated Gort since the British divisions assigned to the attack were already hard-pressed and short of ammunition, and the French divisions were either depleted or exhausted. Then Weygand reduced the forces committed to it. Gort gave up on the plan, ignored orders and rushed two divisions up to plug up a gap in the line left by the Belgian surrender.

A newly constituted French armored division under the command of Colonel Charles de Gaulle, long an exponent of the kind of mobile warfare that the Germans were practicing, and the British Forty-first Highland Division attacked from outside the ring near Abbeville and destroyed German tanks and captured prisoners, but they could not hold their gains. Gort established a defensive line in the flat marshland from Gravelines to St. Omer. Rear-echelon troops were sent up as reinforce-

---

* By convention, cabinet minutes do not use direct quotes. This, like other quotes from cabinet meetings, is from the minutes. However, it sometimes seems apparent that the words used are those of the minister.

ments to hold this line. Behind this line, the encircled British and French troops drew back toward the nearest French port to the Belgian border, Dunkirk.

* * *

Churchill was sending more messages to Roosevelt. On May 18 he said Britain expected to be attacked very soon "on the Dutch model" and added: "If American assistance is to play any part, it must be available soon."

His next cable, on the twentieth, contained a warning. He promised that whatever happened his government would never surrender. But he went on: "If members of the present Administration were finished and others came in to parlay amid the ruins, you must not be blind to the fact that the sole remaining bargaining counter with Germany would be the fleet, and if this country was left by the United States to its fate no one would have the right to blame those then responsible if they made the best terms they could for the surviving inhabitants. Excuse me, Mr. President, for putting this nightmare so bluntly."

He explained his intention in sending this and similar messages to the Canadian prime minister, Louis Mackenzie King: "We must be careful not to let the Americans view too complacently the prospect of a British collapse."

Actually, there was no danger of this. The prospect of British collapse was fearful to the administration. With all but a small part of the American navy in the Pacific, the defeat of Britain, removing the British navy from the scene and leaving the Atlantic open to German domination, would be a dangerous situation for the United States. If Germany acquired the British fleet and this was added to the German strength, this would indeed be a nightmare situation.

Churchill did not know it but his warning was echoed by Ambassador William Bullitt in Paris. Bullitt said in one of his personal cables to Roosevelt: "I think it may possibly be of the utmost importance for the future of the United States that you should have in mind the hypothesis that, in order to escape from the consequences of absolute defeat, the British may install a government of Oswald Mosley and his Union of British Fascists which would cooperate fully with Hitler. That would mean that the British Navy would be against us."

Roosevelt said to Interior Secretary Harold Ickes, "Suppose Hitler offered Britain generous peace terms but said Britain must hand over its fleet, to replace the German fleet that Britain had seized in 1919. What would Britain do?"

Ickes, a self-styled curmudgeon with a tendency to hold strong views on any topic, had moved from being unconcerned about foreign affairs to sounding the tocsin about fascist aggressor nations. He had likened them to the Ku Klux Klan with the phrase "nations in nightshirts." He had used his position at the Interior Department to argue for an embargo on oil and other materials for Germany and Japan. After the conversation with Roosevelt about the British fleet he was even more alarmed. In his diary he contemplated a situation in which Britain sent its fleet to Canada and Hitler said, "Bring back your fleet and hand it over or we will bomb England from end to end for six days." He wrote: "There is no doubt in my mind that this country is in the most critical situation since it won its independence."

Roosevelt was very worried indeed. He asked Mackenzie King to send a personal envoy to Washington for a secret conversation. Hugh Keenleyside of the Canadian foreign service went to Washington, spoke with Roosevelt and Hull, and sent his report to King. King wrote an account of this in his diary:

"The President and Mr. Hull were doubtful if England would be able to bear up under attack, and the President has it from what he believes good authority from Germany that Hitler will make a peace offer based on . . . the turning over of the fleet to the Germans." King said the president wanted him to line up the dominions to bring pressure on Britain not to accept such a peace offer, "even though it might mean destruction of England comparable to that of Poland, Holland and Belgium [and] the killing of those who had refused to make peace, but to have her fleet make its way to different outlying ports away from Europe, and send the King to Bermuda."

Mackenzie King was outraged at the suggestion. His diary entry went on: "For a moment it seemed to me that the U.S. was seeking to save itself at the expense of Britain. That it was an appeal to the selfishness of the Dominions at the expense of the British Isles . . . I would rather die than do aught to save ourselves or any part of this continent at the expense of Britain."

The German advance had an immediate impact on American defense plans. The administration had been increasing defense spending for the past three years. As in Britain in the 1930s, most defense spending had gone on the navy and the air force, leaving the army at the back of the line. This accorded with Roosevelt's own proclivities as well as his appreciation of strategic needs. In one discussion General George Marshall, who had been appointed army chief of staff at the beginning of the year, said to him, "At least, Mr. President, please stop speaking of the Army as 'them' and the Navy as 'us.'" Marshall, an upright, formal military figure, never established with Roosevelt the casual, good-fellow relationship that Roosevelt liked to have with those around him. He refused to call Roosevelt "Franklin," and insisted on using "Mr. President."

Back in February, Marshall had suggested shrewdly to his staff that it would be better if congressional hearings on defense appropriations were delayed. "It is probable that events in Europe will develop in such a way as to affect Congressional action," he told them. They certainly did.

Roosevelt hurriedly prepared a new defense program in cooperation with the service departments, and Congress began hearings immediately. Whatever one's view about America's stake in Europe, it was clear that with Nazi Germany bursting out of its frontiers the world had become a more dangerous place. Roosevelt put the program before Congress on May 16. He asked for $1.18 million. He said he wanted an air force and navy with 50,000 planes. The air force was to have 12,835 planes by April 1942, of which 4,000 would be combat aircraft. Legislators of both parties interrupted his address from time to time with applause.

Roosevelt gave an alarming picture of an America vulnerable in the world of the blitzkrieg. "Motorized armies can now sweep through enemy territory at the rate of 200 miles a day," he told Congress. "Parachute troops are dropped from airplanes in large numbers behind enemy lines. Troops are landed by planes in open fields and on highways . . . If the British colony of Bermuda fell into hostile hands, it is a matter of less than three hours for modern bombers to reach our shores. From a base in the outer West Indies, the coast of Florida could be reached in 200 minutes. The islands off the West coast of Africa are only 1,500 miles from Brazil."

Major General Henry Arnold, the Army Air Corps commander, told the Senate Appropriations Committee that some American bombers were so old compared with modern air forces that it would be suicide to send them against an enemy. He said the Flying Fortress, the B-17, was as good as any bomber in the world, but the air force only had fifty-two of them. He realized that a new day had dawned for the services when Senator Henry Cabot Lodge Jr. told him: "It is the general feeling of Congress, and as far as I can gather among public opinion throughout the country, to provide all the money necessary for the national defense, and all you have to do is ask for it."

Two weeks later, on May 31, Roosevelt sent a second message to Congress asking for more funds, and asking also for authority to call up the National Guard. He told Congress: "The almost incredible events of the past two weeks in the European conflict, particularly as regards the use of aviation and mechanized equipment, necessitate another enlargement of our military program."

• • •

It was in this situation that the administration considered Churchill's plea for help. Treasury Secretary Morgenthau consulted with General Marshall. Marshall was torn between America's needs and a desire to see Britain and France prevail. He asked General Arnold how much it would set back the air force's training program if they sold 100 airplanes to the Allies, as Churchill wanted. Arnold said it would set it back six months. Marshall decided that he could not agree to the sale of any modern aircraft. "It is a drop in the bucket on the other side and it is a very vital necessity on this side, and that is that," he told Morgenthau. He pointed out that they had already bent the law to get war material to the Allies.

Marshall illustrated the army's shortage when he pointed to the Allied request for antiaircraft guns. "We have no ammunition for antiaircraft guns, and we won't have for six months," he told Morgenthau. "So if we gave them the guns they couldn't do anything with them." However, he conducted a survey clearly biased in favor of Britain, and concluded that they could sell 500,000 World War One Lee Enfield rifles, 500 field guns, 35,000 machine guns, and 500 mortars, plus ammunition. Marshall signed a document saying these were surplus.

The War Department acted quickly. On June 4, as soon as the sale was approved, telegrams went out to army depots and arsenals, and within days the weapons were on their way by rail to the army docks at

Raritan, New Jersey. There men worked day and night unloading the six hundred freight cars. Meanwhile the British government had diverted twelve merchant ships already at sea to Raritan.

However, under the neutrality legislation, the government was not allowed to sell military equipment to a belligerent nation. Only a private corporation could do that. So the government went through the charade of selling the weapons to an American company so that the company could then sell them to Britain. The company chosen was United States Steel. On June 11, Secretary of War Woodring signed a contract with the chairman and the president of U.S. Steel selling the entire arsenal for $37,619,556.60. Then the two U.S. Steel executives taxied across Washington to the office of the Allied Purchasing Commission. There they signed a contract selling the material to the British and French governments for $37,619,556.60, Arthur Purvis and Jean Block-Lainé, the heads of the Allied Purchasing Office, signing for their governments.

Five minutes later a senior army officer telephoned the docks at Raritan and said, "Go ahead and load." Stevedores started loading the guns and ammunition onto the British freighters for the dangerous journey across the Atlantic. The first ship to sail, the *Eastern Prince*, left two days later with a cargo of field guns, machine guns, rifles, and ammunition.

Many people had misgivings about the sale. Roosevelt's military aide, Lieutenant General Edwin Watson, asked Major General Walter Bedell Smith what he thought about selling five hundred 75mm. field guns before the 105mm. gun that was to replace them was fully ready. Bedell Smith replied: "If we were required to mobilize after having to release guns necessary for this mobilization and were found to be short, everyone who was a party to the deal could expect to be found hanging from a lamp post."

The navy also, at Morgenthau's prompting, did its best. Fifty Curtis Wright Scout dive bombers were sold back to the Curtis Wright company so that they could be sold to Britain. They were flown up to Halifax, Nova Scotia, where they were put aboard a British aircraft carrier. The services scoured their bases for ancillary equipment, locating 500-pound and 1,000-pound bombs at several bases, and fuses in Panama. Naval officers told Morgenthau that the Army Air Corps had realized the importance of dive bombing from reports from Europe and wanted to borrow the Scout bombers to practice with. "Nuts on the army," Morgenthau said.

Anxious to give all help possible to Britain, Morgenthau raised the subject of the overage destroyers with Admiral Harold Stark, the chief of naval operations. Stark was adamantly opposed to transferring them. He said the World War One four-stackers were not obsolete even if they were in mothballs because others of the same type were in commission, and more were going to be put into service.

At the end of the month Roosevelt prevailed on Admiral Stark to agree to the transfer to Britain of twenty of the newest motor torpedo boats, which were under construction and due to be delivered to the navy in July. This caused trouble. The chairman of the Senate Naval Affairs Committee was Senator David I. Walsh of Massachusetts, an Irish-American, anti-British and isolationist. When he found out about the motor torpedo boats he was furious. A Roosevelt aide reported that the senator was in a "towering rage" and threatening to introduce legislation banning the sale of anything. "The whole committee is in a lather," he said. Walsh insisted that the matter be passed to the attorney general, Robert Jackson. Jackson concluded that the transfer would contravene a law of June 15, 1917 prohibiting the sale of U.S.-built warships to a belligerent nation, and the sale was rescinded.

At Walsh's urging, the Senate passed an amendment to the Navy Expansion Bill saying that no military equipment could be sold abroad unless the army chief of staff or the chief of naval operations said it was not necessary for the national defense.

The administration was doing what it could. The Canadian government asked the administration what it should tell Americans who were volunteering for the Canadian air force. The State Department said the president's "informal view" was that they could join and remain American citizens providing they did not take an oath of allegiance to Canada.

Prime Minister Reynaud was sending frantic messages through Ambassador Bullitt. On May 18 he told Bullitt that he wanted Roosevelt to declare publicly that America would not allow Britain and France to be defeated. Bullitt told him this was out of the question but he passed on his message anyway. A few days later Reynaud warned that if America did not give military help now it would have to face the Germans in America. He said he knew the American people did not want to send troops, but he wanted America to declare war and send ships and aircraft and turn its industry over to war production. As Bullitt reported, Reynaud said, "The only real guarantee that the United States could have today that Hitler would not some day be in the White House would be a combination of the American, British and French fleets."

Many Americans, and particularly Americans in Europe, were identifying with the cause of the democracies. The U.S. naval attaché in Brussels, Captain John A. Cade, wrote to a friend, "I am becoming ashamed to wear my uniform in the company of French and British officers who are fighting honorably."

The man in charge of the U.S. embassy in Berlin was First Secretary Alexander C. Kirk, for the ambassador, recalled at the time of the *kristallnacht,* had never returned to his post. Kirk cabled the State Department on May 28 saying that he wanted to return to America by air to explain his views. He gave a summary of them in the cable. He said America should propose a plan for peace, and if Germany did not accept, it should declare war immediately. He explained his reasons. "I am convinced that a continuation of the progress marked during the past two weeks by German arms will destroy the kind of world that is essential to the existence of our national life, and that consequently the fight is our own. If Germany wins a quick war and dictates peace, there will be no place for us in the kind of world that will follow." Hull agreed that he could return to Washington to put forward his view.

The U.S. Army's War Plans Division drew up a memo on the army's posture in the new situation for General Marshall, pointing out the weakness of American forces and the multiplicity of threats. The memo suggested that Germany would probably win the war in Europe. It said that America then faced the possibility of Nazi-inspired revolt in Brazil, disorder in Mexico, and Japanese aggression in the Far East. It said that with its limited resources America must decide what it was *not* going to do as well as what it was prepared to do, and establish priorities. Marshall agreed with this thinking and took the memo to Roosevelt, and he approved it in essence.

Under this guideline, the United States would make its priority "the defense of the continental United States and its overseas possessions east of the 180th meridian." It called for a plan for "such limited operations in Mexico as the situation may require," and also possible "protective occupation" of European possessions in the Western Hemisphere. The stance in the Pacific would be defensive and amounted to a major withdrawal. The defense zone would include Hawaii but would leave out the Philippines and Guam. The possibility of sending troops to Europe was not even mentioned.

The concern about Latin America amounted to alarm. On May 31 the navy sent the cruiser *Quincy* hurrying to Brazil and Uruguay on a goodwill visit. The Navy Department made it clear to reporters that the real purpose was to foil a possible pro-Nazi coup in those countries. Brazil's president, Getulio Vargas, was already uttering friendly words about Nazi Germany. Roosevelt told the navy to draw up plans to send 10,000 troops to Brazil by air, to be followed by 100,000 to be transported by sea.

Three days later Sumner Welles wrote in a memo to Roosevelt: "I am sure you will agree that if we acquiesce in the creation, through the connivance of non-American powers, of governments in some of the American republics subservient to Germany, the Monroe Doctrine would be rendered non-existent and the majority of the American republics would run helter-skelter to Hitler just as so many of the remaining small neutral nations of Europe are doing today."

• • •

If the impact of the German advance on official Washington was to be expected, the impact on the American public was a surprise. For many, the shock seemed to be almost as great as the shock felt in Britain. It was as if the Atlantic were hardly wider than the English Channel and provided hardly more protection.

Many Americans took to heart Roosevelt's alarmist talk about the new danger to America. The Jeannette, Pennsylvania, Gun Club announced that it was forming the first American civilian antiparachutist defense unit. Others followed suit. Several hunting clubs in Chicago called for the organization of the seven million members of rifle clubs into a civilian army of modern-day Minutemen. The National League of Mothers of America announced the formation of the Molly Pitcher Rifle Legion, named after the woman who fought beside her husband in the War of Independence; members would be given rifle instruction once a week. The General Federation of Women's Clubs meeting in Milwaukee passed resolutions approving the government's defense program and rejected one opposing any American participation in a foreign war.

At McGinniss's Restaurant at the New York World's Fair, notices were put up saying: "Please refrain from discussing the war situation at the bar," and bartenders were instructed to enforce this. The management explained that heated arguments were breaking out and these disturbed the atmosphere.

And this item appeared in the Sunday *New York Times* Book Section on May 19: "The team of Joseph Alsop and Robert Kintner, Washington columnists and authors of *American White Paper,* has asked Simon and Schuster to hold up printing a postscript to the original book until this weekend is over. The authors are now concerned with the policy of the United States if Germany wins quickly."

The stock market also reacted with alarm, registering a fall from 145 to 128. War might be good for the American economy; a German victory would not be. It would end the Allies' purchases of aircraft and other war material and it might close European markets to commodity exports.

Newspapers all over the country reported a change in the public perception. F. Lauriston Bullard, reporting in the *New York Times* on the feeling in New England, wrote on May 26: "An army of parachutists landing from the skies on Boston Common could not have startled these states more than did the German penetration of the Allied defenses. What some men had feared for many months was now occurring at last to the whole population. Germany might win, the British fleet might be swept from the seas, an enemy might appear on this side of the Atlantic."

In the West, the *Idaho Statesman* noted: "The American attitude to the war is fast changing from that of the disinterested spectator to that of a possible victim of the Nazi military machine."

From St. Louis, Roscoe Drummond reported in the *Christian Science Monitor:* "The grave peril which faces the Allies has almost overnight reversed the nation's thinking about the war. There is far less dissent today from the proposition that a Nazi victory menaces the security of the United States."

Republican Party leaders in the Midwest said privately that sympathy for the Allied cause was spreading and that foreign affairs issues favored the Democrats. They said every German advance made a Democratic victory in the coming presidential election more likely, particularly if either Roosevelt or Cordell Hull were the candidate. This was borne out by the Gallup poll, which showed a 5 percent jump in support for the Democrats in the two weeks after the German attack began.

Ohio Senator Robert Taft, a leading candidate for the Republican nomination in the coming election, tackled the issue head on when he spoke in Topeka, Kansas. "This is no time for the American people to be wholly absorbed in foreign battles simply because the newspapers with screaming headlines devote the first three pages to news from Europe," he insisted. "Under cover of war, the New Deal domestic program is sneaking up."

Isolationists hit back at the president's alarmism. Lindbergh said: "We need not fear foreign invasion unless the American people bring it on through their own internal quarrelling and meddling with affairs abroad . . . Let us stop this hysterical chatter of calamity and talk of invasion that has been running rife these last few days." The *St. Louis Post-Dispatch* ran an editorial headed: "Whoa, Mr. President," warning that if Roosevelt continued on his present course unchecked he would lead the United States into war. The editors said letters were eight to one in approval.

Stuart Chase, a onetime member of Roosevelt's brain trust and a prominent writer on national affairs, had a prescient warning: "If we help France and England to win, we shall certainly be called upon to guarantee the peace. That puts us into European power politics, perhaps so deep that we can never get out."

Yet most Americans seemed to be sharing some of the president's anxieties. They had been taught in grade school that the Monroe Doctrine was a proud declaration of hemispheric independence, not that it was dependent for its effectiveness on the British navy. But they were reacting now as if they had internalized the prevailing geostrategic view of the foreign policy specialists. They had accepted the protection of the British navy and the European democracies without acknowledging it, but seemed to recognize it now that this protection might be swept away.

Americans seemed to accept what Roosevelt had been saying for months: that America had a stake in the survival of the Allies. A Gallup poll published on June 10 found that 62 percent believed that if Nazi Germany defeated Britain and France, it would attack America next.

Walter Lippmann, the most influential of American foreign affairs commentators, wrote in his syndicated column: "The rest of the world will do well to recognize what is happening in the United States. The American public is changing its mind profoundly . . . The American people know now that if the Allies begin to fail, there will come into being an alliance of aggressive powers — Nazi Germany, fascist Italy, Soviet Russia and imperialist Japan — which the United States alone is incapable of dealing with."

Adolf Berle wrote in his journal on May 29: "The country has at last got the idea that the war may end in a smashing German victory — so smashing that the British might surrender their fleet. For the first time in over a century, the country is getting a little frightened."

5

RETREAT AND DELIVERANCE

On May 25, the British chiefs of staff produced for the cabinet a confidential report entitled "British Strategy in a Certain Eventuality." The "certain eventuality" was the fall of France, something still so awful to contemplate that it was to be referred to only indirectly and spoken of figuratively in whispers. It is a curious document. It is a strategic assessment by military men but the principal factors it cited are not military.

It began: "We make two assumptions. A. That the United States of America is willing to give us full economic and financial assistance, *without which we do not think we could continue the war with any chance of success.* [Italics in the original!] B. That Italy has intervened against us."

The British public did not know it, and even the American government seems not to have fully appreciated it, but in the eyes of the British military chiefs, the outcome of the war depended on financial and economic aid from the United States. Long before Pearl Harbor, the United States was a crucial actor in the war.

The report went on to say that if France fell, Britain's ability to avoid defeat rested on three factors. First: "Whether the morale of our people will withstand the strain of air bombardment." Second, whether Britain could import essential commodities. And third, Britain's capacity to resist invasion. This was an assessment by military chiefs, but only the third of the three factors they cited was military.

The report concluded: "Germany might still be defeated by economic pressure, by a combination of air attacks on economic objectives in Germany and on German morale and the creation of widespread revolt in the occupied territories." It forecast food shortages in Germany in the winter of 1940–41 and a shortage of oil. However, it said, this view rested on advice from the Ministry of Economic Warfare and added: "We cannot emphasize too strongly the importance of the substantial accuracy of this forecast, since upon the economic factor depends our only hope of bringing about the downfall of Germany."

It is just as well that the chiefs added this qualification. The forecast by the Ministry of Economic Warfare was not accurate. Germany did not face shortages of food or oil that winter, nor was there any chance of widespread revolt in the occupied territories.

Its conclusion also emphasized morale once again: "*Prima facie* Germany has most of the cards, but the real test is whether the morale of our fighting personnel and civilian population will counter-balance the numerical and material advantage that Germany enjoys. We believe it will."

However, at this point France had not fallen but was still fighting. In the north of France and Belgium, more than half a million British and French troops, including some 250,000 of the 350,000 British troops in France, were encircled in an area some twenty-five miles long and thirty miles deep around the port of Dunkirk. They were pulling back before the advancing panzers and were hard-pressed. A British artillery captain rushing to set up his guns in a field before the German onslaught was berated by a farmer, who pointed to a white sheet hanging out of his window as a flag of surrender and begged the British soldiers to go away. The captain told him, "My advice to you is, take the washing in. It may rain tonight."

The expected onslaught did not come that night. The German tanks halted, obeying an order from the high command confirmed by Hitler. Historians have speculated about this halt order. A few have suggested that Hitler wanted to allow the British Expeditionary Force to escape so that he could make peace with a Britain that was not totally defeated and helpless. But there are military reasons why Hitler might have been cautious about pressing home the attack earlier. Men and machines were fatigued; they had been surprised themselves by the rapidity of their advance. Many tanks were already out of action. The battle in the north seemed to be all but over, and it would be sensible for the panzers to harbor their strength for the next phase, the advance on Paris. Also, Hitler had promised the Luftwaffe's Marshal Hermann Göring that he would let his airmen win this battle alone and destroy the encircled forces from the air.

The two-day halt gave a rest to the British and French forces and allowed them to establish perimeter defenses. If the panzers had pushed on, it is likely that they would have reached the port of Dunkirk before most of the British forces and cut off their escape route, and the course of the war would have been very different.

Boulogne had fallen, and the British troops in the other channel port, Calais, thirty miles from Dunkirk, were encircled and hard-pressed. Destroyers were sent in to take them off. Then the evacuation order was rescinded and the destroyers sailed away. The troops were to fight on to protect the southern flank of the Dunkirk perimeter. Another reason was that the French were angry about the evacuation of Boulogne, and the abandonment of a second channel port would not look good. A message went out from the War Office to Brigadier Claude Nicholson, commander of the British troops at Calais, saying they must remain and fight on "for the sake of Allied solidarity."

When Churchill saw the message he was furious that men were being asked to die for Allied solidarity. He sent a telegram to Nicholson saying: "Every hour you continue to exist is of the greatest help to the B.E.F. Government has therefore decided you must continue to fight. Have greatest admiration for your splendid stand. Evacuation will not (repeat not) take place and craft required for above purpose are to return to Dover."

The German commander at Calais sent an emissary under a flag of truce with a surrender offer. Nicholson sent back a soldier's reply: "It is the duty of the British Army to fight as it is of the German Army." And fight they did, for forty-eight hours. When artillery and dive bombers pounded much of the town into rubble, they fought in the rubble, and when they were split up into small groups these fought on, keeping German divisions away from Dunkirk. Nicholson himself was wounded and was to die in a prisoner-of-war camp.

Others also fought. At Lille, inland from Dunkirk, several French divisions, entirely surrounded, held off the Germans for four days, winning the admiration of the German commanders, while the British and other French troops escaped to the coast.

As usual when an army retreats, there was a lot of confusion. A British infantry officer, Captain Roy Blew-Jones, wrote in a letter to his sister:

> It was all pretty bloody and rather vague and disjointed . . . I never caught up with my own battalion, but had a body of 40 men from 25 different regiments. None of us had ever met before, but I do not think any of us will ever forget the faces of the others; in my mind they are imprinted for life. We fought in France and then north of Ypres, and then all the way back to Dunkirk, taking a week over the journey without food or sleep. By a miracle only two were lost, and they because they refused to obey my order to retire from a very difficult position in order to cover the retreat of the rest of us.

Gort and the French general Blanchard conferred in the visitors' room at the Vimy War Memorial, a site that commemorated the thousands who had died there in the First World War, and they coordinated their defense of the perimeter. But they had different aims. So far as Blanchard was concerned, the Dunkirk pocket was to be a redoubt from which forces would eventually mount new attacks. For Gort, it was to be a point of embarkation for the British troops, from where they could reach home. Churchill had told Reynaud that the plan was to get the British troops out, but this was not passed down to Blanchard.

The chance of many of the British troops getting away under fire did not seem good. Gort warned war minister Anthony Eden in a cable: "I must not conceal from you that a great part of the B.E.F. will inevitably be lost." Ironside thought they might get 30,000 men away at most. One of Gort's commanders, Major General Sir Alan Brooke, expressed the general view when he wrote in his diary: "Nothing but a miracle can save the B.E.F. now, and the end cannot be very far off."

In Britain the government declared that Sunday a national day of prayer, and the churches were unusually crowded. The BBC broadcast the morning service from Westminster Abbey, and the country heard the Archbishop of Canterbury, the primate of the Church of England, pray for "our soldiers in dire peril in France."

The war situation acquired a new urgency. The country was faced with the prospect of a Nazi-dominated continent and invasion. Measures were taken in a mood that sometimes bordered on panic.

The War Office told the cabinet that all Germans and Austrians in Britain were a threat. The vast majority were refugees from Nazism and they had already been required to register, and the few suspected Nazis had already been interned, but the government heeded the War Office warning. Some seventy-four thousand Germans and Austrians, most of them Jewish refugees, were rounded up in a peremptory manner and bundled off to makeshift camps, many on the Isle of Man off the northwest coast. Public anxiety about these aliens spread, tinged with anti-Semitism, and it was encouraged by some newspapers. Stories circulated that supposed refugees in Holland had turned out to be fifth columnists aiding the invaders (there had to be *some* explanation for the German success). The returning British ambassador said German parachutists had landed disguised as nuns, peasants, and policemen. Paratroops in nuns' habits became a stock joke for a while, but the stories were believed.

Many internees were sent to Canada and Australia. Some sailed for Canada on the liner *Arandora Star,* which carried German prisoners of war as well as the internees. It flew a German flag beside the British flag in an attempt to let enemy submarines know that it was carrying Germans, but it was torpedoed and sunk nonetheless, with the pointless loss of some six hundred lives. Later calmer heads prevailed, and most of the internees were returned to Britain and released.

In this crisis Britain became, on paper, a dictatorship. On May 24 Parliament passed, without much dissent, the Emergency Powers (Defense) Bill, which, with other wartime legislation, gave the government unlimited power over individuals. It said the government could pass regulations "requiring persons to place themselves, their services and their property at the disposal of His Majesty, as appears necessary for defense or maintaining public order." The Ministry of Labor was empowered to "direct any person to perform any service required." This meant that in the name of defense, the government could do anything with anybody and their property. It could commandeer buildings, direct shipping, tell farmers what to plant, and regulate prices, all of which it did. It could also imprison people without trial.

Under the British system of government, Parliament is sovereign. There is no written constitution guaranteeing the rights of citizens, no Supreme Court to restrain Parliament. The only thing that prevented dictatorship becoming tyranny in 1940 was the democratic tradition and the conventions of political life. This was sufficient. There were few instances of the emergency powers being exploited.

Another example of Parliamentary sovereignty was the postponement of the election. A British government remains in office for a maximum of five years. Within that period, it must resign and call a general election. The last election was in 1935 so one was due in 1940, but Parliament decided to postpone the next election until the end of the war. In theory the majority party in Parliament could vote to postpone an election and keep itself in power indefinitely. In practice Parliament would only postpone the election if all parties agreed, as they did.

One regulation made spreading rumors or defeatist talk a crime, and a few people were arrested under this. A charity collector was jailed for spreading rumors about air raids on the doorstep. A man was fined for saying Germany would win the war. The organizing secretary of the Women's Peace Campaign was jailed for a month for saying at Speaker's Corner in London's Hyde Park that people should lay down their arms. But voices were raised against these arrests, and some newspapers protested against the suppression of free speech; democratic instincts prevailed. There were few other arrests. The Communist Party still argued in its daily newspaper that this was the bosses' war. Pacifists spoke from public platforms.

Prominent members of the British Union of Fascists including its leader, Sir Oswald Mosley, and some Nazi sympathizers were arrested under the emergency regulations, and this met with general approval. Unexpectedly, this led police to a U.S. embassy official.

One of those arrested was a member of Parliament, Captain Albert Ramsay, long known to have pro-Nazi sympathies. Police were surprised to find in his home copies of confidential American embassy documents. Some of these were cables to President Roosevelt signed "Naval Person." It turned out that a code clerk at the embassy, Tyler Kent, had given the documents to another Nazi sympathizer who had shown them to Ramsay. Security police, accompanied by an American embassy official, went to Kent's apartment and found there 1,500 embassy documents, photographic plates, and keys to the embassy code room.

Ambassador Kennedy waived Kent's diplomatic status, and he was arrested and prosecuted under the Official Secrets Act of 1911. This meant that he could be tried in secret. His trial took place in October and he was sentenced to seven years' imprisonment. Kent had served previously in the U.S. embassy in Moscow. He said later that he thought Communism was a greater danger to America than Nazism. He had come to feel there that the administration was not telling the people the truth, and it was taking actions which could involve America in a war.

Had his diplomatic immunity not been waived, he would have been sent home and tried in America. The trial would be open, and the nature of the documents he copied might have been revealed. Cordell Hull said in a cable to Kennedy, "In the circumstances, publicity in connection with the charges would be undesirable." This was an understatement. If Roosevelt's isolationist opponents had discovered that he had been in secret correspondence with Churchill, the result would have been explosive.

The American ambassador to Belgium, John Cudahy, arrived in London and met a group of British and American journalists for an off-the-record talk at the U.S. embassy. He told them that the Germans were behaving well toward the civilian population in Belgium, in fact, he said, better than American soldiers would have behaved. This was received with mixed disbelief and anger. Some Americans felt this was a slur on American soldiers. One said he had been there and had seen German aircraft machine-gunning fleeing civilians. Ambassador Kennedy, as host, tried hinting to Cudahy that he should temper his remarks and then terminated the meeting. (Cudahy, who made a lot of money in real estate in Wisconsin before going into diplomacy, seems to have had a soft spot for Germans in uniform. His first diplomatic posting was to Warsaw, and he stopped off in Germany on his way there in December 1933. He wrote to Roosevelt that Germany was characterized by "national solidarity and patriotic buoyancy," and said the Brownshirts were "a social organization comparable to the Elks.")

The Allies were still anxious to dissuade Italy from entering the war. Churchill sent a warm message to Mussolini talking about the friendship between their two countries and asking him to stay out. France was keeping ten divisions on its border with Italy and wanted to release these to fight the Germans. Reynaud suggested that they approach Mussolini yet again through Roosevelt. Ambassador Bullitt supported this and cabled Roosevelt on May 29: "Al Capone will enter the war about fourth of June unless you can throw the fear of the USA into him." He suggested that the Pope might be persuaded to threaten Mussolini with excommunication.

President Roosevelt took up a suggestion of Reynaud's. He sent Mussolini a note on May 26 saying he would pass on to France and Britain any territorial claims he wanted to make, and that Mussolini would be welcomed at the conference at the end of the war, where these claims would be considered sympathetically. This meant that Italy could be in on the peace settlement and might gain territory without going to war. It also implied that America would be a guarantor of a settlement.

The British ambassador in Rome, Sir Percy Lorraine, gave his opinion of this and other approaches: "Their success presupposes a degree of reasonableness and moderation on the part of Mussolini which in my opinion he does not possess." Mussolini did indeed reject these offers. He was evidently determined to go to war.

Churchill injected some harsh realism into the talk of bringing Germany down by economic pressure, pointing out to the cabinet on May 26 that if Germany controlled resources from Brest to Vladivostok, it did not seem likely that a blockade would win the war. But outside the cabinet he put on an optimistic face. He assured the dominions in a cable the next day: "If we can hold out for some time, there are a good many factors which may produce a state of affairs where the enemy cannot carry on the war, *e.g.*, effects of our blockade on Germany on economic position there, particularly as regards foodstuffs and oils, dissatisfaction and loss of morale in Germany."

■　■　■

Everyone who knew the situation believed that most of the British Expeditionary Force, which meant most of Britain's trained soldiers, would be lost. A compromise peace seemed a way to avoid defeat. The fighting then did not seem like the opening battle of a world war. Unconditional surrender had not been enunciated as a war aim, nor was there an acceptance of the moral absolutism that lay behind it. Although Nazi Germany was seen as an aggressor, which was why Britain and France went to war, it had not yet perpetrated the large-scale cruelties with which it will always be associated, the Holocaust and the barbarous treatment of the Polish and Soviet populations. A peace that would leave in power a dictatorship, one of several in Europe at the time, albeit a particularly brutal one, might be preferable to a probably hopeless struggle if it enabled Britain to keep its independence and its empire.

Since the war began, there had been those in Britain who were unhappy about it and sought an end by compromise. Some were prewar appeasers, temperamentally inclined to fear Communism more than Nazism. Halifax received letters from aristocratic friends urging him to seek peace with Hitler and establish a front against Communism. There was also a group of about twenty members of Parliament, led by Richard Stokes, a Labourite, who wanted peace. These had no sympathy whatever with Nazism but were pacifists of the 1930s who regarded war as the greatest evil and felt that differences could be resolved by compromise. The Communist Party, in obedience to the line from Moscow, was organizing "peace now" rallies.

There was in effect a peace party, although it was never organized into a bloc, and as the war situation became worse, their belief that the war should not continue gained strength. They hoped for a government headed by Lloyd George. He himself gave no encouragement to this idea, although some of Churchill's friends suspected that he did.

The peace party even had, or at least some people might have thought they had, the possibility of an alternative monarch if King George VI refused to head a country that sued for peace. This was the duke of Windsor, who had abdicated as King Edward VIII in 1936 in order to marry the American divorcée Wallis Simpson. The duke had always favored friendship with Nazi Germany. Soon after he abdicated and went to live in France he paid a visit to Hitler. On the outbreak of war he was made a major general attached to French army headquarters. When the Germans overran France he and his American duchess fled to neutral Portugal and then to Madrid.

There, he told U.S. embassy officials that America should help end the war before thousands more were killed to save the face of a few politicians. Reporting this to Washington, Ambassador William Weddell commented: "These observations have their value, if any, as doubtless reflecting the views of an element in England, possibly a growing one, who find in Windsor and his circle a group who are realists in world politics and who hope to come into their own in the event of peace."

The British ambassador to Spain, Sir Samuel Hoare, cabled Churchill saying that the duke "had always disapproved of the war and considered it even a greater mistake to go ahead with it." He advised strongly getting him out of Madrid. Churchill took his advice and made the duke governor of the Bahamas, a post safely removed from the theater of war. Even then, care was taken to insulate him from anything that could affect the course of the war or public opinion. Ships that went from Europe to the Bahamas called at New York first. The duke and duchess sailed on the American Export Line ship *Excalibur,* but the British government did not want to expose them to the questioning of American reporters, so it arranged for the ship to go directly to the Bahamas and paid the extra cost.

Churchill warned the duke about speaking out of turn in a cable that contained only the barest note of deference to a royal figure. "The freedom of conversation which is natural to anyone in an unofficial position, or even a major-general, is not possible in a direct representative of the Crown," he reminded him. "Many sharp and unfriendly ears will be pricked up to catch any suggestion that your Royal Highness takes a view about the war, or about the Germans, or about Hitlerism, which is different from that adopted by the British nation and Parliament. Many malicious tongues will carry tales in every direction. Even while you have been staying in Lisbon, conversations have been reported by telegraph through various channels which might have been used to your Royal Highness' disadvantage."

From London, Ambassador Kennedy cabled his assessment of Britain's situation.

> Only a miracle can save the B.E.F. from being wiped out or, as I said yesterday, surrender . . . There will be a row among certain elements in the cabinet here; Churchill, Attlee and others who will want to fight to the death; but there will be other members who realize that physical destruction of men and property in England will not be a proper offset to a loss of pride. In addition to that the English people, while they suspect a terrible situation, really do not realize how bad it is. When they do I don't know what group they will follow, the do or die or the group that wants a settlement.

The issue of a compromise peace arose when Lord Halifax, the foreign secretary, met with the Italian ambassador, Giuseppe Bastaniani, on Saturday, May 25, with Churchill's approval. They talked about British-Italian differences and some possible compromise.

This began as one more attempt to buy off Mussolini and keep him out of the war. Then Bastaniani, treading gingerly, suggested that a settlement of Italian claims might be a part of a general settlement of European questions, in other words, a peace conference. Halifax agreed; and he assured Bastaniani that the British government would always be willing to consider any proposal likely to lead to a peaceful Europe. It seems that he had this in mind from the start. To underline the point, he said it was difficult to visualize such wide discussions while the war was still going on. Bastaniani appeared to agree.

The next day, Sunday, May 26, was the National Day of Prayer, and the atmosphere was grave. Churchill and his wife went to Westminster Abbey along with the king and queen and other leading figures. Queen Wilhelmina of Holland, who had arrived in London a week earlier as a refugee, was there, and the small crowd outside gave her a sympathetic cheer. Twenty minutes later, as the voices of the choir rose up to the magnificent vaulted ceiling, Churchill slipped out, to attend a morning meeting of the War Cabinet, the first of three that day.

Halifax reported on his meeting with Bastaniani. They discussed the possibility that France might quit the war and the terms Germany might offer it. Then they broke off and Churchill and Halifax went to lunch with Reynaud, who was visiting London. Reynaud reinforced their anxieties by saying that the French army's position was near-hopeless. He wanted to offer territorial concessions to Mussolini to persuade him to stay out of the war. Churchill told him he thought this would be useless. Reynaud agreed now that the BEF should make for the coast, although there was no talk of evacuation.

Reynaud went back to Paris and told his cabinet, "The only one who understands is Halifax. He is clearly worried about the future and realizes that some European future must be decided. Churchill is always hectoring and Chamberlain undecided."

When the War Cabinet met again in the afternoon, they discussed Halifax's talk with Bastaniani and the possibility of a peace settlement. Halifax proposed approaching Mussolini again, this time to suggest that he mediate with Germany. He said Mussolini would not want Hitler dominating Europe and might persuade Hitler to take a more reasonable attitude. He said that "we had to face the fact that it was not so much a question of imposing complete defeat on Germany but of safeguarding the independence of the empire and if possible that of France." There was no dissent to this. Chamberlain agreed that Mussolini would not want Germany the dominant power, and this would be an incentive for him to try for a settlement.

Churchill thought Britain would not be offered decent peace terms. He said Britain could not be truly independent if Germany controlled the European continent. If France could not defend herself, "it would be better that she should get out of the war rather than that she should drag us into a settlement that involved intolerable terms." Of Halifax's proposal, he said, "We must take care not to be forced into a position in which we went to Signor Mussolini and asked him to go to Herr Hitler and ask him to treat us nicely."*

Halifax insisted that there was no harm in trying. He said it was not in Hitler's interest to make outrageous terms. Churchill said such an approach implied that if Britain was prepared to give Germany back her colonies and make certain concessions in the Mediterranean, it could get out of its difficulties, but no such terms were offered. He said the peace terms would certainly prevent Britain from completing its rearmament program. But Halifax argued, "If we could get terms which do not postulate the destruction of our independence, we should be foolish if we did not accept them." They met a third time in the evening, and Churchill said it was best not to decide anything until they saw how much of the British army could be brought out of France.

There was no question now of demanding that Germany give up its prewar conquests or that Hitler must go. Germany was winning the war and the discussion was about what terms Britain might be offered, not what terms it would offer Germany.

These discussions were secret, but in the inner circle there was gossip about the attitudes of the leading figures. John Colville, Churchill's private secretary, wrote in his diary: "The cabinet are feverishly considering our ability to carry on the war alone, and there are signs that Hali-

---

* At this stage of the war even the London *Times* observed the courtesies of "Herr" Hitler and "Signor" Mussolini. This quote is taken from the cabinet minutes. It does not mean that Churchill necessarily referred to the German and Italian leaders in these terms. As was said before (see the footnote to page 115), the cabinet minutes never quote directly, although it can sometimes be inferred that the words used were the words spoken.

fax is being defeatist. He says our aim can no longer be to crush Germany but rather to preserve our own integrity and independence."

A hint of what was happening even reached Washington. The two correspondents of the *Chicago Daily News* in London cabled their publisher, Frank Knox, saying that political news from London was being strictly censored and nothing reflecting on the will of the British people or certain politicians to continue the war was allowed to pass. Knox knew Roosevelt and passed this message on to him, commenting that the wording of the cable led him to believe that a group of British politicians was talking of a possible negotiated peace.

When the War Cabinet met the next day, Chamberlain said the government should tell the dominions that even if France were out of the war Britain would fight on. He then added significantly, "This statement would apply, of course, to the immediate situation arising out of the hypothetical collapse of France. It did not mean that at any time that terms were offered, they would not be considered on their merits."

They were told about Roosevelt's approach to Mussolini. They discussed Reynaud's suggestion of offering concessions to Mussolini. Sir Archibald Sinclair, the sec_____ _____ _____ bout this. "Being
in _____ _____ courage the Ger-
_____ Mussolini would
_____ hat the best help
_____ tain would fight

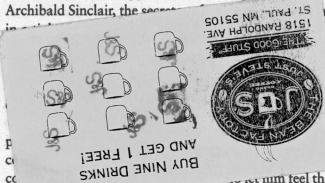

_____ abinet minutes
p_____ _____ nce would be-
c_____ _____ ie best help we
c_____ _____ _____ ___ ___ feel that, whatever hap-
pe_____ ____, we were going to fight it out to the end. Even if we were beaten, we would be no worse off than we should if we were to abandon the struggle. Let us therefore avoid being dragged down the slippery slope with France."

Now Halifax's disagreement with Churchill came to the fore. Halifax said that the previous day, when he had asked Churchill whether he would be willing to accept terms that left Britain independent even if it meant ceding some territory, Churchill said he would. (The minutes do not show him going that far.) Now he seemed to be saying that he would contemplate no course except fighting to the bitter end.

Churchill said there was no point in discussing an issue that was unlikely to arise. "If Herr Hitler was prepared to make peace on the terms of the restoration of the German colonies and the overlordship of central Europe, that was one thing. But it is unlikely that he would make such an offer." With these words, Churchill was implying that he would accept some part of Germany's prewar conquests in exchange for peace.

Halifax put the question to him. What if the French army collapsed and Hitler offered peace terms, and the French government insisted that any offer must be made to Britain and France together? And suppose Hitler then offered terms to the two allies. Would Churchill be prepared to discuss them? Churchill replied cautiously that he would not join France in asking for terms, but that if terms were offered he would be prepared to discuss them.

Chamberlain took up the Chiefs of Staff report of Britain's situation after "a certain eventuality," meaning the fall of France. He pointed out that it assumed American financial support if Britain was to fight on, but Britain might not get this in the immediate future. Churchill agreed. Regarding Roosevelt's anxieties about the fleet, Churchill said Roosevelt "seemed to be taking the view that it would be very nice of him to pick up bits of the British Empire if this country were overrun."

The minutes do not record every word spoken, nor do they always convey the flavor or the tone of what was said. Some indication of Churchill's tone, and perhaps of other talks out of cabinet, can be guessed at from an entry in Halifax's diary that day: "Churchill does drive me to despair when he works himself up into a passion of emotion when he ought to make his brain think and reason." He even suggested in his diary that he might resign, but Churchill took him into the garden and apologized for any harsh words and talked him out of any thought of resigning.

At the meeting the next day, Churchill said the position would be entirely different once Germany had made an unsuccessful attempt to invade Britain. Halifax said Britain might get better terms now, when France was still fighting and Britain's aircraft factories were intact, than in three months' time.

Churchill said Reynaud wanted to get Britain to the conference table with Hitler. "If we once got to the conference table, we should then find that the terms offered touched our independence and our integrity. When, at this point, we got up to leave the conference table, we should find that all the forces of resolution which were at our disposal would have vanished."

This was the "slippery slope" that he had warned of earlier. The Chiefs of Staff had cited morale as a crucial factor in the war. One can see what would happen to British morale if the government went to the conference table with Germany. The British people might be resolved to fight to the death for their country and its freedom. They would not be equally willing to fight for one set of armistice terms as against another. One cannot wage war with fine calculations of advantage and disadvantage.

Attlee took up this point. He pointed out that the public still did not know the real situation of the British army. When they learned how bad things were, it would be a severe shock, and negotiations would make it impossible to rally morale.

In prewar days, Chamberlain had been the architect of appeasement, but now he sided with Churchill and opposed an approach through Mussolini. He said that if Britain held out she should be able to get terms which would not affect her independence. This was not rejecting peace terms entirely, only saying that the time for asking for them was not ripe.

Churchill said: "A time might come when we felt that we had to put an end to the struggle, but the terms would not then be more mortal than those offered to us now . . . Those nations which went down fighting rose again, but those which surrendered tamely were finished."

Churchill had the War Cabinet with him, but only just. He did not have their unqualified support for his evident determination to fight on. He had been prime minister for less than three weeks, and his position was far from assured. However, he still had a card to play.

The meeting adjourned, and Churchill went into another room to address a meeting of the thirty ministers who were not members of the War Cabinet, and there he found new allies. These ministers knew nothing of the discussions in the inner War Cabinet, nor that the issue of peace terms had ever been raised. We have Churchill's own account of this meeting, but also a more objective one from the minister for economic warfare, Hugh Dalton, a Labourite and no friend of Churchill in past times. He writes in his memoirs:

"He [Churchill] was quite magnificent. The man, and the only man we have, for this hour. He gave a full, frank and completely calm account of events in France. Now it was necessary to fight our way to the channel ports and get away all we could. How many we would get away we could not tell. We should certainly be able to get 50,000 away. If we could get 100,000 away, that would be a wonderful performance. Only Dunkirk was left to us." Churchill then said that they could expect an attempt to invade Britain.

Dalton goes on:

> And then he said, "I have thought carefully in these last days whether it was part of my duty to consider entering into negotiations with That Man." But it was idle to think that if we tried to make peace now, we should get better terms than if we fought it out. The Germans would demand our fleet — that would be called "disarmament" — our naval bases, and much else. We should become a slave state, though a British Government which would be Hitler's puppet would be set up — "under Mosley or some such person." And where would we be at the end of all that? On the other hand, we had immense resources and advantages.

Finally, Churchill spoke what must be the most melodramatic words ever spoken in a British cabinet meeting: "I am convinced that every one of you would rise up and tear me down from my place if I were for one moment to contemplate parley or surrender. If this long island story of ours is to end at last, let it end only when each one of us lies choking in his own blood upon the ground." There were cries of approval all around the table and, Dalton says, not one flicker of dissent.

The War Cabinet reconvened immediately. Churchill went back strengthened. He told the other four that the members of the full cabinet had all expressed great satisfaction when he said there was no question of giving up the fight. As the minutes report, "He did not remember ever before having heard a gathering of persons occupying high places in political life express themselves so emphatically." Halifax said no more about peace terms.

Was Churchill ready to consider reasonable peace terms if they had been offered, as he implied to Halifax? Chamberlain wrote in his diary on May 26: "The PM dislikes any move towards Musso . . . though if we could get out of this jam by giving up Malta, Gibraltar and some African colonies he would jump at it."

The minutes do not report Churchill saying anything like this. It seems more likely that he either suggested this, out of the War Cabinet meeting, or allowed some people to believe it, as a tactical maneuver to placate Halifax and those who thought like him, confident that acceptable terms would not be offered. He was not a man to settle for a compromise peace with the enemy. If a British government ever had to ask for peace terms, it would not be one headed by Churchill.

It is easy with hindsight to hail Churchill's resolve and to condemn Halifax and the peacemakers for wanting to compromise with evil. But at this time there seemed no way that Nazi Germany could be beaten, certainly not by Britain alone. It is humane, and not dishonorable, to want to halt bloodshed when there seems no hope of victory.

Churchill had said, "Even if we were beaten we would be no worse off than we should be if we were to abandon the struggle." But it is likely that the terms Hitler imposed would be much harsher after Britain had fought on and lost than they would be if it sought a compromise peace now. Germany would not try to impose an occupation in any peace terms she offered while the fighting was still going on in France. And Britain would be worse off in one important way: many more British people would be killed; there would be more grieving parents and more orphans, as indeed there were. If Britain had continued the war and had been defeated in the summer of 1940, it would be said that the defeat was inevitable and that these dead were victims of Churchill's stubborn refusal to face reality.

Churchill did not use the same language in the War Cabinet that he used to other ministers but they knew his cast of mind. Halifax and those outside the cabinet who thought like him might well have felt that if someone has the responsibility for the welfare of a people, he has not discharged that responsibility properly if they end up choking in their own blood, even if the manner of their death wins the admiration of future historians. One has the right to choose martyrdom for oneself, but does one have the right to choose it for others?

It is clear from this that if Halifax and not Churchill had become prime minister, he would have wanted to seek accommodation with Germany, or at any rate considered peace terms if Hitler offered them. He would have had some support outside the cabinet. Some ministers would have followed him.

And what about the public? We have been left two means of gauging public feeling in Britain at this time. They are surveys that are deeper than opinion polls, with their yes-or-no responses to questions, although also less precise, qualitative as well as quantitative, relying on collections of anecdotes rather than statistics.

One is a regular survey of morale prepared for the Ministry of Information. These were secret at the time but have since been declassified. The other is the work of Mass Observation. This was an extraordinary project begun in 1937 by Tom Harrison, a British anthropologist, and Charles Madge, a journalist. They set out to record the day-to-day activities and feelings of British people as they would a native tribe they were investigating. It was a part of the trend, in America as well as Britain, to pay new attention to the kind of people whose voice is rarely heard, a trend seen also in the work of some documentary filmmakers and photographers. Harrison and Madge enlisted the help of several hundred people to take notes on what people said and did, at work, in buses, in pubs, and in their own homes. They produced reports on specific areas: attitudes to work and leisure in one town, for instance, or behavior in pubs. Throughout the war, MO collected thousands of pages of reports which give a view of British public opinion, which were not published at the time.

Both these sources indicate that a lot of people were confused and anxious, partly because they knew they were not getting the full picture from their newspapers. Thus, the Ministry of Information summary said on May 22: "Considerable depression." On May 24: "Optimism slightly down, anxiety slightly up. London lower morale than the provinces." May 28: "Public opinion stunned, bewildered, anxious, recriminatory." One report said that working-class men were the most optimistic, and added, "the whiter the collar, the less the assurance."

Mass Observation surveys bear out this picture and strengthen it. They note violent swings of mood. One report on May 18 says: "The old complacency has been shaken, but it persists. If suddenly shattered, there could be a morale explosion." One report even has some women saying that they would more or less welcome Hitler — "They say it couldn't be worse and they'd at least have their husbands back." This was certainly a minority view, but one survey on May 25, admittedly the most extreme, concludes: "The public mind is in a chaotic condition and ready to be plunged into the depths of an utterly bewildered, shocked, almost unbelieving dismay. The whole structure of our national belief would seem to be rocking gently."

Confusion and anxiety do not indicate defeatism. They indicate a malleable mood, a public no longer certain what to believe and ready to follow a strong lead if it was given to them, even if they were told that the country must accept defeat. As things turned out, they were given a lead, by Winston Churchill. The public had no idea until years later that a compromise peace was ever considered.

The issue of peace with Germany would arise again in the coming weeks, but this was the only time it was discussed at cabinet level. The decision was taken that the war would continue.

• • •

While this group of men were deciding the fate of Britain and much else besides in the cabinet room, others were also deciding it just a few dozen miles away, in the French port of Dunkirk and the seas around it. The cabinet decided that Britain would fight on. What happened at Dunkirk ensured that it would have an army to fight with. The epic of the evacuation of the army from Dunkirk has been told and retold, mythologized, and deconstructed. It is a part of the British national story.

Admiral Bertram Ramsay had been ordered earlier to prepare to evacuate troops from France, and he established his headquarters in rooms in a tunnel in Dover's white cliffs. For days, British troops in France, some of them lost from their units and disorganized, were making for Dunkirk, and it was now clear that this was to be the port of embarkation.

The BBC had broadcast an announcement on May 14 asking all owners of "self-propelled pleasure craft" between thirty and one hundred feet long to send particulars to the Admiralty, to add to their roster of ships. Using this register, Ramsay's men scoured harbors, boatyards, and yachting marinas. They commandeered rusty weather-worn fishing boats and luxury motor yachts, cross-channel ferries, paddle steamers, and launches that had never been away from the river. They also commandeered forty Dutch *schuyts,* flat-bottomed boats that had come over from Holland, useful because of their shallow draft. Owners were told only that the boats were needed for an urgent mission. The navy also asked some civilian crews to be ready to help.

The order to begin the evacuation was issued by the Admiralty to Admiral Ramsay on the evening of Sunday, May 26, the National Day of Prayer. It showed that the Admiralty was as doubtful as everyone else about getting off many of the 250,000 British troops. Ramsay was told that it was imperative that the operation was "implemented with the greatest vigor, with a view to lifting up to 45,000 men of the British Expeditionary Force within two days, at the end of which time it is probable that the evacuation will be terminated by enemy action."

Lieutenant Colonel John Austin, an artillery officer, described the scene in France: "Every road scouring the landscape was one thick mass of transport and troops, great long lines of them stretching far back to the Eastern horizon, and all the lines converging towards the one focus, Dunkirk. Ambulances, lorries, trucks, bren gun carriers, artillery columns, everything except tanks, all crawling along these roads in well-defined lines over the flat, featureless country."

A traffic jam built up around Dunkirk, and men were told to abandon their vehicles on the outskirts and destroy them so that the Germans could not use them. Most pushed them into the canal outside the town, and soon it was choked with trucks, armored personnel carriers, and even civilian cars, two and three deep.

The Germans attacked Dunkirk from the air, first with high explosives, then with thousands of incendiary bombs. Some two thousand civilians were killed as well as many soldiers, French, British, and Belgian. Royal Navy Captain William Tennant, sent to Dunkirk to organize things from that end, found some British soldiers left in a stunned, dazed state by the bombing, and others roaming the streets in marauding gangs.

The port facilities had been wrecked and were unusable, the locks that changed the water level smashed. Tennant told ships to go to the beaches outside the town to take off men. Ships took up positions and lowered boats to transfer men from the beaches, and small boats came in to ferry men out to the ships. The flat-bottomed Dutch *schuyts* were particularly useful here. Men converged on the sand dunes, stretching along nine miles of front including the vacation villages of Malo, Bray Dunes, and La Panne and in the villages themselves. The navy had put supplies of water in cans along the beach for the men.

German planes dive-bombed and machine-gunned men on the beaches, in boats, and in the water. Soft sand cushioned explosions on the beach so that they had less impact than they would have had on hard ground. Men waited at the water's edge for boats, or waded out and stood in line in their sodden uniforms. Most kept in order. Some fought others to get ahead. Some tried to clamber into boats, threatening to capsize them, and officers had to restore order at gunpoint. Others waited on the beach. Many men wandered about trying to find their regiments. A few units, mostly Territorials, were demoralized, some because of the fighting they had gone through, others because they had retreated for two weeks under attack from the air and had never fired a shot. The older regiments were disciplined and held together. One man recalls a company of the Guards marching down the pier to await evacuation "as if they were on a parade ground." Meanwhile a rear guard, British and French, still fought the Germans on the shrinking perimeter.

French troops also were pouring on to the beach. Marc Bloch, a French army captain, said of his regiment, "The one thought in everybody's mind was to get clear of this damned stretch of coast . . . A sort of escape-hysteria had got hold of this mob of men. They were to all intents and purposes disarmed."

British troops created some organization on the beaches. Quarrels broke out between British and French officers. Some of the French did not like being told where they could and could not go in their own country, particularly by people who, so far as they could see, were abandoning the fight and running for home. The French naval officer in charge at Dunkirk, Admiral Jean Abrial, did not even know that the evacuation was going on for the first two days although French naval officers in Dover were working in cooperation with Ramsay, partly because he spent most of his time in his underground bunker. The British were putting the safety of their troops ahead of Allied cooperation. Churchill told Gort not to delay the movement of British troops to conform with French plans.

Sergeant John Bridges was with a group of men who rowed a lifeboat out to a destroyer. They had no experience of boats and they allowed it to drift too close to the destroyer's propeller and it capsized. He swam over to a motor launch. The naval officer in charge of it called out, with what seemed like astonishing politeness, "Can you swim? If you can I'd rather you let someone else come aboard because we haven't got much room here." Bridges swam to the shore.

Taking men off the beaches in small boats was slow and it was clear that only a small number would get away in this way. After a day of this, Tennant decided to try taking men from the breakwater in the harbor that extended nearly a mile into the sea. It was about eight feet wide and had never been intended as a pier but Tennant thought ships might be able to tie up there. This was what made most of the evacuation possible; the mole was the embarkation point for most of the men who got away from Dunkirk. Men were ordered from the beaches on to the makeshift pier as ships arrived. At high tide the ship's deck was usually somewhere near level with the breakwater, and they clambered across makeshift gangplanks. At low tide they climbed down ladders onto the decks. More than any other single factor, the success of the evacuation was made possible by the men of the Royal Navy, their courage, endurance, and brilliant improvisation.

Captain Blew-Jones, who reached Dunkirk with his men after a fighting retreat, wrote in a letter: "It is very difficult to write on paper all that happened, but the most vivid thing was at the very end. We reached the mole at Dunkirk — dead beat, filthy and only half-conscious. Six ambulances were standing there and they called for volunteers for stretcher bearing to the hospital ship right at the end of the mole. Without a word each man took his place and the journey was accomplished twice amidst a shower of bombs and shells."

Because of attacks from the air, the Navy decided that civilian passenger ships, having no antiaircraft guns, would go into Dunkirk only at nighttime. German submarines and motor torpedo boats operating out of newly captured Dutch ports moved up to attack the rescue ships, and mines were an added hazard. German artillery moved closer and began shelling the harbor. Soon ships entering the harbor had to maneuver around wrecked and burning ships.

More and more civilian boats joined the armada, usually with navy crews, but civilians also were taking part. Thames fire ships from the London Fire Brigade that had never been in the open sea sailed down the river to take part. The navy commandeered the *Bee,* a seventy-ton coastal transport boat. The engineer, Fred Reynard, a chirpy little man, said to an admiral, "Beg pardon sir, but what do your young gentlemen know about Swedish engines? I've been handling this one since 1912." The officer told him about Dunkirk and said, "Ever been under shellfire?" "Ever heard of Gallipoli?" Reynard shot back. He and his crew took the *Bee* to Dunkirk with a navy sub-lieutenant nominally in command.

Then the Navy said civilians could take their own boats over. Civilians who took part were asked to sign a form putting them under navy discipline, and if they were lucky they were given a steel helmet. In British harbors the navy was handing around charts where they had them, provisioning boats with a minimum of red tape, updating information on minefields, taking over boats. Men worked day and night to repair damaged boats. It was a blessing that throughout this time the sea was calm and the weather clear, although the hot sun on the beaches was intensifying men's discomfort and thirst.

C. H. Lightoller, who had been an officer on the *Titanic,* took over his fifty-nine-foot motor launch with his teenage son and a sea scout. It had never carried more than twenty people before but it brought back 130 soldiers crammed in below decks, exhausted and vomiting in the suffocating heat, the more so because Lightoller at the helm was zigzagging to avoid bombs.

Raphael de Sola, a London stockbroker, went across wearing the blazer of the Royal London Yacht Club, with his yacht towed behind a fishing vessel. He and his crew were told to take the yacht's lifeboat to a spot on the beach where soldiers were signaling with a lamp. When they got there they found that the lamp was on an abandoned truck and no soldiers were about. They came under attack from the air, and only hours after leaving his London home, de Sola was sheltering under his upturned lifeboat from machine gun fire.

At night on the beach at La Panne, an army officer called out to a boat, "I cannot see who you are. Are you a naval party?"

"No sir," came the reply. "We are members of the crew of the Ramsgate lifeboat."

"Thank you," the officer called back. "And thank God for such men as this night you have proved yourself to be."

The smallest boat known to have made the journey to Dunkirk is the *Tamzin,* a seventeen-foot fishing smack. It is now in the Imperial War Museum in London.

The shortest route from British harbors took ships through French minefields and within range of the biggest German guns, so ships were directed out into the North Sea to come in at an angle, a journey of eighty-five miles. The crossing was hazardous and often horrific. The destroyer *Wakeful* was torpedoed and sank within seconds, drowning all the estimated 700 soldiers crammed below her decks. Another destroyer, the *Grafton,* was torpedoed while searching for survivors. As she went down her gunners fired on what they took to be a German motor torpedo boat but was actually a British drifter that was also looking for survivors. She was taken in tow but sank on the way back. On the *Mona Queen*, which was built to take passengers across the twenty miles between the English coast and the Isle of Man, twenty-three men were killed and sixty wounded when German planes machine-gunned the crowded decks.

Dunkirk was an inferno. Crews setting out from England saw black smoke rising above the fires from thirty miles away. It is not surprising that some men, perhaps thinking of wives and children, refused to go, or having set out turned back. It is noteworthy that many men who had not expected to go to war and were not trained or prepared for it did go into that raging battle, and in some cases went back again, to bring back soldiers.

In the Admiralty files in the Public Records Office in London, there is a folder containing reports written immediately after the Dunkirk evacuation by men who were there, naval and civilians. Some are typed in formal style, some handwritten, the writing faded now and difficult to read; some of them are accompanied by pencil-drawn sketches or crude maps. The parts that can be picked out say much about conditions at Dunkirk and the mentality of the men who went there.

From navy lieutenant J. A. Simmons, in command of a trawler that had been commandeered: "The embarkation was carried out smoothly and swiftly and the naval officers and ratings who were on the quay and actually assisted in making fast the ship, letting go ropes and putting ladders ashore etc. were among the best chaps I ever wish to meet. Hungry, tired and constantly under fire, they had a cheery confidence and the ratings an endless flow of repartee which I shall never forget."

Others: "There was a rumor around the harbor just before lunchtime on Sunday that volunteers were wanted to fetch the last of the Dunkirk troops off the jetty. This cleared all the pubs around the harbor in about two minutes and a seething crowd gathered around the Naval office." "The *Bonnie Heather* behaved like a perfect lady in spite of the treatment she received, and never let us down." "I went across on my yacht with two naval ratings but they had never been to sea before. We followed a destroyer in." "The crossing was like the main street in a busy town, traffic several abreast going each way."

"I should like to mention Harry Brown who did a brave action. We just loaded boat with troops. We saw a pontoon with soldiers being swamped with waves. Brown being the swimmer decided to go over the side with a rope, he tied it to the pontoon and saved the soldiers from being drowned."

The captain of the *Shamrock,* which for years had taken vacationers around a seaside harbor at Folkestone, wrote: "We had our load but then I realized it would be selfish to clear off when several destroyers were waiting in deep water to be fed by small craft, so I decided what our job was to be. We could seat sixty men, and with those standing we had about 80 weary and starving British troops, some without boots, some only in their underpants, but with enough life left in them to clamber on board the destroyers with the kind hand of every available seaman." Eventually, the *Shamrock* foundered. He concluded: "This was the last straw, having to leave my boat, which constituted my life savings."

For most of this time the public had no idea that the troops were being evacuated. George Kimber, a civil servant, asked for an extra day off at the weekend. He came back with a suntan and his boss, Geoffrey Shakespeare, the Dominions undersecretary, asked whether he had been sunbathing in Hyde Park. "No sir," Kimber said. "I've been with my small sailing boat to rescue survivors from the beaches near Dunkirk."

The RAF provided air support. Bombers attacked German troops and transport around Dunkirk. Fighter patrols were sent over the beaches from airfields in England, not only Hurricanes but also the newer, faster Spitfires. The Fighter Command chief, Hugh Dowding, always reluctant to use his fighter planes for any purpose other than defending the home island, now allowed these to go into battle for the first time.

The fighters, flying out of England, carried only enough fuel to operate for a limited time over the beaches. Forced to choose between having a small number over Dunkirk all the time and larger numbers for less of the time, the RAF chiefs opted for the latter, so that they would not always be outnumbered when they met the Luftwaffe. This meant that much of the time the troops on the ground were exposed to German air attacks without seeing any opposition, and even when air battles took place they were mostly out of sight. Many came back complaining bitterly that the RAF was nowhere to be seen.

The RAF lost 99 fighters over Dunkirk, 42 of them Spitfires, as well as bombers, but they shot down 132 German planes. As was to happen later on, RAF pilots exaggerated their success, usually unwittingly, and the official account said they had shot down more than 300 German planes. Churchill told the cabinet that this first real trial of strength between the British and German air forces was "a signal victory, which gives cause for high hopes of our success in the future."

. . .

Churchill went over to Paris along with Attlee and some military chiefs on June 1. He was elated to learn that by now 165,000 men had been taken off, and he woke up his private secretary in the night to tell him. Reynaud pointed out that only 15,000 of the men evacuated were French. Churchill assured him that from now on they would be embarked in equal numbers, and he sent instructions to this effect to Gort. He then said, with tears in his eyes according to Reynaud's account, that he did not want to see any more French troops sacrificing themselves, and British divisions would make up the rear guard (which is not what happened). However, from that point on most of the troops brought off were French.

Now the British public were told that the BEF was being evacuated and the exhausted soldiers were arriving back, bringing the war and its disasters home. People greeted them with placards saying "Well done, B.E.F." and "Thumbs Up." Members of the Women's Voluntary Service, formed two years earlier to help the civil defense, worked all night to provide sandwiches and tea at the railroad stations.

Captain Bloch, who came with the French troops, recalled their arrival:

> We landed at Dover. Then came a whole day traveling by train across Southern England. The journey has left in my mind the memory of a sort of drugged exhaustion broken by chaotic sensations and images which like the episodes of a dream, rose to the surface of my consciousness only to sink again almost immediately: the pleasure of devouring ham and cheese sandwiches handed through the windows by girls in multi-colored dresses and clergymen who looked as solemn as if they were delivering the Sacrament; the faint sweet smell of cigarettes showered on us with the same generous profusion; the acid taste of lemonade and the

flat taste of tea with too much milk in it; the cozy green of lawns; a landscape made of parks, cathedral spires, hedges and Devon cliffs; groups of cheering children at level crossings. But what struck us more than anything else was the warmth of our reception.*

The evacuation was terminated in the early hours of June 4. The official tally shows 338,226 Allied troops brought out, 228,500 British and the rest nearly all French. An estimated 2,000 were killed during the crossing. Most of the French troops evacuated were sent back to France to continue the fight, and it was expected that they would be joined by British troops.

The record says 861 ships, naval and civilian, took part in the evacuation, 693 British and the remainder French and Belgian, but so ad hoc were the arrangements that the official account admits that the participation of some other small craft went unrecorded. More than a quarter of these, 243 ships, were sunk, all but 17 of them British, including 6 destroyers. Nineteen destroyers were damaged. The army left behind almost all its heavy equipment.

No reporters were at Dunkirk, but reporters in England saw the men coming back. E. A. Montague wrote in the *Manchester Guardian:* "One watched them with a pride that became almost pain as one cheerful, patient figure succeeded another . . . Their eyes were red with weariness above dark bags of tired skin, but they were still soldiers and still in good heart." Hilde Marchant wrote in the *Daily Express:* "It is the greatest sight I have ever seen . . . The men came ashore in heaps, barely able to stand. Yet they pulled themselves in straight lines and walked to the harbor gates."

The men were coming from a raging battlefield to a country just across the channel that barely knew it was at war. A lieutenant in an antiaircraft unit, Alun Lewis, wrote in his diary about a group he saw: "The boys just back from Dunkirk, bearded and dirty and slightly wounded and tired to death. I shall never forget how quiet their voices were, amenable as children, waiting for an hour and more until the

---

* Marc Bloch was in civilian life a distinguished historian whose books on medieval Europe are read today. He returned to France and was demobilized and joined a resistance group in Lyons. Shortly after finishing his personal account of the battle of France he was arrested by the Gestapo, and was executed by a firing squad in June 1944.

bacon was cut and fried, or talking about it all as they lay in the sun outside the pub. 'It's marvellous seeing the houses all standing and the milkman coming down the lane there,' one of them said."

Not all the men were in good heart. Many men arrived back demoralized and with shattered nerves. Some threw their rifles out of train windows. A psychiatrist in a London hospital reported: "Men swarmed into the hospital, some raging mutinously at their officers for having deserted them, and others swearing that they would never fight again. So complete a loss of morale was scaring to witness." This was not reported. The British people did not need more bad news.

Others reached this conclusion. The theater director Basil Dean, on a mission with a colleague for army entertainment, found a pub in a seaside town crowded with soldiers seething with anger at their officers who, they charged, had abandoned them and boarded boats to England. His reaction and that of his colleague was patriotic self-censorship. "We promised each other that while the war lasted we would never speak of what we had seen and heard that night, and we never did," Dean wrote later.

With Dunkirk, the war became a people's war. The whole nation was praying for the men on the beaches. The inhabitants of seaside towns watched the boats going and coming back. The trains carrying the returning troops crisscrossed the country. Crowds at railroad stations welcomed the troops. Soldiers wrote notes on scraps of paper addressed to wives or parents with an address and a brief message, something like "Back home safe," and threw them out at stations, and people delivered them.

Everyone felt a part of what was happening. Harold Nicolson, who a few days earlier had urged his wife to prepare a suicide pill in case of defeat, wrote to her: "My darling, how infectious courage is. I am rendered far stronger in heart and confidence by such bravery."

In a more humble stratum of society, the Barrow housewife Nella Last wrote in her diary: "I forgot that I was a middle-aged woman who woke up tired and often had back-ache. The story made me feel part of something that was undying and never old — like a flame to light or warm, but strong enough to burn and destroy trash and rubbish. It was a very hot morning and work was slowed a little, but somehow I felt everything to be worthwhile, and I felt glad I was of the same race as the rescuers and the rescued."

It was not only British people who were inspired. The *New York Times* said in an editorial on June 4: "So long as the English language survives, the word Dunkirk will be spoken of with reverence. For in that harbor, in such a hell as never blazed on earth before, at the end of a lost battle, the rages and blemishes that have hidden the soul of democracy fell away. There, beaten but unconquered, in shining splendor, she faced the enemy."

The country was mobilized psychologically now. John Colville, Churchill's private secretary, wrote in his diary: "The war has now for the first time become the question of paramount importance to the average Englishman." There was much truth in a cartoon by David Low in the *Daily Express* at this time that showed Göring telling Hitler, "We've gone too far, Adolf. Der British have declared war."

The role of the little ships seized the popular imagination. These ships were familiar to many people. A holiday in those days normally meant a holiday by the seaside, and this usually included a trip in a little steamer or motor launch that gave its passengers a brief taste of the briny. A popular music hall song went: *"Any more for the Skylark, for a quick trip round the bay. / Any more for the Skylark, if you don't come back don't pay."*

The popular novelist and playwright J. B. Priestley had no illusions about the glory of war. He had served in the trenches in the First World War, and he wrote bitterly about the men who sent his generation into that carnage. But he used the word "glory" in a moving broadcast about the Dunkirk evacuation in the days following the event that became famous.

He talked about these ships: "We've known them and laughed at them, these fussy little steamers, all our lives. We have watched them load and unload their crowds of holiday passengers — the gents full of high spirits and bottled beer, the ladies eating pork pies, the children sticky with peppermint rock."

He eulogized the paddle steamer *Gracie Fields*, which used to ferry him across the few miles from the mainland to his home on the Isle of Wight, sunk at Dunkirk:

> Never again will we board her at Cowes and go down into her dining room for a fine breakfast of bacon and eggs. She has paddled and churned away forever. But now, look, this little steamer,

like all her brave and battered sisters, is immortal. She'll go sailing proudly down the years in the epic of Dunkirk. And our great grandchildren, when they learn how we began this war by snatching glory out of defeat, and then swept on to victory, may also learn how the little holiday steamers made an excursion to hell and came back glorious.

These were stirring words. The Dunkirk evacuation was certainly an epic and there was plenty of heroism there. But war is usually glorious or dramatic only when seen from a distance, not for those at the center of violent action. For the onlooker, whatever glory or drama he perceives in it provides a cost-free thrill. To balance J. B. Priestley's picture, one should, for the sake of honesty, look at the center also.

Priestley did not say what happened to the *Gracie Fields* beyond the fact that she was sunk. She was hit by a bomb which burst her boiler, and men on the decks were scalded by steam. Some were scalded to death, others were taken off by another ship with hideous wounds. The ship was taken in tow, but sank on the way back. It is likely that men who were on the *Gracie Fields,* or who saw what happened to those who were, would have recoiled from the use of the word "glorious," perhaps with revulsion. So would many others who experienced the Dunkirk evacuation.

But no one view of war can encompass it, and no one view can prevail to the exclusion of all others. Priestley was passionately sincere, but he was also a patriot and a democrat who believed that democracy had to be defended, and he knew that the British people at this dark moment needed something to cling to, something to be proud of. To celebrate the heroism without spelling out the price is a half-truth, the kind of half-truth that people must tell themselves when they have to go to war.

A statement by the Ministry of Information said the returning men were "undefeated, in good spirits, wanting only to have another crack at Jerry." This was comic book stuff. It is usually civilians who want to have another crack at the enemy.

Churchill reported to Parliament in more somber tones. He hailed the achievement, but he warned: "We must be very careful not to assign to this deliverance the attributes of a victory. Wars are not won by evacuations." He pointed out that the British Isles were now threatened with invasion. He ended with famously eloquent words of defiance:

Even though large tracts of Europe and many old and famous states have fallen and may fall into the grip of the Gestapo and all the odious apparatus of Nazi rule, we shall not flag or fail. We shall go on to the end. We shall fight in France, we shall fight in the seas and oceans, we shall fight with growing confidence and growing strength in the air; we shall defend our island whatever the cost may be.

We shall fight on the beaches, we shall fight on the landing grounds, we shall fight in the hills; we shall never surrender; and even if, which I do not for one moment believe, this island or a large part of it were subjected and starving, then our empire beyond the seas, armed and guarded by the British fleet, would carry on the struggle, until, in God's good time, the New World, with all its power and might, steps forward to the rescue and the liberation of the Old.

This was Churchillian oratory at its most powerful, the manner stirring, the message urgent. It energized people in Britain in a way that seems to have been almost palpable. An official British history said: "So profound were the effects of Mr. Churchill's words that their delivery can be reckoned a major step towards the better defense of the United Kingdom."

The speech went around the world. *Time* magazine carried the text in full, over two pages. The passage about fighting on the beaches and in the hills was quoted more widely and more often than the last words, about the New World coming to the rescue. But to more and more Americans, the idea was coming to seem less strange.

6

THE GREAT DEBATE

In the first week of June 1940, the secretary of Harvard University, Jerome Green, wrote to an old friend in England, Lionel Curtis, a professor at Balliol College, Oxford University. He said:

> The attitude of the college and university students of this country is, in my opinion, one of the most extraordinary social phenomena that has ever occurred. The genesis is not unlike that of the movement in England a few years ago when quantities of students bound themselves to a pledge not to fight for King and country. I dare say most of those young men have thought better of that pledge during the past years . . . A curious antagonism has developed between the attitude of our students and most of their elders, and their apparent blindness to the social issues involved is very distressing. What makes it difficult to change their attitude is that however mistaken they may be, they are also taking a stand over what seems to them to be a moral issue.

May and June are the end of the college year and exam time, and for some it means the celebrations of commencement and the end of college days. But in 1940 other concerns were pressing on students. They heard the distant sounds of war and saw a possible future for themselves as soldiers, willing or unwilling. The student-faculty split that Green observed, with students opposed to any involvement in the Allied war effort, was seen on many campuses.

Presidents James Conant of Harvard and Charles Seymour of Yale both came out in favor of aid to the Allies whatever the consequences. The *Harvard Crimson,* the student magazine, criticized them for speaking out "so early and so soon the words that may send to destruction the lives in their charge." Three hundred Harvard students signed a petition telling President Roosevelt that "never under any circumstances will we follow in the footsteps of the students of 1917."

In the last two weeks of May, fifty-five members of the Northwestern University faculty sent a letter to the White House urging all-out aid to the Allies. Yale undergraduates sent a petition with 1,486 signatures saying America should "grant no credits, give no supplies and send no men" to either side, and should refrain from war "even if England is on the verge of defeat." The petition was drawn up by the editors of the *Yale Review,* the student newspaper, F. Stuart Hughes and Kingman Brewster. Brewster later became president of Yale and ambassador to Britain. Others who signed the petition and later played a part in American public life include Gerald Ford, R. Sargent Shriver, Chester Bowles, and Philip C. Jessup.

Princeton undergraduates were already in the field with the satirical Veterans of Future Wars. These demanded an immediate bonus of $1,000 for all men between eighteen and thirty-six, since they would be unlikely to survive a war and should be able to spend it, and asked the president to name an unknown soldier. They staged a parade in New York accompanied by a coed auxilliary, the Future Gold Star Mothers, who demanded free trips to Europe to see their future husbands' and sons' graves.

At the University of Kansas, the *Daily Kansan* pointed out in an editorial that the lives of students, not faculty members, would be at risk if war came. The *Oberlin Review* complained about a French faculty member who it said had brought his interventionist views into the classroom. Students from the City College of New York walked out of school to parade with banners reading "Better Stop a Class Than Stop a Bullet" and "Let God Save the King. The Yanks Aren't Coming."

Fortune conducted a poll in June on whether the United States should avoid war at all costs. The magazine reported that 40 percent of those polled answered "yes," but 60 percent of college students did so. The same generational breakdown was seen off campus as well. The American Institute of Public Opinion reported that more under-thirties were isolationist than their elders. It also found that those in the upper income groups were more likely to be isolationist than others.

When a writer in the *Atlantic Monthly* accused student anti-interventionists of lacking ideals, two prominent ones, Kingman Brewster of Yale and Spencer Klaw of Harvard, responded in the following issue rejecting the idea that intervention was a moral imperative and saying: "We can by no means accept that the defense of England is the automatic measure of our loyalty to American ideals."

Leaders of the American Youth Congress, which was active in the antiwar demonstrations, were summoned before the House of Representatives' Committee on Un-American Activities to be quizzed about alleged Communist leanings. Eleanor Roosevelt had encouraged the formation of the congress and she gave them moral support by sitting in the committee room. Afterward she invited them to dinner at the White House, where the president questioned them over the dinner table. Since they had opposed not only aid to the Allies but also aid to Finland to help it fight the Soviet invasion, she asked them whether they were Communists, as the House committee had suggested. They told her they were not. Some of them were lying. Evidently, young people who could justify the invasion of Finland and the bombing of Helsinki as means to a morally right end would have no qualms about lying to a president's wife who had befriended them.

There were exceptions to the pattern. At Williams, the small, ivied Massachusetts college, argument over the war swept the campus, much of it swirling around the head of political science professor Robert Schuman. The author of a book on Nazi Germany who took a strong interventionist stand, he was accused in an article in the student newspaper, the *Williams Record*, of imposing his views on students, and was defended by colleagues. Later, the *Record* reversed its stand. It published as a front-page article a letter written by a group of Williams undergraduates to President John Adams in 1798, pledging their support in any struggle against the dictator Napoleon, and this was reprinted as an editorial in the *New York Herald Tribune*.

Archibald MacLeish, the poet and writer who would soon be appointed librarian of Congress, had some apt words about the antiwar sentiments of students and those who thought like them, in a speech to a conference of educators that was widely reprinted. MacLeish came of age as a writer in the period of disillusion that followed the First World

War, in which his brother was killed, and he wrote bitterly of the futility of war and the lies that had sent young men to fight. He saw behind the antiwar sentiments of students the influence of the writers of his generation who wrote with disillusionment and cynicism about the war, a group that included Hemingway and Dos Passos and, as he admitted, himself. He said of their writing:

> However noble it may have been as literature, however true as a summary of experience, it was disastrous for a generation that would have to face the danger of fascism in its adult years. The inevitable and natural effect of [their] words upon the generation that read them in childhood was bound to be what we now witness. That generation was inoculated against any attempt in its own country by its own leaders to foment a war by shouting rhetorical slogans or waving moral flags. But it was left defenseless against an aggressor ready to force war upon us. Above all, it was left defenseless against an aggressor whose cynicism, whose brutality and whose stated intention to enslave presented the issue of the future in moral terms — in terms of conviction and belief.

. . .

Arthur M. Schlesinger Jr., who was a junior fellow at Harvard at the time, wrote in his autobiography: "There have been a number of fierce national quarrels in my lifetime — over Communism in the late Forties, over McCarthyism in the Fifties, over Vietnam in the Sixties — but none so tore apart families and friendships as the great debate of 1940–41."

The passions unleashed were not surprising. An argument over whether millions of young Americans should go to war is not just another argument over politics. If one believed, as many did, that powerful figures were whipping up war fever and manufacturing dangers in order to drag the country down the war path and send its young men away to foreign battlefields, this was something deserving of strong feelings.

Among the families it tore apart was the Morrows. Anne Morrow Lindbergh, like her husband, was anti-interventionist. She went beyond that. In her book *The Wave of the Future* she showed that, like some others, she had just about given up on democracy in favor of Nazi and even Communist dictatorships. "They have felt the wave of the future and they have leaped on it," she wrote. "The evils that we deplore in their systems are not in themselves the future. They are the scum on the wave of the future." *The Wave of the Future* was reviewed widely and published in condensed form in the *Reader's Digest*. Anne Morrow's mother, Celia Dwight Morrow, at that time acting president of Smith College, was a very public advocate of more aid for the Allies.

A new pressure group for aid to the Allies sprang up, created by William Allen White. He was the editor of the *Emporia Gazette* of Emporia, Kansas, and his writing, of books, articles, and a syndicated column, had made him a national figure. His base was always Emporia, population 15,000, and he was often said to represent the decency and commonsense wisdom of small-town America. He was a Republican with a political background going back to Theodore Roosevelt's Progressive movement, but he was also a friend of Franklin D. Roosevelt and supporter of many of his New Deal policies.

White and Clark Eichelberger, the director of the League of Nations Association, had set up a committee to call for more aid to the Allies. They discussed it with a few like-minded people in both political parties who agreed to press the case in their own parties. They called their group the Committee to Defend America by Aiding the Allies, and William Allen White was chairman. It soon came to be called simply the White Committee.

It organized newspaper articles and paid advertisements and broadcasts by prominent people pushing its view. White wrote to a friend: "Our idea is to fill the radio and the newspapers and the Congressional mail with the voices of prominent citizens urging America to become the non-belligerent ally of France and England. I am afraid it is too late, and I stand aghast at what will happen if the English either scuttle their ships or turn them over to Germany." The committee had three hundred chapters across the country by the end of July, six hundred by September.

It was pressing the administration for more aid to the Allies, but its real aim was not to influence Roosevelt but to influence the public and Congress on behalf of Roosevelt's policies. In relation to the administration, it acted as a kind of partisan band alongside the regular uniformed army, fighting for the same cause but out of uniform. White said of Roosevelt: "I knew I had his private support. I never did anything he didn't ask for, and I always conferred with him on our program."

In Chicago, the argument over the war became known as "the battle of the colonels." Colonel McCormick's *Chicago Tribune* argued the isolationist line, and Colonel Knox's *Chicago Daily News* argued for all-out aid for the Allies. The editorializing was not always limited to the editorial columns. A *Tribune* photographer was sent to a rally organized by the White Committee in Stagg Park (Adlai Stevenson was chairman of the local chapter) and told to photograph rows of empty seats to show the lack of support. He reported that he could not find any rows of empty seats.

Even the *Ladies' Home Journal* weighed in, taking the anti-isolationist side. It quoted one of Hitler's more savage utterances under the headline "Memo to Pacifists," and ran a long account of the fall of France, which it said was the story of: "France — a nation that made the fatal mistake of preparing for war by saying 'We love peace.'"

The Communists' new line, post–Nazi-Soviet pact, that the war was just an imperialist war and America should stay out of it, added a new twist. The Communist Party had attracted a number of prominent intellectuals in the 1930s when capitalism seemed to be failing so catastrophically, but many now quit. The party's attitude to the war and to Finland lost it just about all its allies on the Left. For many left-wingers the split was painful and was done in sorrow as much as anger. They had always believed that they were on the same side as the Communists fundamentally with the same enemies.

Some anti-Stalinist left-wingers, while conceding that Nazism was worse than capitalist democracy, were against intervention. A group of writers for the *Partisan Review,* the literary/intellectual monthly, including Dwight Macdonald, published an open letter to the magazine declaring: "Our entry into the war under the slogan 'Stop Hitler!' would actually result in the immediate introduction of totalitarianism over here."

Even many American liberals who hated fascism were not sure whether this war was worthy of their partisanship. Rallying to the defense of the Spanish Republic was one thing; defending Britain, an imperialist, class-ridden monarchy that had failed to stand up to fascism until the last moment, was another. One writer in the *New Republic* justified his call for support for Britain by concluding: "Britain at its worst is better than Nazi Germany at its best," which could be seen as an apotheosis of faint praise. Liberals also felt all the old qualms at spending money on armaments while there were hungry people in America. The magazines of the liberal intelligentsia, the *New Republic,* the *Nation,* and the *Partisan Review,* reflected these arguments.

When Ralph Ingersoll, the editor of the new New York liberal tabloid *PM,* went to Britain, he said he was going to find out "whether the war is on the up and up." By this he meant "whether it was an honest war against what was evil, or a dishonest war whose British makers would be quite willing to settle for the right to co-exist with fascism or make a fascist state themselves and live as simply another gangster in a world governed by gangsterism." In other words, whether it was a war for democracy or just one more fight for power between two European governments, unworthy of American concern. A lot of Americans wanted to know whether the war was on the up-and-up.

Others were against involvement because they saw among its supporters the same imperialist impulse that carried America across the Pacific to annex Hawaii and conquer the Philippines forty years earlier. In small towns and in some big cities people worried about what the eastern sophisticates who determined foreign policies were up to, and wondered whether recruiting posters would soon go up with images designed cleverly to lure away to danger the more adventurous and more patriotic of their sons.

. . .

After the Dunkirk evacuation there were still nearly 100,000 British troops in France, and Churchill ordered two more divisions over to join them, the only two fully formed and equipped British army divisions left, plus a Canadian division.

The German commanders gave their troops a brief respite and then, on June 5, they began their next offensive, driving down from the north. The British reinforcements had not arrived yet. Weygand had withdrawn twenty-five divisions from the Maginot line to meet the attack, but the Allies were still outnumbered and outgunned at the points where the armies clashed. Some French troops fought tenaciously. At other places, stunned by the rapidity of the German advance, they simply waited for the panzers to arrive so that they could surrender. In some places the tanks streaked ahead of their supply units leaving gaps of twenty or thirty miles behind them with no German troops. The Fifty-first Highland Division was cut off at St. Valéry and most of the men captured, the worst defeat yet for the British army.

Weygand had already decided that the position was hopeless. He told ministers several times that France should not have gone to war. The Germans advanced on Paris, and German aircraft bombed the city. Reynaud cabled Churchill: "Paris, the Paris area and industrial targets have just been bombed by 300 German planes. A similar treatment meted out to Berlin would be *greatly appreciated*." Churchill did not reply.

On June 10, Italy made its long-awaited declaration of war and Italian troops attacked France from the south. Three French divisions held off ten Italian divisions, and the Italian army made no headway. British aircraft flying from Britain bombed Milan and Turin. The RAF planned to attack Italian cities from airfields in southern France, but the French government refused to allow it for fear of Italian retaliation against undefended French cities. When Churchill protested and the French government reversed its decision, local authorities blocked the runways, preventing the British planes from taking off, and in the disintegrating situation of the time the government in Paris could do nothing about it.

On the morning of June 10, President Roosevelt conferred with Jay Pierrepont Moffat, who was about to leave his post as head of the European Affairs Section in the State Department to become minister to Canada. The appointment of such a high-ranking figure to the Ottawa post was an indication of the new importance of Canada in American eyes. The previous minister, James Cromwell, was a political appointee who resigned after three months to run for the Senate. Roosevelt told Moffat to tell the Canadians that America could give just as much help to the Allies as a neutral as it could if it became a belligerent.

That afternoon Roosevelt was due to go to Charlottesville, Virginia, to give a talk to the graduating class of the University of Virginia. He had on his desk thirty petitions from college student organizations urging him to avoid involvement in the war, and he planned to lecture the Virginia students on the dangers abroad in the world. Just before he left, Bullitt telephoned him from Paris with the news that Italy was about to declare war. Bullitt relayed Reynaud's comment to him: "What really distinguished, noble and admirable people the Italians are, to stab us in the back at this moment." Later in the day Reynaud used almost the same phrase in a message to Roosevelt. "Another dictator has just struck France in the back."

Roosevelt inserted into the script of his address that phrase "stab in the back." Sumner Welles, ever the cautious diplomat, persuaded him to remove it, saying it would complicate needlessly relations with Italy. On the journey down to Charlottesville with his wife, Eleanor, he received confirmation that Italy had now declared war. Sitting in the train in the afternoon heat, he grumbled about the weather and brooded on the Italian action, and on the rejection of his appeals to Mussolini not to go to war. With Eleanor's encouragement, he put that phrase back in.

Roosevelt's speech that day was a foreign policy statement. He once again ranged America unequivocally on the side of the Allies, and said a victory for Hitler would be a disaster for the Americas. He castigated Mussolini's Italy, and used the phrase for which the speech is most remembered: "On this tenth day of June, 1940, the hand that held the dagger has struck it into the back of its neighbor." (The phrase brought him some hostility from Italian-Americans. When the election campaign was under way in the autumn he seems to have given some consideration to this. He made three speeches in New York City on the day that Italy invaded Greece and made no reference to the fact.)

He concluded with what amounted to a call to arms: "We will pursue two obvious and simultaneous courses: we will extend to the opponents of force the material resources of this nation, and at the same time we will harness and speed up the use of those resources in order that we ourselves in the Americas may have equipment and training equal to the task of any emergency and every defense . . . We will not slow down or detour. Signs and signals call for full speed — full speed ahead."

John Wheeler-Bennett, then an official at the British embassy in Washington, was in the audience, and his heart leaped up when he heard these words. As he wrote later: "This was it; this was what we had been praying for — not only sympathy but pledges of support. If Britain could only hold on until these vast resources could be made available to her, we could yet survive and even win the war. It was the first gleam of hope."

Supporters and opponents both recognized the importance of the speech. The *Washington Evening Star* said: "President Roosevelt has at last cast aside America's pretense of neutrality in this war to destroy democracy." The *St. Louis Post-Dispatch* said it was "one of the most reckless speeches ever made by an American statesman."

Churchill welcomed the speech, telling Roosevelt in a cable: "Your statement that material aid of the United States will be given to the Allies in their struggle is a strong encouragement in a dark but not unhopeful hour." Then he went on to specifics: "I have already cabled you about airplanes, including flying boats, which are so needful to us in the impending struggle. But even more pressing is the need for destroyers. The Italian outrage makes it necessary to cope with a much larger number of submarines which may come out into the Atlantic and perhaps be based in Spanish ports. To this, the only counter is destroyers. Nothing is so important for us as to have 30 or 40 old destroyers you have already had reconditioned."

The German government entered the debate with an attempt to dismiss fears about incursions in Latin America. The Hearst newspaper chain carried what it said was an interview with Hitler by its chief foreign correspondent, Karl Wiegand, in which Hitler said he had no ambitions in Latin America and that the idea was "fantastic." He said he believed in "Europe for the Europeans and America for the Americans." In fact Wiegand never saw Hitler; the questions and answers were concocted by the German Foreign Ministry. The German embassy in Washington produced 100,000 copies, and Senator Jacob Thorkelson of Montana inserted it into the congressional record.

Roosevelt was asked about this at a press conference and said only, "It brings back recollections." He invited reporters to enlarge on this themselves with dates and nations.

Public opinion seemed to be moving in the same direction as the president. The *Philadelphia Inquirer* switched from its isolationist policy with an editorial on the front page headed: "America Must Help the Allies to Beat Hitler."

Turner Catledge reported in the *New York Times* a survey by political observers across the country. He wrote: "A sentiment is spreading with the rapidity of wildfire throughout most of the country, including the strongholds of post World War isolationism, for more aid by the United States to its sister democracies in Europe, not merely as a matter of idealism, but as a measure of insuring our safety." He went on to say that if these observers were correct, "Congress is thirty days behind the trend, and even the President for once is being outdistanced in the demand for aggressive action."

William Allen White reached the same conclusion. He wired Roosevelt: "My correspondence is heaping up unanimously behind the plan to aid the Allies by anything other than war. As an old friend, let me warn you that maybe you will not be able to lead the American people unless you catch up with them."

• • •

Reynaud was now desperate and he wanted more than Roosevelt could give, even in the rapidly changing climate of American opinion. On the day that Roosevelt made his Charlottesville speech, the French leader sent the president a message asking for all the help America could send short of an expeditionary force before it was too late. He promised, in terms that were almost Churchillian: "We shall fight in front of Paris, we shall fight behind Paris, we shall fortify ourselves in the provinces, and if we are chased from there we shall go to North Africa and if need be to our American possessions." He did not promise to fight *in* Paris. He was about to declare it an open city, promising that it would not be defended, to spare it from becoming a battleground.

The government left the city for Tours, some one hundred miles to the southwest. Reynaud left in a car shortly before midnight, taking with him the newly promoted brigadier general Charles de Gaulle, whom he had just appointed undersecretary for defense. He wanted to fight on and he had brought in de Gaulle to strengthen his position against those in his cabinet who were already talking about seeking an armistice. De Gaulle recalls in his memoirs driving through the night past lines of refugees. "Suddenly, a convoy of luxurious, white-tired American cars came sweeping along the road, with militiamen on the running-boards and motorcyclists surrounding the procession; it was the Diplomatic Corps on its way to the chateaux of Touraine."

One prominent member of the diplomatic corps who was not in this convoy was Ambassador William Bullitt. Bullitt, who had always acted as Roosevelt's personal envoy rather than a member of the State Department team, had told Roosevelt when the war began that if the Germans captured Paris he would remain in the capital. He cited previous American ministers and ambassadors in Paris who had remained at their post through the revolutionary Terror in the 1790s and the siege in 1870–71. Anthony Drexel Biddle, who was the American representative with the Polish government in exile in Paris, followed the government as acting American ambassador.

As the Germans approached Paris, Roosevelt told Bullitt he should leave, but he did not actually order him to do so. "Because it is impossible here to know last-minute developments or the wishes of the French Government," he said, "I must rely on your discretion and assume you will make your decision in the best interests of the United States and humanity." He told him that if he remained he could be killed by either the Nazis or the Communists. It was a mistake to give such a warning to a man with Bullitt's ego and sense of drama. Bullitt replied: "Since the age of four I have never run away from anything however painful or dangerous when I thought it was my duty to take a stand."

Hull believed that Bullitt should have gone with the government and that his remaining behind had serious consequences. He thought that with his close relations with French ministers, Bullitt might have influenced the decisions they took in the following days. He might, Hull believed, have persuaded the government to continue the war from the French territories in North Africa — Algeria, Morocco, and Tunisia. Certainly Bullitt's decision was a curious one. He was not, after all, ambassador to his beloved Paris but to the French government.

Churchill flew over for a meeting of the Allied War Council, and Reynaud said they should meet outside the town of Briare, near Tours, where the military headquarters was now situated. Churchill and his small party met with the French political and military leaders in a country house, a place unsuited for a summit meeting; it had only one telephone, situated in the toilet.

Also present was Major General Sir Edward Spears, whom Churchill had sent over as his personal representative with the French government. Spears, who was bilingual and had a deep knowledge of France, had served as a liaison officer in World War One and was a Conservative member of Parliament. He recalled the meeting in his memoirs: "The Frenchmen sat with set white faces, their eyes on the table. They looked for all the world like prisoners hauled up from some deep dungeon to hear an inevitable verdict."

Churchill told the French ministers that a Canadian division was embarking for France that night and another British division would follow in ten days' time. He said that if they could hold out until the following spring Britain would have twenty or twenty-five divisions in France. He was unhappily aware that so far Britain had made a relatively small contribution to the battle and France had borne most of the burden and most of the suffering. Nonetheless, he tried to revive the French fighting spirit. He wanted the French to defend Paris street by street, house by house, as the Spanish Republicans had defended Madrid. Weygand objected: "Reducing Paris to ashes won't affect the final result."

Weygand asked for all British fighter planes to be thrown into the battle. "Here is the decisive point," he said. "Now is the decisive moment. It is therefore wrong to keep any squadrons back in England."

Churchill's reply showed the gulf between British and French perceptions. "This is not the decisive point and this is not the decisive moment," he insisted. "That moment will come when Hitler hurls his Luftwaffe against Great Britain. If we can keep command of the air, and if we can keep the seas open, as we certainly shall keep them open, we will win it all back for you." For Churchill and the British government, Britain's survival and ultimate victory would decide the outcome of the war, not what happened in France.

Over dinner that evening, Churchill tried to ease the atmosphere by recalling to Pétain the days of 1918 when Britain and France had faced together the German advance. Pétain replied, "In 1918 I gave you forty divisions to save the British Army. Where are the forty British divisions that we need today?" Churchill had no answer. Pétain was deeply mistrustful of Britain. He had told Bullitt a few days earlier that he thought the British would allow France to fight to the last drop of its blood, and then, with its air force and fleet largely intact, would make a compromise peace with Germany, perhaps under a fascist government.

Reynaud had a plan for a Brittany redoubt; the French could establish a defense line on the Brittany peninsula, supplied by sea from Britain. Churchill was enthusiastic. But Weygand poured cold water on the idea from a military point of view. Churchill raised the crucial question of what would happen to the French fleet in the event of an armistice, and the French naval commander, Admiral Jean Darlan, assured him that it would never be handed over to Germany.

Weygand wanted an armistice and he was supported by Pétain. He held the traditional attitudes of the conservative French officer class. He distrusted politicians, he disliked the British, and he feared revolution above all else. He worried that if the French army were to be shattered it would be unable to maintain order and the Communists would stage an uprising. He reminded the others that in Russia in 1917 when the front collapsed, mutinous soldiers formed Soviets and spearheaded the Bolshevik Revolution. He also no doubt had in mind the events of 1870–71, when defeat by the Prussians led to revolutionaries seizing Paris and establishing the Paris Commune, which was suppressed with appalling bloodshed. This had been in Weygand's lifetime, albeit when he was a small child.

Churchill went back to London and cabled Roosevelt: "There must be many elements in France who will wish to continue the struggle either in France or in the French colonies or both. This therefore is the moment for you to strengthen Reynaud the utmost you can, and try to tip the balance in favor of the best and longest possible French resistance."

Three days later he was back in France again. Reynaud asked him to come to Tours, and he went with Halifax and Lord Beaverbrook. Churchill talked about fighting on, waging large-scale guerrilla warfare and carrying on the war from North Africa. Reynaud asked Churchill to release France from the promise it had made in March, when the two governments pledged that neither would sign a separate armistice. Churchill said he wanted to talk to his colleagues before answering. He, Halifax, and Beaverbrook went into the garden and talked for half an hour. When they returned, Churchill said the British government could not release France from its promise, but that whatever happened, there would be no recriminations.

The fact that this was an election year in America came into their considerations. Reynaud said there was no chance that America would enter the war before the election in November. Churchill suggested that electoral considerations might actually favor intervention, although this was not what he had said to the War Cabinet in London. He suggested that Reynaud make one more appeal to Roosevelt. Reynaud said he would do this, and would hang on until Roosevelt replied.

Reynaud wanted to fight on but he was under pressure from those who wanted to seek an armistice, and unlike Churchill he had no large political party behind him. As well as Weygand and Pétain, Paul Baudouin, secretary to the War Cabinet, said the position was hopeless. Behind Baudouin stood the countess Hélène de Portes, who had been Reynaud's mistress since he separated from his wife. The widow of a count, Hélène de Portes was a player on the political scene; it was at her instigation that Reynaud had appointed Baudouin. Before the war she had held a salon in Paris at which the German ambassador, Otto Abetz, was a frequent and welcome guest. She was a representative of that part of the French *haute bourgeoisie* that had said, "Better Hitler than Blum." She advised Reynaud on appointments, read confidential messages, and interfered in every area of politics. She nagged at Reynaud and weakened his resolve. She was energetic, shrewd, and strong-willed, yet curiously for one who exerted influence through a man, no one seemed to have found her either beautiful or alluring. Clare Boothe said she looked "as much like a *hausfrau* as a French *maitresse* can."

The French cabinet moved the seat of government still farther away from the advancing Germans, to Bordeaux, with such civil servants and support staff as it could manage in the chaotic conditions that prevailed. U.S. ambassador Biddle went with the government. So did the British ambassador, Sir Ronald Campbell, and Sir Edward Spears, driving in the ambassadorial Rolls Royce. They drove along roads clogged with refugees and through villages, Spears noted disapprovingly, thronging with French soldiers apparently with nothing to do.

This was a trail marked by history. Seventy years earlier the government had fled to Bordeaux when the Prussians besieged Paris, and there it had accepted the humiliating Prussian peace terms. Again in 1914 the government retreated to Bordeaux when the advancing German forces drew close to Paris, but that time the Germans were halted just short of the capital. Now Bordeaux was host to a refugee French government again, and in that port city, the capital of a wine-producing area, the French Third Republic died, day by day, hour by hour.

• • •

The issue of whether France would fight on was reaching its climax, with messages crossing one another and being overtaken by events. Roosevelt replied to Reynaud on June 13 paying tribute to French resistance and welcoming Reynaud's assertion that France would continue to fight on. He promised that America would redouble its efforts to send more aid. He said, "It is important to remember that the French and British fleets continue mastery of the Atlantic and other oceans, and also to remember that vital materials from the outside world are necessary to maintain all armies." He sent the message through Ambassador Biddle, and told him to make it clear that it was personal and private and not for publication.

He also sent a copy to Kennedy and told him to give it to Churchill immediately. Kennedy took it to Admiralty House, where Churchill was still living. Churchill was having dinner with his wife and two daughters — an entrée, fish, jellied chicken, and strawberries, Kennedy noted in his diary. Kennedy read him the message. His account in his diary goes on: "He then read it himself three or four times during dinner and was visibly moved by, I think, excitement but possibly by champagne, which he was drinking, and told me he would immediately convey to Reynaud that his understanding of the message was that America assumed a responsibility if the French continued to fight and finally moved out their government. This was the point he stressed most strongly."

Desperate to keep France fighting, Churchill read more into the message than Roosevelt intended, or appeared to do so. So did his cabinet when they discussed it. Beaverbrook thought an American declaration of war was now inevitable. Churchill told Reynaud in a message: "If France on this message of President Roosevelt's continues in the field and in the war, we feel that the United States is committed beyond recall to take the only remaining step, namely, becoming belligerent in form as she has already constituted herself in fact. Constitution of the United States makes it impossible, as you foresaw, for the President to declare war himself, but if you act on his reply now received, we sincerely believe that this must inevitably follow."

Evidently unaware of Roosevelt's instructions to Biddle that the message be private and personal, he cabled Roosevelt: "I must tell you that it seems to me absolutely vital that this message should be published tomorrow 14 June in order that it may play a decisive part in turning the course of world history. It will I am sure decide the French to deny Hitler a patched-up peace with France."

Ambassador Kennedy passed on the message and Roosevelt replied to him immediately: "My message to Reynaud is not to be published under any circumstances," he told Kennedy. "It was in no sense intended to commit and does not commit this Government to the slightest military activity on behalf of the Allies . . . If there is any possibility of misunderstanding, please insist that Churchill at once convey this statement to the appropriate French officials."

Kennedy telephoned Churchill with this message. He reported: "Churchill was obviously terribly disappointed as he had counted on publication of this message to put a little stiffening into the French backbone. He . . . said he was afraid conveying such a message now to the French would merely dampen what fires remained."

Reynaud cabled Roosevelt again, putting the fate of France, indeed of European democracy, in American hands, in a message of eloquent desperation. France had a choice, he said. She could fight on from North Africa or ask Hitler for armistice terms. "We can only choose the first path, that of resistance, if there is a chance of victory in the long term, if there is light at the end of the tunnel . . . If you cannot give to France the certainty that the United States will come into the war within a very short time, the fate of the world will change. Then you will see France go under like a drowning man and disappear, after having cast a last look towards the land of liberty from which she awaited salvation."

On that day, June 14, German troops reached the eastern suburbs of Paris, and since it had been declared an open city, two French officers came out under a flag of truce to arrange its peaceful surrender. For such an earth-shattering event, the fall of Paris was undramatic. As the blue skies of the past month clouded over and a drizzle came down, German infantrymen marched in unopposed and paraded down the Champs Élysées. The next day German soldiers were already behaving like tourists, sitting in the sunshine at outdoor cafés and photographing each other in front of the Eiffel Tower.

The fall of Paris touched an emotional chord everywhere. Paris was closer to London than Glasgow and more familiar to many Londoners, for the better-off a place for a weekend jaunt. Two million Americans had seen Paris in the army in World War One, and for many of them it was a high point of their youth. For these and many others, Paris was the city of culture and light, of art and gaiety, and the stamp of German jackboots on its boulevards seemed like a violation. Archibald MacLeish was found at his desk in tears at the news. The next day he told Harold Ickes over lunch that he was in favor of declaring war. Ickes was astonished, but decided that he agreed with him. "We could not send soldiers but we could send munitions and ships and airplanes, and permit volunteers," he wrote in his diary.

Tin Pan Alley, in the person of two of its most sophisticated songwriters, Jerome Kern and Oscar Hammerstein, rushed out a song called "The Last Time I Saw Paris" with elegiac lines:

> *The last time I saw Paris,*
> *Her heart was warm and gay.*
> *No matter how they change her*
> *I'll remember her that way.*

• • •

The British government was planning to send yet more troops to France. But when Field Marshal Sir John Dill telephoned the British commander on the spot, Major General Alan Brooke, who had gone back to France after Dunkirk, Brooke told him French resistance was crumbling and he was pulling back British troops. Dill said, "The Prime Minister does not want you to do that."

"What the hell does he want?" demanded Brooke. "He wants to speak to you," Dill replied, and gave the phone to Churchill, who was standing next to him.

Brooke had never met Churchill (although his two brothers had served in the army with him). He found himself talking to the prime minister now and arguing with him. Churchill said they should send more forces to make the French feel that Britain was supporting them. But Brooke, a man who knew his own mind, told him that the French army was to all intents and purposes dead. "You cannot make a corpse feel," he insisted. They argued for nearly half an hour, and in the end Churchill said, "All right, I agree with you." The Canadian troops who had just landed got back into their ships. (Churchill liked people who argued with him constructively. He promoted Brooke, and the following year he made him chief of the Imperial General Staff — he later became Lord Alanbrooke. They had some furious arguments over strategy.)

Churchill cabled Roosevelt again the next day expressing disappointment that he had refused publication of the earlier message. His tone was hardly less urgent than Reynaud's. "I understand all your difficulties with American public opinion and Congress," he said, "but events are moving downward at a pace where they will pass beyond the control of American public opinion when at last it has ripened.

"Have you considered what offers Hitler may choose to make to France? He may say: 'Surrender the fleet intact and I will leave you Alsace-Lorraine,' or alternatively: 'If you do not give me your ships I will destroy your towns.' I am personally convinced that America will in the end go to all lengths, but this moment is supremely critical for France. A declaration that America will if necessary enter the war might save France." He summoned up the picture of a defeated Britain, a "vassal state of the Hitler empire," with its fleet passing into German hands, with all the consequences for America.

This was said to scare Roosevelt, but he believed in this possibility. He said in a cable to Lothian that he thought that if Britain were defeated a "quisling government" might hand over the fleet, and the Germans would rule the Atlantic. "If we go down," he said, "Hitler has a good chance of conquering the world." He added a whimsical sentence which he crossed out before sending the cable: "How else would he pass away his time?"

More immediately, the fate of the French fleet weighed heavily on British and American minds. With 11 battleships, 5 aircraft carriers, and 101 submarines, it was the third largest in the world. German control of it would be a disaster.

Churchill sent another message to Roosevelt saying he had just learned of Reynaud's desperate message, virtually saying that continued French resistance depended on an American promise to enter the war. "When I sent you my message just now I did not know that Mr. Reynaud had stated the dilemma in these terms," he said, "but I am afraid there is no getting away from the fact that this is the choice before us now."

But Roosevelt had already sent a preliminary answer to Reynaud through Ambassador Biddle. He followed this up with a message expressing once again enormous sympathy for French suffering, admiration for French resistance, and the promise of still more aid. But he insisted again: "I know that you will understand that these statements carry with them no implication of military commitments. Only the Congress can make such commitments."

British ministers were still discussing unrealistic possibilities of American action. Halifax suggested that Roosevelt might be ready to tell Hitler, if he offered harsh peace terms to France, that if he insisted on them America would declare war.

The French cabinet debated whether to seek an armistice. Reynaud pointed out that the promise to Britain that it would not seek a separate armistice was still binding. He said the honor and interests of France required it to continue the struggle. Pétain said that a common obligation implied a common effort, and Britain had not made the effort that France had. Vice Premier Camille Chautemps suggested that they ask the Germans what armistice terms they would offer, without making any commitment. Reynaud used the same argument Churchill had used in a similar situation: that simply asking about terms would sap the will to resist. He had several ministers on his side, but Pétain and Pierre Laval, a minister of state, were all for seeking an armistice.

The pressure on Reynaud was enormous. He was aware that while the cabinet debated French soldiers were dying. Chautemps reminded him of this at one point and said he had two sons at the front. Reynaud wanted Weygand to order a cease-fire. Weygand retorted that this would cast shame on the French army, that the government had started the war and the government could finish it. The difference between a cease-fire and an armistice was important. An armistice would mean terms agreed by victor and vanquished, which would preserve some kind of French government in France. If the army surrendered on the battlefield but the government did not, there would be no agreement, and the Germans would rule France as a conquering army while the government was elsewhere.

On June 16, in response to yet another query, the British cabinet changed its mind about releasing the French government from the agreement about seeking a separate armistice. It knew Reynaud was struggling to remain in power, and decided that if he was ousted another government would seek an armistice with or without British consent. Ambassador Campbell told Reynaud that the French government could ask the terms of an armistice provided that the French fleet immediately sailed to British ports, pending any negotiations. Reynaud pointed out that this would leave French North Africa exposed to the Italian navy.

Meanwhile, British forces in France were being evacuated under fire, along with twenty thousand Polish troops. At St. Nazaire, the liner *Lancastria,* packed with British troops, was bombed and exploded in flames. An estimated three thousand men died, making it one of the worst maritime disasters of all time. Churchill ordered that this be kept secret, telling his officials: "The newspapers have got enough bad news for today."

. . .

Then there occurred one of the most extraordinary episodes of this extraordinary period. The British government proposed to join together the British and French nations. This episode is forgotten now and is hardly mentioned in the history books, understandably because it was something that did not happen, a proposal that was not accepted. But the fact that it could have been put forward seriously says something about the atmosphere of the time, when things were possible that at any other time would not even have been thinkable.

It is particularly striking placed against the argument that has been running through British political life since the early 1960s over relations with the entity that began as the European Common Market and became the European Union. There has been passionate debate between and within the two main political parties about how much sovereignty Britain was surrendering or should surrender, centering on one issue after another — criminal law, armed services, currency. If this proposal had been followed through in 1940, it would have meant a far greater surrender of sovereignty than any that has been contemplated in the contemporary debates. It would virtually have meant the end of Britain as a separate sovereign nation.

The proposal was a desperate measure designed to keep France in the war, grappling a sinking ship to one that was still afloat. The idea came from Jean Monnet, who had been in America negotiating the purchase of weapons. He was then in London as the chairman of the Anglo-French Coordinating Committee, which was concerned with economic warfare. He steered the proposal to the British war cabinet with the same drive and politicking skills that he was later, in the postwar world, to bring to the creation of the European Common Market.

On June 13, Monnet and Arthur Salter (later Lord Salter), another member of the committee, drew up a five-page memorandum. This put the breathtakingly radical proposal last, not even in a separate sentence but in a subsidiary clause, as if it were a mere detail. The memorandum talked about the need for French forces to continue the war alongside Britain even if the entire country were occupied, and said America had to come in (without explaining how this should be brought about). It concluded with this sentence: "There should be a dramatic declaration by the two governments of the solidarity of the two countries' interests and of their mutual commitment to restore the devastated areas, making clear also that the two governments are to merge and form a single cabinet and to unite the two parliaments."

They wanted this brought up in the cabinet. An official friend of Monnet advised him to give it to Neville Chamberlain, saying Churchill had a lot of respect for him, so the next day, June 14, he took it to Horace Wilson, who was still Chamberlain's private secretary. The news that the Germans were about to enter Paris gave a dramatic emphasis to the proposal. Wilson seemed astounded by the last phrase. "You mean," he said, "real unity, complete unity? One parliament, one army?" "Exactly," Monnet said.

Wilson agreed to put it to Chamberlain, and Chamberlain put it to Churchill, who agreed to place the proposal before the War Cabinet the next day. At a midnight meeting, he and Conservative Party chief whip David Margesson told Monnet that he had to get it to Lord Vansittart, the foreign affairs advisor to the cabinet, so that he could draw it up as a cabinet document. Vansittart had gone to the country for the weekend but they tracked him down. He wrote a proposal for a customs union, common currency, and merger of the functions of government.

De Gaulle had come to London ostensibly to organize the transport of French troops to North Africa, so Monnet invited him to dinner at his apartment along with René Pleven, a colleague. He was not there when de Gaulle arrived, and his wife asked de Gaulle how long he expected to be in London on his mission. De Gaulle showed that he had other things besides transport in mind. He replied, "I am not here on a mission, Madam. I am here to save the honor of France."

He warmed to the idea of union when Monnet told him about it over dinner, perhaps surprisingly since he was later to become the very symbol of French nationalism. He was realistic about the proposal and seems to have thought that it could not be brought about in its totality. He wrote in his memoirs, "It was obvious that one could not, by an exchange of notes, even in principle, fuse England and France together, including their institutions, their interests and their empires, supposing this were desirable." But he saw that such a bold statement at this time might strengthen Reynaud.

De Gaulle was right. The details of the proposal had not been thought through. Like many another wartime proposal of marriage, it was made in haste to meet the urgent needs of the moment, without serious consideration of the long-term commitment that was implied.

The next morning, Sunday, Vansittart telephoned Monnet and told him that the document had been circulated among the War Cabinet and would be discussed that afternoon. He invited them to look at the final version.

The document began with a sonorous declaration: "At this most fateful moment in the history of the modern world the governments of the United Kingdom and France make this declaration of indissoluble union and unyielding resolution in their common defense of justice and freedom against subjection to a system which reduces mankind to a life of robots and slaves." The next sentences contain the kernel:

"The two governments declare that France and Britain shall no longer be two nations but one Franco-British union.

"The constitution of the union will provide for joint organs of defense, foreign, financial and economic policies.

"Every citizen of France will enjoy immediate citizenship of Great Britain; every British subject will become a citizen of France."

It went on to declare that there would be a single war cabinet and all the armed forces of Britain and France would come under its direction. The two parliaments would be "formally associated."

De Gaulle and Monnet were due to have lunch with Churchill that day. De Gaulle wanted to strengthen Reynaud's hand immediately and he telephoned him. It is symptomatic of the depth of division and mistrust in the French government that Weygand had his intelligence section tap Reynaud's telephone, and it is because of this that we have a record of their conversations.

DE GAULLE: "I have just seen Churchill. There is something stupendous happening that affects the identity of our two countries. Churchill proposes the establishment of a single Franco-British government, perhaps with you as head of a Franco-British war cabinet."

REYNAUD: "It is the only possible solution for the future. But it must be done on a large scale and very quickly — above all very quickly. It is a question of minutes. I give you half an hour. It would be splendid."

When de Gaulle demurred at this timing Reynaud told him a decisive cabinet meeting was scheduled for that afternoon. "I can delay it a little, but not beyond five o'clock," he said.

De Gaulle and Monnet talked it up to Churchill over lunch. "It's an enormous mouthful," Churchill said. De Gaulle agreed. Churchill said it would take a lot of time to bring it about, but he thought the gesture should be made immediately. Then he went into the cabinet meeting. De Gaulle and Monnet went with him to 10 Downing Street and waited in an anteroom outside the cabinet meeting.

The cabinet papers show that the proposal for a union, which was intended to change the British nation forever, was not the first topic on the agenda. Ministers discussed Roosevelt's message to Reynaud and Roosevelt's reply. They agreed to invite Reynaud to establish a government-in-exile in London.

Then Chamberlain raised the proposal for unity, which the others had already seen. Summarizing it, he said the memo's main points were that it was essential that France remain in the war, that the United States enter the war, and that Germany be prevented from successfully invading Britain. To attain these objectives, "the indispensable condition would be real unity between Britain and France, dramatically expressed and fully realized by the two peoples." He observed that the proposals for a joint cabinet and joint Parliament did not seem to have been fully thought out, which was certainly true.

Churchill said his first instinct had been against the idea, but they must not allow themselves to be accused of lacking imagination. If a statement of unity would appeal to the French, so much the better. As for the form of government, if the French government moved to London they could have frequent meetings of the French War Council, which would seem to cover the situation. This was treating it as if it were simply a matter of enhanced cooperation instead of union.

The cabinet agreed to put the proposal to the French government with minor alterations. Churchill came out of the meeting smoking a cigar and told de Gaulle and Monnet, who had been waiting impatiently, that the document had been approved.

John Colville, Churchill's private secretary, had no doubt about its significance. He wrote in his diary: "It is a historic document and its effects will be more far-reaching than anything that has occurred this century — and more permanent?" And in a lighter tone: "The King does not know what is being done to his empire . . . Who knows, we may yet see the 'fleurs de lys' restored to the Royal Standard." (The *fleur de lys* was the emblem of the old French monarchy.)

It was now just before four o'clock. De Gaulle telephoned Reynaud immediately with the news. But Reynaud had a cabinet meeting scheduled for five o'clock, and he knew that the issue of whether to fight on could be decided then.

De Gaulle said: "There is going to be a sensational declaration."

REYNAUD: "But after five o'clock it will be too late."

DE GAULLE: "I will do my best to bring it to you by plane."

REYNAUD: "Yes, but that will be too late. The situation has deteriorated seriously within the last few minutes. Unforeseen events have occurred."

Pleven sat down and translated the proposal into French, and de Gaulle telephoned Reynaud at 4:30 to say the proposal was ready and would be coming soon. Reynaud said the cabinet meeting was about to begin and they could not wait. So de Gaulle read out the message there and then and the French prime minister took it down in longhand, writing in pencil in an excited scrawl. Sir Edward Spears stood beside him, handing him more paper when he had filled a sheet.

Churchill came on the telephone and said de Gaulle would come over with the declaration, and he would meet him the next day at Concarneau, a port in Brittany. He immediately made plans to go to France, taking with him his deputy premier, Clement Attlee, and also the secretary for air, Sir Archibald Sinclair. Sinclair was not in the War Cabinet but he was the leader of the Liberal Party, the smallest of the three parties represented in Parliament. With an issue of such a fundamental nature, affecting the nature of the British state, Churchill wanted the involvement of all three political parties.

In Bordeaux Reynaud seemed to be, in Spears's words, "transfixed with joy . . . happy with a great happiness that France would now stay in the war." He told Campbell, "I will fight to the death for these proposals" and hurried off to the cabinet meeting. Reynaud reflected on the effort of imagination that it must have taken for a British government to come up with such a proposal: "One has only to consider the insular mentality, the individuality and the pride of the British people, reserved to the point of isolation."

Campbell and Spears went over to the Hotel Montré, where they were staying, to wait for the result. While they waited they amused themselves by picturing a meeting of an Anglo-French Parliament at which British and French members would not understand one another.

In the cabinet, reaction was divided. Edouard Herriot, the president of the National Assembly, was enthusiastic. So was Georges Mandel, the minister for the interior, who had been in favor all along of continuing the fight from North Africa. But Camille Chautemps said he did not want France to become a British dominion. Navy secretary Jean Ybarnegaray agreed. "Better to be a Nazi province. At least we know what that means," he said. Reynaud retorted, "I prefer to collaborate with my allies rather than my enemies." Pétain said Britain was finished, and that joining with Britain now would be "fusion with a corpse."

The division was a familiar one. Those who wanted to fight on favored the proposal; those who wanted an armistice were against. During the meeting, word arrived that the Germans were now in Besançon and Dijon. Reynaud guessed that Weygand had held back this news for the moment when it would have the greatest impact.

Hélène de Portes, who knew about the British proposal as she knew everything that passed through the prime minister's office, sent a note for Reynaud into the cabinet meeting. It said: "I hope you are not going to play at being Isabella of Bavaria." Isabella was the Queen of France from 1389 to 1435 who gave her daughter in marriage to Britain's King Henry V and recognized him as heir to the French throne.

Confronted with all this opposition, Reynaud threw in the towel. He did not even put the union proposal to a vote. He resigned, and the president of the republic, who steps in when a government falls, asked the eighty-four-year-old Marshal Pétain to form a government. Reynaud told Ambassador Biddle that he hoped the Germans' armistice terms would be harsh, because then the government might reject them and decide to fight on.

Churchill and his colleagues were on a train at Victoria Station that night about to leave for Southampton, where a destroyer would take them to Concarneau, when they received a message from Campbell saying Reynaud had resigned. They left the station dejected.

• • •

Pétain sent a message through the Spanish ambassador asking for an armistice. The Germans said a French delegation should go to a site near Tours, and four French senior officers went. From Tours the Frenchmen were whisked off to a staged event that dramatized German triumph and German revenge. They were driven to the forest of Compiègne, fifty miles east of Paris. There they were taken to the railroad carriage in which, in 1918, representatives of the German army had surrendered. It had been kept there at the same spot to commemorate the French victory in 1918. A monument celebrating the German surrender was draped with a swastika (and later blown up).

Hitler himself was present, wearing a military uniform with his Iron Cross, along with Hess, Göring, and Ribbentrop. They watched the French delegates sign the armistice document in that historic railroad carriage, reversing the defeat that had overshadowed German life. Then Hitler left for a visit to the battlefields of World War One where he had served, before being driven back to Germany. Hitler's journeys outside Germany were few and brief.

The French surrender was a shock to the British people. France had been their front line. Now it was gone, and they were in the front line.

Nella Last, the Barrow housewife who kept a diary, was alone when she heard the news of the French surrender on the radio, and she records: "My faith, my philosophy, my courage left me . . . Never have I felt so naked, never so alone."

Moyra Charlton, who was now working as a nurse's aide in a military hospital, wrote in her diary: "So we are left alone to champion the cause of truth and beauty and all that makes life worth living. It makes one dread the endless future and the menacing present, but one must be proud."

Churchill spent the following morning working on the speech he would make to a tense and anxious Parliament, dictating it to his typist, reworking one sentence after another until he had the note he wanted.

"What General Weygand called the Battle of France is over. I expect that the battle of Britain is about to begin," he said. He spelled out what was at stake in grave tones. "Hitler knows that he will have to break us in this island or lose the war. If we can stand up to him, all Europe may be free and the life of the world may move forward into broad, sunlit uplands. But if we fail, then the whole world, including the United States, including all that we have known and cared for, will sink into the abyss of a new Dark Age, made more sinister, and perhaps more protracted, by the lights of perverted science."

He concluded with the phrase that has often been attached to the succeeding months: "Let us therefore brace ourselves to our duties, and so bear ourselves that, if the British Empire and its Commonwealth last for a thousand years, men will still say, 'This was their finest hour.'"

Drew Middleton, then an Associated Press correspondent, was in the press gallery, and he recalled: "At the end there was a roar of cheering. I felt a buoyant emotion that banished all I had seen and heard in France in the preceding six weeks. Somehow these incredible people were going to do it. I felt great gratitude for being there that day, confidence in the future. When I emerged into the street the sunshine seemed brighter." That evening, Churchill repeated the speech on the radio, and millions, sitting in their homes, heard the same message and felt encouraged.*

The German armistice terms were not as onerous as they might have been. Germany would take back Alsace and Lorraine. German forces would occupy all of northern and eastern France, three-fifths of the country. The Germans wanted the fleet to remain in French ports and to be disarmed under German or Italian control, but the French government rejected this at Admiral Darlan's insistence. The ships sailed to North Africa or remained in the unoccupied area of France. Darlan gave secret orders to the fleet that the warships were to be scuttled if the Germans tried to seize them, and these orders were obeyed. When the Germans marched into unoccupied France following the Anglo-American invasion of North Africa in November 1942 and occupied the port of Toulon, all the Navy's ships in Toulon were scuttled.

---

* After the war a radio actor, Norman Shelley, said he had delivered the speech on the radio, imitating Churchill's voice, and a recording was found that seemed to substantiate this. The story is complicated. It turns out that Shelley may have recorded the speech later but evidence shows that what the British people heard on June 18 was definitely Churchill's voice. The point was established by the *Economist*, issue of Dec. 4, 2000.

The French government described the armistice terms as "hard, but honorable." It said that had they not been honorable, it would have continued the fight.

Pétain set up a government with its capital in Vichy which, it was clear, would have to be compliant with German wishes. It was not to be a democratic government. *"Liberté, Egalité, Fraternité,"* the slogan of republican France since the French Revolution, was replaced by *"Patrie, Famille, Travaille"* — "Country, Family, Work," and new coins were minted carrying these words. Marshal Pétain, a traditional French conservative, was content to head an authoritarian government; he had been appointed ambassador to Spain following General Franco's victory because it was assumed that he would be in sympathy with the Spanish leader. Baudouin sent a message to London saying the new government wanted to remain on friendly terms with Britain. The United States, like most other countries, gave it partial recognition as the government of France.

Reynaud drove south from Bordeaux with Hélène de Portes. Just outside the town the car skidded and hit a tree. The crash broke her neck, and she was killed instantly; Reynaud suffered only minor injuries. A few weeks later he was arrested by Pétain's government and spent the rest of the war years in prison.

General de Gaulle, in London, denounced the armistice. He was the senior French figure in London and he was willing to continue the war. But, although Churchill had met him in France and had been impressed by his vigor, he was an unknown quantity to British ministers, a brigadier general who had been in the French government as a junior minister for only a few weeks.

With Churchill's permission, he gave a broadcast speech to France over the BBC calling on French soldiers to rally around him and continue the struggle. "France has lost a battle. It has not lost the war," he declared. The text of this broadcast is now historic, and is engraved on the side of the Arc de Triomphe in Paris.

Churchill decided to back him and with this support de Gaulle created the Free French Movement. Soon he and Pétain, to whom he had dedicated his book containing his military philosophy, headed rival French governments, the one in exile in London, the other in Vichy, and each denounced the other as a traitor.

To many British people their country's plight seemed the end product of years of muddle and mistakes. The political cartoonist David Low had drawn for years cartoons with comic caricatures pointing to the growing menace of Nazism and the folly of appeasement. Now he drew a cartoon with nothing comic about it, that seemed to be a culmination of all his warnings. It showed a British soldier, rifle in hand, on a beach facing a darkening sky and a stormy sea, raising his fist in defiance. The caption said, "Very well then, alone."

7

THE WHITE CLIFFS

Germany's next move seemed clear. After polishing off Western Europe, it would cross the stretch of water that separated Britain from the Continent, twenty-two miles across at its narrowest point, and invade Britain. This was what the world now expected and it was what Britain expected. This danger was something new in the British national experience. The last time British people had to face a threat of invasion was when Napoleon assembled his ships at the channel ports. The last time a foreign invasion force actually landed in Britain was nearly nine hundred years earlier, in 1066. For British people, wars were fought somewhere else. Now the German army was on the French shore, a coastline visible from Britain on a clear day, and Britain was vulnerable.

The writer H. M. Tomlinson tried to get across the feeling to American readers in an article in the *Atlantic Monthly:* "It is hard to explain what that means to us. We still ponder it with incredulity. For long and easy years, we looked to the French cliffs as to the porch of another home, and a welcome; but now the enemy is there."

The southeast and east coast seemed the likeliest invasion area. People living near these coasts saw them transformed into potential war zones. Holiday beaches were covered with barbed wire and mined. Booms were built in harbors so that they could be blocked to enemy ships. Holiday hotels were taken over to house troops. Gasoline stations in coastal towns were kept in low supply so that invaders could not use the gasoline. In some areas, a curfew was in force and foreigners were barred. Two hundred thousand civilians were evacuated from likely invasion zones. Children who had been moved from London to the east coast at the beginning of the war because of the danger of air raids were moved again because of the danger of invasion.

Some moved farther away still. Many who could afford to do so sent their children to safety in America or Canada. Sir Henry Channon, the wealthy American-born Conservative member of Parliament, sent his son Paul to relatives in America. He recorded in his diary the scene when he went to see him off: "At the station there was a queue of Rolls Royces and liveried servants and mountains of trunks. It seemed that everyone one knew was there on the very crowded platform."

In America, a Committee for the Care of European Children was set up with Eleanor Roosevelt as honorary president. There was tremendous sympathy for this project. The *New York Daily Mirror* editorialized: "Hitler may hurl hell at Britain at any moment. America must say to Britain: 'Our barriers are down to your children. Send them by the thousands.' It is our duty and privilege to give them a new home." American businesses with branches in Britain made fostering arrangements for children of their British staffs. Several American and Canadian universities brought over the children of British academics. Thousands of British children went to America and Canada, some to return years later with changed accents and attitudes.

There was resentment that the wealthy and certain professional families were able to send their children to safety while others could not afford the expense, so the War Cabinet approved a scheme whereby the government would send children to the Dominions where hospitality was offered. Children aged five to sixteen were eligible, and there were 210,000 applicants. But many shrank from parting with their children when the time came. For parents, wealthy or otherwise, it was an agonizing choice: whether to send their children overseas, and probably not see them for years, or keep them at home and expose them to danger.

Many, and not only parents, were in tears on the docks at Liverpool as the liner *Batory* pulled out bound for Australia with six hundred children singing, "There'll always be an England." Children going overseas were told that they were going as ambassadors for Britain and should be on their best behavior, and most took this to heart. One reporter saw a seven-year-old girl at a railroad station in Toronto sobbing, when a girl of eleven went up to her and said, "Stop it at once and be British!" The little girl stopped crying immediately.

Churchill did not like the scheme. The War Cabinet approved it on the day that France surrendered when he was too preoccupied to voice his opposition. It was suggested that he send a message with a child to the Canadian prime minister, and he replied in a memo: "If I sent any message to anyone it would be that I entirely deprecate any stampede from this country at the present time." A schoolboy, David Wedgewood Benn, wrote a letter to the *Times* rejecting evacuation and saying, "I would rather be bombed to fragments than leave England." Churchill sent him a signed copy of his autobiographical book *My Early Life*.

Some twenty-six hundred children went overseas under the government scheme, mostly to Canada. Then the liner *City of Benares* was torpedoed in the Atlantic in September and seventy-three children were killed, and the transport scheme stopped.

Harold Nicolson was not alone in contemplating suicide rather than live in a world in which Britain was occupied. Britain had fought wars in most parts of the globe over the centuries and won some and lost some, but it had not been conquered for nine hundred years. France, Germany, and other countries on the Continent had been conquered and had emerged again, but Britain was protected by the sea and conquest was not part of the British national experience. Most British people simply could not envisage living beyond it.

Britain's army was much smaller than Germany's; conscripts and even volunteers were still waiting to be called up. It was woefully short of weapons. The army did a tally and found that it had left behind in France 880 field guns, 700 tanks, and 40,000 other vehicles, which was most of the artillery and tanks that it possessed. The home forces consisted of fifteen infantry divisions, but many of these were half their normal strength of 15,500 men. They had only 160 tanks, and most were light tanks armed with machine guns, not cannon. The army was short of trucks, and an arrangement was made to assemble civilian buses and drivers at short notice to transport troops. Factories were turning out tanks and artillery but they could not catch up with demand.

General Ironside was appointed commander of Home Forces. He established a static defense line covering all the eastern and southeastern part of England, thirty to seventy miles in from the coast, starting up in Yorkshire and running down to Cambridge and Kent and along the

south coast over to Bristol in the west, shielding all the main manufacturing centers. Workmen were rushed in to build antitank obstacles
along this line. He stationed what artillery he had near the possible invasion beaches and kept most of his meager supply of antitank guns
with the mobile reserve.

Naval guns were also sited near likely invasion beaches, manned by
sailors. These had a range of 12,000 yards, about seven miles, but because of the shortage of ammunition they were told to hold their fire until the enemy was within three or four miles. When Churchill visited
beach defenses at St. Margaret's Bay, near Dover, the brigadier in command of the sector said he had only three field guns in his brigade and
only six shells for each gun. He asked Churchill whether he thought he
should let his men fire a single round each for practice so that they
would at least know how the guns worked. Churchill replied that they
could not afford practice rounds, that the guns should be fired only at
the last moment and at close range. Thus did Britain face the most powerful army in the world.

General Ironside's message to his officers was characteristically aggressive. He wrote: "If the Germans ever attempt a landing here they
will put the utmost energy into establishing what might be called a
'bridgehead' in England. All our energies must be put into stopping
them. No waiting for more troops to come up. Our mobile forces must
attack at once regardless of losses and nip the landing in the bud. We
cannot inculcate that idea too much into everybody concerned."

When the first shipments of American rifles and ammunition arrived
from Raritan, special trains were waiting at the ports to rush them to
army units immediately. Troops and in some cases women volunteers
spent days wiping off the grease in which they had been kept since
1918. Soon, thanks to these shipments, the army had enough rifles.
Field guns and tanks followed as the summer weeks went on.

What stood between Britain and defeat was the navy and the air
force. The Chiefs of Staff made this clear in a report on the prospects as
early as May 26. It said that the RAF and the navy together stood a
good chance of preventing a landing. "The crux of the matter is air superiority," it said. However, it went on, "Should the Germans succeed
in establishing a force with its vehicles in this country, our armed forces
have not got the offensive power to drive it out."

The navy patrolled the area with destroyers and some seven hundred small craft. It kept battleships and large cruisers away from those waters because they would be vulnerable to air attack, but they were ready to move up to deal with an invasion force. Some of the small craft were very small. Petty Officer David Mayhew, still new to the navy, was put in charge of a requisitioned forty-two-foot motor boat in Lowestoft harbor and given a crew of two. He wrote to his mother: "We have a machine gun and a rifle and I have a revolver. If they try to invade this place or the immediate neighborhood we beat it out to sea with all the other ships in port and (in the Captain's words) use our own wits and make as much trouble as we can."

Experiments were made with setting the sea on fire, by spreading oil on the top and igniting it. They were not successful, but rumors went around that a raiding party had been driven off in this way and charred bodies of German soldiers had been washed up on the beach. The authorities did not deny this, assuming that the rumors would reach the Germans and might present some discouragement to German soldiers.

There was one other anti-invasion tactic that was never admitted officially, at the time or later. Churchill ordered his military chiefs to investigate the possibility of drenching the beaches with mustard gas if the Germans landed. He said to one of his generals, "I have no scruples, except not to do anything dishonorable." Plans for using gas were made.

RAF bomber crews flew practice runs low along the beaches, without being told what these were for. Very little was said about this, either at the time or since, and no official documents on the subject have been released. Long after the war General Brooke, who succeeded Ironside as commander of home defense forces, published his diary and wrote in a note attached to an entry about invasion preparations: "I was also relying on heavy air attacks on the points of landing, and had every intention of using sprayed mustard gas on the beaches."

The government was not going to declare London an open city as Paris was. London would be defended street by street even if this meant reducing it to rubble. An outer ring of pill boxes, tank traps, and trenches was built, and inside this a second defense line running through suburbs whose very names signify placid, uneventful living, such as Enfield, Harrow, and Norwood. An inner ring was to be manned by a crack Guards regiment. Churchill wrote to a member of Parliament: "You may rest assured that we should fight in every street in

London and its suburbs. It would devour an invading army, assuming one ever got so far."

Desperately aware of their shortage of soldiers and weapons, the British underestimated the difficulties facing the Germans. We tend to think of a 1940 invasion of Britain as D-Day in reverse four years earlier. But amphibious warfare had not been developed in 1940. The only landings in army manuals of tactics were river crossings. There were no purpose-built landing craft, no way of getting tanks on to beaches. Troops would have to be brought ashore in motor launches and barges and heavy equipment landed at a port.

General Sir Hastings Ismay, secretary to the War Cabinet, told the prime minister in a memo: "In view of past experience in Norway, Holland and France, it can be taken for granted that the Germans have the plan for the invasion of this country worked out to the last detail, and have provided all necessary special equipment, such as motor landing craft etc." In fact the Germans had no plans worked out. Hitler had not planned for a war against Britain. His aim was to dominate the Continent and he had achieved this, and more quickly than he could have anticipated. After this he expected Britain to agree to peace. Only when Britain failed to do so did he begin to think about what he should do next.

Paratroops, as a novel form of warfare, seized the popular imagination, and the official one as well. Although paratroops had been used only in Holland and played no part in the main campaigns in France, it was assumed widely that an invasion force would be accompanied by a mass drop of parachutists and probably gliders. The Air Staff calculated that 5,000 paratroops attacking seven airfields in southern England could temporarily paralyze air defenses, and then bombers could pave the way for 20,000 troops landing with armored vehicles.

Measures were taken to prevent planes or gliders from landing. The army put obstacles on commons and cricket fields. Everything was done to frustrate paratroops. Road signs were taken down, as were signs at railroad stations, and even some shop signs which gave the location, all making life difficult for travelers. People were instructed to immobilize their cars when they were not driving them by removing the rotor arm of the distributor. If police found a car that was not demobilized they might deflate the tires and fine the owner. Car radios were banned —

they could be used as transmitters — and so was carrying a radio in a car.

It was assumed that fifth columnists would play a part in the attack. No less a person than the Dutch foreign minister gave credence to the myth that German troops had descended from the skies over Holland disguised as monks, nuns, and nurses. People were told constantly to be on the alert for anything unusual. Everyone now had to carry an identity card, and anyone who hesitated to show his to a policeman might be arrested on suspicion.

The authorities decided that the ringing of church bells would be the signal that an invasion had begun, so church bells were silenced. If the message "Cromwell" went out to military units, it meant that an invasion fleet was on its way or had landed.

The government produced leaflets with instructions, which were carried in the newspapers. Mindful of the difficulties caused in France by refugees clogging the roads, the government urged people not to take to the roads if invasion came but to stay put.

One leaflet said encouragingly: "Remember that if parachutists come down near your home they will not be feeling at all brave. They will not know where they are, they will have no food, they will not know where their companions are." It went on with instructions:

> Do not give the German anything. Do not tell him anything. Hide your food and your bicycles. Hide your maps. See that the enemy gets no petrol. If you have a car or a motor bicycle put it out of action when not in use. It is not enough to remove the ignition key; you must make it useless to anyone except yourself.
>
> The time may come when you will receive orders to block roads or streets in order to prevent the enemy from advancing. Never block a road unless you are told which one you must block. Then you can help by felling trees, wiring them together or blocking the road with cars. If you keep your heads you can also tell whether a military officer is actually British or is only pretending to be so. If in doubt ask a policeman or the A.R.P. warden, or use your common sense.

Another leaflet urged resistance: "The Government has always expected that the people of these islands will offer a united opposition to an invader, and that every citizen will regard it as his duty to hinder and frustrate the enemy and help our own forces by every means that ingenuity can devise and common sense suggest."

People were having to think how they would behave in circumstances that seemed almost unimaginable. One woman in a country village, the wife of an Auxiliary Fire Service officer with a new baby and a three-year-old son, wrote in her diary: "I pictured myself with my young baby in my arms and Michael beside me trying to fulfil what was asked of me in the leaflet about invasion, e.g., refusing water to the enemy, and the obvious result, and wondering how it would help my country to make my children motherless."

The writer Rebecca West fairly burned with patriotic zeal when she gave a stern admonition to her fellow countrymen in an article in the magazine *Time and Tide*. "Don't give way to fear," she instructed them, even if friends were killed and homes destroyed.

> It might be worse. It would be much worse, to take one possibility, if we behaved badly . . . We should all of us go to our doors and say to ourselves, "If the village were set on fire, I should be inclined to run away along that road. I must not do that if there are German troops on that road, for then our troops and aircraft might be afraid to bombard it. Even if there is no other way, I will not go along that road." The problem will differ in every locality; but we must always find a like solution. Otherwise we will be as dangerous as cowards and traitors.

• • •

Soon after the attack on France began, War Minister Anthony Eden announced the formation of a force of Local Defense Volunteers. "Men of reasonable physical fitness and a knowledge of firearms" who were willing to take part were asked to report to local police stations. The first volunteers arrived as the broadcast finished. Churchill, with his feel for words, changed the name to Home Guard. This became the civilian defense force that would face an invasion. Young men waiting to join the army, old soldiers happy to be shouldering a rifle again, civilians exempt from conscription because they were engaged in defense work or agriculture eager to play a part, all volunteered. There were 250,000 within twenty-four hours and 2.5 million within a few weeks.

They were to supplement the regular forces, each unit operating in its own locality. Their task was said to be to guard utilities, freeing up regular army units for training, prevent an enemy from using the roads, and possibly be the first on hand to meet invaders from the sea or air or fifth columnists. From the first days, they carried out guard duties and patrolled beaches and moorland.

Home Guard units were raised locally, with a minimum of direction from above. The author Charles Graves recounts the formation of a Home Guard unit in the village of Wilmington, which began with a meeting in the village pub.

> There were shepherds, farm hands, gardeners, village shopkeepers, a retired civil servant from India, a retired schoolmaster and one or two folk who worked in London and had cottages in downland. We held a subsidiary meeting at another village over the hill. Men came in from their work in the fields, and we stood around a farm wagon in a farmyard and discussed things and elected a local section leader, calling him corporal. Communications were the difficulty so we went to the big house of a local colonel to get him to agree to let us use his telephone. The corporal's wife (a maid there) could answer if need be.

Soon, every district had its Home Guard unit, in the countryside and in the cities, although there were no weapons for most of them. Members wore armbands identifying themselves, some issued by the War Office, some sewed by wives. Later they were issued khaki uniforms and steel helmets, and organized into platoons, companies, and battalions. The local commander was usually a retired army officer or a local figure high in the social hierarchy, a landowner or bank manager, but it might also be an old soldier from the ranks, and there was some mixing of the classes. A former ambassador to France, Sir George Clarke, joined his local unit and took orders from his butler, who had been a sergeant major in the regular army.

Some factories created their own units. The miners of South Wales, according to their union leader, had plans to blow up the pits if the Germans reached them and take to the hills "to fight German tanks with picks and shovels." The men of Bolshover Colliery designed an antitank gun to be made out of a boiler tube, and they were proud of their weapon and manufactured twelve. The Home Guard platoon based in the village of Farningham, Kent, provided evidence of the continuity of

English rural life. Seven members were descended from men who answered a muster to raise local levies to meet the danger of invasion from Spain in 1545; the names of these earlier volunteers are in a roll in the church.

The Fifth City of London (Press) Battalion consisted mostly of journalists and other newspaper workers. It was commanded by John Astor, the proprietor of the *Times,* who converted his Rolls Royce into an armored car. Americans in London formed what they called a "Mobile Defense Unit," which was a Home Guard company in all but name. It was organized by Charles Sweeney, a socialite and polo player, and commanded by retired brigadier general Wade Hayes, who had served in the Spanish-American War.

People were moving ahead of the authorities. The weekly magazine *Picture Post* carried a series of articles about irregular warfare by Tom Wintringham, a burly, bespectacled left-winger in his forties who had fought in the International Brigades in the Spanish Civil War. *Picture Post,* a large-circulation illustrated magazine started in 1938, was socially conscious, liberal, and frequently critical of the government. Following these articles and the readers' response, the editors started their own Home Guard school with Wintringham in charge. He believed in a people's army, and although he also believed in discipline, he said parade ground drill taught men "how to walk stiffly, stand up straight and be shot." They brought in as instructors a few people who had served with Wintringham in Spain, and also a scientist who was expert in explosives, the chief instructor of the Boy Scouts, and the surrealist artist Roland Penrose to advise on camouflage. "I am trying to do what I advise everyone to do — get on with the job of defense against invasion without waiting for official approval," Wintringham wrote.

The publisher of *Picture Post,* Edward Hulton, was a friend of the earl of Jersey, and the earl offered the use of his country estate, Osterley Park, outside London. "Could we dig weapon pits there?" Wintringham asked, thinking of the effect on the manicured grounds. "Loose off mines? Set fire to old lorries?" The earl said they could do anything that would be useful. So they taught people how to shoot, make their own explosives, make and plant mines, and decapitate a motorcyclist. The army first tried to close down the school on the ground that it was illegal, then took it over, retaining the staff.

The *Home Guard Training Manual* reflected the influence of the school. "The tasks you must carry out in cooperation with the army and the armed forces are, many of them, quite new to British military experience," it said. "No British road or street has had to be barricaded for centuries. No British subject living in Britain has had to be called upon to destroy an invader in our own countryside. Moreover, our army has not been trained for this sort of war. This means that the Home Guard offers you a real opportunity for adventure. We are faced with a menace. There are no answers in the older military textbooks. We are, in fact, in the same position as the militiamen in Republican Spain, or the Finnish soldiers in the war with Russia." It says something about the atmosphere of the time that a government pamphlet could tell people to look to the example of the Spanish people's militia, who represented a revolt against the hierarchical structure that characterized traditional armies in Britain as elsewhere.

Today the Home Guard are the subject of a comic TV series in Britain called *Dad's Army,* and some of them must sometimes have seemed a clownish lot. But they served a useful function from the first days, patrolling coastlines, moorland, and airfields and manning roadblocks, freeing soldiers for training. They were determined and made serious plans for defending their own part of the homeland to the death, devising homemade tank traps and barricades. Home Guard units were to play a part in the fire barriers that the army planned. The army lined some short stretches of roads near coastal areas with perforated pipes, instructing the local Home Guard on how to flood the roads with gasoline and set them alight. Some created a store of homemade Molotov cocktails. Vita Sackville-West wrote in her journal: "I had never thought to spend an afternoon filling old wine bottles with petrol, paraffin and tar and finishing them off with two of Messrs. Brock's gay blue squibs* bound tightly to the sides . . . This novel form of bottle party is conducted with the usual supply of English chaff and good humor. It is quite difficult to detect the underlying grimness."

Official advice was supplemented by suggestions in the press. In the *Daily Telegraph,* the favorite newspaper of country gentlemen, one letter writer suggested that tractors could be employed as gun platforms, another extolled the shotgun as a weapon — "A charge of shot through a parachute will rip up the material." Another, looking back to the cav-

---

* Brock's were leading manufacturers of fireworks.

alry, said armed horsemen were the answer: "I defy a dozen parachutists to get to their objectives cross-country if chased by a dozen volunteers well-armed and well-mounted." One letter from a writer who had seen the war in Holland contained a dash of harsh realism: "My conclusion is that men armed with rifles are no match at close quarters for an enemy firing machine guns."

The Home Guard were told to be constantly on the alert for fifth columnists, who might be found anywhere in any disguise. They were authorized to stop cars at night and demand anyone's identity cards. General Ironside, addressing a group of Home Guard commanders, told them, "My experience is that the gentlemen who are the best behaved and the most sleek are those who are doing the most mischief. We cannot be sure of anybody."

When you arm civilians and tell them to be suspicious of everyone, accidents are going to happen. Sometimes a driver failed to see a stop sign at night or ignored it, and sometimes anxious Home Guard sentries opened fire precipitately. Four people were killed by Home Guard sentries, one of them a young woman who was a passenger in a car that failed to stop, before the War Office tightened the rules about signaling and stopping cars.

Home Guard stories abounded. Charles Graves reports that one unit near his village found a man and a young woman in a parked car at night in a coastal area that had just been declared off-limits. They pulled them in and the Home Guard officer said to the man, "You've just been in a prohibited area." "Oh no he hasn't," the young woman snapped.

The secret resistance network that was set up to operate behind enemy lines in case the Germans conquered part of Britain developed differently. Created to practice the most unconventional kind of warfare, it was established in the conventional British way, its leaders recruited through the "old boy network" of social and professional ties, like the intelligence service of the time. Its commander was an intelligence officer, Colonel Michael Gubbins, a dapper, gentlemanly figure who had gained his spurs fighting the IRA in Ireland in 1920.

It was organized into cells of five or six men each, mostly civilians, many of them countrymen, farm workers, or poachers. They were trained in the arts of sabotage and assassination, operating in their home areas. Under Gubbins, these men trained with new weapons to be used behind enemy lines: plastic explosive, tire-bursting mines disguised as horse manure, a .22 caliber rifle with a telescopic sight that fired small, high-velocity bullets that could kill at a range of a mile, and a time pencil to detonate a bomb that had no moving parts and worked by acid.

These were called Auxiliary Units, and few people at the time knew of their existence. Members were instructed to resume their normal lives in the event of enemy occupation and carry out acts of sabotage and resistance. Women also were members, trained as radio operators. The only time Gubbins spoke about this, long after the war, he agreed that the activities of his resistance groups would have brought reprisals against civilians. "There had to be a cabinet decision there," he said. "There was nothing for it, we were facing total war."

No one has written more bitingly of Britain's class divisions than George Orwell, but of this period he wrote: "There are moments when the whole nation suddenly swings together and does the same thing, like a herd of cattle facing a wolf. There was such a moment, unmistakably, at the time of the disaster in France. After eight months of vaguely wondering what the war was about, the people suddenly knew what they had to do: first, to get the army away from Dunkirk, and secondly, to prevent invasion."

. . .

People were exhorted to adopt Spartan attitudes: to work hard producing what the nation needed, to forsake pleasure and put their country before their own concerns. The parliamentary secretary to the Ministry of Food, Robert Boothby, said hotels and restaurants should stop serving luxury meals. The minister of supply, Herbert Morrison, told the British people: "If we waste a minute at our desk or bench we sacrifice a life. If we put our personal rest or ease or comfort before the needs of the job we increase the risk of our own and our family's survival."

Engineering factories producing armaments worked flat out, in response to appeals from the government. Many summer holidays were canceled; the eleven-hour day and the seven-day week became the norm. An atmosphere of urgency prevailed, in aircraft production more than anywhere else under the dynamic leadership of the minister for aircraft production, Lord Beaverbrook. Beaverbrook inspired his managers with zeal, poached materials from other industries, and ignored civil service guidelines to produce more aircraft at whatever cost. These methods worked, but in the long run they would have caused industrial chaos. However, Britain needed aircraft to survive in the short run.

One Friday it emerged that there was a shortage of the fabric used for barrage balloons, which came under the aegis of aircraft production. On Beaverbrook's orders, police in cotton mill towns called at workers' homes on Saturday asking people to return to work, and notices were flashed on the screens at movie theaters. More than 90 percent of the cotton workers, mostly women, reported for work. One industrial reporter observed: "To meet men and women who had worked on special rush jobs continuously for thirty-six hours was a commonplace experience." However, working at this pace is counterproductive in the long run, and the minister of labor, Ernest Bevin, urged industry to limit the working week to sixty hours maximum.

There were constant exhortations. Grow food — "Dig for Victory." "Don't eat more than you need. You'll save yourself money; you'll save valuable cargo space which is needed for munitions; and you'll feel better than you've ever felt before." "Save and Mend," "Don't Be a Rumor-Monger," "Walls Have Ears." The accepted social pattern of the time was seen in one popular poster slogan on the "walls have ears" theme: "Be Like Dad. Keep Mum."

After years of unemployment and low wages, industrial workers welcomed the plentiful jobs and overtime pay. Some unions took advantage of the situation to make new demands. But people were conscious of their part in the war effort. The official economic history of the war, like the official military history, gives great importance to morale as a factor. Of the period beginning in the spring of 1940 it says: "The British people had been throughout the past winter too much detached from the war. Now they passionately attached themselves to it. This was the great transforming fact, the motive power of subsequent achievement."

Most people who could grew food, even if only in tiny back yards. Vegetables were planted in London's Hyde Park. Women knitted. Lord Beaverbrook started a "Spitfire fund" — £5,000 would pay for a Spitfire — and offices, factories, village communities, and even union branches raised money for the fund. One firm making metal office equipment evaded an official order to retool and make shells. The union representatives complained to the management, and when the management tried to buy them off with longer holidays, they wrote to their member of Parliament and got the ruling enforced.

That summer was a strange, possibly unique period in the British national experience. It was a time of heightened emotion and awareness of the common danger, the knowledge that great things were at stake in the outcome of events. One must make allowances for the tendency of memory to create narratives and dramatic structure, but it is clear from contemporary writings and observation that the sense of national danger gripped people and bound them together.

People did not live in a perpetual spirit of selflessness and high heroism. No doubt their predominant day-to-day concerns were with events in their own lives. But people invested much more than the usual amount of their individual thoughts and feelings into the collective psyche, and much of their energies into the collective effort. They felt and functioned, not only as individuals, but as part of a nation under threat. Like anxious members of a family, people listened to the news on the radio continually to check on the nation's condition. Fifty percent of people listened at least three times a day.

Many found in themselves an attachment to their country now that it was threatened that they had not known they felt. This is a theme that emerges often in diaries and letters written at the time.

Alfred Duff Cooper, the minister of information, wrote to a friend about flying back from Gibraltar: "As I looked down on the sea there suddenly was England under my eyes — Cornish fields, little white cottages, the coastguard stations, small roads running into coves by the sea. I was so foolishly moved, perhaps because it was unexpected. This passionate patriotism is, I suppose, rather nonsense, but so too I suppose is passionate love. I think I should die if we had to surrender."

Harold Nicolson, a member of Parliament, wrote in his diary: "I have always loved England, but now I am in love with England. What a people! What a chance! The whole of Europe humiliated except us. And the chance that we shall by our stubbornness give victory to the world."

The writer and onetime pacifist Vera Brittain, returning from a lecture tour in America in May, wrote in her journal: "No wonder men, and women too, are prepared to die in the service of this peaceful, patient country without enquiring too closely into the motives and methods of her government; to lay down their lives

> *. . . for some idea but dimly understood*
> *Of an English city, never built with hands,*
> *Which love of England prompted and made good."*

Duff Cooper, Vera Brittain, and Nicolson were far from typical. They all belonged to a particular stratum of British society — privileged, educated, humanist, with cultivated sensibilities. But there is ample evidence that their feelings of passionate patriotism were shared by others less articulate and less likely to put their sentiments in writing.

Many people even felt satisfaction in the fact that Britain stood alone, something which in any rational calculation could only be a cause for dismay if not despair. King George wrote to his mother: "Personally, I feel happier now that we have no allies to be polite to & pamper." A woman in Oxford wrote to friends in America: "Now we have got our expeditionary force back, we feel we are sharing the dangers here, and there is no one to let us down."

The American writer Clare Boothe was in Britain for some of that spring and summer. When she left in July an oil company executive drove her to the airport. She told him she did not understand the British. They did not seem to realize what they were facing.

He asked, "Do you think they'll take it when it comes?" She said, "Why yes, of course." "I mean really take it, from John o'Groat's to Land's End, until there's hardly an English home left standing or an Englishman left alive?" "You know, I think they will," she replied. "Then," he said, "you've found the only fact worth knowing here."

· · ·

On the Continent, governments accommodated themselves to the German victory. The Romanian government allied itself with the Axis, which guaranteed Germany access to Romanian oil, and the Hungarian government made friendly overtures. Some Dutch politicians who had fled the country returned to join a national unity government to serve under the German occupation. Sweden allowed German troops limited passage through Swedish territory. The president of Switzerland said on June 25 that the Swiss people should "adjust themselves to the new realities," and Switzerland closed its borders to Jewish refugees. Most French people accepted defeat and adjusted to life under the Vichy government or under the German occupation, finding that German soldiers were behaving properly and paying for things they bought.

The Soviet Union took advantage of the situation to occupy the three Baltic states of Estonia, Latvia, and Lithuania, confident that it would encounter no serious opposition, and seized the adjacent Romanian territory of Bessarabia.

Even some German-Americans felt strengthened by the German victories and found them a source of pride in their ethnic roots. In Chicago German-Americans organized a German Day picnic, and the German consul, Ernst Baer, spoke about the achievements of the German armed forces and was applauded. A new radio station in Hammond, Indiana, WHIP, began broadcasting Nazi propaganda programs.

The British government, and the American, were still worried about the French fleet. Despite the French promise that it would not be surrendered to Germany, it seemed possible that Germany might get control of it. The British government decided to take over all French warships within reach. Lord Lothian told Roosevelt of the plan; Roosevelt did not tell the State Department. Early on the morning of July 3, Royal Navy boarding parties seized the French warships in Portsmouth and Plymouth. In the Egyptian port of Alexandria, dominated by the British navy, the French admiral was compelled to demobilize his ships.

The most critical situation was at the Algerian port of Mers el-Kébir, or Oran. A sizeable French fleet was there including two of the world's finest battle cruisers, the *Dunkerque* and the *Strasbourg*. A British naval force sailed to Mers el-Kébir and presented the French admiral with an ultimatum: join the British, neutralize the ships, or else scuttle them, otherwise they would be taken by force. It was a painful step to take against a fleet that until a few weeks earlier had been an ally. The British vice admiral on the spot recommended that force be avoided at all costs, but he was overruled by the government.

The ultimatum was rejected. The British ships attacked, the largest French warships were sunk or put out of action, and some one thousand French sailors were killed. Five ships escaped and sailed to unoccupied France. Churchill regarded the attack as a tragic necessity, and when he announced it to Parliament he was fighting back tears. The Vichy government was furious and broke off diplomatic relations with London.

Churchill made the point in his war memoirs that the action produced a profound impression abroad and showed that Britain "feared nothing and would stop at nothing" in this struggle. It seems that this was an important consideration. Certainly it was hailed in Washington as evidence of British resolve. President Roosevelt told the French ambassador that even if there was a remote chance that the fleet would come under German control Britain was right to act as it did. Senator Key Pittman, the chairman of the Foreign Relations Committee, said: "Every member of the Senate approves Churchill's course and applauds his courage in preventing the use of the French Navy by Hitler. It was the fear that this step would not be taken that shook the confidence of some as to the power of British defense."

The Royal Navy, although still the largest in the world, was stretched thin. Nine destroyers had been sunk during the Dunkirk evacuation and twelve others put temporarily out of action; its destroyers had to patrol the invasion coast, face the Italians in the Mediterranean, and escort convoys. Arthur Purvis, the head of the British purchasing mission in America, asked Morgenthau on June 5 whether Britain could have the aging destroyers it had asked for earlier, and Morgenthau asked Roosevelt. Roosevelt said, "There's a slight ray of hope. The trouble is with Admiral Stark." He said Stark, the chief of naval operations, had told congressmen that he needed all these destroyers. Purvis, a Scottish-Canadian businessman, former president of Canadian Industries Ltd., was dedicated to his mission for the British government and was establishing good personal relations with Morgenthau and some other important people in Washington.

Roosevelt told Ickes that the ships would not be much use to Britain since they lacked antiaircraft firepower. He also indicated that he was uncertain about whether Britain would hold out. "We can't tell what turn the war will take," he said, "and there is no use endangering ourselves unless we can achieve some results for the Allies."

Churchill wrote to him about the heavy burden the navy was bearing. He went on: "We must ask therefore as a matter of life or death to be reinforced with these destroyers. We will carry on the struggle whatever the odds, but it may well be beyond our resources unless we receive every reinforcement, and particularly do we need this reinforcement on the sea."

Morgenthau read this letter and sent Roosevelt a memo saying: "Unless we do something to give the English additional destroyers, it seems to me it is absolutely hopeless to expect them to keep going."

King George added his voice. He wrote to Roosevelt on June 26 thanking him for a letter of encouragement sent eight weeks earlier, and then went on: "As you know, we are in urgent need of some of your older destroyers to tide us over the next few months. I well understand your difficulties, and I am certain that you will do your best to procure them for us before it is too late. Now that we have been deprived of the assistance of the French fleet — to put the least unfavorable interpretation on the present position — the need is becoming greater every day if we are to carry on our solitary fight for freedom to a successful conclusion."

Those fifty destroyers were becoming the crucial item of aid that America would or would not give, and a test of America's commitment.

Kennedy reported in a cable to Washington that there was a lot of anti-American feeling in Britain although Roosevelt personally was very popular. He said if the British were defeated, "they will never forgive us for not having come to their aid."

• • •

Many European powers had overseas territories, and those bits left over when their colonial rulers were conquered caused problems for Washington. The American republics had declared in Panama the previous November that they would not allow any territories in the Western Hemisphere to change hands, and this clearly applied to the French and Dutch islands in the Caribbean.

The French Caribbean island of Martinique was home to several French warships including the aircraft carrier *Béarn*, with 106 American-built planes which it had collected at Halifax. The British wanted the ships to go to British ports or join de Gaulle's Free French forces; America wanted them neutralized or the planes turned over to Britain; Germany threatened the French with "grave consequences" if the ships and planes were surrendered. For a time both British and American warships hovered off Martinique.

The U.S. Navy prepared a plan to land marines, and Cordell Hull warned the French ambassador that the situation was serious. Rear Admiral John W. Greenslade was sent from Washington to talk to the French high commissioner on the island, and he warned him that any French warships that tried to leave would be sunk. Eventually, the French agreed to demobilize the ships and allow a limited American presence in exchange for American help for the island.

Greenland, the huge island inhabited by a small number of Inuits, belonged to Denmark, which was now under German occupation. The State Department declared that on its maps Greenland was in the Western Hemisphere and so came under the Monroe Doctrine, and presumably the Panama declaration. To underline the point, after the Germans seized Denmark, America established a consulate in Greenland and sent a Coast Guard ship from time to time. Britain landed troops in Iceland, which also came under the Danish Crown, when Germany occupied Denmark.

Lothian, in an address to Yale alumni, gave the American public the warning about the British fleet that Churchill had given Roosevelt in private. "Let me be blunt," he said. "Many people in the United States believe that somehow or other, even if Great Britain is invaded and overrun, the British Navy will cross the Atlantic and will still be available through Canada or otherwise as part of your own defensive system. I hope you are not building on that expectation. If you are, you are building on an illusion."

He was equally blunt before a much larger audience when he was asked in an interview on NBC radio what would happen if Britain were defeated. "Then both your prospects and ours are very bad," he said. "You have not got an army or an air force of modern size and you have only one navy for two oceans. Hitler will then have double if not treble the ship-building and aircraft capacity you have."

Roosevelt, who tended to think of geostrategy in naval terms, hankered after bases in the British West Indies to extend American control in the Atlantic, all the more so as the possibility arose that Britain might be defeated. He had told King George this during the king's visit the previous year. A keen sailor until he was crippled by polio, he had sailed in those islands and swum from their beaches. When he discussed the subject with Hull, Hull was amazed at his intimate knowledge of the islands and their harbors.

At that time, the American navy, with its limited resources, was making very little use of the bases it already had in the Caribbean. There were few naval facilities either on Puerto Rico or at Guantanamo Bay, Cuba, and no dry dock facilities between Charleston and the Panama Canal.

Lothian was aware that Roosevelt wanted bases in the West Indies, and he suggested that the British government offer them to him. The British cabinet discussed this. Halifax thought the idea should be considered. "The aim should surely be to assist America in the task of assuming a new and heavy responsibility for which so little in her tradition and history has prepared her," he said, showing the handing-on-the-torch attitude and patronizing tone that characterized much of the British aristocracy's thinking about America.

Churchill was against it unless there was a quid pro quo. He said America had given Britain practically no help in the war, and "now that they saw how great the danger was they wanted to keep everything that would help us for their own defense." Others were also opposed. Some said they should ask for the cancellation of the World War One debts in return. The cabinet asked Lothian what reason he had for thinking that if they did make the offer, "really substantial advantages would accrue to us." Lothian said he would not pursue the matter.

Germany's conquests seemed to embolden Japan, which was taking a more aggressive line in diplomatic exchanges, and raised the possibility that it might try to seize the Far East colonies of countries Germany had conquered — French Indochina and the Dutch East Indies (Indonesia today) — and perhaps British colonies also. Most of America's rubber and tin came from the East Indies and Malaya. The administration had moved its Pacific fleet from San Diego to Hawaii the previous year, sending a message to Japan that it meant business. It decided to keep it there. As Roosevelt said to Admiral Stark: "When I don't know where to move, I stay put."

Attitudes to the war in Europe were changing. In polls tabulated by the American Institute of Public Opinion, the percentage of people who favored more aid to the Allies shot up from 15 percent at the beginning of 1940 to 70 percent after the attack on Norway and to 78 percent after the attack on France and the Low Countries. Half of those questioned thought Germany would be a threat to the United States if it won the war in Europe, and 42 percent thought it would try to invade America.

On July 20, after the fall of France, 73 percent of respondents said America should do everything possible to help Britain except go to war. Most significantly, 37 percent now said it was more important to help Britain win than to stay out of the war. Far more people were willing to take measures to halt Germany than to halt Japan.

Three academics working on public opinion wrote an article in *Public Opinion Quarterly* analyzing these results. The group they defined as isolationist was reduced by half its early summer size. The biggest shift was in the Rocky Mountain states; more people from small towns had joined the interventionist camp. Young people were more ready than their elders to say that the war was a purely European matter, and particularly young people in the upper-income group. In this group, 30 percent of people under thirty were ready to call themselves isolationist, but only 17 percent over fifty. In the lower-income group, the figures were 22 percent and 34 percent.

A public-opinion analyst, Hadley Cantril, thought young people in the upper-income group were looking after their own future. Writing in *Public Opinion Quarterly* he said: "These young people are well aware that they would have a good deal to lose by active intervention. Not only would they have to fight on what they now regard as the losing side, but, unlike the less fortunate members of their generation, they would have to give up the relatively bright futures which loom ahead for them in a country that remains at peace." This was not the view that was generally taken of college students opposed to the war, who were thought to be motivated by idealism more than selfish concerns.

∎ ∎ ∎

Britain had an asset that became increasingly important as the war went on, the existence of which was only disclosed thirty years after the war ended (Churchill did not mention it in his history of the war). With the help of Polish intelligence, the British had acquired the basic German military coding machine, called Enigma. Using Enigma, they were learning to decode German military and naval messages, which they could intercept when they were sent over the air waves. A Victorian country mansion at Bletchley Park, in central England, became the headquarters of the operation, and eventually hundreds of people, men and women, intelligence specialists, linguists, mathematicians, crossword enthusiasts, and other puzzle solvers, would be working there on decoding everything that elements in the German armed forces were saying to each other.

This decoding was so secret that it was given the name "Ultra" standing for ultrasecret, more secret than top-secret. Very few of the military commanders who were receiving reports on German activities from Ultra knew where they were coming from. They were only said to be from "a reliable source."

On July 16, the Bletchley Park decoders picked up an order from Hitler to his armed forces. It said: "As England, in spite of the hopelessness of her position, has so far shown herself unwilling to come to any compromise, I have decided to begin to prepare for, and if necessary carry out, an invasion of England." Any doubts that Churchill and the Chiefs of Staff had about whether they would have to prepare for an invasion were removed with this message. They also learned the code name for the invasion plan: Operation Sea Lion.

Some people suggested after the war that Hitler never really intended to invade Britain, that he was bluffing to try to persuade Britain to surrender. The phrase "if necessary, carry out" made the invasion plan conditional. It denoted hesitancy, possibly even reluctance, something far from the aggressive vigor which characterized Hitler's other military orders. He had ordered the demobilization of thirty-five army divisions, which did not indicate the intention to engage in a major campaign. Hitler's navy chiefs warned of the dangers.

Nonetheless, during July and August German military chiefs worked out plans for Operation Sea Lion. Troops and tanks were to land at two points on the southeast coast, paratroops were to drop north of Dover, and a bridgehead fifteen miles deep was to be established before pushing on. Ships and barges were on the move through the rivers and canals of Europe toward the English Channel ports, and troops were being assembled.

Plans were drawn up to administer conquered Britain. There was a list of people to be arrested. Able-bodied males were to be sent to Germany for forced labor. Dissent was to be suppressed ruthlessly. Even two years later, at the Wannsee conference of Nazi officials, when plans

Prime Minister Neville Chamberlain had a promise of peace from Hitler.

President Roosevelt and Cordell Hull, though smiling here, worried that approaching war clouds threatened America.

Children were evacuated from Britain's cities to keep them safely away from the expected air raids.

A trawler loaded with troops heads out of the burning port of Dunkirk.

With America facing a world in crisis, Roosevelt wanted bipartisan support for his foreign policy and thus took Frank Knox (*above*) into his cabinet as navy secretary and (*below*) Henry Stimson as secretary of war, seen here with General George Marshall.

"Very Well, Alone."
Cartoon by David Low
in the *Evening Standard*,
June 1940.

German planes attacking
ships in the English Channel.

Winston Churchill
with Lord Halifax,
who wanted to
consider a compromise
peace with Hitler.

The government prepared the British people for invasion, a possibility they had not had to face before.

"If the invader comes." A Home Guard unit trains on a factory roof.

A German bomber over the London docks, photographed from another bomber.

IMPERIAL WAR MUSEUM, LONDON

The target: London's riverside ablaze.

STOP HITLER NOW!

A message for Americans from the White Committee.

Antiwar demonstrators carried their message to the White House.

FRANKLIN D. ROOSEVELT LIBRARY

Charles Lindbergh urged America to stay out of the European conflict.

Raiders approaching! RAF fighter pilots race to their planes.

For many Londoners, subway stations became bomb shelters.

Wendell Willkie campaigning. His surprise nomination meant that Roosevelt was free to help Britain.

As you know, we are in urgent need of some of your older destroyers to tide us over the next few months. I well understand your difficulties, and I am certain that you will do your best to procure them for us before it is too late. Now that we have been deprived of the assistance of the French Fleet - to put the least unfavourable interpretation on the present position - the need is becoming greater every day if we are to carry on our solitary fight for freedom to a successful conclusion.

I am
Yours very sincerely
George R.I.

King George VI asked for destroyers in a private letter to President Roosevelt.

After transfer of the destroyers, American sailors showed the workings of the guns to the men who would soon be using them.

were drawn up for the "final solution," the extermination of European Jewry, British Jews were included in the tabulation (and those of Eire).

What did Hitler intend? In a system of cabinet government one would seek the answer by looking at different opinions and counting votes. Since the decision rested entirely on one man, any divisions existed only in the one man's mind. It is unlikely that the movement of ships and troops was simply a bluff and that he had no intention of invasion. It is more likely that he intended to invade but felt less than determined.

He offered Britain peace as an alternative to invasion. Several emissaries dropped private suggestions in neutral countries that Hitler was willing to make peace with Britain on the basis of being given a free hand on the Continent and some changes in the British cabinet. Then, three days after his order to his armed forces to prepare for invasion, Hitler offered peace publicly. This came at the end of a long speech blaming the war on others and paying tribute to the German armed forces.

There was no mention of what might be the peace terms, but Hitler said that if the war continued, "a great empire will be destroyed, an empire which it was never my intention to destroy or harm." He went on: "This struggle, if it continues, can end only with the complete annihilation of one or the other of the two adversaries. Mr. Churchill may believe this will be Germany. I know it will be Britain. I feel it to be my duty before my own conscience to appeal once more to reason and to common sense in Britain as much as elsewhere. I consider myself in a position to make this appeal since I am not a vanquished foe begging favors but the victor, speaking in the name of reason. I see no reason why this war need go on." This sounded so reasonable that Hitler was sure that Britain would accept.

In Washington, Lothian was in contact with the German embassy's chargé d'affaires through an American Quaker, Malcolm Lovell. Lothian showed that he still retained some of the attitudes of appeasement. He telephoned Halifax entreating him not to reject the peace offer out of hand, because he knew the terms and they were reasonable. Halifax and the cabinet ignored Lothian's entreaty and instructed him to have no further contact with the German embassy.

Churchill gave the task of rejecting the offer to Halifax, who had earlier been ready to consider a compromise peace. Halifax did so in a broadcast saying Britain would never accept the Nazi conquests. The Germans dropped leaflets with English translations of Hitler's speech over southern England. People collected these and auctioned them to collect money for the Red Cross.

Ultra picked up and passed on other orders about invasion plans, for the requisitioning of motorized barges and the assembling of air and sea transport at the channel ports. Spitfires modified as reconnaissance aircraft, stripped of their guns for speed and equipped with cameras, flew over these ports almost daily. Their photographs showed a buildup of forces there.

In order to invade Britain Germany first had to gain command of the air, and this meant defeating the Royal Air Force. The RAF was conceived as a bomber force. Its raison d'être when it was established as an independent service was its ability to strike at an enemy's homeland. Bombers, the RAF believed, could win a war. But in the summer of 1940, it was the RAF's fighter planes that stood between Britain and defeat.

The head of the RAF Fighter Command was Air Chief Marshal Sir Hugh Dowding. Nicknamed "Stuffy," he was an austere, remote figure, very different in temperament from most of the young pilots he commanded, but they looked up to him. He was thirty-one when he joined the Royal Flying Corps in 1913, and he was due to retire in July and had been asked to stay on only at the beginning of the month. Dowding believed in his mission above all else. He had argued doggedly for more fighters and more pilots. He had argued against sending them to France; he thought their sole purpose should be to defend the homeland.

Since the French collapse the German air force had been moving aircraft, fuel, and ground staff into airfields in northern France and Belgium. Luftwaffe chief Hermann Göring moved his regally appointed headquarters train, with its movie theater, dining car, and wine collection, to Beauvais, thirty miles from the English Channel, so that he could direct personally the air assault on Britain. By the second week of July, the Luftwaffe was ready to begin the attack.

Germany had 1,480 bombers, including dive bombers, and 980 fighters on the coasts facing Britain. The RAF had available 900 fighters, but it could put only 600 or at most 700 in the air at any one time. It was outnumbered. Germany wanted to destroy Fighter Command. The

Luftwaffe wanted the air battles to be fighter against fighter. The RAF wanted to avoid German fighters and to make the air battles fighter against bomber.

Britain was producing aircraft faster than Germany; under Lord Beaverbrook, the aircraft industry produced 1,200 fighter planes in the three months after May 10, more than twice the number in February, exceeding the RAF's expectations by one-third. German industry was still not geared completely to the war effort and was producing only 156 planes a month. (Beaverbrook's son Max was a fighter pilot. As one of Beaverbrook's biographers observed, father and son were both engaged in changing the imbalance between the British and German air forces.)

In the week that France surrendered, a senior civil servant was heard to say reflectively, "It may well be that the continued existence of this country depends on a few thousand pink-cheeked young airmen."

The fighter pilots were almost all under twenty-five as a matter of policy. Some were regular RAF. Some had come from the Auxiliary RAF, weekend fliers in peacetime. This had a social cachet; most members had a private school background and many came through the university air squadrons. They had a dashing image, young men with fast sports cars, driving up to London for a night's leave to go to their favorite bars and night clubs; for many their unofficial uniform included a flying jacket with red silk lining and a silk scarf. Alan Henderson recalled, "One of the best reasons for choosing to be a fighter pilot was that you were only shit-scared for forty minutes at a time. The other was that we were the kings of everything. Girls were flinging themselves at you all the time."

Other pilots came from the Volunteer Reserve, which was established in 1936 to swell the ranks, civilians who did most of their training on weekends. Most of these did not come from a privileged background and could not afford cars. Most were not commissioned and became sergeant pilots. J. E. "Johnny" Johnson, as a twenty-one-year-old graduate with an engineering degree, tried to join the Auxiliaries in 1938, but his interviewer lost interest in him when he said he did not go fox hunting. He joined the Volunteer Reserve and rose to be a wing commander. They were segregated socially although they were flying the same missions. The sergeant pilots were supposed to eat in a different mess and live in different quarters, although in practice this was often not possible where an airfield was thrown up hastily with minimum facilities. Class distinction existed alongside the natural camaraderie of flying men sharing the same dangers.

More than half flew Hawker Hurricanes. These planes were not quite as fast as Germany's best fighter, the Messerschmitt 109, but they were resilient, able to fly after suffering a lot of damage, and therefore easy to repair. The Supermarine Spitfire was the RAF's favorite plane — "beautiful" was a word pilots often used about it. It was the fastest war plane in the air with a top speed of 355 miles per hour, and very maneuverable, although the ME109 had the edge in altitude. Another fighter in use was the two-man Defiant, with no forward guns and a heavy rear turret, but this was no match for the German fighters. Nor was the Blenheim light bomber, adapted as a fighter to try to make up the deficit.

The German air force, because of its commitment to aid ground operations rather than operate independently, did not have long-range heavy bombers. Its biggest, a Dornier, carried a bomb load of 2,200 pounds, less than the B-17 and much less than the heavy bombers the British were building. Of its two principal fighters, the Messerschmitt 109 was almost as fast as the Spitfire; the twin-engined Messerschmitt 110 was not as fast but still formidable. Both were limited in the fuel they could carry, which normally allowed them to spend only half an hour over Britain.

Radar was more developed in Britain than anywhere else. When bombers were expected to fly from Germany, a journey of several hours, it was important. When they were coming from just across the channel, minutes from the British coastline, it was the difference between victory and defeat. An official history explained: "Where the speed of an enemy's advance was reckoned in hundreds of miles an hour rather than ones or tens, the time left for decision would be very short; and only the information provided by the radar chain could help them decide swiftly and correctly. If the oracle spoke clearly and was understood, they might win with their six or seven hundred fighters; if it failed them or if it mistook their message, then defeat was almost certain."

A Spitfire or Hurricane could only remain in the air for an hour or so. If too few were sent up to meet enemy bombers, they would be outnumbered in battle. If too many were sent up, or if some were sent to the wrong place, they could be back on the ground refueling when a large enemy force of bombers came over. Much depended on ground commanders making the right decision quickly.

Radar was principally the work of Robert Watson-Watt, a British scientist, later knighted for his contribution. In the 1930s, with RAF backing, he built a device which detected aircraft seventy-five miles out at sea. By the summer of 1940 there were twenty scanners along the south and southeast coast linked to RAF stations. Radar could spot enemy aircraft when they were still over France.

The radar posts were backed up by the Royal Observer Corps, civilians serving part-time, stationed at lookout posts, each equipped with a pair of binoculars, an aircraft identification manual, and a telephone line leading directly to an RAF base. These were important in tracking the path of enemy aircraft across Britain, where they were no longer visible on radar.

Dowding developed a system of what in today's military terminology would be called command and control. His headquarters was an underground plotting room in a country mansion south of London called Bentley Priory, the ancestral home of the marquess of Abercorn, which had been turned into a hotel. Dowding divided responsibility for British air space among four groups, and within these there were sector stations each controlling a smaller area. All information about incoming aircraft came to Bentley Priory. From there it was passed on to the group controllers and the sectors, who would make the decisions on how many planes to scramble and where to send them.

In operations rooms, WAAFs — members of the Women's Auxiliary Air Force — would move counters around a board showing the positions of British and German aircraft like croupiers in a casino, and the controller would give them their instructions, putting them on course to meet the enemy. "Vector" was the term used — "You're vectored at 230 degrees" or "at angels eighteen," which meant at 18,000 feet. "Bandits" were enemy planes. "Tally ho!" was what the pilot said going into the attack. The lone pilot up was never really alone. He would be guided on to an enemy force, and with any luck guided back home again, by a controller who was himself a pilot and understood the situation of the man in the sky.

It was not always exact. Radar sightings were not precise; the operators could make a mistake about the number of planes or — and this very often — the altitude. Nearly half the time pilots were sent up after enemy planes they did not make an intercept. Sometimes it was a false alarm and there were no enemy planes, sometimes they missed them. When intercepts did not work out and pilots found themselves in empty sky, they tended to blame the operations officers. "Instead of thinking about plotting the fuckers, they're thinking about fucking the plotters," went one crack. This was usually unfair, but lives were at stake and feelings ran high.

• • •

The first serious attacks came in July. Groups of five or six bombers attacked convoys in the English Channel and five south coast ports. Ocean shipping had already been transferred from the south coast to west coast ports, partly to put it farther away from the newly established submarine bases on the French Atlantic coast, but British industry relied on the transport of coal and other essentials by coastal shipping. The Germans attacked military targets, including aircraft factories, but these were situated in or near towns.

This was the start of what historians, using Churchill's terminology, call the Battle of Britain, the struggle for control of the air space over Britain. If Germany won the battle, its bombers could pave the way for an invasion force unimpeded, or else its air force would be able to bomb Britain continually, which, combined with a blockade, would bring it to its knees.

Historians generally give July 10 as the opening date, but the attacks were building up in the week before that. On the morning of July 10, radar reported that German planes were up over the French coast, and six Hurricanes went up to meet them. They saw the German bombers and fighters stacked in three tiers "like the Eiffel Tower," one pilot said. They were twenty Dornier bombers with ME109s and 110s above. The Hurricanes were still climbing when they were told that the convoy was already being bombed so they attacked immediately, ignoring the heavy odds. They shot down three German planes and had no losses. One small ship was lost. First blood went to the RAF.

Hitler had ordered the Luftwaffe to attack the RAF but ordered that "before everything, the inflicting of great damage on the civilian population must be avoided." People in the towns that were being bombed did not know this, and would probably not have believed it had they been told.

In the weeks that followed, the sound of sirens, the thud of bombs, the sight of buildings reduced to rubble and houses with the sides ripped out, the sense of fear, all became familiar in southern and eastern England. People learned to take to the public shelters, and air raid wardens were no longer something to joke about. Sixty-two people were killed in raids on Norwich and Southend. In Chatham, the site of a naval base, members of four generations were killed in a house by a single bomb. In nearby Medway, an eighteen-year-old Boy Scout leader, Donald Jones, crawled into a bombed house and lay with his body shielding the upturned faces of two trapped men from bits of falling rubble and dirt for four hours while rescuers dug the wreckage away; he was awarded a medal for bravery and the Boy Scout Silver Cross.

A German pilot parachuted out of a burning Messerschmitt to become the first German airman captured on British soil. He presented himself to a tractor driver plowing a field, who said, "Well you'd better come with me," and took him home. His wife made the German a cup of tea while he called the police.

Another German pilot shortly after this was wounded when he came down and was treated on the spot by a paramedic. The sight provoked a conversation among two women watching, which an observer recorded:

FIRST WOMAN: "Poor boy. You can't help feeling sorry for him."

SECOND WOMAN: "Can't you? What do you think he came here for, except to bomb and machine gun some people like you and me and perhaps our children."

FIRST WOMAN: "He was only carrying out orders, and after all, he's some mother's son."

SECOND WOMAN: "Look here. I've got a boy in the army, and I'd rather see him in his grave than doing the kind of thing that young Nazi there has been taught to do. Although of course he would never be ordered to do it."

Bombing civilians was still something of a novelty back then.

A local reporter recorded an event in the town of Havering near the mouth of the Thames:

One man thought he heard an unexploded bomb fall in his back garden but was too frightened to look, so he sought advice from the nearest air raid warden. The warden, believing it to be in the next district, disclaimed all responsibility for the bomb and told him to go to the Town Hall. There he was told that they did not deal with unexploded bombs and he should go to the Auxiliary Fire Service for help. They thought it fell under the jurisdiction of the police and so he dutifully sought their assistance. They in their turn thought it a job for the military authorities, who fortunately accepted that the matter fell within their province.

It turned out that there was no bomb. The reporter concluded: "The civil defense organization should not yet be accorded the label of a well-oiled machine that subsequent sustained bombing helped it achieve."

The fighter squadrons were now permanently on the alert, the young men living in their flying suits on the tarmac, ready to rush to their planes when the alarm sounded, what they called the "scramble," and be off the ground within minutes, trying to gain height before the enemy planes were over the coast. Their airstrips were often a farmer's field hastily converted, their living quarters a hut or even, in the first weeks, a tent.

It was a strange life for these young men in their late teens and early twenties, some of them only recently out of school. Most days they were in combat; most days one or more among them was missing, sometimes to turn up after parachuting down, perhaps into the channel, sometimes not. In the evenings there were sometimes riotous parties in the mess, at which WAAFs stationed on the base were much in demand. Or there would be schoolboyish games — rugby using a cushion as the football, or wrestling. They developed their own folkways. The pilots always wore the top buttons of their tunics undone. They displayed a marked disrespect for formal discipline. Battle, narrow escapes, achievements, were all recounted, if at all, in an off-hand way. Understatement was their style. Anything that sounded dramatic or could be interpreted as verging on the boastful — "shooting a line" — exposed the perpetrator to hoots of ridicule.

The RAF's basic operating unit was the squadron, consisting of twelve planes. When combat was taking place almost daily, a squadron needed eighteen planes if it was to have twelve ready to fly. There were always repairs to be done on the others, sometimes bullet holes to be patched up, sometimes just wear and tear.

The pilots learned quickly about the war in the air that was beginning. They had been taught how to attack bombers from the rear but not about the fighter escorts. But the German bombers always had fighter escorts. Squadron Leader James Leathart recalled in exasperation: "All our attack practice had been designed for us to meet unescorted bombers. There had been years of a complete bloody waste of time. We had to learn from scratch." They had been taught to fly in three-plane V-formations. A squadron would consist of four of these Vs. But soon some squadron leaders found that trying to keep in formation was distracting when the enemy was approaching and abandoned the V-formation. The most important thing was to keep alert and keep watching on all sides — "Watch for the Hun in the sun," pilots were told.

The eight machine guns on the wings of Spitfires and Hurricanes were placed so that their fire converged at 650 yards. This gave a spread and it was good for the pilot who was not such a good shot. The aggressive fighter pilot with the killer instinct, like the aggressive fighter in any combat, wants to get in close ("The nation that shortens its swords lengthens its boundaries" was an old Roman military maxim). They adjusted their guns so that they converged at 450 yards or less.

The Germans also learned lessons. They learned that the Stukas were very vulnerable where there was fighter opposition and withdrew them after the first few weeks. They learned that the ME109 was the only fighter that matched the Hurricane and Spitfire in performance, and that bombers should ideally have three times as many fighters escorting them. The weakness of the ME109 was its short range; it could spend only twenty minutes in the target area, which limited the bombers also.

Air battles were fought over the channel almost daily. The Germans had organized air-sea rescue, which the British had not. They had Heinkel planes marked with a red cross and fast boats operating in conjunction with them to rescue downed pilots. The Air Ministry announced that the red cross would not be respected because the German aircraft were being employed for other purposes, which, it was explained, meant reconnaissance, and RAF fighters shot down four rescue planes. Dowding said the planes should be intercepted because the pilots they rescued would go on to fight another day. This was logical, if harsh, and he followed the same logic in his attitude to pilots shot down over Britain. He said the Germans would be justified in shooting at RAF pilots as they came down by parachute since if they survived they would continue to fight, but German pilots should not be shot at since they would become prisoners of war. There were at least two instances where German planes shot and killed airmen as they came down, but it did not happen often.

At the end of July the assistant air attaché at the U.S. embassy in London, Captain Ben Kelsey, wrote an assessment of the situation of Britain and in particular of the RAF. It is worth quoting at length, both as an objective view and for the admiring tone, rare in a diplomatic dispatch.

It is apparent that this war is being fought on the basis of complete participation of every individual in the country in the war effort. The meaning of the phrase "total war" is that every action or thought of every individual has a bearing upon the outcome. This is now realized pretty generally throughout England although such realization apparently has occurred only in the last two weeks, that is, some time after the evacuation from Dunkerque. The possibility of immediate invasion has been a sufficient incentive to the general populace so that they are all cooperating to minimize the possible danger of such a move. There is no attitude of defeatism evident among the ordinary citizens or those elements of the fighting forces with which I came into contact . . .

Observations of the Royal Air Force indicate that the individual Royal Air Force pilots and commanders will not be beaten and will carry the struggle to the enemy regardless of the odds . . . The excellence of the R.A.F. training system and the quality of the product leads to the conclusion that the R.A.F. will continue to be stronger in every way.

There are innumerable examples of individual or unit activities in which the English pilot and crew have been able to counterbalance tremendous force on the other side. Taken alone, no one of these instances has a bearing on the final outcome. Taken collectively they indicate a point of view that is immediately apparent when contacting the operating units. That point of view is a sincere and enthusiastic entirely voluntary willingness to accomplish any mission and determination to complete such missions. In addition, there is a large measure of individual initiative exemplified . . . The general attitude of personnel in the R.A.F. is that they can successfully counterbalance opposition if not outnumbered by more than four or five to one, and with odds of one to three that they are superior.

Captain Kelsey concluded that the British had a good chance of defeating an invasion attempt, and like others, he cited the importance of morale:

> With the availability of all the resources of the R.A.F. for the counteraction of an attack on England, it is possible that such an attack would either be impossible or too expensive to be carried to a completely successful conclusion. It is difficult to explain the importance of the psychological attitude connected with the conduct of the war but one definitely obtains the impression that any thrust against England can be completely absorbed without upsetting the national will to carry on regardless of the extent of the material damage.

The German attacks were concentrated on the southeast corner of England, Dover and the towns nearby and the waters offshore. Half the population of Dover left. Defense headquarters were established behind the thick stone walls of the 700-year-old Dover Castle, from where observers could look through telescopes and see the boats moving about in the harbor at Calais.

As bombs crashed down on Dover one day, a World War One veteran serving with an AA battery said to Lieutenant Ray Rayner, "Sir, I'll eat my hat if that one wasn't a shell. I've heard plenty in my time and I know the difference." The Germans had begun shelling Dover with long-range guns on the French coast.

The whole area, in peacetime a popular place for seaside holidays, became known as hell-fire corner. Barrage balloons were brought in to protect Dover from air attacks. One day German fighters attacked them, shooting down five, and townspeople watched the deflated gas bags sink to the ground. Destroyers were withdrawn from Dover harbor.

Reginald Foster, a reporter for the London *Daily Herald,* watched with others at Dover harbor as a Hurricane and a Messerschmitt chased each other around until the German plane took a burst of gunfire and spiraled down in flames, and he wrote: "It seemed rather indecent to stand lamely on the ground and gaze at the efforts of two men about to give and avoid death. For us spectators, it is a grim thrill, but there's nothing one can do but stand and watch. It is quite beyond the control of human expectancy not to do so."

And watch they did. In Folkestone, twelve miles away, in peacetime a holiday town looking down on a popular beach, a chemist recalled: "Rumors would sweep through the town that a convoy of ships was going through and we'd all rush down to the front to watch. The atmosphere was just like a football match. We would cheer every time a German plane went down. Of course we didn't feel so pleased when one of ours was hit."

BBC reporter Charles Gardner threw away his prepared script one afternoon to give a running account: "There's somebody's hit — a German — and he's coming down, there's a long streak, he's coming down completely out of control, a long streak of smoke, ah, the man's bailed out by parachute, the pilot's bailed out by parachute, he's a Junker 87 and he's going slap into the sea and there he goes — *sma-ash!* . . . Oh boy, I've never seen anything as good as this! The R.A.F. fighters have really got these boys taped." Some listeners cheered at this broadcast but others found the reporting of a life and death struggle in sporting terms bad taste, and Gardner was told not to do it again.

The battles over the channel and over southern England went on intermittently through July and the first days of August. The Germans scored occasional victories, particularly when the attacks on the convoys were joined by motor torpedo boats. Convoys took to going through the channel at night only, but they were not stopped. Nearly a million tons of shipping passed through the channel in the following month, with the loss of only 30,000 tons. The RAF lost 150 aircraft, the Germans twice as many. Antiaircraft guns as well as British fighters took their toll. In this first phase of the battle, the Germans did not succeed in their aims.

American correspondents and British reporters gathered at Dover to watch the battles. They sat on the grass on top of the cliffs with their binoculars by day, frequenting the town's pubs in the evening.

Ben Robertson, a reporter for the liberal New York tabloid *PM*, came to Britain with a hostile attitude to the British Empire and no great affection for Britain, but he saw these battles overhead as battles for freedom as much as Lexington, Concord, and Gettysburg.

Vincent Sheean was also watching from the Dover cliffs, and he wrote later: "High in the wind and the sun, in the most brilliant summer weather for many seasons, we watched that assault in awe, conscious that the whole destiny of Mankind was in all probability being decided above our heads . . . There were times when an episode brought us to our feet with the constriction of the throat that might have been a cheer if it had dared — if it had dared run the risk of turning into a sob."

It was a dramatic time, and a dramatic place as well. The white cliffs of Dover have always had a symbolic significance as Britain's protective wall, the battlements of

> This fortress built by nature for herself
> Against infection and the hand of war . . .
> This blessed plot, this earth, this realm, this England.

Now the symbolic had become actual. As German planes roared overhead and German forces gathered on the opposite shore in preparation for an invasion, these steep chalk cliffs gleaming in the summer sunshine really were the ramparts over which Britain was defending itself. More than that, for many, they were the ramparts of democracy, of decency, of civilization itself against a threatening barbarism. The stark simplicity of the image, the high white cliffs and the dark seas pounding against them, seemed to mirror the simplicity of the national life-or-death struggle, and the moral simplicity of what was at stake.

8

PANZERS IN PHILADELPHIA

Roosevelt wanted some bipartisan participation in the administration's foreign policy making. The previous autumn he had offered the post of secretary of the navy to Frank Knox, the publisher of the *Chicago Daily News,* a Republican who supported all-out aid to the Allies. Knox had turned it down, saying that his disagreement with Roosevelt's domestic policies was too great. On June 18, Knox made a speech in Detroit calling for compulsory military training, vastly expanded defense expenditure, more aid to Britain, and cooperation with the British navy. It is indicative of the rapidity with which American thinking had changed that two months earlier, in a speech in Cleveland, Knox had said, "After our experience in the last war, it is simply unthinkable that we will ever again send overseas a great expeditionary force."

Roosevelt called him and again invited him to join his cabinet. He offered him the choice of the War or Navy Departments. Knox had turned down the offer of a cabinet post before, but he decided that in this crisis in world affairs he could not refuse to serve, and he chose the navy. However, he said he wanted to wait until after the Republican National Convention, which was to open in a few days. He wanted to attend the convention and fight against the isolationists in the party.

Roosevelt argued that the announcement of his appointment should be made before the convention. He said that if Knox attended the convention and an isolationist candidate was adopted, his joining Roosevelt's cabinet would be seen as the action of a disgruntled loser. If his candidate won the nomination, then he could hardly desert the candidate he had fought for by joining the administration. His joining the cabinet should be seen as an act of patriotism unaffected by party considerations. Knox accepted this argument. Roosevelt had already arranged for the present navy secretary, Charles Edison, to get the Democratic nomination for the governorship of New Jersey.

Knox, a native Chicagoan who began his working life as a reporter, had fought in the Spanish-American War in Theodore Roosevelt's Rough Riders. In World War One he enlisted as a private and rose to the rank of lieutenant colonel, and he was Alfred Landon's running mate in the 1936 election. He admired Theodore Roosevelt, and some said he modeled himself after him, with his fierce patriotism, his strong opinions, and even his ruddy complexion and bristling red hair.

That left the War Department. Roosevelt had to replace his secretary of war, Henry Woodring, who had tried to obstruct every move to get help to Britain. He did not like to sack anyone but he could find no way to ease Woodring into another post as he had Edison, so he simply asked him to resign.

Two people who were to influence events pressed him to offer the post to Henry Stimson. They were Felix Frankfurter, Supreme Court justice and advisor to presidents, and Grenville Clark, a lawyer and protegé of Frankfurter's. Roosevelt offered the post to Stimson, and he accepted.

Stimson, a lawyer and a vigorous man at seventy-two who still rode regularly, had been governor general of the Philippines and secretary of state under Hoover, where he closed down the department's codebreaking department saying, "Gentlemen do not read each other's mail." He was the son of a wealthy family and a graduate of Yale, where he was a member of the secret society Skull and Bones. He had long argued for opposition to fascism and aggression in Spain and China as well as France. The previous week he had spoken at the Yale commencement and urged help for Britain, to be sent in American ships if necessary.

Later, Roosevelt asked William L. White to help ensure that the two appointments were confirmed by the Senate. White asked South Carolina senator James F. Byrnes for a list of those who were doubtful on the issue, and then made sure through local chapters of his committee that when the appointments came up these senators were bombarded with telegrams from their constituents.

Stimson made several new appointments to the War Department, people he knew and who shared his background and outlook. Robert Lovell, another Wall Street banker, Harvey Bundy, who had worked with Stimson under Hoover, George Harrison, former president of the New York Federal Reserve Bank, and John McCloy, a Wall Street lawyer, all joined the War Department.

John Kenneth Galbraith said that the ideal American establishment figure would be a Republican called to service in a Democratic administration. Now there were to be a number of them. These were men who had known each other professionally and socially for many years and belonged to the same clubs. Including Stimson, four of them had been members of Skull and Bones at Yale, and five were graduates of the Harvard Law School. Along with Knox and James Forrestal, a Wall Street investment banker who was appointed navy undersecretary, they formed a Republican clique within a Democratic administration, but they could be counted upon to support a defense buildup and aid for Britain.

• • •

In the early summer, the American election scene was as full of uncertainties as the international scene. Presidential election campaigns then were shorter than today, and in the spring it was not at all clear who the candidates would be. Both parties had several potential candidates. In the Democratic Party, the figure of Franklin Roosevelt hovered over them all, for he had not yet said whether he would run for a third term.

Throughout the spring there were three main candidates for the Republican nomination. They all held similar views on America and the war. Ohio senator Robert Taft, although he was still a freshman senator, was a member of a distinguished Republican family and the embodiment of conservative Republican values, an opponent of the New Deal and of involvement in Europe's affairs. He said American entry into the war would be "even worse than a German victory." Michigan senator Arthur Vandenberg was the leading isolationist in the Senate — Borah had died of a brain hemorrhage in January. Thomas Dewey was the New York State attorney general who had acquired a national reputation for breaking up some big criminal gangs and had narrowly lost the New York gubernatorial race. He warned that Roosevelt wanted "to tie the future of the United States to the fate of Britain." Others were considered as outside possibilities, including newspaper publisher Frank Gannett and Pennsylvania governor Arthur James.

Until May, everyone had assumed that the campaign would focus on domestic issues, particularly the success or otherwise of the New Deal, but the Nazi victory in Europe changed that. Now the war was uppermost in people's minds. For the first time since 1916, foreign affairs were to be the key election issue.

The man who was to win the Republican nomination was the darkest of dark horses, an outsider who had not entered any of the primaries. His nomination was one of the most extraordinary events in American political history. Wendell Willkie was a registered Democrat in 1938 and only joined the Republican Party when he became the presidential candidate. He had never run for political office. He was an internationalist who favored all-out aid to the Allies, and his nomination both signified and accelerated a shift in national attitudes.

Willkie was a lawyer from Elwood, Indiana, his German-American father and his mother both lawyers, the fourth of six children in a bookish household. He was on the Indiana delegation to the 1932 Democratic National Convention, at which he supported Roosevelt's candidature. He moved to New York, joined a law firm representing utilities, and became president of the Commonwealth and Southern Corporation, a holding company that controlled six utilities. In this capacity he came into conflict with the Tennessee Valley Authority and New Deal legislation. He came to believe, as he said, that big government, and not big business, was the principal threat to freedom in America. He was never a primitive laissez-faire capitalist but always maintained that business must be socially responsible, and he approved of much of the New Deal's welfare legislation.

Willkie began to write articles and speak at public forums and on the radio. He was a particular success in a discussion program, *Town Meeting of the Air*. He was an attractive speaker, enthusiastic, witty, speaking his mind freely, a burly, disheveled figure with rumpled hair (Dewey was voted best-dressed man in America by the Merchant Tailors and Designers). Older than Dewey and Taft, Willkie somehow seemed younger.

He was married but was carrying on an affair fairly openly with Irita Van Doren, the literary editor of the *New York Herald Tribune* and divorced wife of the writer Carl Van Doren. She groomed him, introduced him to newspaper publishers and columnists, and urged him to consider himself a candidate. From the beginning of the year he began to cultivate journalists and to hone his off-the-cuff remarks.

But he refused to play it safe. He wrote a magazine article criticizing the courts and saying people had been victimized, and he named as victims two of the most unpopular figures in America, Earl Browder, the Communist Party secretary, and Fritz Kuhn, leader of the pro-Nazi German-American Bund. He once began an address to a group of supporters with the words "Fellow amateurs . . ." Dewey's campaign literature portrayed him as a model citizen, boy and man. Willkie's showed him as a bit of a rebel, getting into trouble as a boy, sassing cops.

He attracted followers and aroused enthusiasm. The managing editor of *Fortune* magazine, Russell Davenport, met him and told his wife Marcia, "I've just met the man who's going to be the next President of the United States. When you see him, you'll know." She met him and said he could charm a bird out of a tree. A well-connected New York attorney, Oren Root, began a campaign with a newspaper advertisement calling for support, and it snowballed. Willkie for President groups sprang up all over the country.

It may have been a grassroots campaign, but the seeds were scattered from on high. Davenport took a leave of absence from *Fortune* to become his campaign manager. Henry Luce and John and Gardner Cowles, powerful newspaper and magazine publishers, supported him. Thanks partly to Irita Van Doren, he acquired the backing of the *New York Herald Tribune,* and one of its editorial writers, Geoffrey Parsons, helped write some of his campaign speeches. People like Henry Luce and Ogden Reid, publisher of the *Herald Tribune,* may have been charmed by Willkie as Marcia Davenport was, but their support was more likely to stem from his views on the war. Stimson would have campaigned for him if he had not joined Roosevelt's cabinet.

Root told his cohorts, "Talk Willkie, breathe Willkie, live Willkie and we'll nominate him." They took him at his word and picked up his fervor, and the campaign to nominate Willkie took on the nature of a crusade. William H. Harman, vice president of an engineering company and president of the Pennsylvania for Willkie Club, told a reporter, "I regard this as a semi-religious movement, and we are trying to get it on a revival basis." An opinion poll showed Willkie's support among the Republican rank and file rocketing up from 3 percent on May 8 to 17 percent on June 12 and to 29 percent on June 20, the eve of the convention. He edged Taft out of second place, but still trailed behind Dewey, who had 47 percent of the support.

Taft wanted the Republicans to campaign as the peace party. The *Chicago Tribune* told delegates that the Republican Party should be "a peace party and not a lesser war party." But Willkie insisted: "Despite the views of the narrow isolationists, America does have a vital interest in the English, French and Norwegian way of life . . . We must send and keep sending aid to Britain, our first line of defense and our only remaining friend."

Many eyes were on Philadelphia on the eve of the Republican convention. The German embassy's propaganda chief, George Viereck, a pro-Nazi German-American, went to work with funding from the German embassy. On his advice an isolationist congressman from New York, Hamilton Fish Armstrong, invited fifty Republican isolationist congressmen to the convention to use their influence on the delegates; their expenses were paid. Fish published a full-page advertisement in six leading newspapers headed "Stop the March Towards War." The National Committee to Keep America Out of Foreign Wars also took out full-page ads urging the convention to adopt an anti-interventionist plank.

On the eve of the convention there was an outburst of press support. Henry Luce's *Time* magazine carried a three-page convention preview hailing Willkie. The *Saturday Evening Post,* published in Philadelphia, devoted much of its issue that week to Willkie. The *Herald-Tribune* carried a front-page editorial in support.

When the Drafting Committee met, the Foreign Affairs Subcommittee argued long after the other planks had been agreed upon. Alfred Landon was the chairman, and he proposed a policy plank of giving aid to the Allies but staying out of war. A group of isolationists headed by Senator Henry Cabot Lodge opposed the first part of this. Congressman Wayland Brooke of Illinois, who was one of the group, told reporters, "We spoke rather bluntly out there in the Middle West. We declared that the blood of America belongs to America even to the last drop, and should not be spilled in foreign wars."

The final statement was a compromise that tried to please everybody although the neutralist-isolationists lost out. It blamed Roosevelt for failing to build up U.S. defenses, said the party was "firmly opposed to involving this nation in foreign wars," but supported aid to people fighting for their freedom "consistent with international law and the needs of national defense."

The convention opened on June 21, sharing the front pages with France's capitulation. It was a wide-open convention, with, as the *Philadelphia Inquirer* said, "barely enough leadership to allow it to coagulate." One of the first items on the agenda, which was not planned, was the decision by Stimson and Knox to join Roosevelt's cabinet, announced the day before the convention opened. It infuriated party professionals, who saw it as a political ploy by Roosevelt to throw the party off balance, and this may not have been entirely absent from Roosevelt's thinking. Dewey denounced the appointments, saying, "It's not a coalition cabinet, it's a war cabinet." The chairman virtually expelled Stimson and Knox from the party.

The party leadership were against the Willkie candidature. When Indiana senator James Watson said it was not appropriate that one who had so recently been a Democrat should be the Republican standard bearer, Willkie said to him, "You're a member of a church council. If a reformed prostitute came to your church, wouldn't you let her in?"

"Certainly," Watson replied. "But I wouldn't invite her to lead the choir."

Thousands of Willkie supporters flocked to Philadelphia to carry their crusading spirit to the convention hall. While others dominated the floor, they crowded the galleries. They claimed theirs was the voice of the people against the politicians. "We want Willkie!" they chanted throughout the day, with such fervor that one reporter called it "a riot for Willkie." They badgered delegates night and day to vote for this man many of the delegates had not heard of two months earlier. A delegate sent a suit to the cleaners and it came back with a Willkie button in the lapel. One Minnesota delegate received a telegram from his doctor saying: "Operation successful stop Daughter doing well stop Drop Taft and vote for Willkie." Pro-Willkie telegrams poured into Philadelphia.

Congressman Sam Pryor of Connecticut, a Willkie supporter who headed the Arrangements Committee, gave preference to Willkie people, allowing them to pack the galleries. There were accusations of dirty tricks when the microphone went dead as Herbert Hoover was making a speech denying that events in Europe threatened America. "The three thousand miles of ocean is still a protection," Hoover said, to an audience most of whom could not hear him.

On the first ballot Willkie came third behind Dewey and Taft. The passion of the pro-Willkie delegates was supplemented as the convention went on by the support of an increasing number of newspaper commentators, including Walter Lippmann and Dorothy Thompson. More and more of the delegates began to think that this might be the man who could win it for the Republicans.

Willkie won the nomination on the sixth ballot. The convention chose as his running mate Senator Charles McNary, a liberal from Oregon (who had never met him). Interior Secretary Harold Ickes wrote in his diary: "Willkie nominated. Nothing so extraordinary has ever happened in American politics."

Willkie's nomination meant that Roosevelt could continue to aid Britain without fearing that every move exposed him to attack by his Republican opponent. Morgenthau commented in private, "The fact that Willkie is running will make it possible for me to continue for the next four months just the same as the last four months to help the Allies, and within the next four months the thing will be settled one way or the other."

The German ambassador to Washington, Hans Thomsen, cabled home: "From the standpoint of foreign policy, Willkie's appointment is unfortunate for us."

Traditional Republicans were furious. One Republican committee woman from the Midwest wrote in a letter: "I have never been more disgusted and disappointed in my life than I have been with the attitude of a great number of educated voters in the East. They are so pro-British they might as well be colonists."

Most observers were agreed on the reason for this unexpected turn of events. *Time* magazine said of Willkie's supporters: "They would not have organized Willkie clubs, badgered Republican delegates, trekked uninvited to Philadelphia, if the voltage of US political life had not been stepped up by Hitler's conquests. Nor would they have blundered ahead to do the impossible if Adolf Hitler had not plunged through the Low Countries into France."

• • •

The country had been speculating for a year about whether Roosevelt would do what no president before had ever done and run for a third term. Among Democrats there was a "draft Roosevelt" movement; many people felt that at this critical time the country needed his experienced hand at the helm. But there were also others who felt that the country would recoil from giving him what George Washington had thought no man should have, a third term as president.

Roosevelt's chosen successor had been Harry Hopkins, the tall, lanky, Iowa-born social worker. Hopkins had headed the Civilian Conservation Corps and then the National Recovery Administration, two key New Deal agencies, and Roosevelt appointed him secretary of commerce in 1937 to give him more political visibility. He shared Roosevelt's views and he would be the one to carry on Roosevelt's work. But Hopkins fell ill the year before with cancer of the stomach and never recovered his full health, and that ruled him out as a candidate. The vice president, John Nance Garner, would be a natural candidate for the nomination, but Roosevelt did not see him as the man to carry on the torch of the New Deal. He dropped hints that he would like Cordell Hull to succeed him; with a record of twenty-four years in Congress and seven as secretary of state, Hull had the requisite experience.

For all his bonhomie, Roosevelt always played his cards close to his chest — he would not allow notes to be taken at cabinet meetings — and he shared his intimate thoughts with no one. Not even his closest friends knew whether he would run again. He had told some friends he was tired of the strains of office and that he looked forward to devoting himself to his Hyde Park estate and his stamp collection. He signed a contract with Collier's magazine to write a series of articles.

A week before the Democratic convention was due to open in Chicago, James Farley, the postmaster general, called on Roosevelt at Hyde Park. Farley was a former chairman of the Democratic Party and a close political friend of Roosevelt from the days of his 1932 campaign, and he was one of those often mentioned as a possible Democratic candidate.

Sitting in his wheelchair in the spacious house that had been his family's home for a century, looking down over the Hudson Valley woods that he loved, Roosevelt told Farley his decision. He had decided to run. He pointed to newspaper headlines over reports from Europe, and said the world situation made it imperative that he remain in the White House. Farley told him bluntly that he was opposed to a third term on principle. But Roosevelt had made up his mind.

He was not going to make it easy for his party. He was going to be a distant figure, above the political fray. He would not put himself forward as a candidate and would not even go to the convention. The party would have to draft him.

On the Platform Committee, the Foreign Policy Subcommittee meetings were a replay of the ones in the Republican Party, with arguments just as fierce. Some members wanted a statement renouncing all "foreign entanglements." Senator Burton Wheeler said: "It's not sufficient to say we will not send troops to fight in Europe's wars. We must make it clear that we will not participate in any way whatever." The Women's Advisory Committee concurred. Others wanted a commitment to aid Britain. Clark Eichelberger argued that this was defending America: "We won't need a large military budget if aggression is stopped at the English Channel."

Feelings ran high. At one point Wheeler threatened to walk out and form a peace party, and five other senators supported him.

The subcommittee reached a compromise on wording. The isolationists got a promise that American troops would not be sent abroad; their opponents got the added phrase "except in case of attack." The statement called for aid for victims of aggression "consistent with the law and with the interests of national self-defense." It sounded like the Republican platform.

When the convention opened in Chicago on July 14 some of Roosevelt's friends pleaded with him to come to it. Harold Ickes, taking an extreme view as usual, sent him a long telegram pointing to the crisis in world affairs and the danger of a Republican victory and said, "Willkie means fascism and appeasement."

Harry Hopkins was in Chicago to organize things for Roosevelt. He used Chicago Mayor Ed Kelly, the corrupt head of the corrupt Democratic Party machine in the city and a long-time ally of Roosevelt in the business of getting elected. Under Kelly, it was difficult to obtain city employment if you were not a registered Democrat, easy if you were a friend of his.

The keynote speaker, Senator Alben Barkley of Kentucky, had a message from Roosevelt. He told the convention: "Tonight at the specific request and authorization of the President, I am making this simple fact clear to the convention. The President has not had, and has not today, any desire or purpose to continue in the office of President, to be a candidate for that office or to be nominated for that office. He wishes in all earnest and sincerity to make it clear that all the delegates to this convention are free to vote for any candidate." This confused the delegates. They did not know what they were supposed to do.

They did not have long to wait. A voice boomed out over the loudspeakers: "We want Roosevelt! Everyone wants Roosevelt!" The voice came from the basement and it belonged, appropriately, to the Chicago superintendent of sewers. The galleries, packed with city employees, erupted in wild applause and, in a demonstration stage-managed by Kelly, delegates swarmed into the aisles carrying Roosevelt banners. The voice from the deep continued: "New York wants Roosevelt! Chicago wants Roosevelt! Everyone wants Roosevelt!" as the demonstration continued. After this there was no other candidate.

Roosevelt, while remaining in Washington, accepted the nomination. He issued a statement saying he had made retirement plans, but went on: "Today all private plans, all private lives have been replaced by an over-riding public danger . . . My conscience will not let me turn my back on a call to public service." His close associates did not doubt that this was sincere. Later Cordell Hull wrote: "Roosevelt's third term was an immediate consequence of Hitler's conquest of France and the specter of Britain alone standing between the conquerors and ourselves. Our dangerous position induced Roosevelt to run."

He had a surprise in store for the party. He let them know that his vice-presidential candidate would be Henry Wallace, his secretary for agriculture. He had earlier asked Cordell Hull to be his running mate, but Hull had declined. Wallace, from an Iowan farming background, was successful as agriculture secretary, creating stable prices and advancing rural electrification, and he was a passionate liberal, representing the most idealistic elements in the New Deal. (He was also cartoonist Al Capp's model for Li'l Abner.) Delegates caviled at this message from Roosevelt, partly because Wallace was not popular with the party professionals and was regarded as politically inept, and partly because they resented Roosevelt's high-handedness in foisting a running mate upon them. It looked as if the convention would reject Wallace. Roosevelt raised the ante: he let it be known that without Wallace, he would not run. Eleanor Roosevelt went to Chicago to plead with the convention to give her husband the man he wanted to help him bear the burden of office. Wallace was nominated with just 627 votes out of 1,100. He was advised not to make a speech to the convention because it might be received badly, and he did not.

The choice of two candidates who thought alike on the European war left the isolationists sidelined. Both were interventionists. The most important issue facing America would not be debated in the election campaign. Senator Robert LaFollette expressed the frustration of many when he said the election was a fixed fight: "The President and Wendell Willkie will vie with one another in protesting their love of peace, only to team up on the road to war once the ballots are counted."

Never before or since have events abroad had so direct an impact on domestic American politics. Hitler's panzer divisions had driven right into the convention halls where the two parties met. Their success on the battlefields of Europe determined the course of the presidential election and who the candidates would be: that Roosevelt would run again, and that the Republicans would choose Willkie.

. . .

One day in late June Frederick Miller, a member of the Council on Foreign Relations, and his wife Helen, the Washington correspondent of the British magazine the *Economist,* invited some friends to their house in Fairfax, Virginia, to talk about the war in Europe. Most were involved in public affairs, although not in government. At the end of the day, they found they had reached the conclusion that the United States should declare war on Germany. They decided that they should press this view on the American public. But first they met again and refined their analysis. Because they met at the Century Club, a socially exclusive club in New York, they became known as the Century Group.

They reasoned that Britain could not win against Germany and Italy without American participation, and if Britain were defeated Nazi Germany would present a direct danger to the United States through Latin

America. They thought the American people would not make the all-out effort required to help Britain unless there was a state of war.

Their analysis went beyond national self-interest. They said that Americans would fight for other things as well, and they prepared a draft statement not for publication setting out what some of these were. This said:

> They have to do in general with our faith in the American way of life. In its idealized social version this way of life stems from the Sermon on the Mount and the French Revolution. Even the lowest levels of American society are rarely free from the camaraderie of the egalitarian or the touch of mercy of the humanitarian. In its political and legal version this way of life is deeply rooted in English soil. It includes the representative form of government, the liberties and obligations of the Bill of Rights and a relatively free system of production and trade.

This analysis linked American values to the British cause, including even the "lowest levels of American society," and if their venue did not indicate the social class of those who drew it up, this phrase would.

The group decided to publicize their conclusion that America should declare war, and they sought signatories for a statement to be published in major newspapers. Some people would not go all the way with their analysis; others agreed with them but thought the public was not ready. One wrote that the time was not ripe but some time soon "the thermometer may have risen to the place where the declaration you propose would have the desired results."

The statement was published with thirty signatures of distinguished people, including Justice Felix Frankfurter and a retired chief of naval operations, Admiral William H. Standley. Headed "A Summons to Speak Out," it linked America's future to the Nazi advance and said: "The United States should immediately give official recognition to the fact and to the logic of the situation — by declaring that a state of war exists between this country and Germany. Only in this constitutional manner can the energies be massed which are indispensable to the successful prosecution of a program of defense."

The Century Group expanded and met regularly to advance their cause, and it included some influential media figures, such as Henry Luce, the publisher of *Time* and *Life*, Herbert Agar, publisher of the

Louisville Courier-Journal and author of a Pulitzer Prize–winning study of the presidency, and Joseph Alsop, the syndicated columnist. They were to have some influence and, like the White Committee, they were to serve as partisans, fighting the political war alongside the administration but without being signed-on, uniformed members of its army for which it would be responsible.

Henry Pitt van Dusen, a member of the group and a professor at Union Theological Seminary, saw Lord Lothian on July 4 and asked what they could do to help. Lothian gave what was now the standard answer, that the most important thing was the fifty destroyers. He cabled London the next day that there were "encouraging developments in informed opinion" in America.

Miller took leave from the Council on Foreign Relations to organize the Century Group's activities and rented an office on Forty-second Street, off Fifth Avenue. Members of the group began nibbling at the body politic and public opinion from several sides. Some talked to administration members and they organized talks on American radio for British figures. Van Dusen arranged a series of talks on the war by British clergymen. This was another group of individuals influencing government policy that summer.

By a happy coincidence, the office of the German Fellowship Forum, a pro-Nazi group supported by the German Embassy, had the office next door in the same building as the Century Group. Century Group staff reported on the comings and goings there to the FBI, and received a note of thanks from J. Edgar Hoover.

The German Fellowship Forum was one of a number of organizations that were not just isolationist but pro-Nazi. These included far-right political organizations outside the mainstream but very vocal. Organizations such as the Knights of the White Camellias and the Silver Shirt Legion published pro-Nazi, anti-Jewish magazines and staged meetings at which "Franklin D. Rosenfeld" was denounced. They had some following in rural areas among the kind of bigots who made up the Ku Klux Klan, and some in the cities. When New York City mayor Fiorello La Guardia found that some New York policemen were members of the Silver Shirt Legion, he insisted they resign either from the Legion or from the force. The Legion sometimes made common cause with the German-American Bund.

The voice on the far right that carried farthest came over the radio from Royal Oak, Michigan. It was a rich, warm, intimate voice with just a touch of an Irish brogue, a voice you could trust, a voice with extraordinary power to charm. It belonged to Father Charles Coughlin, a priest who brought his politics to the pulpit and to the air waves.

He began by preaching sermons, and, relayed over the CBS network, he acquired a nationwide audience estimated at 30 million, Catholics and non-Catholics, drawn by his persuasive radio manner. In the early 1930s, in the depth of the Depression, he started telling his listeners that it was the international bankers and the Communists who had wrecked the country. He asked them to send in donations to support his National Union for Social Justice, and they came in tens of thousands. Usually the donation was just a dollar or two dollars, because he appealed to the little man, to the poor, not to the rich and comfortable. At one time he was receiving eighty thousand letters a week, more than any other person in America.

He was always on the side of the little man, the common people. He began by defending them against the bankers and Wall Street; he supported Roosevelt and the New Deal in the early days, and Roosevelt invited him for a chat at the White House. He went on to defend them against the Jews and liberals and international financiers. He turned against the labor unions. CBS stopped carrying his broadcasts. He created a new organization, the Christian Front, and a magazine, *Social Justice*, which carried his views, along with articles supporting General Franco in Spain and now Hitler. "Must the world go to war for a hundred thousand German Jews?" he asked. He called the White Committee and its allies "gold-protected, Government-protected, foreign-protected snakes in the grass."

He had a lot of support in the isolationist heartland in the Midwest, particularly among the German-American communities there. But increasingly, his following came from the big cities, particularly among working-class Irish-Americans, for whom anti-British sentiments were part of their history and anti-Semitism part of their street culture. Christian Front members were formed into platoons of twenty-five. They went out on to the streets taunting or beating up Jews and trashing Jewish-owned stores, sometimes with police looking the other way. Father Coughlin claimed to have no knowledge of this. Members of the Catholic hierarchy were slow to denounce him — they agreed with his support for Franco — but eventually most did, including his superior,

Archbishop Edward Mooney of Detroit. (When, years later, Mooney died suddenly on a visit to the Vatican, Coughlin said, "It's my birthday. My Father has given me a birthday present." Forgiveness was not conspicuous among his Christian virtues.) A Committee of Catholics for Human Rights was set up in opposition to Coughlin.

There was some accidental conjoining of left-wing isolationism and the far Right. Coughlin had some support from a few national figures who agreed with his opposition to war and ignored or were hazy about his other views. Senators Borah and Homer Bone and New York congressman Hamilton Fish contributed articles to *Social Justice*. A few others in Congress supported him right down the line, including racists such as Mississippi senator John Rankin and Michigan congressman George Dondero. He may never have been in the political mainstream, but Coughlin and those who thought like him had an input into national opinion, if not to any serious degree in Congress then in a lot of living rooms and on the streets.

National mobilization went ahead. On July 10, Roosevelt put his defense program before Congress. He wanted equipment for an army of 1,200,000 men and reserve stocks for an additional 800,000, the largest naval expansion ever, and an air force of more than 20,000 aircraft. "The principal lesson of the war up to the present time," he said, "is that partial defense is inadequate defense." The total cost would be $4.848 billion. General Marshall said in testimony to Congress that a 2-million-man army would be needed to meet a Nazi attack on Latin America. Congress voted the funds for the naval expansion immediately, and after hearings lasting eight weeks voted more funds for the army than Marshall had asked for.

Industry was being mobilized also. In May Roosevelt revived the moribund Council on National Defense, which he had established the year before. He had been urged to do so but had delayed, probably because he was anxious about giving more power to businessmen. Now he created a powerful Defense Advisory Commission to the council. William S. Knudsen, vice president of General Motors, was put in charge of industrial production and the president of U.S. Steel, Edward R. Stettinius, of industrial raw materials. Other leading figures from industry and labor were members. They were dollar-a-year men, remaining on the payrolls of their corporations but receiving a dollar a year as a nominal salary from the government to give them a formal status within the bureaucracy, and they brought in other business executives to join them. They planned the transition of civilian industry to military production, which, they warned, would not be rapid.

Scientists were being organized. The president of the Carnegie Institute, Vannevar Bush, suggested to Harry Hopkins that there should be an organization to tap the brains of American scientists for national defense, and the National Resources Defense Council came into being, with Bush as its president.

New factories were built and jobs were created. Because the German armies now stood on the shores of the English Channel, Detroit and Pittsburgh hummed with new energy, and men found jobs making warships in Newport News, Virginia, guns in Springfield, Massachusetts, airplane engines in East Hartford, Connecticut, and explosives in Allentown, Pennsylvania.

Harry Hopkins worked with Major General James H. Burns of the army's Ordnance Department on material for the army, and he found that the services, accustomed to the lean years, were slow to ask for things. He told Burns to be more ambitious and raise his requests. Others did also. The air force said it wanted 9,000 parachutes by 1941. Robert T. Stevens, a leading textile manufacturer, called in to estimate service needs in textiles, told the air force it would need 200,000. Asked how he arrived at that figure, he said he calculated that the average crew of a military aircraft was four, so: "The President has asked for 50,000 planes by the end of 1941. I just multiplied that by four."

Morgenthau also was thinking big. Knudsen balked at accepting an order from Britain for more planes. Morgenthau advised Purvis, the head of the British purchasing mission, to tell Knudsen that he was ready to order 3,000 planes a month now. "You've got to bluff," he said. "After all, part or all of your British production facilities will be bombed — this country has got to take care of it. Tell Knudsen you want 3,000 planes and I'll back you up. I'll tell him it would be suicidal if this country didn't do it." Purvis took his advice and Knudsen agreed.

Not everyone was behind the government. Henry Ford, isolationist, anti-Semitic, and anti-British, the recipient of the Grand Cross of the German Eagle from the German government in 1938, canceled a program to manufacture Rolls Royce airplane engines in his factories when he found that some of them would be for Britain. They were manufactured in the Packard plant instead.

Congress passed legislation in July allowing the government to control the export of strategic materials, and the Defense Council drew up a long list of items that might be required for defense and could not be exported without a license, including aluminum, petroleum products, and iron and steel scrap. Congress also authorized it to stockpile strategic materials such as rubber and steel, and Roosevelt pressed it on this.

• • •

It was all very well for Congress to vote funds for an army of 2 million men. The present strength of the army was half a million and it was unlikely that 1.5 million more men could be persuaded to enlist.

The answer was conscription, and a private citizens' campaign for conscription was already under way. A prime mover was Grenville Clark. Again and again that summer, people outside the government, individuals or groups, exerted an influence on events, moving America closer to involvement in Britain's struggle.

Most of the prominent ones among them were associated with the old east coast establishment or else were interested professionally or personally in international affairs and had an Atlantic focus. These made up most of the Executive Council of the White Committee, although the council members made sure that the most prominent figure was the small-town newspaper editor from Kansas; most of the Century Group; and many of Willkie's prominent supporters. Among these, Grenville Clark, educated at private schools and Harvard, once a law clerk alongside Roosevelt and now a partner in a leading New York law firm, was an exemplary figure.

Clark had urged Roosevelt to appoint Stimson to the War Department partly because he knew Stimson approved of the idea of compulsory military service. Back in 1915 Stimson had said, "Every man owes it to his country not only to die for her if necessary, but also to spend a little of his life in learning how to die for her effectively."

The movement for conscription grew out of the Association of Military Training Camps begun in 1915, otherwise known as the Plattsburg movement. These camps were established on the initiative of Theodore Roosevelt to train young men to be military officers, in the expectation that America would enter the European war; the first was at Plattsburg, New York. Grenville Clark organized one of the camps, and the list of its trainees was said by a contemporary observer to look "like *Who's*

Who and *The Social Register* combined." Stimson, McCloy, and Forrestal, new appointees in the War and Navy Departments, were all veterans of Plattsburg, and all had been combat officers, McCloy one of the first navy pilots. At a twenty-fifth anniversary reunion of Plattsburg men in June, Grenville Clark proposed a motion favoring compulsory military service, and it was passed. The meeting also passed a motion favoring all-out aid to Britain.

Roosevelt wanted conscription, but he let others put their heads above the parapet first. As his speech writer Robert Sherwood wrote later, "There was more than one occasion when Roosevelt wanted to be attacked for inactivity and goaded into action by public demand." At Clark's instigation, a bill was introduced in Congress calling for selective military service on June 21, by Nebraska senator Edward R. Burke and Congressman James W. Wadsworth from New York. Burke was an anti–New Deal Democrat and Wadsworth was a Republican, so the bill could be presented as a measure for the defense of America rather than a Roosevelt project to get America ready to go to war.

For some time Roosevelt backed away from giving an opinion on conscription. Finally, on August 2, when he was asked at a press conference about the selective service bill, he said he was "distinctly in favor." He need not have been so cautious. Polls showed that public opinion was behind the idea. Sixty percent of people thought that twenty-year-olds should be conscripted. Public opinion was behind other defense measures also. The number of people who said they would be willing to pay more taxes for a larger army rose from 68 percent to 85 percent in the six weeks after the attack on France and the Low Countries.

Isolationists in Congress and elsewhere rose up in opposition. Wheeler poured scorn on the idea that Germany could invade America and keep open a 3,000-mile supply line. The Mothers of America demonstrated on the steps of Congress with placards saying "Kill the Bill, Not Our Sons." Some students said they would refuse to register.

Many were not so much against having a large army as worried about what the president would do with one if he were given it. He had said in asking Congress for funds that the army would be used for hemisphere defense, but some people feared that he would send it to fight in Europe's war. The president of the American Federation of Labor, William Green, said that if men were to be drafted, "an absolute guarantee should be accorded them that their services would be used only for the protection of the Western hemisphere, our homes, our homeland and our governmental institutions."

Willkie refused to play politics with the issue and came out in support. Largely because of this, McNary and Martin, the Republican leaders in the Senate and House, did not oppose it. A disappointed Senator Hiram Johnson said Willkie "broke the back of the opposition." Then the president backed the Wadsworth-Burke Bill. Congress finally passed it in September, and men between the ages of twenty-one and thirty-five registered for one year's military training starting October 16.

· · ·

Along with industrial mobilization went psychological mobilization. There was a surge of conspicuous patriotism. The record of Kate Smith singing "God Bless America" made the popular music charts. "Nation Discovers It's Smart to Be Patriotic" *Life* magazine said in a headline on July 22. It reported: "Red, white and blue gallantly gleamed on lapels, umbrellas, hats and suspenders," and pictured a bracelet with letters spelling out "America," and a "God Bless America" plastic bracelet.

President Roosevelt warned about a Trojan horse, and there was a scare about a Nazi fifth column that at times came close to hysteria. The Immigration Department announced that it was doubling the number of border guards because of the danger of fifth columnists. San Antonio mayor Maury Maverick said he was equipping the police force with submachine guns because of the danger of fifth columnists from Mexico. The term was heard constantly. The FBI said it was reinforcing its Pennsylvania office with "experts on sabotage and subversion" because of the number of armament plants in the state. A book called *The Fifth Column Is Here* by George Britt became a big seller.

Fifth-column fears were reinforced when a suitcase bomb planted in the British pavilion at the New York World's Fair on July 4 exploded, killing two detectives who had gone to investigate it. The bomb, containing twenty pounds of explosive, had been moved out of the pavilion after being spotted by a diligent employee. If it had exploded where it had been placed it could have killed many more. The culprit was never found.

Foreigners became objects of suspicion. Congress passed a law requiring all aliens to be finger-printed. Several states passed laws barring aliens from employment in defense industries or state programs, and from receiving state benefits. Seventy bills on the regulation of aliens were introduced. As an article in the monthly magazine *Harper's* said: "Every home with a foreign-born head is believed to be the nucleus of a fifth column, and a hue and cry is aroused about the alien which is amounting to proportions unheard of since World War One."

Roosevelt insisted that the fifth column was a reality. When a reporter expressed skepticism at a press conference he said: "I will give you a very simple example. There are at the present time, within the last couple of months, I suppose there are at least forty — that is a guess on my part but I think it is about right — about forty or fifty factories in this country where somebody in the factory has tried to destroy tools. That is fifth column. Those are perfectly known cases." He was not challenged on this. No one asked whether these attempts to damage tools were successful, or how the authorities knew that this was done on the orders of the German Intelligence Service and not by a disgruntled employee.

In fact Germany had no saboteurs in the United States. Hitler had ordered that there be no attempts at sabotage on the sensible ground that the political risks outweighed any possible benefit. The FBI found no sabotage in the 20,000-plus cases they investigated.

However, there was a fifth column, that interfered in the political process, suborned news media, sabotaged the campaigns of some congressmen and supported covertly others, and spread false information. It was run by British Intelligence, from the British passport control office in downtown New York. In June 1940 it expanded its offices and its activities when a Canadian, William Stephenson (later Sir William), arrived in New York. His brief was "to do all that was not being done and could not be done by overt means to ensure sufficient aid for Britain and eventually to bring America into the war."

Stephenson was an adventurous man. In World War One, as a fighter pilot, he was shot down and captured and escaped from a German POW camp. He won a lightweight interservice boxing competition on the same program as Gene Tunney, boxing with the U.S. Marines, and they became lifelong friends. He designed a radio set and made a fortune selling it, and another dealing in steel. Traveling in Germany in the 1930s, he carried out covert surveillance for the British government.

In America, Stephenson created an organization which he called British Security Coordination and took offices in Rockefeller Center in

New York. Soon after arriving, Stephenson was introduced by his old friend Gene Tunney to FBI Director J. Edgar Hoover. He told Hoover he wanted the FBI's cooperation. Hoover told him that only Roosevelt could give him that. Roosevelt gave the green light and BSC worked with the FBI's help. Sometimes this meant the FBI turning a blind eye to BSC activities; sometimes it involved more active cooperation. Stephenson maintained a link with the White House through Ernest Cuneo, a Washington lawyer who had worked on New Deal projects.

Stephenson reported to Churchill: "The President has laid down the secret ruling for the closest possible marriage between the FBI and British Intelligence. The fact that this cooperation was agreed upon is striking evidence of President Roosevelt's clarity of vision. The fact that it has to be kept secret even from the State Department is a measure of the strength of American neutrality."

Some of the BSC's activities were normal for a foreign quasi-diplomatic service. It cultivated press contacts. Through its influence with friendly newspapers, notably the *New York Herald Tribune* and the *New York Post,* it urged support for Willkie in the run-up to the Republican convention as the only candidate who would not follow an isolationist line, and worked behind the scenes for the same end. Sam Pryor, the pro-Willkie congressman who was accused of packing the convention with Willkie supporters, was in the construction business and he was later given a contract by a British firm to build airfields in Brazil.

Ernest Cuneo was a friend of the columnists Drew Pearson and Walter Winchell and lawyer to them both, and he was able to feed them BSC material. Pearson wrote a Washington column that was more gossip than punditry. Thanks to BSC it now carried more and more items about the German threat to Latin America and the murky links of some isolationists.

Winchell, a Broadway gossip columnist, was the most widely read journalist in America, with a daily syndicated column and a weekly radio program, both of them with a zippy, slangy, original style. Just as political Washington turned to see what Walter Lippmann was saying in his column, so millions of other Americans turned to Winchell. Along with news about who was about to get married ("Adam-and-Eveing it") or divorced ("Reno-vating") they also got his political opinions.

It was not difficult to get Winchell on their side. He was pro-Roosevelt, although his column was carried by the anti-Roosevelt Hearst chain, and he castigated Hitler from the time he came to power when most of his readers were barely aware of who Hitler was. Winchell was Jewish, and although he played no part in Jewish affairs he responded vigorously to anti-Semitism. Now, under Cuneo's guidance, with BSC in the background, he attacked the isolationists savagely and carried BSC-inspired stories.

One example: Winchell warned his readers who might receive letters from relatives in Germany that every German writing overseas was forced to be a propagandist. Each month Germans corresponding with foreigners were given by the authorities some sentences that had to be included in every letter. Winchell knew this because an American merchant seaman who had been in Hamburg had written to him with a copy of some obligatory sentences and also a letter that had been returned by the censor because it did not contain these. The story and the material supposedly from the merchant seaman had been fabricated, although of course Winchell did not know this.

BSC reached American minds through many and diverse channels. It persuaded Ham Fish to introduce pro-British, anti-Nazi elements into his comic strip "Joe Palooka."

BSC subverted a radio station, WRUL, which broadcast around the world from New York by short wave. WRUL was founded by a businessman, Walter Lemmon, with the aim of "spreading international goodwill." BSC, working secretly through intermediaries, provided additional financing and recruited staff, and soon it was broadcasting overseas in twenty-two languages, putting out stories designed to meet the British needs of the moment. Arthur Schlesinger Jr. gave some broadcast talks over WRUL having no idea of the BSC connection, and was surprised, years later, to find the scripts in the Public Records Office in London.

BSC helped set up and finance secretly several supposedly independent anti-Nazi organizations, among them the American-Irish Defense Committee and the Inter-Allied Information Committee, representing the governments of German-occupied countries; these had the same address in New York City, 8 West Fortieth Street, which was also the New York address of the White Committee. Sanford Griffith, the head of Market Analysts Inc., a leading opinion-polling organization, served BSC in secret. His assistant, Francis Adams Henson, had worked for organizations favoring aid to the Allies before joining Market Analysts Inc.; he said later that part of his job with Market Analysts was to get some results of their opinion polls into sympathetic newspapers. He also provided BSC with reports on antiwar groups at the party conventions.

BSC was also very active in Latin America, spreading covert propaganda, gathering information on shipping, and trying to frustrate German business. In August it acquired an ally in this work. Nelson Rockefeller set up the Office for Commercial and Cultural Relations Between the American Republics. This gathered intelligence on German business and persuaded American companies to sever links with commercial agents in Latin America who were linked to German business.

It operated against the French embassy when a new pro-Pétain ambassador, Gaston Heury-Haye, arrived in Washington and immediately began gathering information on Frenchmen in America sympathetic to de Gaulle. It intercepted embassy mail and countered its reporting activities.

It forged documents. One was a German plan for extending control over South America, which Roosevelt produced at a press conference. Another, probably produced in Britain but distributed in America by BSC, was a supposed diary of a Stuka pilot that was published as a book and reviewed widely and seriously. It had friends in high places. Robert Sherwood, the playwright and Roosevelt speech writer, had a home in England and had served in the Canadian army in World War One. He showed Stephenson the draft of some speeches he had written for Roosevelt before they were delivered.

BSC was to step up its duplicitous activities later on. It organized the harassment of isolationist meetings and set out to brand isolationists as pro-Nazi, often quite unfairly. It worked for the election defeat of isolationist congressmen. It set up a rumor factory that sent rumors about Nazi activities around the Americas. It campaigned covertly against German businesses in America, particularly I.G. Farben.

Roosevelt gave a green light to a foreign intelligence service which suborned elements of the American press and interfered in congressional elections. Most people would forgive him in retrospect because the ultimate cause — the defeat of Nazism — was right. Many would have forgiven him at the time, had they known, who in any other circumstances, or with another president, would have found such a betrayal of his office akin to treason and grounds for impeachment.

. . .

Sumner Welles wrote in his book *Seven Major Decisions:* "In July 1940, very few of us in Washington believed that Britain, even under Winston Churchill's inspired leadership, could hold out long against Nazi Germany." Many, particularly among the military, worried that sending weapons to Britain could only prolong the agony and the weapons might end up in German hands, weapons that would be needed for the defense of America.

Senator Pittman, chairman of the Senate Foreign Relations Committee, said Britain's position was so obviously hopeless that it would be better if the British government accepted Nazi domination and sent its fleet to North America. He hoped this would not be "too long delayed by futile encouragement to fight on."

Others were thinking along the same lines, including even Stimson. Stimson told Morgenthau that while he wanted to continue to send war material to Britain, they had to think now of the possibility of British defeat. "We must be sure," he said, "that the contracts contain provisions which will save us against such a situation that we've seen in France, where the Germans have taken over a lot of our American airplanes and they are using them against Britain and eventually against us."

As Welles indicated, the pessimism about Britain's chances was widespread. A magazine editor cabled Vincent Sheean, a writer and war correspondent who was now in Britain, offering substantial payment for 25,000 words on the entry of German troops into London. When Quentin Reynolds sent *Collier's* magazine a report from London titled "Britain Can't Lose," the editor cabled him, "You are probably crazy," adding, however: "But call the shots as you see them." The treasurer of Harvard, William Clafflin, told President James Conant, who was campaigning for aid to Britain: "Hitler's going to win. Let's be friends with him."

This was the message that Germany was sending to American business. On June 26, 1940 Gerhard Alois Westrick, a German trade official, organized a private dinner at the Waldorf Astoria for some of America's leading industrialists. He promised them that Britain would soon be finished, and then there would be good prospects for trade with Nazi-ruled Europe. In the meantime, he wanted them to stop trading with Britain. Among those attending were Sosthenes Behn, the chief executive of IT&T, James D. Mooney, chief of overseas operations for General Motors, Edsel Ford, Ralph Beaver Strassburger, who had investments and property in Germany and France, and Torkild Rieber of Texaco, who was shipping oil and petroleum products to Germany via South America. Westrick wanted them to stop trading with Britain and look to Germany.

(Westrick became the target of BSC's attention. BSC persuaded the ever-friendly *New York Herald Tribune* to run a series of articles about his activities that gave his address in suburban Westchester County and carried headlines such as: "Hitler's Agent Ensconced in Westchester." Westrick was abused and threatened, he had to leave his house, and many of his business friends broke off contact, unwilling to be linked to a fifth columnist.)

Lothian was worried about this kind of talk. He cabled London on June 26 that most Americans seemed to regard Britain's defeat as inevitable, and this "might affect Roosevelt's efforts to provide help." William Stephenson also was worried about it. To help counter the idea that Britain faced certain defeat, he turned to William Donovan.

Donovan had a career as adventurous as Stephenson's own. The two men had first met in 1916, when Donovan visited Britain on a Rockefeller Foundation war relief mission. He was an Irish-American from a working-class background, hardly a natural ally for Britain. In World War One he commanded the Sixty-ninth Division, the "Fighting Irish," made up mostly of Irish-Americans from New York, and he won the Medal of Honor and acquired the sobriquet "Wild Bill." Between the wars he was a successful lawyer and was Republican candidate for governor of New York. He also carried out missions for the government as an unofficial observer, with Mussolini's army in Ethiopia and in Spain during the Civil War.

He had been a classmate of Roosevelt's at the Harvard Law School, and Roosevelt had offered him the post of secretary for war although he was a Republican, but he turned it down, saying his differences with the administration on domestic issues were too great. But he agreed with Roosevelt about the war. He believed that America had a stake, not only in the survival of Britain, but in the survival of democracy in Europe.

Donovan was a close friend of Navy Secretary Frank Knox. He arranged a meeting for Stephenson with Knox and Stimson. The four men discussed aid for Britain. The others suggested that Donovan go to Britain and talk to military people and report. It was put to Roosevelt and Roosevelt agreed. He was getting mixed signals from the London embassy. Ambassador Kennedy was pessimistic about Britain's chances, as was the naval attaché, Captain Allan Kirk, but the military attaché thought Britain might win through. He would welcome a report by Donovan.

Roosevelt gave Donovan credentials as his special emissary and a letter of credit for $10,000, and Donovan left by clipper on July 14. Roosevelt did not consult Kennedy about Donovan's mission or even tell him that Donovan was going. Kennedy was understandably annoyed at this discourtesy. When he learned of Donovan's presence in London he told Roosevelt that the mission was "the height of nonsense and a blow to good organization."

Stephenson cabled London on the importance of Donovan's mission: "The American Government is debating two alternative courses of action. One would keep Britain in the war with supplies now desperately needed. Other is to give Britain up for lost. Donovan is President's most trusted personal advisor despite political differences and I urge you to bare your breast to him."

The government took Stephenson at his word and Donovan was given red-carpet treatment. He met the king, who joked with him that Buckingham Palace was an obvious target for German bombers. He visited RAF fighter stations and was particularly impressed with the role radar was playing. Churchill discussed the prospects with him. But Churchill did much more than butter up an important visitor. He ensured that Donovan was initiated into some of the innermost secrets of British intelligence. He was shown things that no other foreigner had ever seen, and told things that even very few Britons were allowed to know.

The king showed him a copy of Hitler's order to prepare for the invasion, which showed him that the British were intercepting and decoding top-secret German messages. He met Colonel Gubbins, who told him about his plans for guerrilla resistance against a German occupying force. He saw the fledgling Special Operations Executive, which was being created to organize resistance in occupied Europe. He met the head of MI6, the secret intelligence service, Colonel Stewart Menzies. The British people were not allowed to know who was the head of MI6. Menzies was a wealthy aristocrat, a colonel in the Life Guards and a high Tory, representing everything that most Americans traditionally dislike about Britain, but he and Donovan formed a friendship.

Donovan arrived back in New York on a British flying boat on the evening of Sunday, August 4. He took a night train to Washington and was in Knox's office on Monday morning. Then, along with Knox, he spent two days with Roosevelt on the presidential yacht *Potomac*. He told Roosevelt he thought Britain would fight on and would not surrender the fleet and that morale was high. He said they could win the air battle and that they could defeat an invasion. But, he stressed, they were short of equipment and should be given help, in particular destroyers.

Stephenson was able to cable London: "Donovan greatly impressed by visit. Has strongly urged our case re destroyers and is doing much to combat defeatist attitude in Washington by stating positively and convincingly that we shall win." From then on Donovan was a powerful partisan for British interests. Soon after his return he and Edgar Mowrer, a reporter on Knox's *Chicago Daily News* who had been in England with Donovan, wrote a series of articles on the Nazi fifth column.

The meetings between Donovan and British intelligence chiefs bore fruit. The following year Roosevelt gave Donovan the innocuous-sounding post of coordinator of information. In fact he was setting up a new intelligence agency with the help of BSC American agents trained in secret in BSC camps in Canada, learning the dark arts of espionage and subversion with some British help. When America entered the war Donovan became director of the new Office of Strategic Services. The lessons learned in these camps, and many of the personnel also, were absorbed into the OSS, and later into the CIA, and along with them something of the British gentleman-adventurer style that drew Ivy League graduates into these organizations.

The British government took a further step in sharing its secrets with America. At the prompting of the minister for air, Sir Archibald Sinclair, the government sent Sir Henry Tizard, a leading government scientist, to America. Tizard took a black steamer trunk containing blueprints and samples of Britain's newest weapons. These included the cavity magnetron, a microwave generator which allowed the miniaturization of radar so that it could be fitted into aircraft, and the Asdic submarine detector.

Tizard found that the British were ahead in most areas of military technology, which was not surprising because Britain was at war. An army technical specialist told Stimson that the United States was "getting infinitely more from the British than we could give them." The visit by Tizard led to the National Defense Research Council setting up a new laboratory at MIT to develop radar technology based on the cavity magnetron.

One member of Tizard's mission was Professor John Cockcroft, a physicist and a member of the Maud Committee who was working on the possibility of a nuclear fission bomb. He met with members of Briggs's Uranium Committee, and found that the British team was further advanced than the American. He told the Americans about the Frisch-Peierls memorandum, and from then on British and American scientists working on an atomic explosive exchanged information. Later the British project was absorbed into the American and all the work was transferred to America, to take advantage of America's greater industrial potential and safety from bombing.

Churchill was not too happy about this visit and was evidently in a mood to keep Americans distant for the moment. In a memo to General Ismay, he said: "I do not see what we are going to get out of this arrangement. Are we going to throw our secrets into the Americans' lap and see what they give us in exchange? If so, I am against it. It would be very much better to go slow, as we have far more to give than they." He suggested a piece-by-piece exchange: Asdic for the Norden bomb sight, radar for microwave technology.

With invasion threatening, the British government worried about the possibility of an attack through the back door, Eire, as Ireland was called. The Irish Army was only thirty thousand strong and had no modern equipment with which to face a German attack. The thought of German forces established in Eire so that Germany could invade Britain from two sides was a nightmare.

In Churchill's first cable to Roosevelt requesting weapons, he said Britain was worried about a German attack on Eire and asked him to send a U.S. naval squadron to Irish ports for a prolonged visit to warn off the Germans, a request he repeated. Roosevelt was sympathetic but said he could not spare the ships. The Irish government recognized the danger, and at the time of the Dunkirk evacuation it called up its small number of army reserves. But President Eamon de Valera rejected a British suggestion that British troops go to Eire to help defend it.

Then the British government suggested that its troops and ships reoccupy the three so-called treaty ports, Queenstown, Berehaven, and Lough Swilly, and de Valera again refused. The British had had bases in these three ports under the 1920 treaty which gave Ireland independence, but it relinquished these in negotiations in 1938, something Churchill opposed. A lot of other people must have regretted this now because ships and aircraft operating out of these ports could have provided better protection for Atlantic convoys.

On June 9 Churchill told Roosevelt in a cable that de Valera and his party were now ready to throw in their lot with the Germans and Eire was in danger of being invaded. "In these circumstances," he said, "it may be necessary for us to forestall German action by a descent on certain ports, and I think it right to let you know this, even if you may feel unable to make any comment on it." He did comment, or at any rate the administration did, in the person of Cordell Hull. Hull told Lothian that a British invasion of Irish territory would be received very badly in America. Lothian said no such thing was being contemplated. Churchill dropped the idea.

The American minister in Dublin, David Gray, tried to get some movement on the issue of unity with Northern Ireland. With the British government's consent he went to see the prime minister of Northern Ireland, Lord Craigavon, but found him stubbornly opposed. When the Irish government asked Washington for at least a single destroyer to defend the coastline, Gray advised Washington: "The Irish Government has no more use for one destroyer than I have for a white elephant. To defend this coast with a navy would require, in the opinion of experts, a fleet of submarines and fast torpedo boats."

In June the British government began secret negotiations with the Irish government, and made an offer that was kept secret at the time and for many years afterward: all-Ireland unity in exchange for Irish participation in the war. Malcolm MacDonald went over to Dublin to put the offer to Irish ministers. As minister of health he had no responsibility for such matters, but in a different capacity he had negotiated the withdrawal from the three Atlantic ports two years earlier, and he had established good relations with the Irish ministers.

De Valera said they were being asked to enter the war immediately in exchange for a promise of all-Ireland unity at some time in the future. MacDonald said no, the machinery to establish Irish unity could be put into motion immediately. The deputy prime minister, Sean Lemass, observed shrewdly that it seemed that Britain was not so much anxious for Eire to take part in the war as to ensure that it was not occupied by Germany. MacDonald said this was true, and it could be achieved by the stationing of British forces in Eire. De Valera said this would be tantamount to declaring war on Germany and it would be unacceptable to Irish public opinion; he warned that if British troops came, the population would fight them.

Lemass asked whether Northern Ireland would agree to steps toward unity. This was the rock on which every proposal for Irish unity has foundered, before and since that time. MacDonald said they would not coerce Northern Ireland but hoped they could persuade them. He said Britain would take full responsibility for seeing that its side of the agreement was carried out. In fact the Northern Ireland government had repeatedly rejected any talk of a united Ireland, and the majority of the Northern Ireland population was solidly behind it on that. MacDonald did not explain how the British government could change their minds.

De Valera suggested instead a united neutral Ireland, with the United States invited to send ships and troops to Eire to guarantee its neutrality. MacDonald pointed out that Northern Ireland, as an integral part of the United Kingdom, was playing a part in the war effort and could not become neutral. He did not even refer to the improbability of America sending ships and troops. He went back to London with nothing accomplished.

. . .

Back in April, when Britain was fighting in Norway, the syndicated columnist Samuel Grafton made a perceptive comment, picking up on an item of news that others had overlooked:

> The British Empire is rendering its own fat. It has put out a list of
> 117 American stocks and bond issues and has ordered English-
> men who own securities on this list to turn them over to the
> British Treasury. The former owners will be paid off in English

pounds, and the Treasury will sell the securities here for dollars with which to buy airplanes. This development is as sensational, in its way, as the battle of the Skagerrak.* It is the first outline for a hungry England after the war. Those stocks and bonds have been her food and drink. They, more than lands, have meant England, Seat of Empire. Now she is shoving these investments into the furnace of the war.

Britain was dependent on imports, including food, and had been for the past two centuries. In World War One it sold most British investments in the Americas to pay for war materials, transforming itself from America's creditor to America's debtor. Now it was having to spend more and more abroad, buying the materials for war and for its daily existence from America and elsewhere, and to pay for them mostly out of overseas reserves. Grafton saw the historic significance of this.

On the eve of war, the British treasury told the cabinet that it did not have enough of these to finance a lengthy war. "Unless when the time comes the Americans are prepared either to lend us or give us money, the prospects for a long war are exceedingly grim," it warned.

On June 30 the cabinet cabled Lord Lothian in Washington: "So long as the gold and other assets at our disposal permit, we shall, of course, continue to pay cash for essential armaments, raw materials and foodstuffs, but we desire to impress on the Administration in the clearest possible manner the utter impossibility of our continuing to do this for an indefinite period in view of the scale on which we shall need to obtain such resources. Our immediate anxiety arises from the necessity of entering into long-term contracts."

Lothian duly conveyed this message to Hull. The British government sent a senior Treasury official, Sir Frederick Phillips, to talk to the administration, in particular the U.S. Treasury.

Treasury Secretary Morgenthau had argued fiercely within the administration for aid for Britain. He advised Purvis on how best to deal with the administration. When Britain and France needed smokeless powder for bombs and shells, he got the navy to give them some from its stocks, and not only facilitated contracts to manufacture the powder with du Pont and Hercules, but beat the price down. He wanted to back the war against Germany to the full. However, he had his own agenda.

---

* A naval engagement off Norway that had just taken place.

He had never liked the domination of the world's financial system by sterling and the finance men in London. Like Hull, he also wanted to end imperial preference, the system of tariffs that linked the commonwealth. He was ready to use Britain's present plight to reduce its economic power.

Sir Frederick told Morgenthau that Britain expected to have a balance of payments deficit in the coming year of some £428 million ($1.07 billion in 1940 terms, worth much more today). Morgenthau said Britain should sell some of the £833 million represented by British ownership of or shares in American companies, such as Dunlop Tire, Viscose, and Brown and Williamson Tobacco. It did sell them, in the case of Viscose at a knock-down price because it was separated from its parent company. This meant the British government ordering the British owners to sell them, paying them in pounds sterling, and then selling them in America for dollars, which could be used to pay for war materials and also raw material and food.

Sir Frederick did not fare much better when he saw Roosevelt. The president said, "How about selling some of these securities you have in Argentina?" When Sir Frederick demurred, Roosevelt pressed him and said, "Take the Queen of the Netherlands. She owns an apartment house here. She could borrow money on that, and I am sure you could borrow money on securities in this country also." Treasury officials continued to press the point, telling Sir Frederick and Lord Lothian that Britain could sell its South American securities and its interests in tin and rubber in Malaya.

For Britain, continuing the war meant watching its economic life blood drain away. Win or lose, Britain would no longer be the world power after the war that it had been before, and certainly not if the U.S. Treasury had anything to say about it.

This thought may have been behind what seems like another attempt on the part of some British ministers to seek a compromise peace, using neutral Sweden as an intermediary. The initiative came from Rab Butler, who was parliamentary private secretary to foreign secretary Lord Halifax. Butler had a long career in British politics before and after this and he had been strong for appeasement. On June 17, Butler met the Swedish minister in London, Bjorn Prytz. After the meeting, Prytz cabled Stockholm: "Mr Butler's official attitude is that for the present the war should continue, but he must be certain that no opportunity should be missed of compromise if reasonable conditions could be agreed, and no diehards should be allowed to stand in the way." There was no doubt who the diehards were.

Later that day Butler told Prytz, according to Swedish documents, that Lord Halifax's attitude was that "common sense and not bravado would dictate the British Government's policy." Churchill saw some telegrams from Stockholm referring to this talk and wrote a note to Halifax. He said Butler seemed to have used "odd language" to the Swedish minister and given an impression of defeatism, and asked him to find out what Butler had said. Butler denied using these terms.

Most of this information comes from Swedish documents. No British papers on exchanges with Sweden have been declassified. From the Swedish papers, it seems that a tentative approach was made by the Foreign Office, with or without the approval of the foreign secretary, and that it was slapped down by Churchill. Later, in December, when Lord Lothian died suddenly, Churchill appointed Halifax to replace him. It was an important position and one that Halifax could not refuse in wartime, but it removed him from the policy-making area.

. . .

The Royal Navy took destroyers off convoy duty and transferred them to the Southern Command to be ready to face an invasion. The German navy began using the French Atlantic ports as submarine bases, which extended the U-boats' reach. Sinkings went up. In March 107,000 tons of British merchant shipping were lost; in July the figure was more than doubled. Churchill messaged the navy chief: "The repeated severe losses in the Northwest approaches are most grievous. No doubt this is largely due to the shortage of destroyers through invasion preparations . . . We can't go on like this."

He cabled Roosevelt asking again for the American destroyers. "We have a large construction of destroyers and anti-U-boat craft coming forward, but the next three or four months open the gap of which I have told you." He said four destroyers had been sunk and seven damaged in the previous ten days and went on:

> We could not sustain the present rate of casualties for long, and if we cannot get a substantial reinforcement the whole fate of the war may be decided by this minor and easily-remediable factor . . .

Mr. President, with the greatest respect I must tell you that in the long history of the world this is a thing to do *now*. Large construction is coming to me in 1941, but the crisis will be reached long before 1941. I know you will do all in your power, but I feel entitled and bound to put the gravity and urgency of the position before you.

Lord Lothian conveyed the urgency of the situation to friendly figures in America. He passed a confidential defense estimate to Henry Luce and to Whitney Shephardson, a Century Group member and former Rhodes scholar. The naval attaché at the embassy gave one to Joseph Alsop. The White Committee and the Century Group made the issue public. They argued for this at meetings and ran a full-page newspaper advertisement headed: "Between Us and Hitler Stands the British Fleet."

Within the administration, people were coming up with ideas. Knox suggested to Roosevelt that, whereas Congress would not allow the sale of the destroyers to Britain, it might allow, at a later date, their sale to Canada, with the proviso that they be used only for the defense of the Western Hemisphere.

Benjamin V. Cohen, a key official at the Department of the Interior and a Roosevelt appointee, produced a plan with Jesuitical logic for handing over the destroyers without congressional approval. Under an act of 1916, the president is allowed to sell "ships of the navy classified as colliers, transports, supply ships, special types and hospital ships" eighteen years old or more. By an act of 1901, the president can reclassify ships. So the president could say he had reclassified fifty destroyers as supply ships and he was giving them to Britain. Cohen admitted that although congressional approval would not be needed, congressional opinion would have to be taken into account. Roosevelt passed this on to Knox, commenting: "I frankly doubt if Cohen's memorandum would stand up. Also I fear Congress is in no mood at the present time to allow any form of sale."

Members of the Century Group drew up a long memorandum for Roosevelt. This said that in its own vital interests America should hand over to Britain 100 destroyers immediately. They suggested that America ask in return for a guarantee that the British fleet would not be surrendered to Germany, and suggested a quid pro quo: "These destroyers should be offered to Britain in exchange for immediate naval and air concessions in British possessions in the Western hemisphere."

On August 1, the day after Roosevelt received the urgent cable from Churchill about the destroyers ("this is a thing to do *now*"), he received three members of the Century Group, Herbert Agar, Clark Eichelberger, and Ward Cheney. These put to him the proposition contained in the memorandum: 100 destroyers in exchange for bases. Roosevelt was noncommittal.

They asked him whether there was anything they could do to make it easier for him to go ahead. He said it would help if they could get General John Pershing to go on the radio and speak in favor of the deal. Pershing, the commander of the American Expeditionary Force in World War One, was now a few weeks away from his eightieth birthday and in poor health, living in retirement at the Ritz Carlton Hotel in Washington. He had never taken part in politics and was much respected.

Agar approached the old general. Pershing said he would be glad to come out for the destroyers deal, and asked whether someone could help him write his radio talk. Walter Lippmann and Joseph Alsop both pitched in. Pershing told a radio audience that numbered millions: "By sending help to the British, we can still hope with confidence to keep war on the other side of the Atlantic Ocean, where the enemies of liberty, if possible, should be defeated." Following this, the *New York Times* and the *New York Herald Tribune* both ran editorials in support.

9

"THE MOST CRITICAL MONTH"

On July 31 the military attaché at the U.S. embassy in London, Major General Raymond E. Lee, wrote in his diary: "Tomorrow, the first of August, is the opening day of the most critical month in history. If the British are standing upright on September 1, I will say there is a good chance of beating the Boches, no matter what may be happening elsewhere."

Hitler seemed to be thinking along the same lines. On August 1 he issued a directive for an all-out air attack on the RAF, which Bletchley Park picked up and decoded immediately. It said: "The Luftwaffe will use all the forces at its disposal to destroy the British Air Force as quickly as possible. The attacks must in the first instance be directed against flying formations, their ground organizations and their supply organizations, and in the second against the aircraft production industry and the industries producing anti-aircraft equipment." It went on to say that once the Luftwaffe had achieved air superiority, air attacks should be continued against ports and food supplies. It added: "Terror raids as revenge I reserve the right to order myself."

The operation was called *Adlerangriff,* "the attack of the Eagles," and the date chosen for the start was to be *Adler Tag,* "Eagle Day." Hitler said in his directive that it could start any time after August 5, the exact date to be left up to the Luftwaffe. Dowding was forewarned.

Even before Eagle Day there were raids on Britain and air battles almost daily. On August 12 the Germans staged a devastating attack on the naval base and town of Portsmouth, and knocked out the radar station at Ventnor, leaving a gap in Britain's southern defenses. Evidently, the Germans did not realize the importance of radar to Britain or they would have followed this up with other attacks on radar stations.

Eagle Day was supposed to be the start of a new phase but it turned out to be a muddle. Göring decided that it would be August 13. Weather arrived to impede visibility, so Göring called off the first raid while the aircraft were in the air. The fighters turned back, but the bombers did not get the message and went on unescorted. They attacked airfields, army bases, and Southampton, but the RAF fighters took a toll on the German planes. At one RAF airfield, Detling, sixty-seven people were killed including the station commander.

When Göring gave the go-ahead in the afternoon, escorting fighters lost their bombers and the RAF shot down six of a group of nine Stukas as well as others. One British pilot exulted at the end of the day, "I missed the 'glorious twelfth' (the official start of the grouse-shooting season) but the thirteenth was the best day's shooting I ever had." At the end of the day the Germans had lost forty-seven planes and the RAF fourteen fighters, but forty-seven other aircraft were destroyed on the ground.

The Air Ministry reported that seventy-eight German planes had been destroyed. This boosted morale, but it was not merely propaganda; the Air Ministry believed it. Throughout this period pilots were exaggerating the number of aircraft they had destroyed. In the confusion of high-speed combat several pilots would claim the same "kill" or would say a plane was destroyed when it limped home. The Germans overestimated even more the number of British aircraft they had destroyed and the damage done to airfields, with serious consequences. Soon they would believe that Fighter Command was on its last legs and could put up little more serious resistance.

The RAF began putting cameras in fighter planes pointing straight ahead and synchronized with the guns, so that they would film an attack on an enemy aircraft. This made a useful training aid, and in many cases it confirmed kills. After a time they also turned some of the film over for showing in movie theaters, and this was something new in war footage.

The Germans went on attacking airfields over the next two days. August 15 saw the biggest battles yet, with the opening of a new front. As aircraft attacked across the channel, others flew from Norway across the North Sea to attack Scotland and the northeast. They did not fare well. They were escorted by the ME110s, slowed down by the extra fuel they had to carry. Some of the RAF squadrons in the north had seen little action; others had been rotated there for a rest after hectic activity in the south. They were eager to get at the bombers. They intercepted them out at sea and dove down from above, shooting down sixteen planes in a few minutes. Most of the remaining bombers jettisoned their bombs and turned tail. This was not cowardice — no one in the RAF accused German pilots of cowardice; they had been ordered to turn away if they looked to be suffering heavy losses. The Germans were more successful in the south with raids on airfields and towns. They wrecked the Short Brothers aircraft factory in Rochester, holding up production of the Short Stirling, the new four-engine bomber.

RAF fighter pilots were keen to fight. Time and time again a small group of fighters or even a lone pilot would dive into a much larger formation of enemy raiders. Alan Deere, a New Zealander who had already been shot down once over Dunkirk, bailed out of a crippled Spitfire and parachuted down with a sprained wrist. An army paramedic drove him to the nearest hospital, where the doctor in charge mended his wrist and telephoned his base to say he was keeping him in for a few days because he needed the rest. Deere slipped out during an air raid and caught a train to his base the next morning.

The knowledge that they were defending their own country was a spur. One pilot, Brian Kingcome, said later: "One used to look down and see one's own country, one's own people, and see these hideous great hordes of aircraft flying over. One thought, 'Bloody hell, you know, one can't allow this to happen.'"

The RAF's sector headquarters for southern England, bearing the brunt of the attack, was at Uxbridge, on the outskirts of London, and the commander there was Air Vice Marshal Keith Park, a New Zealander and the most important person in the Battle of Britain after Dowding. One day Churchill drove to Uxbridge with General Ismay and stood in the underground operations room as waves of German bombers came on, and he followed the course of the battle. The fighter squadrons were Britain's first line of defense and nearly its last as well, and they were stretched to the full. For Ismay, and evidently for Churchill, it was an emotional few hours.

After watching operations Churchill drove away with General Ismay, and said, "Don't speak to me. I have never been so moved." It was five minutes before he spoke again, and when he did he had worked out a phrase to express his thoughts: "Never in the field of human conflict has so much been owed by so many to so few." Ismay remembered the sentence and relayed it to his wife when he got home. Churchill used the phrase again four days later when he addressed Parliament on the subject of the air force, and it became one of his most famous.

Most of August was warm with sunny skies, and there were dogfights over southern England nearly every day. This was an area of gently sloping landscapes, genteel homes with lovingly tended gardens, and farming villages where farmers still plowed fields with horses and men played dominoes on wooden tables outside pubs on warm evenings. From here people on the ground followed the air battles through the vapor trails against the blue, watched an aircraft on fire plunging earthward, and prayed to see a parachute emerge. Home Guard units rushed to the scene of a wrecked airplane, British or German, or to find crew members who had parachuted down. Schoolboys collected souvenirs: shrapnel was okay but pieces of German aircraft were a real prize.

Pilots based in southern and eastern England were sometimes scrambled five and six times a day. Sometimes they took off with a flying jacket thrown over pajamas, or in their shirt sleeves. Ground crews also worked at a punishing pace, and learned to refuel and rearm a Spitfire or Hurricane in minutes. For those on the ground, fighter pilots were heroes, defending them and the homeland literally and visibly. Lydia Lopkova, the Russian-born ballerina and wife of J. M. Keynes, wrote to a friend, "We hear all day bombs and anti-aircraft guns, feel while it lasts a bit reckless, but English airmen are wonderful and protect us."

The RAF counted scores, and a few with a high kill-count acquired fame. Prominent among them was Squadron Leader Douglas Bader, who flew with two artificial legs, a brilliant if reckless pilot (he lost his legs before the war doing an aerobatic stunt too close to the ground). There was "Sailor" Malan, a South African who bore the nickname because he had formerly been a merchant navy officer, and may have preferred it to his real first name, Adolf. Malan had an aggressive attitude to fighting the Germans; he said it was better to aim at crewmen in a bomber than the engine, since its arrival home with dead and wounded men on board would be a blow to morale. There were also Ernie

Mayne, who had flown as a fighter pilot in World War One, a forty-two-year-old flying with eighteen- and nineteen-year-olds; and Frank Carey, who left school at fifteen and joined the RAF as a mechanic, argued his way into flying, and was to rise to the rank of group captain and shoot down eighteen German planes.

Among the most aggressive fighter pilots were the 146 Polish pilots in the RAF and a number of Czechs who had made their way to France and then to Britain. The Poles found, as one of them said, that British food was even worse than they had expected but British girls prettier and more agreeable. They were taught English and formed into two fighter squadrons and two bomber squadrons, under British command. Their top scorer was Josef Frantisek, a Czech who had flown with the Polish air force and then with the French air force, winning the Croix de Guerre. Frantisek was a superb fighter pilot but totally undisciplined and incapable of playing the role assigned to him. So they kept him on as a "guest of the squadron," allowing him to attack German planes on his own.

A few Americans were in the RAF. One was Billy Fiske, as William Fiske III was known, a partner in a finance house who lived in London and was married to the countess of Warwick. A Spitfire pilot, he was credited with shooting down four German planes. On August 17 his squadron attacked a group of Stukas and his plane was hit by bullets from one of their fighter escorts and caught fire. He landed the burning aircraft but died in hospital the next day, becoming the first American to be killed in action in the war. Another was Michael "Red" Tobin, a tall, lanky Californian who used to play up to the American image by telling his fitter: "Saddle up, boy, I'm riding out." The following year American volunteers would be formed into a squadron, the Eagle Squadron.

The battlefield was everywhere. When Flight Lieutenant Michael Constable's plane was hit the engine cut out over the little town of Herne Hill. If he bailed out, the plane would have landed on houses so he crash-landed in a field. He walked away from the wreck, took a train to London, a taxi across London, and another train to his base at North Weald. The taxi driver refused a tip, saying he would not take one from a man who was risking his life for him.

With the country alert for German paratroops, anyone parachuting down was an object of suspicion. Richard Lee bailed out of a burning

Hurricane over Kent and landed in a cornfield, bleeding from the impact of bits of an explosive bullet. He had not expected to fly so he was not in uniform. He was confronted by an old man brandishing a rifle who refused to believe that he was a British pilot, and marched him off at gunpoint and handed him over to some soldiers. Their officer took him for a recuperative drink at the local golf club. Lee heard someone say, "Who's that chap in a dirty shirt? I don't think he's even a member."

Harry Deacon bailed out of his crippled Hurricane with a bullet in his leg to be faced by a young man who thrust a shotgun in his face and demanded to know whether he spoke English. Deacon's brief reply using an Anglo-Saxon word effectively answered the question. There were a lot of stories like this.

The Germans concentrated on airfields, so airmen were under attack on the ground as well as in the air. Two JU88s sneaked in to the training base at Brize Norton behind some British planes, put the wheels down as if to land, and then dropped their bombs, destroying seven planes on the ground. At Biggin Hill, a sector station, thirty-nine people were killed when the main shelter took a direct hit. WAAFs were trapped by debris, and when they were rescued one was dead and most of the others covered in blood and dirt. A WAAF was awarded a medal for manning the switchboard through the raid even though bomb blasts were bringing bits of the ceiling down on her. After this, senior RAF figures no longer worried that women would go to pieces under pressure.

Squadron Leader Johnny Johnstone recalled what it was like when an attack came without warning. Pilots were sprinting to their planes as bombs crashed around them: "It was a complete panic take-off with Spitfires darting together from all corners of the field, and it was a miracle that no one collided . . . The air was a kaleidoscope of airplanes swooping and diving around us for a moment. I felt like pulling the blanket over my head and pretending I wasn't there." Johnstone got his plane off the ground and shot down an ME110.

Craters on the runways were filled in quickly, but aircraft and communications equipment could not easily be replaced. At Kenley, four planes and three of the four hangars were wrecked, and nine people were killed. The operations room was destroyed and a temporary one was set up in a butcher's shop in the village. Manston was in a vulnerable position, situated on a cliff top overlooking the channel. It was bombed and strafed several times and had to be abandoned after its buildings were set on fire. Firemen from nearby Margate fought the blaze while some nearby residents looted store rooms. Altogether fifty-six planes were destroyed on the ground.

Civilians played a part in the battle. Apart from the Observer Corps, maintenance workers worked through air raids to repair telephone lines and other facilities at RAF stations, although others refused to leave the shelters. Others repaired damaged planes in record time, working twenty-four hours a day, sometimes pulling planes away from airfields while bombs were still falling.

In the operations room the radio connection with the planes was open so that the controllers could be in constant touch, and they could hear the sounds of combat as the pilots talked to one another in the air. "A swarm at Angels 16. Looks like a fighter and bomber mix." "Tally ho!" "Red 2's been hit." "There's a parachute." "Dickie's pulling away." "Watch out, Mike, there's one on your tail!"

Officers were worried at first because WAAFs in the ops room would hear unsuitable language. The WAAFs could take the language. Other things were more difficult to take. Sometimes they would hear a pilot giving a warning to another and repeat it involuntarily, calling out "Look out!" although no one could hear them, or, when a plane was going down, "Jump, please jump!" Worst of all were the sounds from men burning to death in the air. Corporal Claire Legge, who worked in the ops room, recalled, "What they heard often distressed the girls very badly. They knew the pilots and heard them screaming and going down. It was horrid."

Burning was a pilot's worst fear. He sat behind eighty-five gallons of high-octane fuel which, if it caught fire, could develop temperatures of several thousand degrees within seconds. Some pilots wrapped themselves in as much clothing as they could to provide some protection. Men who survived bailing out of a burning plane often did so with agonizing burns that turned them into monstrous beings, with faces swollen to three times their normal size, holes for ears and eyes, no lips, and stumps for fingers.

Geoffrey Page, a twenty-year-old Spitfire pilot, bailed out over the channel suffering burns and was rescued by a fishing boat and taken to hospital. He recalled a moment in the operation theater:

One of the prettiest girls I'd seen in my life came into the room. Attired in the cool, colorful uniform of a V.A.D. Red Cross nurse, she personified the wounded warrior's vision of an angel of mercy. Standing beside the dressing trolley assisting the professional nurse, she was unable to hide the expression of horror and loathing that registered on her lovely face at the sight of my scorched flesh. From the depths of my soul I longed for Beauty to cast me a friendly glance, even if it came in the shabby guise of pity, but the first expression remained constant.

Then he caught a glimpse of himself in the reflector mirrors of the overhead light, and saw "the hideous mass of burnt, swollen flesh that had once been a face." Some young men paid a high price for the British government's decision to fight on.

At the Queen Victoria Hospital in East Grinstead, a special burns unit was set up where Archibald McIndoe (later Sir Archibald), a New Zealand surgeon, developed new techniques of skin grafting. He believed the psychological cure was important as well as the physical. Mirrors were barred. The nurses were instructed always to be cheerful. A group of patients would sometimes be taken to a nearby pub where the regulars had learned not to flinch. Later, McIndoe's guinea pigs, as they called themselves, formed a club and held regular reunions, always with McIndoe as their guest of honor.

• • •

Roosevelt also thought this was a critical time. After receiving Churchill's desperate cable about the destroyers and the Century Group's proposal, he discussed the subject with his cabinet at length on August 2. Unusually, he kept his own notes of this meeting. These read in part: "It was the general opinion, without any dissenting voice, that the survival of the British Isles under German attack might very possibly depend on their getting these destroyers. It was agreed that legislation to accomplish this is necessary. It was agreed that such legislation, if asked for by me without any preliminaries, would meet with defeat or interminable delay without a vote."

The cabinet agreed that the British would be asked to guarantee publicly that their fleet would not fall into German hands in the event of defeat and would not be scuttled, but would sail to North American or British Empire ports where they would be available.

Roosevelt wanted to get Republican support for the move in advance, or at least a guarantee that they would not oppose it in an election year. The notes show that Roosevelt decided to approach Willkie through William Allen White. White had supported Willkie at the Republican convention and was on good terms with him. The cabinet agreed that Roosevelt would ask White to come to Washington to see him, and then to see Hull, Stimson, and Knox. White would be asked to see Willkie and ask him to try to get McNary and Joe Martin, Republican leaders in the Senate and the House, to support the plan. Roosevelt said he thought legislation would fail unless it had the support of the Republicans.

Roosevelt's notes go on: "At 8:30 P.M. I talked to William Allen White, who was in Estes Park, Colorado, explained the above to him, and asked him to come East. He told me he was sure that his attitude in this matter was the same as mine. I explained to him that this was wholly insufficient, and that Willkie's attitude was not what counted, but that the Republican policy in Congress was the one essential. White told me he would get in touch with Willkie and let me know at the earliest moment."

Curiously, there is no mention in these notes of the acquisition of bases from Britain in exchange for the destroyers, but we know from Harold Ickes' account of the meeting that this was discussed at length.

The proposal for a deal was put to Lothian. Roosevelt assured Lothian that all he wanted was bases. He said he knew how poor these islands were and he certainly did not want any part in governing them. Lothian passed on the proposal to Churchill, who cabled back that the granting of bases in exchange for the destroyers and flying boats was acceptable. "Go ahead on these lines full steam," he concluded.

But the administration could not yet go full steam ahead. Roosevelt wanted congressional support, and he wanted Willkie's assurance that he would not oppose it and make it an election issue. Senator Claude Pepper of Florida, who favored unlimited aid for Britain, told Stimson he thought Congress would not pass the necessary legislation in an election year.

Willkie's brief vacation in Colorado Springs was getting a lot of interruptions. White saw him and then two emissaries from the Century Group who also wanted Willkie's approval: Lewis Douglas, the Arizonan heir to a mining fortune from an Anglo-American family (and future ambassador to Britain), and Russell Davenport, who had been Willkie's campaign manager. He also received a visit from Arthur Krock, a Washington columnist for the *New York Times*, who opposed many of Roosevelt's policies, an august figure who was often ready to impart advice as well as to receive information.

Shortly after his visit Krock wrote in his column that Russell Davenport had asked Willkie to say he would not oppose the destroyer deal. He said Willkie had replied that "to make such a promise . . . was virtually to urge such an action on the President," and that he was not sufficiently familiar with the background to reach such a decision. He said Willkie did not want to prejudice the freedom of action of Republican members of Congress on the issue. Krock also said the navy high command opposed the transfer of the destroyers. Douglas and Davenport thought Krock had influenced Willkie. Francis Miller wrote to another member of the Century Group: "He has really done us dirt."

Receiving conflicting advice, Willkie was sending out conflicting signals. A week after the cabinet meeting Willkie came out with a disappointing statement. He said his general views on foreign policy were well known, but: "As to specific executive or legislative proposals, I do not think it appropriate for me to enter into advance commitments and understandings."

He seems to have spoken differently to White. White told Cordell Hull in a telephone conversation that Willkie had agreed to the destroyer deal in principle but would like to see a draft of the proposed agreement before approving it. He said he had not talked to Willkie about McNary and Martin's attitude but would do so. A few days later White telegraphed Roosevelt: "I have talked with both of you on this subject in the last ten days. I know there is not two bits difference between you on the issue pending. But I can't guarantee either of you to the others. Which is funny for I admire and respect you both. I realize you in your position don't want statements but Congressional votes. Which, by all the rules of the game, you should have. But I've not quit and, as I said, it's not as bad as it looks."

Nonetheless, Willkie would not commit himself publicly. In his opening campaign speech on August 17 in his home town of Ellwood, Indiana, he stressed foreign affairs but made no mention of the destroyers. He made it clear that he was in favor of aid to the Allies and military preparedness, but criticized the president. "He has courted a war for which this country is hopelessly unprepared . . . He has seriously meddled in the affairs of Europe, and has even unscrupulously urged other countries to hope for more help than we are able to give." Willkie was a popular candidate and opinion polls showed him gaining on Roosevelt rapidly.

Felix Frankfurter, who was also associated with the Century Group, set some more wheels in motion. He suggested to Ben Cohen that he get together with Dean Acheson and try again to find a legal way to transfer the destroyers without going to Congress for new legislation. Acheson, also a Century Group member, was former assistant secretary of the Treasury. They spent several days in Cohen's apartment and in the New York Bar Association library working out an argument to this effect. Then they wrote it as a letter to the *New York Times*, and Acheson signed it along with three other prominent members of the bar. Acheson contacted the editorial page editor on the *Times*, Charles Mertz, an old Yale classmate, and Mertz agreed to publish it prominently on the editorial page on Sunday, August 20. This letter proved to be the breakthrough.

It was one-and-a-half columns of closely reasoned argument, citing the Neutrality Acts, precedent, and international law. It argued that the act of 1917, which prohibited the sale of the motor torpedo boats, "is obviously not applicable to ships which were neither built nor equipped with a view to their entering the service of a belligerent power."

It said that to seek the approval of Congress would be to risk a delay which could affect America's vital interests. "There is no reason to put a strained or unnecessary interpretation on our own statutes contrary to our national interests," it went on. "There is no reason to extend the rules of international law beyond the limits generally accepted by other nations, to the detriment of our own country."

Stimson read the letter and told Lothian: "This adds a speck of light on the situation."

As Acheson said later, the letter was written for only two readers, the president and the attorney general, Robert Jackson. But Jackson was away on a camping trip with his daughter in the Pocono Mountains in Pennsylvania, getting away from it all. Jackson was an old political friend of Roosevelt from New York State politics, and Roosevelt had brought him to Washington in the early days of the New Deal. He was also a friend of Acheson, and Acheson knew that quite apart from his formal role, he had Roosevelt's ear.

Acheson wanted Jackson to see the letter immediately. He called his office and his secretary said he could not be reached by telephone but if it was urgent a message could be sent calling him to the nearest telephone, which was several miles away. Taking his cue from his British contacts, Acheson said it was urgent. Jackson was not happy about having his vacation interrupted, but he listened. Acheson pleaded the importance of the matter and outlined the legal justification. Jackson promised to consider it. He cut short his vacation, came back to Washington, and wrote an opinion for the president reaching the same conclusion, which was delivered five days later.

Roosevelt was still worried about congressional opposition, and he tried to win over David Walsh, the chairman of the Senate Naval Affairs Committee and an isolationist who had stopped the sale of motor torpedo boats. He took him on a three-day cruise on the presidential yacht. At the end of it Walsh remained unconvinced. He wrote Roosevelt a letter, saying that the American people shared his sympathy for the Allies and abhorrence of dictatorship, but most felt it was too late to help Britain and trying to do so could get America into a war.

Roosevelt wrote back saying Britain could use the destroyers and America could use the bases. He said the navy had been selling destroyers of this type for scrap metal at four and five dollars a ton, so acquiring bases in exchange was a bargain. As for the possibility of German retaliation: "I think you can rest quietly on that score. If Germany, at the conclusion of this war or before that, wants to fight us, Germany will do so on any number of trumped-up charges."

Lothian gave Hull a memorandum setting out what Britain would offer, and another stating what the British government expected in return: twelve flotillas of eight destroyers each, with torpedoes and ammunition; thirty motor torpedo boats; fifty PBY-5 flying boats and some Vought-Sikorsky dive bombers; and 250,000 Lee Enfield rifles. Roosevelt told Lothian what he wanted in return, and this was passed on to London.

The bases presented no problem, but the promise about the fleet was another matter. The first lord of the Admiralty — equivalent of Navy secretary — A. V. Alexander was furious at this request. He found the request "an impertinence" and defeatist, and persuaded Churchill of this view. Churchill dictated a letter to Lothian telling him to make it clear to Roosevelt that Britain would "never agree to the slightest compromising of our liberty of action nor tolerate any such defeatist announcement." Halifax persuaded him not to send it, neither the first nor the last time that he exercised a restraining influence on Churchill's impetuosity.

Instead, Churchill assured Roosevelt that the present government would neither sink nor surrender the fleet, but said he was loath to raise the issue publicly. To do so, he said, might create the impression "that the Government viewed collapse as a possible contingency."

He pointed out to Halifax in a memo that with invasion expected, a public discussion of what would be done if the country were defeated would be damaging to morale. He also worried that such a promise would be surrendering Britain's freedom of action. As he wrote in the memo: "We must never get into a position where the United States Government might say: 'We think the time has come for you to send your fleet across the Atlantic in accordance with our understanding of agreement when we gave you the destroyers.'"

On August 13, with the air attack on Britain under way, Roosevelt conferred with Stimson, Knox, Morgenthau, and Welles. All agreed that Britain's situation was desperate and the destroyer deal would have to be put in motion. Even without domestic support assured, Roosevelt began negotiations with a cable direct to Churchill.

He said America might be able to supply at least fifty destroyers and some motor torpedo boats, and a small number of flying boats. He spelled out what he wanted, including an assurance that "if the waters of Great Britain become untenable" the fleet would be sent to other parts of the empire. He recognized Churchill's point about the damaging effect of a public announcement on this point, and said a simple reiteration of his early statement to Parliament saying his government would never surrender the fleet would be sufficient.

Churchill replied to Roosevelt welcoming his message and agreeing to the bases, and said: "You know well that the worth of every destroyer that you can spare us is measured in rubies. But we also need the motor torpedo boats which you mentioned, and as many flying boats and rifles as you can let us have."

In public, prime minister and president both denied that any deal was in the offing. On August 16 the president told a press conference that America and Britain were holding negotiations on the acquisition of bases for the protection of the Western Hemisphere. Asked whether the question of giving destroyers to Britain was involved in these discussions, he said it was not.

Churchill spoke in the same vein, albeit more oratorically. He told Parliament on August 20 that the government was willing to grant America a ninety-nine-year lease on the bases in the interests of the two countries' defense. He made no mention of the destroyers; he said the bases were being offered "spontaneously and without any inducement." This was in the same address on the war situation in which he made his famous statement about "the few."

As always, he was looking at the larger picture of Anglo-American cooperation. He concluded the passage in his speech about the bases with a characteristic peroration: "Undoubtedly, this process means that these two great organizations of the English-speaking democracies, the British Empire and the United States, will have to be somewhat mixed up together in some of their affairs for mutual and general advantage. For my part, looking out on the future, I do not view the prospect with any misgivings. I could not stop it if I wished; no one can stop it. Like the Mississippi, it just keeps rolling along. Let it roll on — full flood, inexorable, irresistible, benignant, to broader lands and better days."

In his car on the way back from Parliament, as his private secretary recalled, he sang to himself, "Ol' man river, dat ol' man river . . ."

In fact Churchill did not like the idea of a deal. It smacked of bargaining, of calculating gains and losses, even of selling bits of the British Empire. He cabled Roosevelt: "I had not contemplated anything in the nature of a contract, bargain or sale between us . . . I see difficulties, and even risks, in the exchange of letters now suggested or in admitting in any way that the munitions that you send us are a payment for the facilities. Once the idea is accepted, people will contrast on each side what is given and received. The money value of the armaments would be computed and set against the facilities, and some would think one thing about it and some another."

Kennedy reported to Roosevelt different views in the cabinet. Beaverbrook had told him: "If we are going to make a gift, well and good. If we are going to make a bargain, I don't want it to be a bad one, and that is definitely a bad one." But Halifax, he said, "wants to do it any way the President wants it done, believing that the England–United States tie-up on anything is of more value than either bases or destroyers." (Chamberlain took no part in these discussions because he was ill with cancer. He died in November.)

Sumner Welles told Lothian and Lothian told Churchill that Roosevelt could not hand over the destroyers as a gift. There would have to be a quid pro quo that he could present to the American public. Roosevelt had to appear as a shrewd Yankee trader, not Britain's savior. Churchill cabled Roosevelt again saying: "I fully understand the legal and constitutional difficulties which make you wish for a formal contract embodied in letters, but I venture to put before you the difficulties, and even the dangers, which I foresee in this procedure." He pointed out areas of possible disagreement, saying Britain was asked to give "undefined concessions" in its territories.

He even said Britain could get along without the destroyers if it had to. It wanted the American destroyers to fill the gap before more came out of British shipyards. He went on: "We should not, however, be justified in the circumstances if we gave a blank check on the whole of our Transatlantic possessions merely to bridge this gap, through which, anyhow, we hope we can make our way, though with added risk and suffering."

Frustrated by Churchill's attitude, Roosevelt told Attorney General Robert Jackson to talk to him on the transatlantic telephone and explain the political and legal constraints. Churchill said he was willing to give the bases but he repeated that he did not want it to be in the form of a deal. "Empires don't bargain," he said. "Well, republics do," Jackson retorted.

Roosevelt went to Ogdensburg, New York, for his meeting with Canadian prime minister Mackenzie King. But first he reviewed the U.S. Fourth Army there and watched maneuvers involving 94,000 men. Their commanding officer, Major General Clifford Powell, told him they were having to use broomsticks to simulate machine guns and drain pipes for mortars. He did not tell reporters this, but he wrote to a friend, L. B. Shelley: "Anybody who knows anything about the German methods of warfare would know that that army would have been licked by thoroughly trained and organized forces of a similar size within a day or two."

While he was in Ogdensburg Welles drew up a draft agreement on the bases listing the items that America was willing to give in return and telephoned the gist of it to Roosevelt.

The U.S.-Canadian summit meeting went ahead. Roosevelt and Mackenzie King set up a Joint Defense Board, a nonneutral act since Canada was at war with Germany, but America had to be involved in the defense of the Western Hemisphere. This was no mere administrative device. The possibility of a sudden German attack on the Canadian coast was in people's minds. Appointments of civilians and military personnel were made immediately. Roosevelt appointed as chief civilian member of the board New York City mayor Fiorello La Guardia, an energetic figure and a longtime anti-Nazi, and the board held its first session within days.

J. Pierrepont Moffat, the American minister to Canada, was present at the Ogdensburg meeting. He had dinner after one of the sessions with four senior administration figures, Major General Edwin "Pa" Watson, the president's military aide; Admiral Ross McIntyre, Roosevelt's physician; Captain John Callaghan, naval aide to the president; and Gene Regnier, the military secretary to Stimson.

At the end of the evening he recorded some impressions in his diary: "All seemed to believe that England would win the war largely because of character; B) that continental Europe was gone and not worth serious worry; C) that we had a holy duty to save England almost irrespective of cost; D) that we would probably be in the war before very long (this last implied rather than expressed)."

. . .

U.S. Navy chiefs recalled that Woodrow Wilson had refused to allow any talks between the American and British services even while war approached, slowing the process of coordination once America entered the war. They asked if they could have talks with the British navy. Roosevelt agreed readily. A committee was set up in London under Admiral Sir Sydney Bailey to plan naval cooperation in the event of America entering the war. They discussed grand strategy. They decided that while the principal role of the American navy would be to deter Japan in the Pacific, it might also be required to help Britain keep open the Atlantic sea lanes.

In August, a delegation of representatives of the three services went to Britain. At their head was the assistant chief of naval operations,

Rear Admiral Robert L. Ghormley, an urbane Virginian with long experience as a staff officer, who had been briefed by Roosevelt. They traveled in civilian clothes aboard the British liner *Britannic*. Their mission was supposed to be secret, but they heard about it in the mid Atlantic on the radio news. Once the news was out it was said that they were going to advise the British on using the American equipment that was being sold to them.

In London they had a briefing from Ambassador Kennedy, who was pessimistic about Britain's plight and blamed Churchill. One thing that came out of their visit was a flood of technical information from the British services that was very valuable to the American services preparing for a war with new tactics and technology. To cope with these the number of service attachés at the American embassy was increased severalfold. The three-man delegation was not told all the secrets that Donovan was, but it was given wide access to the services and sat in on staff conferences. When Major General Delos Emmons, the USAF chief of planning, attended one top-level RAF conference, he saw a cultural difference from the American services. As General Lee recorded his reactions:

> What amazes Emmons is first, the apparent calmness and unhurried manner of speech and action among these high commanders, and second, their deference to ideas other than their own. In the United States, where commanders and executives are so hardpressed that they never have time to think and where movement is mistaken for efficiency and where each member of a conference tries to impose his ideas *in toto* by persistence, by shouting and by repetition, or finally, by downright refusal to play, such a reasonable and cooperative attitude is almost never found.

The Americans visited Northolt air base to see the life of a fighter squadron. When the "scramble" order came over the loudspeaker, they started a stop watch and were impressed when they found that all twelve Hurricanes were off the ground within four minutes and fifty seconds. It was a busy day. The Hurricanes were scrambled four times while they were there, and shot down two bombers.

The visit by these men and the exchange of information that followed, like Donovan's mission, established a relationship of intimacy and confidentiality. In the government and among the military, Britons and Americans became used to sharing ideas, attitudes, and secrets. This relationship was supported by the sympathies of the peoples. There was never total identity. The two governments had different and sometimes conflicting policies. Military men were not always comradely — some military men on each side disliked and suspected the other nation. But the habit of cooperation continued, the sense of a shared culture was recognized more, and the knowledge of shared fundamental political principles became more important in the face of the threat to them.

Towns in most parts of Britain were being bombed. This was a new experience for most people, and one long anticipated. People were curious to know what it would be like and recorded their response. The novelist Margery Allingham was woken by bombs and found she was short of breath. "It got worse and worse and I suddenly thought, 'My God, I'm gassed,' and I shot out of bed and took a deep and gasping breath, suicidal had I been right. This woke me completely and I found I was better and that I must have caught my breath on the first crash, which half woke me, and not had the sense to go on breathing again. Other people say they noticed the same sort of phenomenon, and the main thing we are all agreed on is that you can never be sure how it is going to take you."

A Mass Observation observer had a different reaction: "A real tremor and shock goes through the house. There is a lot of gunfire, bombs some way off . . . I cannot keep awake — yet a feeling of exhilaration that the war has come here too, that we are sharing in it, and a distinct warlikeness that is perhaps primitive, a desire to fight, to kill, even."

A woman who was a volunteer teaching assistant in Bristol recalled: "I heard a bomb in the distance so I said, 'Come on, can't you children sing louder than that?' So the children shouted the songs. The head said to me, 'You're much more useful than your predecessor. He got under the table and cried and called on the Virgin Mary.'"

Newspapers reported the daily tally of losses like scores in a sporting event, using the exaggerated figures that were being put out. Because of the paper shortage, newspaper posters were banned and newspaper sellers wrote their own: "R.A.F. 17, Huns 9." "Biggest Raid Ever — Score 78 to 26, England Still Batting." People talked about it constantly. Farm delivery man: "Here's your potatoes. Didn't we get a lovely bag yesterday, fifty-three against sixteen. He'll soon find out what he's in for." Policeman: "We got a lot of them yesterday, didn't we." Pub owner as a man orders a drink: "Nice bag yesterday."

People were personifying the enemy as Hitler. "Do you think he'll pay us another visit tonight?" "Our lads gave him a bad time yesterday."

Only London was spared bombing, but it was coming closer. German bombers attacked the docks just downriver from London and Croydon airfield in an outer suburb. The first raid on Croydon killed sixty-two people, including the entire management board of a factory near the airfield who were meeting at the time.

The Croydon town clerk recalled:

> The air battles by day were a marvel to behold. If one were near the aerodrome at almost any hour, one would hear from the loudspeaker the order to the action squadron prefaced by such words as "Fifty bandits approaching from the Southeast" . . . The air would throb invisibly with sound as one looked up to the dazzling heights; then, like minute glittering swarms of flies, the squadron would momentarily come into sight, the roaring and rattling noise reaching the ground being their engines and the sound of their machine-guns.

The writer Vita Sackville-West, watching from her famously elegant country garden, Sissinghurst, could view an air battle with detachment as an aesthetic spectacle:

> Then the planes arrive. They fly overhead in a great flight like geese, and people looking up from the fields wonder vaguely whether they are Germans or ours. We then observe that one goose has become detached from the flight and that two fighters are tumbling around it in the summer sky. Machine-guns crackle. The goose wavers in its flight; it banks; it sinks; it is wounded; its great wings flag. We hear later that it has been brought down at Appledore, ten miles away.

A few German bombers flew over and dropped bombs at night, often flying alone. RAF scientists worked out what they were up to: trying out a new directional beam that could guide bombers to their targets, something that would play a part later on. These had a serious nuisance value. The air raid sirens would sound when one approached, and as it often crossed a good part of England, they would sound over a wide area. Some people went to shelters, others just lay awake and worried.

Nella Last noted in her diary:

> We are going to bed after the news at 9:30, to try to get some sleep before the planes or air raid warnings come. I've averaged only three hours sleep all week. I seem to be lying fully awake at 11:30, straining my ears for the sound of the planes. When they come they circle round and round over the fields and the countryside, looking for us — like a dog trying to pick up scent. I lie tense and still, expecting to hear the crash of bombs. When they have gone I still listen, listen; and if I doze I wake with a start and a feeling of *what's that.*

After a while the authorities decided not to sound the siren for one or two planes, but this meant that bombs occasionally came down without any warning.

People kept going. A woman in a village in Sussex writing to a friend in London described an air raid six days before the annual village festival, and said:

> But we held our fête on Saturday with stalls, side shows, dancing on the lawn and the acting out of scenes from *Twelfth Night* under the old mulberry tree, which is a stone's throw from the path still called Princess Gap because Princess Elizabeth used to walk there when she stayed in our village in the days before she became Shakespeare's Queen Elizabeth. So it was all very much in the English order, and we felt quite secure with one foot in the Sixteenth and the other in the Twentieth Century . . . Just when the clown was singing "Come away, come away death," the sirens wailed. Not a soul moved; the play went on.

This was the authentic voice of the educated British middle class, unshakable in its tone, meeting the war with light-hearted fortitude and an insistently civilized response.

It is seen in the opening of a man's letter to a friend: "I think I can claim to be the only person in Southern England to have been blown off a lavatory seat while reading Jane Austen."

It is seen in a paragraph from a letter written by Christopher Mayhew to his mother on learning that his brother Patrick, a Christian pacifist and conscientious objector serving as an ambulance driver, had been decorated for bravery at Dunkirk: "It is the most delightful incident of the war so far. One's faith is simultaneously strengthened in democracy for allowing Pat to object; in the army for decorating an objector to itself; in Pat himself; in religion for helping him not to run until the time came; even in compulsory games for training him to run so fast when the time did come."

Being bombed, or knowing that you are likely to be bombed, simplifies issues. The doubts and confusion that were heard in May and June were almost entirely absent from conversation and comment now. The Ministry of Information was monitoring public opinion constantly, and their reports show a firming up of attitudes. One report said: "Every bomb Hitler drops strengthens ordinary people's determination."

The U.S. embassy in London asked the American consuls in different cities to report on the effects of bombing, and their reports bear this out. The reports were sent to Washington on August 16, and the summary on the first page said: "Considered reports from U.S. consuls throughout Great Britain indicate that there is a strengthening of civilian morale rather than a weakening, and that German air raids have done little damage, while rousing British determination to resist."

The author also says: "My own observation is that the principal (and almost the only) weak spot in this respect is among the commercial element in London, who think only in terms of pounds, shillings and pence and whose existence centers around 'deals' of one sort or another. These people have some foggy idea that the issue between this country and Hitler can be made a matter of accommodation, and that they would be able to keep their property."

The reports from the consuls all speak of calm, high morale, and a desire to win the war. Glasgow: "The morale of the civil population here is excellent." Plymouth (a south coast navy port which had been bombed repeatedly): "The people in this area have withstood their ordeals very well and there is every reason to believe they will give a good account of themselves in any future crisis." Cardiff: "The morale of the Welsh people is high and will continue to be unmoved by enemy operations." Liverpool: "In my opinion the people in this area will not be stampeded however serious the raids become . . . enthusiastic about doing everything possible to win."

General Lee, forwarding these reports, added his own comments, which reflect some puzzlement about British calmness in their plight: "I am convinced that the average man who admits that the situation is serious does not really believe it. Even many of those quite capable of thinking do not believe it. The Ministry of Information does not intend that they shall believe it. Possibly the Ministry itself does not believe it."

He concluded on the note of admiration which is to be found in most Americans' comments on Britain at this time. "But against this 'wishful thinking' is the fact that the people are sturdily British in the best sense of the word. They will meet the test with courage and philosophy. They will face it, perhaps, better than the politicians in office."

Lee's puzzlement about British insouciance was shared by others at this time. Mollie Panter-Downes, writing from London in the *New Yorker,* told her readers: "It would be difficult for an impartial observer to decide today whether the British are the bravest people in the world or just the stupidest."

The Hungarian-born writer Arthur Koestler asked himself the same question when he encountered what appeared to be an insanely casual attitude to the war. Having fled Nazi Germany and then escaped from occupied France, he volunteered for the British army. But when the call-up order came two months later, he was finishing his book *Scum of the Earth*. He said it would take him two weeks to finish it, so his publisher wrote to the recruiting office asking whether he could have a deferment. He received a reply from the recruiting center agreeing to the request and saying: "I am therefore postponing Mr. Koestler's calling-up, and would suggest that he calls at this center when he is at liberty to join His Majesty's forces." Koestler recounts this in his autobiography and says: "Having read this remarkable document, I was more than ever convinced that England must lose the war."

Harold Nicolson put it another way in a diary note: "My reason tells me that it will be almost impossible to beat the Germans and that we shall be bombed and invaded . . . Yet these probabilities do not fill me with despair. For the moment, we are all anaesthetized."

One person who was certainly not anesthetized was Sir Alexander Cadogan, the head of the Foreign Office, as his diaries reveal. Cadogan was an aristocrat and an experienced diplomat. Government-speak seemed his natural language. His diaries, published after his death, reveal another side, which he allowed out only in the privacy of his study. They are full of gloom, bile, and xenophobia, a counterpoint to the high-mindedness of official pronouncements. The Sir Alexander of the diaries is a grouchy Sancho Panza to Churchill's Don Quixote.

On May 16 he wrote: "The blackest days I have ever lived through. But there are doubtless worse to come."

A characteristic entry on June 29: "Everything is as gloomy as can be. Probability is that Hitler will attempt invasion in the next fortnight. As far as I can see we are completely unprepared. We have simply got to die at our posts — a far better fate than capitulating to Hitler as those damned Frogs have done."

Also: May 19, when Samuel Hoare, a former minister, left to take up an ambassadorial post in Madrid: "Dirty little dog has got the wind up and wants to get out of this country." The following day: "Another glorious day. Only man is vile . . . One bright spot — lots of Germans and Italians in Madrid and therefore a good chance of SH being murdered."

May 29, after discussions of delicate moves designed to keep the Italians out of the war: "Cabinet discussion of what to do with the ice cream vendors. Drown the brutes is what I should like to do."

June 2: "French howling for assistance on the Somme. Perhaps we should give them a token but it's so much down the drain. It won't prevent the French reviling us. I'd rather cut loose and concentrate on the defense of these islands."

June 10: "Musso declares war. Am rather glad. Now we can say what we think of these purulent dogs."

June 15: "We'll all fight like cats or die rather than submit to Hitler. U.S. looks pretty useless. Well, we must die without them."

•   •   •

The Ministry of Information had another source or insight into people's feelings about the war. It censored letters going overseas and read what people were writing. In August it produced a confidential report on this for the cabinet. It said: "Civilian morale in this mail is outstandingly good. Complete confidence in ultimate victory and a pleasurable anticipation of the excitements that must come first are the key note in almost all letters . . . Recent intensification of air raids seems to have had almost exhilarating effect on people's spirits, and the general impression given is of a large and united family, looking forward to a great adventure which they will go through together."

As an account of national morale, this sounds too good to be true. But quotes from some of the letters, which the ministry produced along with its report, support it.

"Now we have got our expeditionary force back . . . we feel we are sharing the dangers with them, and there is no one to let us down." "We certainly are a wonderful people and we are pleased to belong to this tight little island." "I would not be anywhere but here for a fortune. Life is full of adventure."

"It's like watching a nation fighting for its life, and being reborn in the process." "We are all facing the same anxieties, and this makes such a wonderful bond between us." "We have dug down deep into the roots of this old country and have rediscovered the spirit of the old yeomen."

Some thought even sending children away was cowardice. "To tear the children away from England now would make me feel I was forsaking her in her hour of need. There are things even children can do to help the national effort, and I think it best for them, morally, to remain here," one said.

What motivated these letter writers and kept them going was not abstract terms like democracy or freedom, nor the fate of democracy in the world. They drew their strength from simple feelings of patriotism, from deep, historic tribal roots. But patriotism is not value-free. This was not the *fuehrerprinzip,* nor was it anything like the emperor worship that inspired the Japanese. The image evoked was not of a king or a military leader but the old yeomen of England. The yeoman is the common man whose principal characteristic is his independence. In Medieval times, in the modified form of feudalism that existed in England, he was a free man who owned his own land, the Englishman whose soul is his own and whose home is his castle, inviolable even to kings. He was partly a caricature, like the sea dogs of old who ruled the waves for Britannia, but this was the image summoned up. British patriotism had some democratic content.

Despite its singleness of purpose, British society was still divided; there was a gap as wide as an ocean between the lives of rich and poor. They may have shared the dangers, but not the hardships.

The wealthy still had servants to cushion their lives, although, with more men going into the services, these now had to be cajoled into service. Advertisements such as these appeared daily in the "Domestic Situations Vacant" columns of the *Times*. "Butler-valet and cook required, Somerset. Two in family, six staff." "Second housemaid of three. Maidenhead, Berks. Eight staff." "Wanted, butler. Good references. One in family, eight staff." Sir Henry Channon, member of Parliament and socialite, recorded in his diary an evening at the Dorchester Hotel with champagne flowing freely and wrote: "London lives well. I've never seen such lavishness." Yet many people, including servicemen's families, could not afford to buy the weekly meat ration of six ounces.

Nor did those running the affairs of state entirely abandon their leisurely pace, even while the masses were being exhorted to work hard. The diary of John Colville, Churchill's private secretary, shows a succession of trips to the country, bridge parties, and visits to the theater, and he read *War and Peace* that summer. General Ironside fumed in his diary on June 22: "We are still a weekending cabinet. This evening I have not been able to get hold of half the people I wanted to get on to. I am sure the Nazi machine works fulltime and at weekends."

At dinner parties, the niceties were retained. People wore evening dress, and at the end of the meal the ladies would retire to the drawing room while the men smoked cigars and discussed serious matters. Major General Sir Edward Spears wrote in his diary, on a dinner with Churchill and others at Admiralty House: "The ladies left and conversation turned to the defense of Brittany."

Yet things were changing. There were increasing demands for more equality of sacrifice. The left-wing magazine *Tribune* said: "If you ration four or five foods that bulk largely in the workers' diet — meat, tea, butter and margarine, sugar — and leave unrationed food that is not so commonly seen on the people's dinner tables, you are cushioning the rich and comfortable from the discomforts that war brings." The *Lancet*, the journal of the British Medical Association, issued a pamphlet called *The Children Must Be Fed*, calling for immediate government subsidies to enable everyone to have a proper diet.

Others also were saying that there was no going back to the old ways. The London *Times*, which had been a strong supporter of the Chamberlain government, now said in a much-quoted editorial that democracy should mean the right to work as well as the right to vote. "The new order cannot be based on the preservation of privilege, whether the privilege be that of a country, a class or an individual," it said.

The government was taking steps in this direction. When milk went on the ration it inaugurated a scheme to distribute free milk to children, followed soon by free orange juice — adults could not get any orange juice at all since oranges were imported. These were the harbingers of larger schemes of food subsidies and benefits for children. It began requiring certain factories to provide canteens for their workers. The welfare state was over the horizon.

. . .

While the public counted the number of British and German aircraft shot down, government ministers were looking at other numbers: the depletion week by week of the overseas assets with which Britain was financing the war and its day-to-day existence. These were now falling so disastrously that Britain faced the prospect of defeat far from any battlefield. August was a critical month for the economy also, and the crisis in this area was just as urgent and just as profound in its implications as in any other.

On August 21 the chancellor of the exchequer, Sir Kingsley Wood, circulated among the War Cabinet a confidential document. It made grim reading. It began: "I am seriously perturbed at the rate at which our gold and exchange resources are now disappearing." It said total resources had shrunk from £775 million ($3.1 billion) in January to £490 million. This decline was much greater than anticipated, partly because with the fall of France Britain had taken over French contracts with American manufacturers. With the orders for aircraft, tanks, and other supplies now envisaged, the adverse balance of payments would be nearly doubled in the next year.

The report made it clear that America was central to all the chancellor's hopes for the future. It said U.S. Treasury Secretary Morgenthau had been told that Britain would want "massive" credits in the following year and went on:

> Mr. Morgenthau made it clear that the Administration would not at present enter into promises or commitments, and it appears certain that no undertaking of any kind could be obtained before the election. That United States help will be forthcoming, however

the election goes, appears to be the view of our representatives in America, though the time, extent and character of the help may depend on factors which cannot be forecast, such as the course of the war and the extent to which that body of opinion in America which is strongly opposed to entanglements succeeds in influencing the electoral campaign.

The conclusion Wood drew from this was: "We are faced with the immediate practical problem of holding out until well into November in the case of a Democratic victory, or until after 20 January, when the new President takes office, in the case of a Republican victory." He went on to say that American financial aid would probably not be given without conditions or limit. "How far those conditions or that limit will interfere with the present tempo of our war effort and how far with our standard of life," he said, "only the future can tell."

He pointed out that Britain could not spend all its gold reserves on armaments from America because it still had to buy food and other raw materials from overseas.

The cabinet discussed this report the following morning, August 22, when Sir Kingsley Wood spelled out again the bad news. He went through various options for obtaining more gold, from India and South Africa or from the governments of German-occupied countries, which, he admitted, might be reluctant to part with it. He said that as a drastic measure, they could requisition gold ornaments including wedding rings, but that would raise only £20 million. Churchill said this was something they could do at a later stage if they wanted to make a striking gesture "for the purpose of shaming the Americans."

Beaverbrook, temperamentally incapable of pessimism, thought the position was not all that bad and said they could get some of the French gold that was held in Canada. He said Britain had enough to meet its needs "until the United States comes out into the open." He recommended filling American factories with British orders. Then, if Britain could not pay, no American government could tell them to halt production because of the unemployment and economic disruption that would follow.

Churchill did not believe in cutting spending on weapons. He said the best way to economize was to shorten the war; nothing could be more extravagant than to create a situation in which they had to fight a

prolonged war "in a broken-backed condition." He concluded by asking all ministries to economize on nonessential expenditures in dollar
areas.

The reality was plain to those in the cabinet room, although it was
hidden from the public. Britain was a great imperial power resting on a
crumbling base. Earlier in the year, the chiefs of staff had told the cabinet Britain could not win the war without American help. In August the
Treasury told it that Britain could not even continue the war without
American help.

The struggle seen in these cabinet discussions was not the one the
world was seeing, nor the one the British public was watching. It was
not a war against tyranny but a war against economic collapse. Britain
was fighting both wars. In order to continue the first, it had to lose the
second. J. M. Keynes, the preeminent economist of the time and a government advisor, said later: "We threw good housekeeping to the winds,
but we saved ourselves and we helped save the world."

In May the cabinet had discussed seeking an accommodation with
Nazi Germany instead of continuing the war. In August it discussed
continuing the war and becoming financially dependent upon the
United States in order to do so. The two were never discussed at the
same time, but in fact they were alternatives: accommodation with Hitler or dependence on America. The government made its choice.

10

THE BIGGEST TARGET

In America at this time there was an upsurge of sympathy for Britain, the plucky little island holding out against the might of Nazi Germany. In movie theaters people watched the young men at British airfields running to their fighter planes as the siren sounded and thrilled at the drama. The postcard images of Britain — the thatched-roof cottage, the London bobby with his tall helmet, the ancient castle — all became symbols of the stand against tyranny. Shakespeare's patriotic speeches were given a contemporary twist. A favorite, quoted often, was "This England never did and never shall / Lie at the proud foot of a conqueror," pulled out from the rarely performed *King John*.

Stereotypes lingered. The *New York Times* carried a photograph to show British women working for the war effort. The three pictured were Viscountess Caroline Bridgman, the marchioness of Reading, and Mrs. Montagu Norman, the wife of the governor of the Bank of England.

Celebrities staged benefit performances for British War Relief, which raised money for ambulances, hospital equipment, and mobile canteens, and women knitted and sewed for Bundles for Britain. An American Committee for the Defense of British Homes collected sporting guns, revolvers, and binoculars to be sent to Britain's Home Guard. These went with messages such as: "To help you in England in your hour of need from Mr. and Mrs. J. B. Harrison and family." "For the defense of the old country from Mr. and Mrs. Jones." Others went further and organized a blood donor scheme called Blood for Britain. People who were proud of the struggle of an earlier generation of Americans to throw off British rule wore lapel badges with joined Stars and Stripes and Union Jack. Winston Churchill became a hero to Americans, his speeches to the British people broadcast on American networks.

New York City mayor Fiorello La Guardia, as president of the annual Conference of American Mayors, invited the lord mayor of London to be guest of honor at their September meeting. He could not come but he sent a message.

Richard Taylor, a schoolteacher in Apponang, Rhode Island, wrote to a British friend: "We listen to the radio constantly and read the papers eagerly and take as much satisfaction in British victories as though we ourselves were British subjects."

Drew Middleton, who was reporting from Britain for the Associated Press, was amazed at the attitude of his family in South Orange, New Jersey, when he went home on leave. They had never shown much interest in Britain before, but at a family dinner to welcome him back, they turned on the radio when Churchill was due to speak and fell silent. When Churchill had finished, an uncle broke the silence saying, "What a great man!" Someone else followed with, "What a great people!"

People who had never had, or at any rate never acknowledged, any affection for Britain found that they liked having it there; that its removal from their landscape or transformation by conquest was something they could not contemplate with equanimity. In 1939 most Americans were anti-Nazi. In the summer of 1940, most were pro-British.

The number in favor of actually entering the war was still small. There is an interesting distinction here. Asked whether the United States should declare war on Germany, fewer than 10 percent answered "yes." But when pollsters asked what they would do if a vote were taken on the issue, 15 percent said they would vote in favor. It seems that some people were willing to go to war but not to let the president take them into war.

The view of Britain's prospects improved. At the end of June only a third of those questioned said they thought Britain would win. By August this had risen to 50 percent, and it continued to rise. Adolf Berle wrote in his diary on September 6: "Our military staff people came in this morning. They are more optimistic about the British fighting than they have been for some time."

At the New York World's Fair, which was in its second and final season, the British pavilion was now the most popular attraction, drawing more customers even than General Motors' Futurama. As in the previous year, its centerpiece was the Magna Carta, presented as a fount of democratic freedoms. Another popular feature demonstrating the ties between the two nations was a family tree showing George Washington's descent from King John, who signed the Magna Carta, and several of the barons who also signed it. This summer in addition it showed documentary films of Britain at war, and these were a big draw.

Titles of magazine articles in August and September show the predominant tone of the media: "John Bull Ready," *Newsweek;* "Rush All Possible Aid to Britain," *Reader's Digest;* "Bulldog Breed," *Collier's* (which, like the *Reader's Digest,* had been isolationist a year earlier); "Cliffs of England Stand," *Atlantic;* "How We Can Help Britain," *New Republic;* "Never Did, Never Shall," *Time* (an echo from Shakespeare).

The Time-Life organization produced a series of short current affairs films for movie theaters called *The March of Time.* Now it produced a full-length *March of Time* about America in World War One, and in contrast to most earlier depictions of America's entry into the war, it celebrated it as progress from neutrality to participation to victory. The British embassy in Washington told the Foreign Office: "The U.S. Press has never been so little critical of Britain and so sincerely concerned for her survival."

The British government stepped up its information services for America. Previously, the BBC's short-wave transatlantic broadcasts were part of its empire service and were aimed primarily at Canada. In 1940 it started a North American service aimed at the United States, and this carried speeches by Churchill and the king and special reports. Producers found they had to try to get Americans accustomed to the British accent, which sounds effete to American ears, and to British modesty also. The director of the North American service, Maurice Gorham, recalled their problem: "We would get hold of some commando with a desperate record, would meet him in the studio, finding an enormous athlete with a face like Victor McLagen — and then over the microphone would come, 'Oh, it's nothing much really,' in a little piping voice."

J. B. Priestley was a popular broadcaster on the BBC's transatlantic service, as he was at home, his Yorkshire accent a counterpoint to the refined standard BBC voices. His message often veered away from the official line. Although he loved the English countryside he dismissed the view of England as a land of quaint villages and stolid country-folk. Such a land would not last ten minutes in a war against Nazi Germany, he said; it could not produce the Spitfire or the Hurricane. When the air raids on London began and one or two American correspondents described it as "hell on earth," he rejected the term, saying he had been in the trenches on the Somme in World War One and he knew what hell on earth was.

Americans welcomed things British. They learned another London place-name when the romantic song "A Nightingale Sang in Berkeley Square" made the hit parade, as the top ten songs were called. The song's lyricist, Eric Maschwitz, was at that time working for BSC in New York, heading a team that forged documents.

Mixed in with the widespread admiration for Britain's stand was an element of gratitude. Americans wanted Britain to survive because they liked Britain and what it stood for as well as disliking Nazi Germany. But they wanted it to survive also because, increasingly, they saw Britain as America's first line of defense, and it was in their own interest that it survive. As retired brigadier general Thomas E. Merrill wrote in a letter to the *San Francisco Chronicle* urging more help for Britain: "Can we afford to indulge in half-measures on behalf of England while she is fighting for our future as well as her own?" Self-interest strengthened the sentiment.

A long poem about America and Britain, *The White Cliffs* by Alice Duer Miller, appeared as a book and shot into the bestseller list, something unheard of for a poem, selling 300,000 copies within weeks. It was autobiographical, telling the story of how this girl from a Rhode Island Yankee background married into the English upper class shortly before the First World War. Her husband was killed in the war but she stayed on, allowing her son to be raised in the traditions of his class. She disliked the snobbery and rigidity of her English in-laws but came to admire their spirit and their sense of duty. She came to see also the historic British commitment to freedom and the British roots of the American tree of liberty. It was not great poetry, but her last lines were powerful because they were terribly relevant:

I am American bred,
I have seen much to hate here — much to forgive,
But in a world where England is finished and dead
I do not wish to live.

• • •

The Italian entry into the war opened up another front, in the Mediterranean and North Africa. This presented a threat to Britain's oil supplies and its position in the Middle East. The small British forces stationed in Egypt faced a force of some 250,000 men in the Italian colony of Libya. Britain reinforced Egypt with Australian troops from Palestine and some South Africans. Churchill wanted to pull more troops out of Palestine and arm the Jews there, but dropped the idea at Foreign Office insistence. Determined to fight on every front, the British government drew from the meager forces defending the homeland to send troops and 100 tanks to Egypt. With the Italian navy and air force roaming the Mediterranean these had to go right around Africa, which kept them out of action for several weeks and made yet more demands on British destroyers, which had to convoy them.

Churchill was unremittingly bellicose. He insisted that the army plan raids on the Continent, and started the Special Operations Executive to organize resistance and sabotage in the occupied countries. He said he wanted the lives of German occupying soldiers to be made "unceasing torment." He discussed with the chiefs of staff plans for offensive operations against mainland Europe in the following year.

He sent a memo to Beaverbrook, in charge of aircraft production, pointing to Hitler's strong position and saying: "But there is one thing that will bring him down, and that is absolutely devastating, exterminating attack by very heavy bombers from this country on the Nazi homeland. We must be able to overwhelm them by this means." Production was going ahead with new bombers which would be the heaviest in the world and would indeed carry out devastating attacks on Germany.

He practiced shooting with a revolver in case the Germans reached London. When he met David Niven, who had returned to rejoin the regiment he had left some years earlier for Hollywood stardom, he said, "Young man, you did a very fine thing to give up a most promising career to fight for your country." As Niven stammered out some words of appreciation he added, "Mark you, had you not done so it would have been despicable."

His daughter-in-law, Pamela Churchill (later Pamela Harriman), says Churchill once told her that every citizen could fight the Germans if they came. When she protested that she did not have a gun and did not know how to use one, he growled, "Well you can go into the kitchen and get a carving knife." As she tells the story, he gave no indication that he was not serious.

Germany still did not have the command of the air that Hitler said was needed for an invasion. The Luftwaffe stepped up its attacks on airfields. The Germans tried to lure fighter planes up to do battle with their own fighters, but the RAF wanted its fighters to attack bombers. On one occasion they sent over a small group of bombers escorted by 500 ME109 fighters, almost the entire force, but the ruse did not work. At the end of the month, they attacked Birmingham and Liverpool, although the ME109s could not fly that far and they had to rely on the slower ME110s as escorts. Losses on both sides mounted.

At Warmwell fighter station in Dorset, the station commander, a martinet, complained that pilots were not turning up at scheduled mealtimes and ordered the officers' mess closed outside regular hours. Squadron Leader George Dailey wrote to him saying he had asked the Luftwaffe to carry out its attacks only between mealtimes so that his pilots would be free to eat on schedule but was receiving no cooperation. The cold war between station commander and pilots continued even after the pilots were scrambled to fight off an attack on the station. Pilots cooked their own breakfasts in the dispersal hut using camping equipment. The kitchen crew purloined a heap of food and left it for them with a note saying they thought they were "bloody marvelous."

Fighter pilots were still being scrambled several times in a day, and the strain was telling. Squadron Leader Peter Townsend described his reaction when his airfield was raided. "Normally as frightened as anyone, not even bombs could move me then. I placed my pillow reverently over my head and waited for the rest. Worsall [occupying the next bed] still had the energy to be frightened, but I was past caring. It was a bad sign. I was more exhausted than I realized."

Squadron Leader Pat Hughes, much admired for restoring his squadron's morale after its losses in the battle for France, was killed six weeks after he was married when he crashed his plane into a German bomber. His squadron intelligence officer, Gregory Kikorian, said: "When he came to see me the night before he died saying he had spots in front of his eyes, it was already too late. How could pilots cope with this tension?"

For a few, reserves of courage were running out. There was at least one instance when a squadron leader had to reprimand his pilots for turning away from an oncoming force, and several when a pilot turned back from a mission because of a malfunction in the plane which the mechanics could not find. Dowding issued an order that all pilots must have twenty-four hours leave each week.

The battles were becoming a war of attrition. Between July 10 and August 12 the Germans lost nearly three hundred planes, the British one hundred fifty. But more British planes were coming off the production lines, and losses were being replaced. Pilots were another matter. In August one-fifth of the RAF's fighter pilots on active service were killed or wounded. New pilots were going into combat with only twenty hours' experience of Hurricanes or Spitfires. Men were being transferred from the Fleet Air Arm.

The RAF was under strain. Park reported on September 5 that damage to communications was extensive, and that "almost complete disorganization of the defense system makes control of our fighter squadrons extremely difficult." On September 7, Dowding called a meeting with senior RAF officers to discuss the deteriorating situation. Figures showed that 348 fighter pilots had been killed or put out of action in the previous month while the training schools were turning out 280 a month. Dowding said the pilots were overworked and overtired. "I want you to take away from this meeting the feeling that the situation is extremely grave," he told the others.

In the last days of August the German aircraft attacked Birmingham, Liverpool, and Bristol, by day and at night as well. The British had no effective defenses against night attacks at this stage, any more than the Germans did. They were working on radar devices that could be carried in aircraft but these were not developed yet. In July 258 British civilians were killed in bombing raids; in August 1,075. More than half were women and children. The Germans were trying to attack British industry, but RAF chiefs saw the attacks on towns instead of airfields as a mistake on Germany's part, dissipating their efforts.

A few bombs fell on London — in the suburb of Wimbledon, fourteen people were killed and fifty-nine wounded — and there were regular air raid warnings and occasional bombs, but the capital was not subjected to sustained raids. On the night of August 24–25, two of a group of bombers attacking the docks dropped their bombs on central London. No one was killed but one bomb damaged the historic St. Giles's church in Cripplegate.

In response, the War Cabinet ordered raids on Berlin and several other German cities, and a group of bombers set out to bomb Tempelhof Airport in Berlin and the nearby Siemens works. They hit neither but dropped bombs in a Berlin suburb, killing no one. They had to fly five times as far to reach Berlin as the German planes, based just across the channel, had to go to bomb London. Berlin was at the limit of their range, and although they encountered no opposition, they ran into a strong headwind and three of them ran out of fuel and had to ditch in the sea. The next night they attacked four other German towns.

Churchill wanted more attacks on Berlin. He wrote in a minute to the chief of air staff: "Now that they have begun to molest the capital I want you to hit them hard, and Berlin is the place to hit them." So the RAF attacked Berlin again, and this time the bombs killed eight people. The British did not need decoded intercepts to know what Hitler's response would be. They heard it from Hitler himself.

In a speech at the Sportzpalast in Berlin to a mass meeting consisting mostly of women health workers, he began in an unusually light tone. He promised that the invasion of Britain was still on the agenda, saying: "The people of England are curious. They ask, 'Why in the world don't you come?' We're coming, don't worry, we're coming." His audience laughed appreciatively. Then he warned that if German cities were bombed then bombs would rain down on Britain's cities and his voice rose to a shout. "If they attack our cities, we will wipe out theirs!" he promised, and thousands of women responded with frenzied applause.

It must have been clear to Churchill that the bombs that landed on London were an aberration and not an act of policy. (In fact Göring ordered the pilots responsible disciplined.) But by bombing Berlin, he provoked Hitler into switching the weight of his attacks away from the airfields, where they were causing the RAF serious damage, to the capital. When the first raid on Berlin produced no response he ordered another, and only then did Hitler respond. He never said that this was his intention, but it would have made grim sense strategically. Dowding admitted that he was "heartily relieved" when the Luftwaffe switched its attack from the airfields to London.

Churchill himself wrote in his memoirs: "Far more important to us than the protection of London from terror-bombing was the functioning and articulation of these airfields and the squadrons working from them . . . We never thought of the struggle in terms of the defense of London or any other place, but only who won in the air." Civilians, it seems, were more expendable than fighter planes.

In fact there are other reasons why the Luftwaffe commanders wanted to bomb London, and they may have urged this on Hitler. They had greatly overestimated the British losses and thought Fighter Command was on its last legs. An attack on London was certain to bring the remaining fighters into the air to defend the capital, and then they could be finished off. If Hitler wanted to reduce Britain by bombardment and blockade, eliminating Fighter Command was an essential step.

Ultra intercepted the order for the first big attack on London. It was to be on September 7, the day of Dowding's meeting with RAF chiefs. The emergency services were alerted.

■ ■ ■

Roosevelt said once that if he could tell an attorney general what he wanted done and the attorney general found a way to do it, that was a good attorney general. He had known Robert Jackson since his days in New York State politics, and Jackson had steered a tortuous path through the law to get some of his New Deal measures through. Now Jackson drew up a memorandum, based on the Acheson-Cohen letter, saying that the administration could transfer the destroyers without going to Congress first.

Nonetheless, the projected bases-for-destroyers deal was at an impasse. Roosevelt wanted a trade, Churchill wanted an exchange of gifts. He cabled Roosevelt: "Our view is that we are two friends in danger helping each other as we can. We should like to give you the facilities mentioned without stipulating for any return, and even if tomorrow you found it too difficult to transfer the destroyers etc., our offer still remains open because we think it is in the general good." (This was not what he had said in cabinet a few weeks earlier, when he rejected Lothian's suggestion that Britain offer America the bases without asking for anything in return.)

Lothian warned the British government that Hull was irritated by British stubbornness on the issue because the administration was putting its political life at stake in trying to hand over the destroyers. "To us, struggling for survival, these points may seem small but they loom large here," he said.

Kennedy, in London, realized that he was being by-passed in these negotiations, as he had been over Donovan's visit. He cabled Roosevelt: "As far as I can see, I am not doing a damned thing here that amounts to anything. To be perfectly honest, I do not enjoy being a dummy." Roosevelt remarked to Hull that "somebody's nose is being put out of joint," but he tried to placate Kennedy by telling him that the talks were being conducted with Lothian in Washington only because American military and naval chiefs had to be on hand. In fact, Kennedy, who was out of sympathy with the administration's view of the war, was being sidelined on all the most important issues that were being discussed between the two governments. When he went home on leave in October, he did not return.

Hull called in the legal advisor to the State Department, Green Hackworth, and Newman A. Townsend of the Justice Department, and asked them to find a way out of the impasse. They came up with a compromise. Since one side wanted an exchange of gifts and the other wanted a trade, they said, why not make some of the bases a gift and some a trade?

Hull took up the suggestion immediately, and he and Lothian drafted a letter for the British government setting out new terms. Naval and air bases in Newfoundland and Bermuda were to be given "as a gift." The bases in the West Indies, which were more important because of their proximity to the Panama Canal, were to be given "in exchange for military equipment." All the bases were to be on a ninety-nine-year lease, and the letter defined and limited American authority so that it did not infringe on British sovereignty. The promise regarding the British fleet remained.

Churchill cabled back that he agreed in general and threw in a base on the island of Antigua for good measure. Roosevelt approved the idea and left Hull and Knox to thrash out the details with Lothian.

The British cabinet approved the new drafts on August 29. Churchill was clear in his own mind that the exchange was an unequal one in America's favor, but he felt Britain had no choice. He wrote in his war memoirs: "There was of course no comparison between the intrinsic value of these antique and inefficient craft and the immense permanent strategic security afforded to the United States by the enjoyment of these island bases. But the threatened invasion, the importance of numbers in the narrow seas, made our need clamant." He also saw the advantage to Britain of such a decidedly un-neutral act on the part of the United States, which he thought would turn America "from a neutral to a non-belligerent."

The terms of the agreement were sent to Roosevelt when he was on a three-day trip through the South by train, dedicating the Chickamauga dam in Chattanooga, Tennessee, and the Great Smoky Mountains National Park, and he approved them. Lothian and Hull signed the agreement on September 2. The following day Admiral Stark formally gave his opinion that the transfer of the destroyers in exchange for the bases would enhance the security of the United States. The State Department prepared a presidential announcement to Congress which would be released the same day, while the president was still on his train.

Despite the opinion polls in favor of aid to Britain, Roosevelt still worried about it. He confided to Bernard Baruch, the financier, that he thought he might be impeached for what he was about to do. To his secretary, Grace Tully, who was traveling with him, he said, "Congress will probably raise hell about this, but even another day's delay may mean the end of civilization. Cries of 'war monger' and 'dictator' will fill the air, but if Britain is to survive we must act."

He decided to give the story to the twenty-three White House reporters who were accompanying him at the same time as the announcement was being made in Washington, on the last day of his journey. As the presidential train was rolling northward through the verdant Virginia countryside, they were summoned to his carriage, where they crowded in, some standing or squatting, for there were not enough seats.

Sitting at his desk with his cigarette holder jutting out of his mouth, he handled the meeting with his usual easy manner, starting with some jokey greetings: "Why, there's old Fred. Fred, who let you come in? Sit on the floor. Now there don't make a lady stand." Then he said, "I have something for you for your own information. It's a Washington story that will be out there in twenty-two minutes, so the story will come from Washington."

Then he read out the message, with occasional interjections, saying that the U.S. government had acquired the right to lease naval and air bases in Newfoundland and the Caribbean islands, which were named. "The rights to bases in Newfoundland and Bermuda are gifts — generously given and gladly received . . . The other bases mentioned have been acquired in exchange for fifty of our over-age destroyers."

Reporters asked about the leases. He said, "They are all ninety-nine years but Newfoundland and Bermuda are gifts. In other words, there is no quid pro quo in relation to them."

"No quid pro quo?"

"No quid pro quo at all. You see the point."

"Mr. President, what is the differentiation between these two?"

Roosevelt replied, "Oh, all kinds of things that nobody here would understand, so I won't mention them. It is a fait accompli. It is done this way."

He read more of the message to Congress: "This is the most important action in the reinforcement of our national defense that has been taken since the Louisiana Purchase. Then as now, considerations of safety from overseas attack were fundamental."

He then gave them, for background purposes, he said, his version of the purchase of the Louisiana Territory from France by President Jefferson in 1803, that first great act of executive authority just fourteen years after the Constitution was ratified. "We were scared to death that there might be, as an outcome of the Napoleonic Wars, some threat or some danger of some power going in there and going up the valley to connect up with Canada, thereby confining the States practically to this side of the Mississippi. There was an awful lot of discussion about it and everybody was yelling, 'For God's sake protect us' all over the country." Jefferson had decided that to put the purchase up to Congress would mean delay, so "he got the opinion of the attorney general that he could do it without a treaty, do it for the national defense as Commander in Chief and do it as President as well . . . There was never any treaty, there was never any two-thirds vote in the Senate." This version placed a greater emphasis on the defense issue than most accounts of the Louisiana Purchase.

He told the reporters that a message from Churchill would be published reiterating that if British waters became untenable the British fleet would not be given to Germany. A reporter asked, "Is that part of the deal?"

Roosevelt said, "No. It happens to come along at the same time."

"Fortuitously."

"Fortuitously, that is the word."

In his message to Congress announcing the deal, Roosevelt said, "This is not inconsistent in any way with our status of peace. Still less is it a threat to any nation." Attorney General Jackson's statement that the transfer was legal was sent to Congress along with the president's statement.

The promise about the British fleet was delivered in the form of an affirmation of an earlier statement. It was a letter from Churchill sent for publication: "You ask, Mr. President, whether my statement in Parliament on June 4, 1940, about never surrendering or scuttling her fleet 'represents the settled policy of His Majesty's Government.' It certainly does. I must however observe that these hypothetical contingencies seem more likely to concern the German fleet, or what is left of it, than our own."

Churchill reported the deal to Parliament and said: "I have no doubt that Herr Hitler will not like this transference of destroyers, and I have no doubt that he will pay the United States out if he ever gets the chance. That is why I am very glad that the army, air and naval frontiers of the United States have been advanced along a wide arc into the Atlantic Ocean, and that this will enable them to take danger by the throat while it is still hundreds of miles away from their homeland."

After all the hesitations and maneuverings and anxieties, it turned out that Roosevelt did not have to fight hard over the exchange. Congress did not raise hell about it. There were no demands for his impeachment. America was not rent by violent dispute. Most people and most of Congress approved the move. They accepted that the acquisition of the bases increased American security, and they supported the transfer of destroyers to Britain.

Willkie showed political courage in refusing to make the destroyers an election issue. His presence as the standard bearer of the Republican Party drew the sting out of the opposition in Congress. Senator McNary was against the deal but as Willkie's running mate he could not oppose it in the Senate, so he did not comment. Willkie had already said he favored aid to Britain and he could hardly attack this.

If an isolationist Republican were running against Roosevelt, Republicans in Congress and out would have been full-throated in opposition to the calls for transferring destroyers to Britain, and the whole party machinery would have been thrown into the battle. Roosevelt would not have dared do it until after the election.

Years later Walter Lippmann wrote: "Second only to the Battle of Britain, the sudden rise and nomination of Willkie was the decisive event, perhaps almost providential, which made it possible to rally the free world when it was almost conquered. Under any other leadership but his, the Republican Party would have turned its back on Great Britain, causing all who still resisted Hitler to feel that they were abandoned." But it was not providence which brought about Willkie's nomination. It came about through a democratic process. The choice of Willkie over an isolationist candidate was partly a result of the influence of some highly placed figures in the media and elsewhere exerted at the right place and the right time. However, it could not have happened without a change in the mood of the American public.

Willkie did criticize the way the deal was done. He said Roosevelt should have asked Congress first and said, "When I am President, you will never hear of any great event after it has happened." This was actually a telling point, because Roosevelt's alleged highhandedness and arrogation of power was going to be an issue in the election.

Most newspapers approved. They did not, however, accept Roosevelt's anodyne assurance that this did not affect America's status as a neutral. The *Baltimore Sun* expressed the view of many: "It makes our official neutrality, already highly diaphanous, a well-nigh transparent cover for non-belligerent cooperation on the side of Britain." The *New York Herald Tribune* said that now, "there is no question whatever about the indissoluble link that binds the United States to the fate of the British Isles and the Royal Navy." Nor did newspaper commentators bother much with the distinction between the leases that were traded and the ones that were a gift.

Although the Republicans as a party did not attack the exchange, die-hard isolationists denounced it. Roosevelt had failed to reconcile Senator Walsh to the idea; he called it "an act of war." The *St. Louis*

Post-Dispatch proclaimed its opposition in a full-page advertisement in leading newspapers. It said: "Mr. Roosevelt today committed an act of war. He also became America's first dictator. Secretly his Secretary of State, Mr. Hull, entered into an agreement with the British ambassador that amounts to a military and naval alliance with Great Britain . . . an edict that may eventually result in the shedding of the blood of millions of Americans."

The Century Group were in no doubt about what they had helped bring about. Herbert Agar wrote later: "We warmongers knew that the enemy was at the gate, that the threat to our life was immediate, and that time was running out; but most of our fellow-citizens did not agree. So all we could do in our frustration was to use our several influences, whenever the chance came, to push the country towards war. The British plea for destroyers was such a chance."

The deal was welcomed in Britain. The London *Times* reassured its readers about British sovereignty: "The British Empire is not for sale, nor does the United States buy citizens. There is no transfer of sovereignty, any more than there is when a West Indian landlord leases a house to an American tourist for the holiday season."

Hull wrote in his memoirs: "To judge from the many cables I received from our diplomatic missions abroad in the days that followed, the effect of the destroyers-bases deal went far beyond the fact that Britain had fifty more destroyers and we had eight more bases. It was a demonstration to the world that this government believed that Britain had a real chance to hold fast against Hitler's might. It showed that we were willing to go beyond ordinary methods and find new means to aid the major democracy fighting Nazism."

The German press played down the importance of the deal, but Germany was already starting on a move to check American power. It was negotiating with Japan to form an alliance, extending the Rome-Berlin axis to include Tokyo. The alliance was announced the following month.

Isolationists saw the hand of the White Committee and the Century Group behind the deal. The *St. Louis Post-Dispatch* learned that Walter Lippmann had written most of Pershing's radio speech. The editor told Lippmann the paper would call for a congressional investigation into a conspiracy to get America into the war, naming him as one of the conspirators. Lippmann asked his friend Joseph Pulitzer, an executive on the *Post-Dispatch,* to dissuade him, and for whatever reason he did not go ahead.

Others also were talking conspiracy. On the Senate floor, Missouri Senator Bennett Clarke asked for an investigation into a network of pro-British propaganda organizations. He felt his suspicions were confirmed by the arrival in Washington, within days of the announcement of the destroyers deal, of a so-called "flying delegation" of people from thirty-seven states to press members of Congress for yet more aid for Britain. Some of these belonged to the White Committee and other pro-Allied organizations, others to no organization, and they included the presidents of Harvard, Yale, Smith, and Bryn Mawr. The Senate rejected Clarke's proposal.

General Robert Wood, the chairman of Sears Roebuck and a campaigner against intervention, had heard rumors of Roosevelt's secret correspondence with Churchill, and when Joseph Kennedy came home on leave he wrote to Kennedy begging him to make this public. But although Kennedy disapproved of these exchanges as well as resenting the fact that he was cut out of them, he refused to betray diplomatic confidences.

It was a coincidence that what was to become the principal anti-interventionist pressure group, the America First Committee, was launched in Chicago on the day after the destroyer deal was announced. It had been planned weeks in advance. The committee grew out of the continuing lobbying work of R. Douglas Stuart and Kingman Brewster, coeditors of the Yale student newspaper who had been campaigning against involvement. They attended both party conventions and talked to like-minded delegates. These referred them to General Robert Wood.

At the end of July they set up the Emergency Committee to Defend America First in an office in the Quaker Oats company in Chicago, which was owned by Stuart's father. Then they shortened the name to the America First Committee and canvassed national figures who shared their view. Stuart was the executive director, at twenty-four. Among the founding members of America First were Avery Brundage, Alice Roosevelt Longworth, Charles Lindbergh, and Senator Wheeler.

They announced a four-point manifesto. "(1.) The United States must build an impregnable defense. (2.) No power can attack a *prepared* America. (3.) American democracy can only be preserved by keeping out of a European war. (4.) Aid short of war weakens national defense and threatens to involve America in war." They said no Nazis or Communists would be accepted as members or allies and they refused donations from pro-Nazi groups. This did not stop some commentators, with BSC encouragement, slandering them by labeling them pro-Nazi.

The committee soon became the principal anti-interventionist pressure group, the counterpart of the White Committee. It had chapters all over the country. It contained Christian pacifists, conservatives and old-time progressives, Republicans and Democrats. It would be simplistic to contrast the two committees as east coast establishment versus Corn Belt isolationism. Both Brewster and Hughes came from wealthy eastern families. Nonetheless, of the nine members of the America First executive committee, seven were from the Midwest, while of the twenty-eight executives of the White Committee, twenty-one were from the Northeast and only four from the Midwest. It was appropriate that the White Committee's headquarters should be in New York and the America First Committee headquarters should be in Chicago.

• • •

"With the conquest of France," the official history of the RAF in World War Two says, "the biggest target in the world came within range of the biggest air force in the world." London sprawled across six hundred square miles and contained then 8.2 million people, more than any other city in the world and a seventh of the population of Britain. It made a uniquely valuable target because it was and is the center of so much in Britain: the government, the royal family, finance, commerce, and entertainment. In American terms it is Washington, New York, and Los Angeles all in one. And more. In 1940 an empire of nearly a billion people was governed from huge, rambling Victorian buildings around Whitehall. The ships sailing up the Thames as it snakes its way to the London docks made it the busiest port in the world. Fifty percent of world trade was financed by money that coursed through the old, narrow streets that constitute the financial district and is known as the City.

The center of London is called the West End, because that is what it was centuries ago when London grew up around the docks. The East End was and is the largely working-class areas that spread for miles to the east of that. On every side of the city, suburbs stretched out, with streets of semidetached houses, homes to the white-collar workers making up the expanding middle class, keeping their privacy behind lace curtains. It was the East End that first received the fury of the Luftwaffe.

They came on Saturday, September 7, in the late afternoon, when many people were sitting down to tea in the garden. Lieutenant Alan Rook was with a searchlight unit east of London when he heard antiaircraft fire. As he recorded in his diary, his colonel burst into his office shouting, "My God, they've started." He went outside to look.

"It was a wonderful summer's day with a clear sky and brilliant sunshine," he wrote. "Coming up the river in close order was the biggest fleet of aeroplanes I had ever seen. White against the blue sky, like cherry blossoms seen from below, in level rows of squadrons, hundreds strong, filling the air with a throbbing roar, they came very slowly, following the river towards London."

Despite the Ultra warning, when radar picked up enemy planes approaching, the fighter command controllers were tentative in sending up planes and were slow to realize the size and nature of the attack, 300 bombers and 600 fighters, all heading for London. Only a small number of fighters were in the right place to meet them. Squadron Leader Sandy Johnson was one of those: "I'd never seen so many aircraft," he recalled later. "It was a hazy sort of day right up to about 16,000 feet. As we broke through the haze you could hardly believe it. As far as you could see there was nothing but German aircraft coming in, wave after wave."

Heedless of the odds, Johnson and his Hurricane squadron and one Spitfire squadron attacked without waiting for others to join them. The German bombers got through to their target. The RAF shot down fourteen German bombers and twenty-eight fighters that day, and lost twenty-eight planes.

The principal target was the Thames docks, where the river curves in a U shape, and the narrow streets of tiny houses and tenement blocks around them. People lived their whole lives in these streets. The glitter of the West End, the majesty of the Houses of Parliament, the gently weeping willows over the duck ponds of St. James's Park, all these were foreign lands to the residents of docklands, which they visited rarely if ever.

Arthur Taylor, his brother Bob, and his daughter Ada were standing in the street when Ada pointed to the sky and said, "What's up there?"

"It's birds," a neighbor said. Arthur looked up, curious, and then yelled at his daughter, "Get inside, now!" and seconds later the first bombs crashed nearby and the sirens wailed.

This was the beginning of London's ordeal of fire and explosives, seventy-six days and nights of bombing, what British people call, giving a new meaning to the word, the Blitz. Some forty-three thousand civilians were killed in London and elsewhere in the Blitz. Twenty thousand were killed later, mostly by flying bombs and then rockets, the V-1s and V-2s, in 1944 and 1945.

London's largely amateur civil defense organization had prepared itself for this for months: air raid wardens, fire services with their auxiliaries, medical and paramedical services. The day and night of September 7–8 was their baptism by fire, as well as that of London's civilian population, and it was a ferocious one.

Air raid wardens, most of them part-timers who still had normal jobs, had steel helmets marked ARP, for Air Raid Precautions, and most wore a siren suit on duty, a one-piece garment like a jump suit — Churchill sometimes wore one. A warden was supposed to go to what was called an "incident," the official term for a bomb, often backed by a policeman, and report back by messenger or in person on what was needed: the fire service, an ambulance, rescue gear, or whatever. He might tackle an incendiary bomb fire himself, throwing sand on it as everyone had been instructed to do, or pull wounded out of the rubble, helped by a policeman or sometimes just passers-by, or escort people to some shelter. He might go into a building looking for survivors. A young woman would be manning the telephone at the warden's post, and often, a teenage boy would be ready to bicycle through the streets with messages. The system was put under heavy strain in those first days. Some telephone lines were cut; in many areas there were far too many "incidents," overwhelming the capacity to manage.

Barbara Dixon, one of the minority of women air raid wardens, was worried about how she would cope with her first bomb. "I was not let down lightly," she wrote later. "In the middle of the street lay the remains of a baby. It had been blown clean through the window and had burst on striking a roadway. To my intense relief, pitiful and horrible as it was, I was not nauseated, and found a torn piece of curtain in which to wrap it up."

Unlike in previous raids, the Germans dropped more incendiaries than high-explosive bombs. These were small, eighteen inches long and weighing about two pounds, and they came down in hundreds. If one was caught quickly, a person could smother it with sand or even carry it away in a wheelbarrow, but many started fires that day and these grew. When night fell more bombers came, flames leaping hundreds of feet upward serving as a beacon.

Four-fifths of the firemen were members of the AFS, the Auxilliary Fire Service, who joined up for the war, and they had had little experience of firefighting. They worked with bombs coming down, struggling sometimes through streets choked with rubble from bombed buildings, with hose snaking around the roadway. In the Surrey docks, 250 acres of timber were ablaze, and the heat blistered paint on boats on the opposite side of the river, 300 yards away.

The fire officer in charge sent a frantic message to his headquarters: "Send all the pumps you've got. The whole bloody world's on fire."* The headquarters' central direction system was overwhelmed. Burning warehouses created their own special conditions to torment the firemen. There were pepper fires, filling the air with stinging particles that made breathing painful; rum fires, with burning liquid pouring out into the street and barrels exploding; and rubber fires, belching out clouds of toxic smoke. Some firemen were cut off and died in the flames, others when a wall crashed down on them.

The glow lit up the sky thirty miles away. The dean of St. Paul's cathedral, W. R. Matthews, wrote later: "Inside the cathedral the light was such that I have never seen the stained glass windows glow as they did then." In many places where there were not fires, gas pipes had been exposed and broken by explosives and jets of white flame were shooting up in the air.

A road sweeper gave the writer Robert Herring his opinion of the auxiliary firemen the next day: "See the fire chaps last night? Coo, I laughed at the AFS like we all did. Called them snobby amateurs. Bleeding 'eroes, they is. Dead beat they was when they came back this morning. At it all night and new to it, too. Bleeding 'eroes."

Four hundred thirty civilians were killed that night, 1,600 others

---

* In firemen's terms, a "pump" is a fire truck containing fire hoses and pumps.

were injured, and many more were made homeless. A Mass Observation note-taker in the East End, Nina Masel, jotted down her observations:

> Warning went at 5 P.M. Almost immediately afterwards terrific crashes, bombs falling all round. Women in shelters stood up, holding each other. Some screamed . . . All clear. Everyone groaned relief, went out and screamed with horror at sight of the damage. Every street was damaged, bombs everywhere. Smoke and flames streaming from the docks. Shouting, finding relatives, chaos.
>
> Unexploded bomb. Building fell on a group of men and women. Screams, groans, sudden rush back of the people followed immediately by a rush forward. Women fainted, mass hysteria, man threw a fit. Men, women and children crying and sobbing. Frantic parents searching for their young. Pub near by full of casualties. Dead and dying on the pavements. Someone sick.
>
> Second warning. People tearing to shelters — soon all full. Gunfire and bombs. Accordion and singing in the shelters. Streets full of people shouting, My house is burning! Call the Fire Brigade! No brigade available for a long time — all down at the docks, where fire still raged.

Part of the East End near the dock area was then a Jewish quarter where a lot of the older people were immigrants from Eastern Europe. The playwright Bernard Kops recalls that night: "Imagine a ground floor flat, crowded with hysterical women, crying babies, and great crashes in the sky and the whole earth shaking . . . The men started to play cards and the women tried a little singsong, singing, 'I saw the old homestead and faces I loved,' or 'Don't go down in the mines, Dad,' or 'Yiddle mit his fiddle.' But every so often twenty women's fists shook at the ceiling, cursing the explosions, Germany, Hitler."

People rushed to the brick and concrete public shelters, whose inadequacies were then exposed. More than fourteen hundred people crowded into one shelter, packed so tightly that some could not sit down and many stood in two inches of water. Many shelters were too small and had no toilet facilities beyond a few buckets. People were used to staying in one of the public shelters for an hour or two, not all night.

Some streets next to the river seemed swallowed up by the conflagration, and one thousand people were evacuated from them. They were taken to a school building where they were to wait for buses to take them to permanent shelter. The buses went to the wrong place and did not collect the people, and the next day the school was hit by a bomb. Some of the survivors dug in the rubble to find pieces of their children's bodies.

In many places individuals or voluntary organizations made up for the failure of the authorities to cope. When people seemed in danger of being trapped by fire on an island in the docks area, members of the Women's Voluntary Service gathered a convoy of vehicles of all kinds and brought a thousand people across the two bridges. A priest, Father John Groser, broke into an official food store and distributed rations to homeless people and organized buses to take them to places of shelter.

With the fires still burning, bombers came over the next night and wreaked havoc once again. Many of the firemen worked forty hours at a stretch, in horrendous conditions, with bombs still falling. Maurice Richardson, an auxiliary fireman, recalled: "It was possible to get too tired to feel frightened. Bombs and flames tended to cancel each other out. Flames were a secondary terror compared with bombs, but if the fire was spectacular enough, and if you were having to work very hard on it, you could sometimes forget the bombs."

* * *

On Sunday afternoon, the day after the devastating first raid, Churchill drove out to some of the bombed areas accompanied by the chief administrative officer of the London Civil Defense Region, Sir Harold Scott. He got out of his car and walked through the streets, looking at the burned-out little houses and the rubble, with the smell of burning lingering in the air. People stopped on the streets and cheered him, calling out, "Good old Winston!" and "Good luck!" A group of people carrying their bedding and paltry belongings to shelters dropped their things to join in the applause. Colin Perry, a local teenager, followed him and wrote in his diary: "He looked invincible, which he is. Tough, bulldogged, piercing."

Playing to the gallery, Churchill put his hat on the end of his walking stick and twirled it around, and called out to the crowd that had gathered, "Are we downhearted?" "No!" they shouted back, standing amid the rubble and broken glass that had once been homes. The next day he toured the East End in his car again, getting out now and again to walk through the streets even after the sirens sounded, ignoring the protestations of his aides. Outside a shelter in which forty people had been killed by a direct hit, people cheered him.

Tears ran down Churchill's cheeks. He turned to General Ismay, who was accompanying him, and said, "Did you hear them? They cheered me as if I'd given them victory, instead of getting their houses bombed to bits."

Churchill's popularity was extraordinary. He hovers over British memories of this period, inextricably associated with it. Opinion polls showed that up to 88 percent of the public approved of him as prime minister, but this says little about his place in people's minds. Servicemen as well as civilian crowds cheered him, not only when they were lined up in ranks and ordered to do so but walking along the roadside when he drove by, waving and calling out, "Good old Winnie!" He conveyed to most people what he did to young Colin Perry, the sense that he was indomitable, that so long as he was at the helm there might be tough times but in the end he and the country could not lose.

Churchill made only five speeches over the radio between May and September, but 70 percent of the population listened to them. Most of his famous speeches were made in Parliament, which was not broadcast at the time. He knew his speeches were important, he knew he could impart strength to the British people, and he worked for hours on them, refusing to be interrupted with what others thought was more pressing business. He would dictate his speech to a typist, going over a sentence again and again, changing it, refining it, having her type it again and going over the new draft. Everyone became familiar with his slow growl, his studied pauses, his occasional idiosyncrasies of speech — "Nahzees," with a soft z — his grave tones, the phrases resonating like drum beats, mingled with irony.

Four days after that first raid on London, with the raids continuing every day, he spoke on the radio. It was a characteristic Churchill peroration, delivered in his customary slow pace and measured but dramatic tones.

Warning that an invasion might be imminent, he placed his audience at the center of great events. "The next week may be one of the most important in British history," he said. "It ranks with the days when the Spanish Armada was approaching the Channel and Drake was finishing his game of bowls; or when Nelson stood between us and Napoleon's Grand Army at Boulogne. We have read all about this in the history books; but what is happening now is on a far greater scale, and of far more consequence to the life of the world and its civilization than these brave old days of the past."

He gave them a role to play. "Every man and woman will prepare himself to do his duty, whatever it may be, with special pride and care."

He told them that hardship and danger lay ahead — "blood, sweat, toil, and tears" was a theme that ran through his speeches. "These cruel, wanton, indiscriminate bombings of London are of course a part of Hitler's invasion plan. He hopes, by killing large numbers of civilians, that he will terrorize and cow the people of this mighty imperial city, and make them a burden and anxiety to the Government, and thus distract our attention unduly from the ferocious onslaught he is preparing."

He assured them that they could endure and prevail. "Little does he know the spirit of the British nation, or the tough fiber of the Londoners, whose forebears played a leading part in the establishment of Parliamentary institutions, and who have been bred to value freedom far above their lives."

It was typically Churchillian with its strong adjectives, "cruel, wanton, indiscriminate," "mighty imperial"; its invocation of history; its demand for steadfastness and self-sacrifice; its promise of ultimate victory. Increasingly, as the raids went on, people in Britain were fearful, tired, suffering privations, having to struggle to get through a normal day. Churchill told them they were playing a heroic role in an epic historic drama, and they believed him.

A Labour opponent, Aneurin Bevan, observing public attitudes to Churchill, said, "In a democracy, idolatry is the worst sin," and made sure that he was not beyond criticism. Those who worked with Churchill could not be blind to his failings and often had to battle against some of his wilder notions.

General Sir Alan Brooke, in charge of home defenses, had his difficulties with Churchill. He was worried about the lack of proper coordination over anti-invasion measures among the three services, and he wrote later: "Had an invasion developed, I feared that Churchill would have attempted as Defense Minister to coordinate the actions of these various commands. This would have been wrong and highly dangerous, with his impulsive nature and tendency to arrive at decisions through a process of intuition, as opposed to a 'logical' approach. Heaven knows where he might have led us!"

The prospect of invasion was occupying people's minds in these weeks. Brooke worried that Ironside's defense strategy was too static, and he strengthened the mobile forces. Britain's defenses were reinforced now by 250,000 rifles and several hundred 75mm. field guns from the United States." These 75s were of World War One vintage and much inferior to other artillery in the British and German armies, but as Churchill said, "When you are fighting for existence, any cannon is better than no cannon at all." But Brooke worried constantly that his troops were underequipped and many were undertrained, although most Home Guard units now had rifles and had their assigned tasks.

The British thought that the Germans would want to invade before the second half of September, when the channel becomes less hospitable with wind, fog, and rough seas. An invasion fleet was assembled in several ports between Ostend in Belgium and Le Havre in France. The RAF bombed these vessels and the ports where they were located continually. Dunkirk burned again, and Calais was battered some more. The RAF reckoned that it destroyed 12 percent of the invasion fleet. Nonetheless, at the beginning of September the naval staff reported that an armada was in place consisting of 168 troop transports, 419 tugs and trawlers, and nearly 2,000 barges, as well as motor boats.

The navy said the tides favored an invasion fleet between September 8 and 10. There were other indications that an invasion might be imminent. Four German agents who landed by boat were captured immediately and said they had been told to report on anti-invasion measures in preparation for a landing. The Chiefs of Staff met to discuss this situation on the afternoon of September 7. The Combined Intelligence Committee gave them photographs indicating advanced preparations in Ostend, Calais, and Dunkirk, and told them that German messages about putting down a smoke screen in the channel had been intercepted. They knew that Stukas had been moved up in numbers near the Dover Straits. As the Chiefs of Staff discussed these reports they could hear the sounds of bombs crashing down all over east and southeast London in the capital's first big day of air raids, and this doubtless heightened their state of tension.

They decided that the army must be placed on the highest state of alert, and the way to do this seemed to be to issue the code message

Cromwell, which signified that an invasion was imminent. Brooke sent out the message when he left the meeting at eight o'clock. It was not intended for the Home Guard but somehow it was passed on to some Home Guard units. These took it to mean that an invasion was underway and spread the word, and units were called out to battle stations. In some places, church bells were rung, which was supposed to happen only when an invasion had begun. Near the east coast local army engineers blew up bridges.

One woman recalls her husband, summoned out in the night by his Home Guard commander, handing her the garden fork as he left and saying, "Don't let anybody in, lovey, but if anybody gets in, don't hesitate to push this fork in his blasted guts." Squadron Leader Bader told his pilots, "So the bastards are coming! Bloody good show! Think of all those juicy targets on those nice flat beaches."

The minister for information, Alfred Duff Cooper, was holding a weekend house party, with everyone in evening dress. At eleven o'clock the butler came in and announced, "Sir, the invasion has commenced." Duff Cooper tried to telephone his office but could not get through. He gave up and went to bed. *New York Herald Tribune* correspondent Whitelaw Reid was spending the weekend at the country home of war minister Anthony Eden and his wife, Beatrice. Eden received the Cromwell message by telephone and dashed back to London. Reid hurried to Dover to wait for the invasion there.

The public were not told what had happened. An official statement said some church bells were rung in error because one Home Guard unit mistook some fishing boats returning for an invasion fleet. It is recalled today, if at all, as a comic episode, but a number of ordinary men left their families that night facing the possibility that they would never see them again and prepared to do their best.

The Cromwell order remained in force for some days with the army on a state of alert. The next day, September 8, General Brooke wrote in his diary:

> I called in at St. Paul's School [where Home Defense had set up its headquarters] on the way back, and found that all reports still point to the probability of an invasion starting between the 8 and 10 of this month. The responsibility of feeling what any mistakes or even misapprehensions may mean in the future of these isles and of the Empire is a colossal one, and one that rather staggers

me at times. I wished I had more adequately trained formations under my orders. But for the present there is nothing to be done but to trust God and pray for his help and guidance.

Two days later he wrote: "Still no invasion today. I wonder whether he will do anything during the next few days."

. . .

Throughout the discussion of the bases for destroyers deal, the two sides had talked about the British getting fifty destroyers plus aircraft and weapons. The agreement that was drawn up spoke only of destroyers. Two days after Churchill made his announcement in Parliament, he memoed Halifax at the Foreign Office: "What is being done about getting our 20 motor torpedo boats, the 5 PBY [flying boats], the 150–200 aircraft, and the 250,000 rifles, and also anything else that is going? I consider we were promised all the above, and more. Not an hour should be lost in raising these questions."

Halifax took up the matter with Lothian, who took it up with the American government. Why had the men drawing up the agreement omitted these items? The answer seems to be as simple as it is astonishing. In their hurry, they forgot.

Hull had taken over the negotiations in the last stages and he said he had been told only about the destroyers. He appears not to have read the earlier draft that Welles had drawn up. Lothian, going through the draft of the letters with Hull, had forgotten about the other considerable number of aircraft and weapons that were to have been included. The British cabinet simply assumed they were to be included.

Stimson said that the only thing to do was to admit that a slip had been made and to say that an amendment to the agreement was now necessary. At first Roosevelt agreed with him, but Hull objected. He pointed out that the destroyers transfer was only possible because the chief of naval operations had been able to certify that their exchange for the bases would be a gain and not a loss for American defense. It would be difficult now for the army chief of staff to say that handing over the other equipment would enhance American security because the bases had already been acquired. Furthermore, he said, adding on some more equipment for Britain after the agreement had been signed would lead to accusations of underhanded dealing. So Roosevelt reversed his stand

and said they would not reopen the issue. Instead, he told Lothian that the other items would be given anyway.

Lothian assured Churchill that he was active on the matter. "Purvis and I have sat on the doorstep of the Administration with a view to getting these articles or their equivalent as soon as possible," he said in a cable. "The President fully admits his obligation and, in association with Purvis, the Administration is trying to work out for the earliest possible delivery which will be as good or even from the British point of view better than the original."

Stimson promised to get the rifles and they were sent the next month. Marshall said the air force had very few B-17 Flying Fortress bombers and could not spare any. Roosevelt told Churchill that when the new B-24 heavy bombers started coming off the assembly line soon, half would go to Britain, and they did. This was the best they could do. The sale of the newest motor torpedo boats had already been blocked by Congress.

The fifty destroyers were to be handed over to the British navy at Halifax, Nova Scotia, and Admiral Stark made sure that the first ones were on their way there when the agreement was signed. On that day, September 3, eight destroyers arrived in Boston from Norfolk, and that evening they were instructed to proceed to Halifax. They arrived on the same day as the ship carrying the British seamen who were to man them arrived from England.

These first eight ships were formally transferred on September 9. In the gray northern waters of the harbor, sailors lined the decks, a bugler played "To the Colors," and the American flags flying from every mast, whipped by the wind, were lowered at the same time. The captains went ashore and British crews went on board, where American officers and men were waiting to show them the workings of their new ships.

The Americans had left the ships stocked with foodstuffs in abundance that the British, coming from a country on strict wartime rations, were not accustomed to: fruit juice; clams; canned ham; canned asparagus; even tea, coffee, and sugar; and some items that most had never seen, such as instant coffee and pumpkins. Some of the American officers told their British counterparts that they wished they could go further than supplying them with goodies and join them in fighting the Nazis.

The British cabinet discussed what they should name the ships. In the U.S. Navy they were named after historic American figures. Churchill decided they should name them after American towns that had taken their names from British towns, emphasizing the historic connection between the two countries. So among the first eight, the *Welborn C. Wood* became the *Chesterfield,* the *Buchanan* became the *Campbeltown,* and the *Crownshield* became the *Chelsea.*

The American officers were frank about their ships' shortcomings. One said the hull of his ship was just thick enough to keep out water and small fish. The British found other defects. They had antiaircraft guns that were calibrated for aircraft flying at World War One speeds.

Some of the four-inch guns were found to have a curious and potentially deadly fault: when elevated to their upper limit they automatically fired. A British captain said: "This was easily corrected when it was discovered, but a lot of rounds were discharged on the initial trials in the most unexpected directions, many of them over the mast of the senior officer's destroyer." The most serious shortcoming was in the steering: maneuverability is vital in antisubmarine work. One British officer said these ships had the turning circle of a battleship.

The British were in a hurry to get them into action and the first five sailed on September 15. But two of them collided in Halifax harbor because of steering problems and had to be repaired before they could sail. Another had to turn back because of generator trouble. When they reached Britain the navy installed radar and Asdic submarine detectors, and the first two were on convoy duty in the Atlantic at the end of October.

More defects continued to be found and corrected. Although most were in service, only a third were at sea at any one time. Only sixteen of them were still on active duty at the end of 1943, and then eight were given to the Soviet navy. The one that distinguished itself most was the *Campbeltown,* and that was by being sacrificed. In June 1942 a daring commando raid was staged on the German submarine base at St. Nazaire. The *Campbeltown* was packed with explosives, driven into the submarine docks and blown up, destroying the docks.

For all their failings, they came at a critical time and served a valuable purpose. The Royal Navy's director of antisubmarine warfare, Admiral Sir George Creasy, said later, "Any destroyer that could steam, shoot and drop depth charges was worth its weight in gold in the heightening strain of the Battle of the Atlantic in the autumn of 1940. Admittedly, many of them were an appalling headache to keep running. But taken by and large, they gave invaluable service at a time of really desperate need."

Negotiations of the details of the bases agreement proved to be surprisingly cumbersome. Initially, there were arguments with the local authorities, who had accepted the idea in principle but were aghast when they realized the size of the bases proposed. The governor of Trinidad, Sir Hubert Jones, objected that the proposed base would cut off the best swimming beaches near Port of Spain.

A conference was organized in London to arrange the details, and there turned out to be a lot to negotiate. Representatives of the Bermuda Assembly went to London to object to almost all the plans and had to be mollified by Churchill himself. Points of sovereignty had to be clarified, local property owners and local councils compensated. It was the following spring before construction began.

Argentia, Newfoundland, became a big air base and the starting point of American convoys to Iceland the following spring. Trinidad was the most important of the West Indies bases. Situated off the coast of Venezuela, it was on the sea lanes traveled by ships carrying oil from Venezuela and Surinam and oil and bauxite from Trinidad itself. Port of Spain became a U.S. naval base, and two air force bases were established on the island, Waller Field and Carlsen Field.

Trinidad and its bases acquired a place in the American consciousness when a Tin Pan Alley songwriter adapted a local calypso tune and the Andrew Sisters made it a hit, their fresh innocent voices negating the salacious implications of the words:

From Chacachacare to Monos Isle, native girls all dance and smile.
Help soldier celebrate his leave, make every day like New Years Eve.
Drinkin' rum and Coca Cola, go down Point Cumana.
Both mother and daughter, workin' for the Yankee dollar . . .

Despite the presence of these bases, in the spring of 1942, after America had entered the war, the Caribbean was a happy hunting ground for German submarines. They took a terrible toll on American shipping, and the bodies of American seamen were being washed up on Florida's beaches. The American navy was stretched thin and could provide only minimal opposition. A high-ranking naval officer wrote to Admiral Stark saying that he wished they had those fifty destroyers now. Stark replied that those destroyers had been fighting German submarines for the past eighteen months.

11

ODDS LONG, STAKES INFINITE

Facing the possibility of a German occupation force ruling Britain with Nazism triumphant, many people who had rejected war up to now accepted it as the lesser evil, along with its inevitable moral and intellectual corruption, and rallied to the flag.

The British philosopher Bertrand Russell, in his late sixties and teaching at Harvard, conscientiously logical in the way he lived his life, publicly abandoned his pacifist stance, deciding that in this situation "I must support whatever is necessary for victory."

Esmond Romilly, a British upper-class rebel who ran away from school and fought with the Republicans in Spain at the age of eighteen, had given up on Chamberlain's Britain and gone to live in America with his young wife, Jessica Mitford. Now he decided that Britain was worth defending and returned and joined the RAF, to be killed in action three years later.

Francis Cammaerts, later a literary critic, then a schoolteacher, was a conscientious objector. In the summer of 1940 he decided that this war was an ethical cause and volunteered; he was parachuted into occupied France and served with the French resistance, earning decorations for bravery.

On a more personal and primitive level, David Dawson, a streetwise cockney, took a job in the civil service in order, he said, to stay out of the army, and scoffed at those who volunteered. Then he found his fiancée's body in the ruins of a trolley car that had been hit by a bomb, recognizable only by the engagement ring on her finger. He volunteered for the RAF and pleaded to get into Bomber Command so that he could bomb Germany in revenge, which he did.

Left-wingers tried to persuade Communists, who had shared some of their struggles in the past, that they should stop opposing the war. George Strauss, a Labour member of Parliament, wrote in the Socialist magazine *Tribune:* "If Hitler wins this war, the British working class will be reduced to a state of slavery. All means of winning through to Socialism will be ruthlessly destroyed. Are supporters of the Communist Party prepared to sacrifice themselves for that?"

There were many reasons to fight Nazism: because it was a threat to Britain, to democracy, to socialism, to the workers of the world, to decency, or to one's loved ones.

The night after that first big raid on London, September 8, 171 bombers came over again, and some 400 people were killed and many more injured. They came again the next day and the next night, and 370 were killed. The fires were as bad as the first night's. At St. Katherine's Docks, next to the Tower of London, warehouses containing paraffin wax were set ablaze, and flames rose 200 feet into the air.

Raiders concentrated again on the East End. Local residents, already angry at the authorities for the lack of proper shelters, commented bitterly that the wealthier districts were being spared. But after a few days bombs fell all over London and destroyed some of Bond Street and Park Lane, London's smartest streets. Clement Attlee said to Harold Nicolson, "If only the Germans had had the sense not to bomb west of London Bridge, there might have been a revolution in this country," an uncharacteristically immoderate remark for Attlee.

The raids went on day and night, taking a toll of nerves as well as bodies. A woman on a bus carrying a suitcase, on her way to stay with her sister, said to anyone who would listen, "I can't stand this. It's not war, it's murder." Defeatist remarks were heard occasionally. "It looks as if all we can do is give up. It's no use throwing away our lives when there's no hope," was one view quoted.

Some people fled pell-mell, going to towns out of London where the local council had to take care of them. Some went to sleep outdoors on Hampstead Heath, looking out over London, or to the nearest open country to the East End, in Epping Forest. Thousands took the train nightly to the Chiselhurst Caves, a tourist site. Some better-off people rented a place in the country within easy reach to spend the night.

Yet the first outbreaks of panic subsided. Celia Fremlin of Mass Observation noted the atmosphere in one shelter:

> At the beginning, when nobody was used to it, the women got absolutely hysterical. They were screaming and saying, "I can't stand it, I'm going to die, I can't stand it." And there was usually one who was saying, "Calm down, calm down." Sometimes the women would be really hysterical, crying and falling on the floor. I only once saw it as bad as that, in a shelter. The next time I went there, four nights later, they were all much calmer, they'd brought stools to sit on, and there was even a bit of community singing. Because once you've been through three nights of bombing, you can't help feeling safe the fourth time.

Antiaircraft guns remained silent much of the time those first nights to leave the field free for the RAF's night fighters. But these were still ineffective, and Londoners complained that they were not being defended. So on September 10 the fighters were withdrawn and General Frederick Pile, in charge of antiaircraft defenses, ordered all guns to fire whenever there was a target, and they blazed away. Falling shrapnel meant that the guns probably killed more Londoners than they did German airmen, but the barrage had the effect of forcing the German planes higher, and it raised morale on the ground. "You can't sleep with the guns going but it's a good sound," one man said. In pubs people bought drinks for antiaircraft gunners.

In every area of life, people struggled to adjust. Nightlife was hit at first, with restaurants and night clubs nearly deserted in the evening. Theaters closed when the bombing started. Most opened after some days, but audiences were down. The only one that stayed open throughout, defying the Luftwaffe, was the Windmill, a burlesque house. It featured scantily clad dancers and an occasional nude who was allowed to pose providing she was immobile. It became a favorite with servicemen, and for years after the war, the Windmill's proud boast was "We Never Closed."

Classical music concerts found a new audience. The pianist Myra

Hess gave lunchtime concerts in the National Gallery, from which the paintings had been removed to a safer place, sometimes solo, sometimes with an orchestra, and they were packed. The performance would move to the basement if an air raid was in progress. Once an unexploded bomb went off in the building during a performance of Beethoven's F major quartet; the players did not miss a note.

Far from the East End socially as well as geographically, Verily Anderson, a young wife living in Mayfair, described a round of parties, and wrote: "An extraordinary mood of exaltation sweetened the air of London at that time. Everything seemed against us . . . And yet there was this strange soaring of the spirits. Even the very colors of the summer seemed heightened, the sky bluer, the clouds whiter and the darkness darker. The combined sense of danger and unity was exhilarating." Yet she was sometimes literally sick with fear during air raids.

One young woman recalled, "It was exciting — a terrible thing to say about a war but it was. After all, when you're twenty-three years old, a stimulus is a stimulus. On the other hand, I was scared stiff of the bombing, I don't mind admitting."

People invited out to dinner took their night things, prepared to stay the night if there was an air raid rather than walk through the streets. Restaurants and night clubs, if they wanted customers in the evening, prepared to double as air raid shelters, opening up basements and store rooms. Basil Woon, a film script writer, wrote: "When you take a girl out for an evening these days, she brings her pajamas and make-up. This has led to some interesting situations."

Many people found in this atmosphere of mingled exhilaration and fear an invitation to live as if there were no tomorrow. People were more willing to spend on luxuries. Joan Wyndham was an art student whose Catholic upbringing kept her chaste even though she was hanging out with a bohemian crowd. But when the bombings began she decided, "I can't die a virgin," and made sure that she did not. The moral standards of the 1930s might have been loosened, but they were not swept aside. People rushed into affairs but also into marriages, and the number hit an all-time high.

A bomb hit Broadcasting House, the BBC's main building, killing six people, as a news reader was reading the news. He paused for just an instant to wipe away from his script dust that had fallen from the ceiling.

Others, not always the expected ones, displayed similar sang-froid. The American attaché General Lee admired the street walkers in Mayfair: "When everyone else is hurrying for the air raid shelters, they are quite indifferent, and stroll on unperturbed," he wrote in his journal.

The director of the London Zoo, Julian Huxley, noted the different reactions of the animals to the bombing. The camels treated bombs with disdain; they did not even get up when one landed ten yards from their cage. Similarly, supposedly sensitive animals like antelopes and giraffes were unperturbed. Chimpanzees ignored bombs and guns but screamed at the sound of sirens. Cranes became very agitated when bombs fell, crying out and flapping their wings. Parrots imitated the sirens. Some hummingbirds escaped when their cage was pierced by shrapnel and were never seen again, the only escapees.

A waitress, Betty Jones, recalled a significant change: "Servicemen had priority until the Blitz started. You had to offer men in uniform two eggs. No one else was allowed more than one. But as soon as the bombing started and the civilians were put through it that all stopped and they were treated the same as civilians." Everyone was in the front line now.[*]

Buckingham Palace was hit a few days later, when the king and queen were in residence. "I'm glad we've been bombed," Queen Elizabeth said. "It makes me feel I can look the East End in the face." When the king and queen toured the bombed areas after this they were cheered wherever they went. Actually, the royal family often slept at Windsor Castle, outside London, during the bombing.

King George and Queen Elizabeth gained in popularity in these months, partly because, unlike many wealthy people, they refused to leave the country or send their two young daughters away. The queen told a visitor, "The children could not possibly leave without me. I would not go without the king. And of course, the king will never leave."

George had not expected to be the monarch; he could hardly have anticipated the abdication of his older brother, now the duke of Windsor. He was not well suited for the role. Unlike his brother, he was not outgoing but stiff and rather shy, and he had a stammer. He was seen as

---

[*] Later even one egg in a restaurant was a rarity.

a decent man saddled with a job and determined to do his best, and he was respected for this.

The Germans were dropping 100-pound, 250-pound, and 500-pound bombs and the incendiaries, and now Londoners were introduced to other kinds of bombs. What came to be called land mines — eight-foot-long cylinders — came floating down by parachute. All London soon became familiar with unexploded bombs, the UXBs. It was a common sight to see an area cordoned off with a sign saying "UXB."

Usually the UXB was a dud which failed to explode. Army sappers and a few trained civilian volunteers would defuse the bomb on the spot. Some of these were conscientious objectors. This was hazardous work, and many of the men doing it were killed when the bomb exploded. If the place was sensitive, an industrial plant or a military base, they would take the bomb to an open space and explode it. Sometimes the UXB was designed to cause havoc. It might have a time fuse or a movement-sensitive fuse that would start operating ten minutes after the bomb fell. Others were fixed to explode when tampered with. A battle was being waged between the ingenuity of the bomb designers and those charged with dismantling their bombs.

These latter acquired expertise, but it was often bought at a price. The man dealing with a bomb would usually work alone with the rest of the team at a distance, and would talk into a telephone saying what he was about to do, so that if he made a fatal mistake, others could learn what it was. There were brave men whose last words were an account of what knob they were lifting or what screw they were unscrewing.

The most famous UXB, a one-ton land mine, landed on September 12 next to St. Paul's Cathedral. St. Paul's, with its huge Palladian dome, is London's most prominent landmark, and was all the more so in 1940 when there were no skyscrapers to share the skyline. The bomb burrowed down twenty-seven feet to the cathedral's foundations. A mixed team of sappers and civilians, led by Lieutenant Robert Davies of the Canadian Army Engineers, set out to remove it. They did not know whether it would explode at any moment. The bomb had hit a gas main, and three of the team collapsed from inhaling the gas before this was realized. Then the leaking gas caught fire and the bomb became warm to the touch. Working for three anxious days, they dug down and put ropes around the bomb, and it was hauled up by two trucks in tandem.

Twice the bomb slipped back into the hole. Sunday services in the cathedral were canceled for the first time in a century. Eventually the bomb was hauled out and driven rapidly through London to some marshland outside the city, where it was exploded and made a crater one hundred feet wide. St. Paul's was saved.

Davies was decorated for this, and the civilians on his team were the first recipients of a new medal created for civilian bravery, the George Cross. They were certainly heroes to Londoners. They had saved the city's most celebrated building. Among others who earned the George Cross this same summer were two gas workers who closed off valves while the gas plant was burning around them, and a sixteen-year-old girl who was a messenger cyclist for an air raid warden's post.

Just as Britain's peril brought out a patriotism in many people that they did not know they felt, so the bombing brought out in many Londoners a new affection for their city and a concern for its landmarks. Joan Bright, who took a wartime job in Whitehall, was unusually articulate but her sentiments were not uncommon: "At this time I was not the only one who hugged London to my beating heart. London was ours from the hour the blacked-out night hid its beauty until the morning siren signaled the coming day, most triumphantly in the hours when the full moon shone on its age-old face and we knew the Germans would not be coming."

As the days of bombing went on the mood of defiance was heightened, but so was the strain. People accumulated debts to the nervous system. A schoolteacher in East London wrote a long letter to a friend who had gone to the country and was helping to organize the evacuation of children. At one point he gave an account of that day:

> This morning on duty at the Herbert Read clearing house. On the way past St. Gabriel's Mr. Sands called out to stop me — aerial torpedo on Belgrave Road — still getting the dead out. In East Ham. Alec Ford stopped me — public shelter gone in High Street — haven't got to the bodies yet. And so it goes on. At this clearing station the refugees panicked during the night and refused to stay, and threatened to sit on the debris of their homes if they weren't evacuated at once. The office in charge is almost hysterical with fatigue and nerve strain.
>
> I'm sorry to have written so depressing a letter, but I've written

cheerfully to most people who have families in London, and the words have stuck in my throat, and it does me good to loosen up a bit. How long we shall be able to keep a stiff upper lip I don't know.

*   *   *

During the first days of the raids people would rush to shelters or at least indoors when the sirens sounded. Department stores and office buildings adapted cellars as shelters for those who wanted to take to them. But soon most people ignored sirens in the daytime, ducking into a doorway if the whine of a bomb indicated that one was close.

Harold Nicolson wrote in his diary: "I am nerveless, yet when I hear a motor in an empty street I tauten myself lest it be a bomb screaming towards me. Underneath, the fibers of one's nerve resistance must be sapped. We are conscious all the time that this is a moment in history . . . I have sense of strain and unhappiness, but none of fear. One feels so proud."

Mrs. Ernestine Cotton, the American wife of a British businessman, kept a journal for her grandchildren. On September 11 she wrote: "I went downtown to get some warm boots — and some of the shops were still burning. Every A.M. there is more devastation to see. It is like going about after an earthquake — some streets look just the same — others are just heaps of brick, big craters here and there. And yet we go about our daily affairs just the same. It is too strange for words — one has to experience it to know what I mean."*

At night people still crowded into the unsanitary brick and concrete shelters where the smell of other bodies mingled with the stench of urine. The deepest public places were subway stations, and people wanted to use these as shelters. At first the authorities resisted, fearing this would be too disruptive of normal life, but crowds gathered outside stations and the police let them in.

Soon there were 170,000 underground people, sleeping regularly on the subway platforms even as the trains went by, and evening travelers had to step across them to get to the trains — travel stopped around midnight. It became a way of life for many families. A community

---

* Mrs. Cotton's unpublished journal, like several others quoted, is in the Imperial War Museum in London.

sprang up with rules that were tacitly understood by most, about what you could and could not do. The platforms were open for shelterers starting at four in the afternoon, and people used to line up to reserve a place for their family, and then go down with blankets, pillows, a vacuum flask of tea, and usually something to read and games for the children. Some people would line up to reserve a place, and then sell it, but after a while squatter's rights were recognized, and families had their regular spots.

In the subways, and in the air raid shelters, people lived as they could not have imagined a few weeks earlier, spending their nighttime hours in close proximity to hundreds of others, talking, reading, sleeping, and, inevitably in some cases, copulating. Toilets were buckets behind a screen, emptied frequently. One young woman, incredulous at the sight, said, "It was terribly depressing. One reads and knows about refugees in other countries, but you never expected to see your own people doing that."

Subways were not always safe. In Balham, in south London, the road above caved in when a bomb exploded and water from a waste pipe and sand poured into the station, and sixty-four people were crushed or drowned. There were other disasters.

Sleeping families sprawled along subway platforms is one of the abiding images of the Blitz, but a survey showed that only 4 percent of people took to the subways. Twenty-seven percent slept in domestic shelters, meaning either Anderson shelters in the yard or those provided in an apartment block, 9 percent in public shelters, and the rest, 60 percent, remained in their homes, often taking shelter in the cellar or under the stairs.

The American journalist Ralph Ingersoll of *P.M.* visited some of the poorly equipped shelters in the East End and then, in the middle of the night, the underground shelter at the smart Dorchester Hotel, which was in the Turkish baths in the basement. He described what he found:

> A neat row of cots, spaced about 2 feet apart, each one covered with a lovely fluffy eiderdown. Its silks billowed and shone in the dim light in pale pinks and blues. Behind each cot hung the negligee, the dressing gown. By each cot the mules and the slippers. Alongside, the little table with the alligator skin dressing case. The pillows on which the heads lay were large and full and white . . .

There was a little sign pinned to one of the Turkish bath curtains. It said, "Reserved for Lord Halifax."

Left-wing groups and some newspapers called on the government to improve conditions in the shelters and build more. One evening local Communists led one hundred East Enders, including a pregnant woman, to the Savoy Hotel, and when the siren went off they demanded admittance to the hotel's well-equipped below-ground restaurant, which doubled as a shelter. They were mindful of the fact that many American correspondents would be at the Savoy and the demonstration would embarrass the government. They were all admitted, but unusually, the all-clear sounded immediately afterward and they left. The point was made.

The government set about improving shelters. They were sprayed with antiseptic. Bunk beds were introduced in some. Toilets and washing facilities were installed in the large shelters. Hot drink was supplied, partly by local authorities, partly by ladies of the WVS. The London County Council organized night school classes in shelters.

Some churches had shelters, and some of these acquired different characters. St. Martin-in-the-Fields specialized in drunks and down-and-outs. St. Paul's, Eaton Square, was posh, with women knitting, tea and lemonade and darts. At Lambeth Palace, the home of the Archbishop of Canterbury, the primate of the Church of England, 200 people sheltered regularly in the crypt, and Archbishop Lang would go there most evenings and take prayers.

Self-help groups sprang up. In one housing project, the residents furnished and decorated their shelter, adding carpets, beds, artificial flowers, and pictures of the king and queen, and invited neighbors in to see. A group of shelterers in the Swiss Cottage station started a magazine called the *Swiss Cottager* with the motto *De Profundis* — "from the depths." In West Ham, a poor area near the docks, they organized a shelter library with four thousand books. Sometimes self-help came up against entrenched attitudes. West Ham people started a scheme whereby they repaired each other's bomb-damaged homes, lending what skills they had, but the unions objected. Local authorities were not always cooperative.

In one East End shelter housing several thousand people, so overcrowded that people were fainting from the heat, Mickey Davis, a small, hunchbacked optician whose shop had been destroyed by a bomb, took charge. Under his leadership a committee was elected, which established standards of cleanliness and hygiene and a rota for housekeeping, separate sections for men and women and families, and a first-aid room. They sought and got help from the local council and organized a canteen and free milk for the children. When the local council appointed a shelter marshal, the committee rejected him and insisted that Davis remain. "Mickey's shelter," as it was known, became a showpiece, and foreign visitors were taken there.

The government had also made inadequate provision for people who lost their homes. It had exaggerated expectations of casualties from air raids and had made preparations for burying hundreds of thousands of bomb victims. Yet for every person killed in an air raid, thirty-five were made homeless; 300,000 people lost their homes in the first six weeks of the Blitz. Others still lived in homes with blown-out windows replaced by cardboard and part of the roof gone, because they had nowhere else to go. The rent collector would still come around each week knocking on the door, gently, because it was fragile.

Most of the bombed homes in those first days of the Blitz were in the poorer areas where homes were smaller. In these areas, their homes and their contents meant most to people; their possessions were hard won, representing years of saving up, and often they had no insurance policies.

When the Murphy family home was hit, sixteen-year-old Kitty Murphy rushed in and, with flames licking around, threw clothes and then a three-piece suite of furniture out of the window, ignoring her mother who was shouting at her to get out. She came out carrying a chair and was about to go back in when her mother grabbed her and held on. Kitty recalled: "She said, 'No more, you're not going in there no more, let it burn.' And I just went to get away from her when the whole house caved in. She saved my life. I would have been in there picking up the clock and the ornaments off the mantelpiece."

One fireman who understood the importance of their homes to these people threw himself on a fire started by an incendiary bomb in the front parlor and smothered it, brushing bits of burning fluff off his uniform. When a colleague asked him why he took this unorthodox method of tackling a fire, he explained that he could see that it was a poor home and "I didn't want to mess it up with water."

People who were made homeless were sent to rest centers, or to a public building, often a school, where there was little preparation for them. Newspapers called for action to improve conditions in these, and Churchill ordered the Treasury to make more money available as compensation for people who had lost their homes.

So far as most people were concerned, the shelter situation was one more failure of the political and military leadership, one more sign also of their lack of concern for the ordinary people. One man told a reporter: "The Government tells me to hate Hitler, and so I do, no need of telling. But I don't hate Hitler for this lot. This here is what Chamberlain has done. Shelters to get drowned in, nothing ready, nothing done for the people. They'll find out their mistake one day. Things won't ever be the same after this lot." People like this felt politicians had failed them and so had the brass hats. They had led the country down the path of appeasement and into a war for which it was ill prepared. The fact that most people had agreed with the short-sighted attitude of their leaders in prewar years was all the more reason to castigate those leaders now.

They were pilloried in a pamphlet called *Guilty Men* that appeared in July and sold half a million copies within weeks. It was written by three journalists who signed themselves simply "Cato"; one of them was the young Michael Foot, who went on to become leader of the Labour Party in the 1970s. This created what became a popular picture of the war. In this version Conservative politicians, blinkered and ruled by outmoded concepts, had blundered into war, leaving soldiers to face panzer divisions with only their rifles and their courage. The ruling class had landed the country in a desperate situation from which the common people now had to rescue it.

The people were certainly behind the war effort. Mickey's shelter and *Picture Post*'s Home Guard school reflect a disinclination to wait for the authorities to give a lead. With or without Tom Wintringham's counsel about a people's army, Home Guard units had been created at the grassroots level. J. B. Priestley, whose broadcasts were becoming more openly political, said in one: "Men and women with a gift for leadership now turn up in the most unexpected places. The new ordeals blast away the old shams. Britain . . . is now being bombed and burned into democracy."

This was part of a current of dissatisfaction and demand for change that led to the rejection in 1945 of Churchill's Conservative Party and the election for the first time ever of a majority Labour government.

• • •

The government had its own shelter, a reinforced warren under Whitehall known as the Cabinet War Rooms, built after the Munich crisis in 1938. Ministers and generals and their staffs would sometimes work there and even sleep there. It was a Spartan world, created only for work and protection, the hard, gray, stone walls unbroken by curtains or pictures or colors. Churchill went down there, but he did not like to and he had to be persuaded. Even when he was there he would sometimes go out during an air raid and look at what was going on from the roof.

The rooms were cramped. The cabinet room was eighteen feet square and often contained ten people sitting around a table. Military men worked in the main war room, which had maps showing the disposition of convoys, and charts showing British and German aircraft losses. They received information and telephoned orders from there. A few generals and top civil servants each had a small room, containing a desk, a telephone, just enough room for a typist to work, and a narrow bed. The more senior personnel had a strip of carpet on the floor. Churchill had a slightly larger room with another room for his valet, but even he did not have the luxury of a separate bedroom. In his case it did not matter so much since even down there he worked in bed in the morning, reading papers and dictating. Nearby was a tiny radio studio, and Churchill did some of his broadcasts from there.

Junior staff often worked down there for days on end, sleeping in a staff dormitory area. Joan Bright recalled: "It was a strange life that we led in those days in our quiet dungeon galleries where the only mechanical sounds were the tap of typewriters and the hum of air-conditioning fans. A notice board showed us if it was 'fine' 'wet' or 'windy' outside, red or green lights if an air raid was 'on' or 'off.' If it was 'on' we heard nothing of it until we were outside the heavy steel doors of our cage. Then we would know by the frequency of crump, boom or crackle whether it was worth going out into the normal 'blitz' life of London." (The War Rooms are now open to visitors and are a tourist attraction.)

As the Blitz went on, everyone had bomb stories that they wanted to tell, usually with a comical aspect. A woman told her friends how a freak bomb blast tore the wall off her home but left her bedroom intact, so that she was lying in bed exposed to the world. A man told how he was on his way to a business meeting when a bomb burst a water main nearby, drenching him. Literary London chortled at the story of Cyril Connolly, editor of the literary review *Horizon,* leaping from his lover's bed as bombs crashed around and crawling under it saying, "Perfect fear casteth out love."

People did not tell so often the tragic bomb stories, of death or the disfigurement caused by flying glass. A history of the borough of Kensington lists some of the cases the local council services had to deal with: "John, aged one year six months; mother killed in air raid, John crawled out of the wreckage the next morning. Father in a pitiable state of distress, too unhinged to work. Terry, aged two years. Both parents burned to death. Terry pulled out of blazing house with one eye gone." The comedian Spike Milligan was serving in the army when one of the soldiers was told that his wife and three children had been killed in an air raid; the soldier became insane and did not speak again. These also paid a price for the decision to fight on.

Some called for revenge. When Victor Cazalet, a member of Parliament, wrote to the *Times* calling for the bombing of German cities to break the German people's morale, some supported him, but others rejected this on practical and also on ethical grounds. "We can at present reasonably believe that we deserve to win because we are upholding a higher standard of truth and justice," wrote F. W. Stokoe. "Murderers of women and children have renounced that standard." A clergyman in Bournemouth wrote: "Britain must keep her hands clean if she is to experience the blessing of almighty God." Polls showed that most people were less high-minded and wanted retaliation on German cities.

In Havering, just outside London, a German pilot landed by parachute with a broken leg, and a couple took him into their house, laid him out on a couch, brought him a cup of tea, and called the police. This was the usual response, even when bombs were falling, but there were exceptions that were not reported at the time. A German pilot parachuted down in south London in the middle of a raid and became entangled in some telegraph wires, and a mob including women with kitchen knives attacked him. He was rescued by police.

As always, difficulties also brought out the nastier side of human nature. There was an increase in anti-Semitism, particularly in parts of the East End that had been a favorite prewar stamping ground of the British Union of Fascists. A confidential Ministry of Information report noted this and said: "Some people seeking an outlet for emotional disturbance pick on the traditional and the nearest one." Refugees from the Continent were another scapegoat, for there were a lot of these about, and some suffered insults and charges that they were being given preference over British people.

There was looting, even looting by civil defense workers. Some of this was almost harmless; when leather goods or cigarette lighters from a shop blasted to pieces were strewn across the street, it was easy to feel that they did not really belong to anyone. Some was more cruelly criminal; people went into bomb-damaged homes to steal the contents, or rifled the purses of the wounded. More government regulations and rationing provided opportunities to exploit for profit.

Accidents increased. People would rush out of the house when a siren sounded, and they sometimes left dinner on the stove, or stumbled downstairs as they hurried, or ran into things in the blackout. Children were less supervised, so more children were killed on the roads or drowned in emergency water tanks, and more broke the law and got into trouble with the police.

Sleep became a major problem. For volunteer civil defense workers out much of the night, and with a daytime job as well, the situation was worse than for others. John Strachey wrote in an account of his life as a part-time air raid warden. "Sleep replaced food as the simplest, most everyday object of desire. Whenever someone had anything over half an hour to spare during the day, he had not the slightest doubt as to what to do with the time. He slept." People dozed on buses, at their office desks and during tea breaks.

A survey found that two-thirds of Londoners were getting less than four hours' sleep a night. The government offered ear plugs, but few wanted them; people had a sense that it was better to be able to hear the danger. One woman explained to her granddaughter that she wanted to be able to know when a bomber was directly overhead so that at that moment she could offer up a quick prayer to the Almighty.

People talked to one another. Everyone noticed this in a country where people normally kept their distance. (One difference between

London and New York subways in those days was that in London there were arm rests separating the seats ensuring that a passenger would not be in physical contact with other passengers.) In buses and on the street, people would exchange remarks. In apartment blocks where people would exchange no more than a brief "Good morning" in normal times, neighbors now slept side by side in the basement shelter and this gave them a new intimacy. The famous British reserve was breaking down. Vincent Sheean came out with one American view. "You know what?" he said to some friends in a pub in London. "The Englishman is becoming a human being!"

A Birmingham man who visited London wrote after he returned: "Considering what they have been through, they appear to be remarkably cheerful and friendly. It was much easier to talk to strangers than it had been formerly, and the worse the conditions, the more laughter there seemed to be."

People were brought together by the common danger and also the common difficulties, for every kind of service was disrupted by the air raids. There would be no gas for cooking one day because the gas pipes had been broken, or no hot water, or no water at all, or no telephone service, or no milk or bread. People helped one another.

The government censored news of the effect of air raids for military reasons. Newspapers and the radio could refer only to "parts of west London" or "a town in southern England." They could only say that casualties were "light" or "considerable." Reports were spread by word of mouth — "Fulham Road got a pasting last night." Inevitably, much of it was inaccurate.

Partly because of this dearth of information, many people listened to the news put out from Germany over the "New British Broadcasting Station"; at the peak of its popularity, a quarter of the population tuned in to it. Its principal broadcaster was William Joyce, a prewar member of the British Union of Fascists, dubbed "Lord Haw-Haw" by the press for the braying tone of the exaggerated upper-class voice. Curiously, this was applied first not to Joyce, whose voice did not have this quality, but to his predecessor, Norman Baillie-Stewart, but it stuck to Joyce. His continual message was that Britain had been led into a futile war by Churchill and the Jews. The tagging of a traitor with an aristocratic title was also symptomatic of the popular attitude to the governing classes.

As the bombing went on, much of London became covered with gray dust, and increasingly, it took on a shabby appearance. A grayness also came over much of the material side of British life. There were no street lights and no glitter in store windows, few luxuries, and those there were had been acquired with effort and ingenuity. People made do with old clothes and mended them. A wedding dress was simple and made with scrounged materials, the wedding cake did not have icing, presents were likely to be useful rather than luxurious. Food rationing became tighter, and many things that were not on the ration became scarce, from whiskey to stockings. Food was only a necessary fuel; traditional British meals were replaced by dishes like parsnip soup and vegetable pie. The frugality of the times is seen in something found years after the war in a desk in the War Rooms when it was being renovated for opening to the public: an envelope with an officer's name on it, and inside, three cubes of sugar.

Bus services would be delayed because streets were blocked by rubble or because some of the buses were damaged by bombs. At one point all rail tracks leading south out of London were cut. But people carried on, and those who had jobs somehow got to them, even if it meant waiting in line for an hour for a bus and walking for two or three miles or hitching a ride.

Going to work seemed to mean clinging to an area of normality while much of what usually constituted normal daily life had been transformed. It also meant getting together with other people and swapping experiences, important in a time of stress. Some people were conscious that their jobs were contributing directly to the war effort and their work was needed. A young office worker, Mary Elsy, emerged from a shelter to find her home in ruins. Despite this, as she wrote for a local historian who asked for accounts of wartime: "I went to work as usual. One always did if one could, on these occasions; it was partly defiance to the Germans, partly one's own small contribution to the war effort." Among everyone there was a sense that failing to get to work would mean a victory for the Luftwaffe.

It was important to keep going to stay cheerful, to keep the collective chin up. A store with its window blown out had a handwritten sign up saying: "Open for Business. Even More Open than Usual." A damaged barber's had a sign saying: "We Are Open. Close Shaves a Specialty." At a wrecked pub where most of the drink supply had been left intact, the manager was saying cheerfully to the locals, "Have a drink on the house. There's no bloody house but have a drink on it anyway."

Richard Titmuss, the sociologist who wrote the official history of social policy during the war, concluded:

> Events showed that most people had a greater ability to adjust themselves than was thought possible: a tough resilience to the changed conditions of life imposed upon them. Nor was it realized that there would be such a widespread and spontaneous development of ways of keeping up morale: friendliness, the constant talk about bombs, the attitude of "If it's got your number on it," and a preoccupation with frivolous activities like going to the pub as usual or having a permanent wave.

London Can Take It was the title of a documentary film about the air raids, made in Britain but scripted and narrated by the American correspondent Quentin Reynolds, and this became a slogan. Londoners, they were told, were taking it on the chin and smiling. The German bombs were not even denting cockney cheeriness. This self-congratulation can reinforce good behavior. If people are told that they are behaving well, that they are brave and cheerful and public-spirited, they are more likely to be so.

London taking it is a part of the story of the Blitz that has been handed down, in America as well as Britain. When the former New York City mayor Rudolph Giuliani visited London in the aftermath of the World Trade Center attack, he said New Yorkers took inspiration from the behavior of Londoners in the Blitz.

Today many people look back with something like nostalgia to the days of the Blitz, for all its horrors. They talk about the fellowship. "People used to help each other then. It's everyone for himself now." "People cared then, no one cares now" — remarks like this were heard often in the years after the war. J. B. Priestley said a few years later that the British character was at its best then, and had deteriorated since.

These were exciting times, when great things were happening in the world and they were a part of it. Vera Brittain wrote in October that she was anxious about her children in America, but otherwise, she said:

"I should almost have enjoyed the peculiar zest of dodging death. For all their boredom and grimness, I would not for anything have missed the past two months." The novelist Margery Allingham wrote, when bombs were still falling, "What an age to have been alive in! Thank God I was born when I was."

People were not just living for themselves. They were part of a collective effort. The air raids appear to have brought people together and given them a sense of purpose that strengthened their defenses against mental collapse.

Just as the government overestimated the number of casualties, it also overestimated the amount of mental breakdown. A group of psychiatrists warned before the war that there would be three psychiatric casualties to one physical one. In fact there was no increase in mental breakdown despite the strain, and a special unit set up to deal with the expected flood of psychiatric cases dissolved itself. The suicide rate went down, and throughout the war years it remained below the peacetime level. An official report said many people showed symptoms of shock after an explosion; they became speechless, or trembled uncontrollably, or had crying spells. But when they were given a cup of tea (applied in any crisis, the British equivalent of chicken soup in Jewish folklore) and perhaps a sedative, a night's rest and some reassurance, most recovered quickly.

Richard Titmuss gave his explanation for the lack of the expected mental breakdowns:

> The proximity of death, the spread of physical hardship, and the ubiquity of destructive forces which were more intelligible to the ordinary man than the workings of economic laws, gave existence a new meaning and old fears and responsibilities less significance ... New aims for which to live, work that satisfied a larger number of needs, a more cohesive society, fewer lonely people; all these elements helped to offset the circumstances which often lead to neurotic illness.

It turns out that the social virtues that were highly developed in the British people at this time were important in maintaining individual discipline and social cohesion in the response to the air raids. But later on,

German society also held together while suffering much heavier bombing than Britain, admittedly under a draconian dictatorship that punished dissent severely, as did Japanese society. Those who predicted complete breakdown under bombing, whether psychologists or strategists of air warfare, exaggerated the vulnerability of modern society and of the modern psyche, and underestimated the resilience and resourcefulness of individuals.

• • •

American correspondents in London were identifying with the British people. For one thing, they shared their experiences and the dangers. Guy Murchie of the *Chicago Tribune* was wounded by a bomb that killed the man he was talking to in a hotel room. The NBC and CBS offices were both bombed, and Kay Campbell, a CBS assistant, was thrown across the room by the blast. Correspondents took their turn fire-watching in the office buildings where they worked. George Lait of the International News Service and Merrill Mueller of NBC worked with firemen and wardens pulling injured people from a bombed building. They dragged a three-year-old girl out from beside the bodies of her parents.

They were able to tell Americans the correct position to take when a bomb is about to land nearby: "Flat on the ground, face down, mouth slightly open and hands covering ears," as Ed Murrow explained. They could describe the sound of an incendiary bomb — "Swish, swosh and then a plunk," according to Ralph Ingersoll.

British officials were good hosts to senior American correspondents in London. They understood, as indeed did the British public, the importance of American public opinion. The Savoy Hotel bar was the correspondents' favorite watering hole — some of them lived at the Savoy — so the official government spokesman took to holding his regular briefing there. They were given access to high places and low; they dined with ministers and were taken to munitions factories, airfields, and bomb-damaged towns. A select few were invited to have tea with Queen Elizabeth at Buckingham Palace, through the good offices of the chief press officer at the Ministry of Economic Warfare, David Bowes-Lyons, who was her brother.

Radio then occupied the role that television does today. This was the golden age of radio, both in news and entertainment. Americans relied on radio more than newspapers for their news. Commentators such as H. V. Kaltenborn, Raymond Gram Swing, Elmer Davis, and Gabriel Heatter were household names. Recording equipment was large and heavy and had to be moved about on wheels and connected by cable to a transmission line, but correspondents in London maneuvered it out on to the streets and on to rooftops so that American listeners became familiar with the wail of the air raid sirens as they sounded over the city.

Ed Murrow of CBS was preeminent among those reporting from London. His evening broadcasts that began "This is London . . ." had an audience of tens of millions. The first of these was much like many that followed. Murrow spoke quietly with frequent pauses. "This is Trafalgar Square. The noise that you hear at this moment is the sound of an air raid siren. A searchlight just burst into action off in the distance, an immense single beam of light sweeping the sky above me now. People are walking along very quietly. We're just at the entrance to an air raid shelter here, and I must move the cable a bit so people can walk in." Then listeners heard unhurried footsteps, and a man asking another for a light for his cigarette.

On September 9, Murrow gave an assessment:

> These people are exceedingly brave, tough and prudent. The East End, where disaster is always just around the corner, seems to take it better than the more fashionable districts in the West End . . . The politicians who called this "a people's war" were right, probably more right than they knew at the time. I've seen some horrible sights in this city these days and nights, but not once have I heard a man, woman or child suggest that Britain should throw in her hand. These people are angry. How much can they stand? I don't know. The strain is very great . . . After four days and nights of this air blitzkrieg, I think the people here are becoming veterans, even as their army was hardened in the fire of Dunkirk.

Murrow, tall, lean, trench-coated, lived through air raids on coffee, whiskey, and cigarettes; fearless, committed to the cause of freedom, he became the archetypical foreign correspondent seen in movies, much as, for an earlier generation, the roisterers of the Chicago newsroom in *The Front Page* set the image of the big city reporter.

Soon correspondents' reports carried a tone of unabashed sympathy and admiration. Raymond Daniell wrote in the *New York Times*:

> This is total war in its most brutal and cruel form. None save those who have lived here, sharing the trouble of the people in this stricken capital since the Blitzkrieg started, can understand what they have been through, and none who has been here will ever forget their cheerfulness and calm throughout this crisis in their history. It takes as much heroism to dig out a delayed 1,000 lb delayed action bomb near the foundations of St. Paul's as it does to hold an outpost in the face of a tank charge, and that is the kind of heroism with which the people of this city are defending their homes and hearths. And they are keeping their sense of humor, ready to laugh through it all.

Ben Robertson of *P.M.* wrote later in the same vein as his newspaper dispatches: "Everywhere there were craters and ruin, but the city in this crisis had rediscovered itself; it was living as it had never lived. Everywhere there was courage, and six million people who had lived humdrum lives now learned what it was like to live for civilization."

Life magazine carried on its cover a photograph by Cecil Beaton of a three-year-old British bomb victim, Eileen Dunn, sitting in a hospital bed with a bandage around her head. She is clutching a doll and looking straight at the camera with large round eyes, and an expression that is questioning, even challenging. Why, she seems to ask, was this done to me? Inside, a *Life* writer said: "In this crisis, the friendly courage of the English is proving magnificent. Motorists drive by with cars full of workers. A woman walked to a delayed action bomb to pick up a foolish kitten . . . The mass heart of England rose to meet the challenge, and hardened in anger."

When Eric Sevareid, another CBS correspondent, left London he broadcast a valediction: "London fights down her fears every night, takes her blows, and gets up again every morning. You feel yourself an embattled member of this embattled corps . . . Someone wrote the other day: 'When all this is over in years to come, men will speak of this war and say, 'I was a soldier' or 'I was a sailor' or 'I was a pilot.' Others will say with equal pride, 'I was a citizen of London.'" One man wrote to Sevareid to say that he was driving in his car when he heard this over the radio and had to stop because his eyes were full of tears.

Hugh Johnson complained in his syndicated newspaper column about the amount of what he called pro-British propaganda on the air. "H. V. Kaltenborn, Raymond Gram Swing, Dorothy Thompson and Gabriel Heatter are constantly pumping into the great still pool of public opinion reckless incitements to a pro-British war," he wrote.

Certainly the American press had a pro-British bias at this time. Given the nature of Britain and of its enemy, it could hardly be otherwise. The correspondents may not have heard a single person talk of giving in but others did, here and there. The RAF was bombing German cities with its continuing policy of attacking railroad marshaling yards and oil installations, albeit not very effectively, for it overestimated the accuracy that can be achieved with nighttime bombing. No doubt some German children were wounded in these raids, but their faces did not appear on the cover of *Life* magazine, and their plight did not draw much sympathy.

The tenor of these reports in the American media, and sometimes the reports themselves, were disseminated in Britain. They brought cheer and encouragement and the sense that they had friends across the ocean, who watched what was happening and cared.

● ● ●

On Sunday, September 15, Churchill was at Chequers, the prime minister's country house. He dictated some letters and then, because it was a fine clear day and good weather for aerial activity, he decided to call in at Fighter Command headquarters at Uxbridge. His wife, Clementine, was with him. Air Vice Marshal Park welcomed them and told his guests, "I don't know whether anything will happen today. At present all is quiet." They were not to stay quiet for long.

This day was to see the climactic German attack, the biggest raids yet. Göring had decided that the RAF was on its last legs and he was now going to deliver the coup de grâce. The first wave came in the morning, 500 bombers escorted by 620 fighters. Against these, Park had 630 Hurricanes and Spitfires in what he regarded as front-line squadrons, with a reserve of 172, mostly with new pilots. The RAF had decided that wherever possible, Spitfires should engage the German fighters and try to draw them off while Hurricanes went for the bombers.

Churchill sat in a visitors' gallery overlooking the Group Operations

Room, and as WAAFs moved counters on the map board he watched the battle develop. Soon after he sat down he saw the messages coming which had been distilled from radar and observer reports. An attack of forty plus was noted, others of twenty plus, forty plus, sixty and eighty plus. A set of lights showed the status of each squadron, and more and more lights went on, showing that squadrons were raised to standby status or had taken off.

Things went well. Radar had spotted the Germans mustering over the French coast. The plotters got the course of the German planes exactly right and vectored the fighters to intercept. The Germans were encountering a headwind, which slowed them down and allowed the RAF to intercept them farther from the target. It also meant that the German fighter escorts, with their short range, would only be able to stay over Britain for a few minutes. By the time the Germans crossed the English coast, eleven of Park's twenty-one squadrons were already airborne. They had time to climb to their full height and dive down on the bombers over Canterbury.

An argument had been raging for some time in RAF Fighter Command. Some, most vociferously Wing Commander Douglas Bader, wanted to adopt what they called the "big wing" tactic: assemble an entire wing of five squadrons to attack the enemy bombers in force. Dowding and Park would attack immediately with whatever planes were available before the bombers could reach their target. Park now called on the squadrons based north of the capital, and Bader formed them into his big wing. When the Germans arrived over London they met what seemed like a phalanx of sixty fighters coming straight at them.

People in the streets watched encounters in the skies all over London. They saw vapor trails, burning planes, pilots parachuting down. They saw one fighter plane — piloted by a Pole, although people on the ground did not know this — press its attack on a Dornier so close that it collided with a German airman parachuting out and broke its propellor; it landed with blood spattered over its engine cowling.

In one bizarre incident, the crew of a damaged Dornier bomber bailed out but the bomber continued on its path. Sergeant Ray Holmes, piloting a Hurricane, attacked it, not knowing that it was crewless, and crashed into it. The tail broke off and the Dornier spun downward flinging its bombs out, and two landed on Buckingham Palace. Holmes's damaged Hurricane went into a spin and he bailed out. He landed on a three-story apartment house with his parachute caught in the guttering, cut himself loose, kissed two girls who appeared in the garden, went to see the wreck of the Dornier outside Victoria Station, and then went off to a nearby army barracks to be treated to drinks in the mess.

Another wave came over in the early afternoon and this contained four times as many fighters as bombers. Park sent up his front-line squadrons and they attacked the Germans over southeast England; then, as he saw how big the enemy force was and also that its target was London again, he committed his entire force. Air battles raged all over southern England.

Churchill, watching in the operations room, felt the tension. He was not allowed to smoke a cigar in the underground control room because of the air conditioning but he clenched an unlit cigar in his teeth. At one point he asked Park, "What other reserves have we?" He received the same reply that had shocked him when Gamelin spoke it in Paris four months earlier. "There are none," Park said. He had staked everything. Churchill was grim-faced and anxious. He wrote later: "The odds were great; our margins small; the stakes infinite."

Churchill did not say it, and perhaps did not know it at this time, but Park had foreknowledge. He knew, because Ultra had intercepted Göring's order, that the Luftwaffe was putting all it had into this second wave and would not be sending another to catch his fighters refueling on the ground. The Ultra team was speeding up its interceptions and procedures now, and got the message immediately to Dowding, who passed it to Park.

The Germans turned back, some of them before reaching London. British fighters harassed them on their return journey. At the end of the day the RAF announced that it had destroyed 185 enemy planes for the loss of 28 planes. The German losses were inflated. Actually the RAF shot down 56 planes. Once again the higher figure was not a deliberate lie, but was drawn from the pilots' reports.

The day was a victory for the RAF, and one that changed the course of the war. As the RAF's official history says: "If 15 August showed the German High Command that air supremacy was not to be won within a brief space, 15 September went far to convince them that it would not be won at all."

The pink-cheeked airmen had turned the tide. The Germans continued to bomb London night after night, and other cities as well, but they never again raided by day in force. They had given up trying to destroy the RAF.

The Battle of Britain was a battle for control of the air space over Britain, and it was clear that the Germans had lost it. This had a psychological as well as a military significance. The onward march of Nazi power, which began when German infantry soldiers marched across a bridge over the river Rhine in 1935 and which had seemed unstoppable, was halted for the first time.

• • •

Mid-September was still the expected time for an invasion. The army units put on alert at the time of the Cromwell order remained on alert. Thanks to Ultra, the British knew Hitler's schedule. In late August, after the initial failure to break the RAF, he put off the date, and said the earliest date would now be September 21. He said he would decide three days in advance. But his navy said it needed a week's notice, so effectively his decision would be ten days in advance of the invasion.

The Chiefs of Staff suggested to Churchill that the timing of meetings of the House of Commons be kept secret from now on, pointing out that the huge Parliament building, a clearly visible landmark beside the Thames, made a tempting target for German bombers. On September 17, the House of Commons went into secret session for the first time. There were five secret sessions during the war; at most of them Churchill gave news to the House that was too grim for the public to be told, but at this first secret session he had little news to report.

He proposed accepting the advice of the Chiefs of Staff that they not present the Luftwaffe with, literally, a sitting target by announcing their sessions in advance. "We ought not to flatter ourselves by imagining that we are irreplaceable," he told them, "but it cannot be denied that two or three hundred by-elections would be a quite needless complication of our affairs at this particular juncture." The proposal was accepted.

Then Churchill turned to the possibility of invasion. He repeated and amplified what he had said earlier in public about the German preparations, giving some figures. "At any moment a major assault may be made on this island," he warned. "The shipping available and now assembled is sufficient to carry in one voyage nearly half a million men. We should of course expect to drown a great many on the way over, and to destroy a large proportion of the vessels. But . . . one must expect many lodgements or attempted lodgements to be made on this island simultaneously."

Even as he was speaking, Ultra was receiving an intercepted message that changed the picture. As they knew, one component of the invasion plan was the airlifting of troops and supplies to Britain on the heels of the invading force, the assumption being that the invaders would seize an airfield immediately. Troop-carrying aircraft and loading equipment were being readied for this purpose at airfields in Holland. On the morning of September 17, a message went to the officer in charge of these loading operations from the General Staff saying that Hitler had ordered the dismantling of the air-loading equipment. The Ultra team who translated the message knew what this meant. Operation Sea Lion, the invasion of Britain, was postponed.

They immediately told F. W. Winterbotham, a long-time intelligence officer who was the Air Staff's representative on the intelligence service. Winterbotham sent the intercepted message over to Churchill along with a note explaining its significance. He also sent a note to the prime minister's private secretary asking him to ensure that Churchill read it immediately.

As it happened, Churchill had called a meeting of the Chiefs of Staff for 7:30 that evening in his War Rooms, and he had asked Winterbotham to be there, along with Sir Stewart Menzies, the head of intelligence. An air raid began as they set out in Menzies's car, and they drove through blacked-out streets to the sounds of bombs and antiaircraft fire. They arrived at the underground War Rooms off Whitehall as the Chiefs of Staff were assembling. Winterbotham describes the scene:

> I was struck by the extraordinary change that had come over these men in the last few hours. It was as if someone had cut all the strings of the violins in the middle of a dreary concerto. Churchill read out the signal, his face beaming; then he rightly asked the Chief of the Air Staff, Sir Cyril Newall, to explain its significance. Cyril Newall had been well briefed; he gave it as his considered

opinion that this marked the end of Sea Lion, at least for this year
... There was a very broad smile on Churchill's face now as he lit
up his massive cigar and suggested that we should all take a little
fresh air.

They went up to find the raid at its height. Churchill ignored the protestations of others on the staff and left the shelter of a concrete wall to
stand in front and watch the action. As Winterbotham recalled:

> It was a wild scene. Standing with our backs to the concrete were
> ranged the three chiefs of staff and Churchill, his chin thrust out,
> the long cigar in his mouth, and just across the other side of St.
> James's Park Carlton House Terrace was ablaze: the boom of
> bombs exploding to the South, the crack and rattle of AA guns
> and exploding shells, the red and white glow of the fires silhouett-
> ing the tall black trunks of the great trees. It was a moment in his-
> tory to remember, and above the noise came the angry voice of
> Winston Churchill: "By God we'll get the B's for this."

The hour of worst peril had passed. Three things had changed the
situation. The Germans had failed to crush the RAF. They had been
forced to postpone their plan to invade Britain. America had decided
that Britain would remain in the war and was worth backing, and it had
committed itself to its defense.

It was by no means certain that Britain would win the war, or even
that it would not lose it. Britain was still outnumbered and outgunned
and its ocean lifelines were threatened. The German invasion plan was
postponed, not canceled, and British home forces remained on alert.
But Britain had survived the summer, and would survive the year. It
would have a powerful ally, although not yet a fighting ally. Britain
would not bear the burden of defending democracy unaided.

After mid-September the Blitz continued. The Germans went on
bombing London but they bombed by night. Night after night the
bombing went on until the following April. They bombed other cities
also. They bombed Coventry, a major manufacturing city, razing most
of the city in a single night including the famous cathedral, and they
bombed Liverpool, Newcastle, and Glasgow.

Britain was committed now to carry on the struggle to the bitter end,
however it turned out. This meant that it was committed to give its life's

blood, literally and metaphorically. It would have to expend all its resources, and in order to continue it would have to turn to the United States for more. Its power would wane as America's grew. America and Britain would become allies, and the relationship between them would deepen and would reach new levels of cooperation and trust. America's active involvement in the fate of Europe would continue.

The events of May and June, when German forces swept across Europe, transformed the world. The events of September transformed the world again.

AFTER THE SUMMER

The British people did not know it but they had five more years of war ahead of them, five more years of death rolls, of the absence of loved ones, of anxiety and scarcity, privation and daily hardship.

The fifty American destroyers did not fulfill all the hopes the British navy had for them. But politically and psychologically, they played just the role that the British government hoped they would play. They marked a new level of American commitment to the British cause and a closer association with the war effort.

As the presidential election campaign got into full swing, the war inevitably became an issue. Isolationists went in for full-throated charges of warmongering against Roosevelt. Willkie went on approving of aid to Britain, but at one point he accused Roosevelt of wanting to lead America into the war, in a speech he later ascribed to the heat of the campaign. Roosevelt was stung into making his oft-quoted promise to the mothers of America: "Your sons are not going to be sent into any foreign wars."

Roosevelt won the election with a comfortable majority. He was helped by the improvement in the economy: unemployment went down by 500,000 in these months, due partly to orders from Britain. However, he lost ground compared to the last two elections. Although Willkie carried only six states out of the forty-eight, he won more electoral votes than any Republican candidate since 1928. His six states were all in the Midwest, including Kansas and Nebraska, which had been Democrat in the last two elections, and North and South Dakota, with their large German-American populations. The balance in Congress changed little. The Republicans had three more seats in the Senate, six fewer in the House.

With his election victory behind him, Roosevelt pursued his policy of aid to Britain with the Lend-Lease Bill, which he introduced in December, its importance underlined fortuitously by its number, bill 1776. This time he did not wait for others to clear the way but led from the front, arguing the case for it himself. This bill would solve the problem of Britain's inability to pay for the war. It gave the president powers to transfer war materials to a foreign power. Roosevelt likened this to lending a neighbor a hose when his house is on fire, a phrase he borrowed, like the earlier one about quarantining aggressor nations, from Harold Ickes.

The debate over Lend-Lease was furious. Opponents argued that it would lead to America's entry into the war, that Britain was taking America for a sucker, that it was giving the president power that belonged only to a dictator. Mothers' groups demonstrated against it on Capitol Hill. Most Republicans opposed it, but Willkie stuck to his principles and supported it. Congress passed the bill, but with a two-year limit.

The U.S. Treasury made Britain pay where it could. While waiting for the Lend-Lease Bill to pass through Congress, Morgenthau insisted that Britain sell interests in America to pay for war materials, and Roosevelt sent a cruiser to South Africa to collect gold to pay British debts. British officials were resentful; so far as they were concerned, America was taking advantage of Britain's financial losses incurred in the common cause. Churchill likened the American attitude to that of "a sheriff collecting the last assets of a helpless debtor," in a message intended for Roosevelt that the Foreign Office persuaded him not to send.

In the ensuing war years, Britain received from America $21 billion in Lend-Lease aid and gave back $7 billion. But the United States imposed conditions that ensured that Lend-Lease did not help Britain recover its prewar economic position.

In the winter of 1940 and the following year, the war continued in North Africa, where Rommel's Afrika Corps reinforced and then largely replaced the Italians, and in the Atlantic, where the Germans stepped up their U-boat offensive. Starting in 1942 the dreams of the founders of the RAF were realized as the biggest bombers in the world struck at the heart of the enemy's society, bombing at night and pounding and setting fire to large parts of great cities. Later they were joined by American aircraft bombing by day. This did not, however, win the war, as some of the more enthusiastic advocates of strategic bombing had thought it would.

Rudolf Hess, the deputy fuehrer, had evidently not given up the hopes for peace with Britain which he expressed to Albrecht Haushofer (see Introduction). In May 1941 he flew a Messerschmitt 110 to Britain — he had been a pilot in World War One — and parachuted onto the Scottish estate of the duke of Hamilton, who in prewar days had been an advocate of Anglo-German friendship. But the duke was absent, serving with the RAF (he had been a pilot before the war, the first man to fly over Everest). It seems to have been a one-man peace mission, taken without authorization. The German government denounced it and said Hess had lost his mind. The British authorities imprisoned him, and after the war he was sentenced to life imprisonment at the Nuremberg war crimes trials. He carried letters which the British government has never released, so there is still some mystery about the affair.

In June 1941 Hitler turned his attention away from Britain and invaded the Soviet Union. He told one of his generals that Britain was relying on Russia, and with Russia defeated Britain's last hope would be shattered. Yet the conquest of Russia was not merely a means to defeat Britain but his ultimate goal for Germany as set out in *Mein Kampf*. He counted on another blitzkrieg victory and hoped his armies would be in Moscow before winter set in. Winter came early, however, and was ferocious, and so was the Russian resistance. The juggernaut of the German army's advance was halted in the snows.

The Russians pushed the German armies back, from the outskirts of Moscow and Leningrad all the way to Berlin. America and even Britain sent Russia weapons. Among the American public and even more among the British, there was heartfelt gratitude to the Soviet Union and its people. They were fighting the German army when most American and British troops were still at home. From June 1941 onward, the war was, for Germany, a war with the Soviet Union more than anything else. Even after D-Day, more German troops were fighting on the Russian front than against the Americans and British. Of all the Allies, the Russians killed the most Germans and suffered the most losses.

Throughout 1941 Roosevelt continued to move the United States closer to war. American warships escorted merchant ships halfway across the Atlantic and gave help to the British navy. Inevitably there were clashes at sea. Two American destroyers were attacked, and one, the *Reuben James,* was sunk. The U.S. Air Force trained RAF air crew. In August Roosevelt met with Churchill aboard a British warship in Placentia Bay, Newfoundland, and the two leaders together announced their war aims in the Atlantic Charter. This was unprecedented: the leader of a country that was technically neutral joining with a war leader in proclaiming war aims.

Congress was still not going all the way with Roosevelt. When the conscription bill came up for renewal in October, it was passed by just one vote.

In July 1941 Japan occupied Vietnam, which was then a part of French Indochina, and Roosevelt responded with a series of measures that in effect placed an embargo on oil and other supplies vital for the Japanese war machine. Isolationists warned that this could lead to war. Senator Taft said, with unintentional prophecy, "American mothers do not want their sons to die for a country in Indochina whose name they cannot even pronounce." The American move forced Japan to either withdraw or go to war. It opted for war and announced its decision in the skies over Hawaii on a Sunday morning in December 1941.

Churchill told General Eisenhower once that in his war memoirs he tried to keep out anything that could disturb Anglo-American relations, but he was candid about his reaction to the attack on Pearl Harbor. With much of the American fleet in ruins and 2,330 Americans dead, he wrote that that night, "being saturated and satiated with emotion and sensation, I went to bed and slept the sleep of the saved and the thankful."

Actually, the issue of American participation in the war was not yet decided. There was still the possibility that Germany would renege on its alliance with Japan and not join in the war on America. If the United States had been at war only in the Pacific, Americans would have been much less interested in Europe. But Germany declared war on the United States four days after Pearl Harbor.

The debate in America over neutrality was ended. Britain was no longer alone. This time the United States did not hold itself aloof from its fellow combatants, as it had in World War One, but became a full-fledged partner. It entered into an alliance with a foreign power for the first time, and it did so again after the war.

The Allies decided to try to win the war in Europe before the war against Japan, and in 1942 American troops started crossing the Atlantic, until there were 3 million Americans in Britain.

Wartime British joke: A G.I. in a pub in London complains, "This beer is flat."

"Not surprising," the bartender says. "It's been waiting for you for three years."

• • •

The relationship between America and Britain became closer. During the war and after it, the public in the two countries recognized a common purpose and a common culture. People in government and in the higher ranks of the armed services developed habits of cooperation and of trust. Even the two intelligence services cooperated, sharing secrets to an unprecedented degree. The alliance of the two countries, going far beyond any treaty, came more and more to seem a natural one.

The relationship was an unequal one, however. America was the stronger partner, and for a long time Britain was the dependent one, a situation that naturally tends to create resentment. Yet with the British knowledge of American economic and military superiority went a belief in their own cultural superiority and greater worldly intelligence — "Greeks among the Romans" was a metaphor for a time. Many Americans accepted this, consciously or unconsciously, what is known as the "colonial cringe." American academics sent to the British code-breaking center at Bletchley Park were cautioned against becoming "slavishly Anglophile."

The relationship operated at several levels, and it still does. As in a close family relationship, it is instinctive rather than reasoned, but is also complex and contains some ambivalence.

The war was unprecedented in its scope and its ferocity. It took more than 50 million lives. Unlike in previous wars in the last three centuries, most of these were civilians. The distinction between combatants and civilians largely vanished, as evidenced in the phrase "home front."

The bombing of civilians was legitimized. Armies swept across vast territories, and savage hatreds were unleashed on populations. The preponderance of civilian deaths over military ones was to be a characteristic of the lesser wars that followed in the rest of the twentieth century.

Britain suffered 300,000 dead, 60,000 of them civilians, the United States 292,000. Soviet losses went uncounted, but they totaled more than 20 million, perhaps more than 30 million. Tens of millions of people were displaced, many of them permanently. Parts of Europe and much of Germany suffered devastation such as no European country had seen since the religious wars of the sixteenth century. The Soviet army brought Soviet domination and Communist government to Eastern Europe and the eastern part of Germany, and it remained for fifty-five years.

At the end of the war in Europe the British people, grateful as they were to Churchill, rejected him as a peacetime leader and elected a Labour government. It carried out a social democratic program and led the world in establishing a welfare state. But Britain was nearly bankrupt. Ten percent of its wealth was physically destroyed: buildings wrecked or damaged; a third of its merchant fleet, before the war the world's largest, at the bottom of the ocean; its overseas assets sold. But its plight seemed to be temporary. No one questioned its position as a great power with worldwide responsibilities.

The United States emerged from the war richer than it went into it, the only country to do so, its economy stronger than ever. War had accomplished what the New Deal had failed to do. Britain was dependent on loans from the United States to keep going, as was the rest of Europe. America came to Europe's rescue with the Marshall Plan, and to its defense with NATO. In both these enterprises, Britain was America's principal transatlantic partner. America's engagement with European affairs became permanent.

When Britain agreed to give America bases in the British West Indies, Hess told Haushofer that Britain was handing over its empire to the United States. In fact Britain did not transfer sovereignty over any territory. Nonetheless, there was some justification for seeing this as symbolic of the start of the surrender of an imperial role. The war had sapped Britain's economic strength. It no longer had the economic foundation for its worldwide role, although this was not appreciated immediately. America took over from Britain in a series of moves to either bolster governments in power or replace them, first of all in Greece and then in Iran.

In the following years the U.S. government moved into areas around the world which had been under British control or influence, developing an imperialist cast of mind, taking it upon itself to decide which governments should rule in other countries. The Cold War provided the context for this. Only a pro-American government could be guaranteed to be anti-Communist. The CIA, which developed out of Donovan's OSS, became the principal instrument for covert action to maintain or install governments that the United States wanted in power.

With hindsight, it is clear that the war hastened Britain's imperial downfall rather than caused it. Colonial peoples in the British Empire, as in the French and Dutch empires, were demanding independence, and they were going to get it. Britain's long-term economic decline relative to other industrialized countries was inevitable due to structural weaknesses. France, Holland, Belgium, and even Germany recovered from the ravages of the war more quickly than anyone expected, and then their economies overtook Britain's.

. . .

Britain, unlike America and some other countries, does not have a foundation story. It has no Revolutionary War, no founding fathers, no storming of the Bastille, no Easter Uprising. There was no single event behind the creation of the British nation. Instead of a foundation story for schoolchildren, a historic event that acquires a legendary status, it has a number of episodes from its history that go some way toward being defining moments: Sir Francis Drake sailing off to meet the Spanish Armada, King Charles the First going to the executioner's block, the Battle of Waterloo.

The period epitomized by Churchill's phrase "finest hour" is one of these, and because it is the most recent, it is the salient one. In the legend, the entire British people stood shoulder to shoulder in resisting the enemy. They were all brave, unselfish, and unfailingly cheerful. A compromise peace was never remotely considered. The Battle of Britain was the RAF David against the Luftwaffe Goliath.

If this is the legend, glossy and romanticized as legends usually are, the kernel is true. Britain did what was right, and it was important that it did so, and most of the British people participated in this effort.

At the end of the war British people were proud. The world said they had reason to be. During the war it had been, for the German-occupied countries, a beacon of hope, the one chance of liberation from Nazi rule. A British prisoner of war, who found himself in a slave labor camp with other nationalities, wrote about the small group of Britons: "Among their fellow prisoners, these men found themselves marked and honored for their particular claim to the word that had become universal in all the slave camps of Europe. Frenchmen, Russians, Serbs, Greeks, Dutchmen, Croats, Norwegians, knowing nothing of each others' languages, had in common the name of 'Churchill' to pass between them as a talisman of hope."

But this pride had a downside. It reduced the incentive to change. The British way of doing things seemed validated by victory in the war, much as the Soviet system seemed validated by its victory over Germany so that the Soviet Union stood high in prestige. Britain had fought on when others had caved in, and it had prevailed. When illogicalities in British life were pointed out to British people, such as the House of Lords and the predecimal monetary system, British people would say their funny old ways had proved to be right for Britain. Muddling through had worked.

When the principal Western European nations met in 1958 to form the European Economic Community, which morphed into the European Union, the British government was not interested in joining with them. Yet Britain's standing was high in Europe, not only because of its behavior in the war but also because of the stability of its democratic institutions in the turbulent postwar years, and it could have had the leadership. But so far as British people were concerned, Continental countries had either been on the wrong side in the war or had caved in, and Britain did not need to unite with them. Later it had the humiliation of having its application to join rejected by President de Gaulle, because he thought Britain's special relationship with America would prevent it from becoming truly European.

For a long time there was nostalgia for the summer of 1940 and the Blitz. Like old soldiers when they get together, people remembered the comradeship, the shared dangers, and the achievement more than the fear and the suffering.

As if to recall that time, hostility to Germany has lingered on. It is seen, for instance, in the frequent identification of Germans today with Nazis — sometimes jokingly, sometimes unpleasantly — a sign of this nostalgia for the days when Germany was the enemy at the gates. For a time, Britain seemed like a veteran fingering his war medals as compensation for disappointments in civilian life.

* * *

Inevitably, as the summer of 1940 has become more distant, there has been some revisionism of the accepted version. The heroism, moral virtue, and community spirit were all called into question in a way they could not have been closer to the time. Pride and righteousness always invite attack, and to some degree they always deserve it. The behavior of British people was not always heroic, and motives were far from pure. No government in 1940 was the embodiment of virtue. When the Soviet Union entered the war, hypocrisies multiplied. The lies and brutalities of its system of government were ignored in praise for its success on the battlefronts, and it was hailed as a partner in the fight for freedom.

But war is always portrayed as melodrama, a simple clash between good and evil, while it is happening, in order to persuade people to fight. It is seen as tragedy only afterward. But despite the moral ambiguities, the fundamental moral issue in 1940 remains as clear as it seemed then.

To see what was at stake, it is worth engaging in some counterhistory, and looking at what would have happened if things had worked out differently.

A German victory could have come about through Britain accepting a compromise peace which left Germany with hegemony over Europe. Or it could have come about by the invasion and conquest of Britain, which would have subjected the British people to the awfulness of Nazi rule. Either one of these could have happened if America had decided that Britain was a lost cause and kept apart from the struggle.

Then the Soviet Union, with no allies and no help from the West, would have been conquered and its people enslaved, at least in the European part of the country. Looking at the Nazi plans for Eastern Europe, and the treatment of those lands during the German occupation, the word "enslaved" can be taken literally. The cruelty of Nazi rule would have been extended in space and time.

Japan emboldened would have continued its expansion and attacked the British and Dutch colonies and the Philippines, as it did after Pearl Harbor. Would it have tried to enlarge its empire still more and tried to conquer India, which at that time included what is now Pakistan and Bangladesh? At first glance the idea of a country the size of Japan trying to rule all the Indian subcontinent seems wildly unlikely. But another island nation even smaller than Japan did.

It may well be that Hitler had, as he said, only European ambitions and was not interested in the wider world beyond. But power has a tendency to flow into areas that open up to it. The Nazi Party already had its offices all over Latin America. Many ethnic German communities in South America reveled in German victories and would have welcomed further victories; they would have wanted closer ties with the fatherland, now more powerful than it had ever been. Would a government in Berlin, given the opportunity and even invitations, not have established governments in South America that would be little more than extensions of itself? The prestige of Germany and its style of government would produce some fascist governments. These would probably be no more repressive than ones that were subsequently put into power by the United States in some Latin American countries. Their leaders might be the same people. A German-dominated Europe would be the principal trading partner of Latin America. The United States would be beleaguered.

All this is guesswork. But a Nazi victory would have changed history in ways more profound than a redrawing of political maps. In a world in which the Nazis won, the democratic idea would be in retreat. Having failed to solve the economic crisis of the 1930s, democracy would have failed also to stand up to the military challenge of a disciplined, totalitarian society. Those who said democracy was not a form of government suited to the modern world would appear to be right.

Fascism would acquire a body of intellectual justification in the Anglo-Saxon world. Anti-Semitism would become respectable and accepted in the mainstream of political discourse. The values of liberalism, humanism, and rationalism that emerged in the European Enlightenment in the eighteenth century would no longer be the dominant values of Western civilization. The continuing evolution of Western societies in a more humane direction, a feature of the decades since the war and, in fact, for the last two centuries, would have been halted and reversed.

It is possible to argue, indeed some historians have argued, that Britain would have been better off if it had made peace with Nazi Germany, if not in 1940 then in 1941. It might have kept its empire. It would not have sacrificed lives and money in the exhausting struggle. It would not have been bankrupt. But the world would have been worse off.

NOTES

SELECT BIBLIOGRAPHY

INDEX

NOTES

Abbreviations

FDRL   Franklin D. Roosevelt Library, Hyde Park, New York
FRUS   Foreign Relations of the United States, State
         Department documents
IWM   Imperial War Museum, London
LC   Library of Congress
MOA   Mass Observation Archives, University of Sussex
NA   U.S. National Archives, College Park, Maryland
PRO   Public Records Office, London
PSF   President's Secretary Files

Introduction

page
2 Haushofer recorded the conversation: quoted in Douglas-Hamilton, 135.
3 Churchill's comment was a private memo: Churchill vol. 2, p. 231.

1. Postwar

5 The poet Rupert Brooke exulted: in the poem "Peace" (1914).
6 "If any question why we died": Kipling, "Common Form."
6 The war produced some fine literature: for example, the American novels *Farewell to Arms,* by Ernest Hemingway, and *Soldiers Three,* by John Dos Passos; the British memoirs *Goodbye to All That,* by Robert Graves, and *Undertones of War* by Edmund Blunden; the French novel *Le Feu* (The Fire), by Henri Barbusse; as well as the war poetry of Siegfried Sassoon and Wilfred Owen.
6 "these unheroic dead": Sassoon, "On Passing the New Menin Gate."

6 American students "lacked the tragic sense of life": Freeman Dyson, *Disturbing the Universe* (New York: Harper and Row, 1979), his collection of essays and memoirs.

13 This has left room for historians to argue: for example, Irving, in *Hitler's War*, and Taylor, in *The Origins of the Second World War*.

15 "Anyone but a half-blind idiot": Wheeler-Bennett 1975, 60.

16 Most foreign diplomats could see: Craig and Gilbert, 445.

16 "a chance to bring them back": Fromkin, 459.

16 "The Hitler regime is composed": PSF, box 45, FDRL.

17 "Even if there was one chance": Churchill vol. 1, 154.

21 "If some of my good Baptist brethren": letter to Josiah Bailey in Elliott Roosevelt, 304.

21 Joseph Kennedy did not want to be chairman: Whalen, 187.

23 "It cannot be to our interest": quoted by Arthur Schlesinger, Jr., in *Patterns of American Foreign Relations*.

2. Prewar

27 He wrote to his sister: McDonough, p 22.

29 Arthur Bryant described children: Roberts 1994, 311.

29 "such order, such discipline": PSF, Navy box 58, FDRL.

30 Lloyd George was impressed by Hitler: Gilbert and Gott, 50.

31 "By far the most powerful weapon": Carr, 47.

32 "Air power can dispense with": quoted in David Divine, 171.

32 "To fire willfully": Churchill's letter is in *Companion Papers* to Gilbert, vol. 3, 148.

33 "Welles' pyrotechnics": Hull, 548.

35 One Austrian who was worried: Gita Sereny tells Stangl's story in *Into That Darkness* (London: Andre Deutsch, 1974).

36 Ribbentrop "saturated with hate": PSF9, box 43, FDRL.

37 "Since my talk with Lindbergh": quoted in Dalton, 192.

38 Alanbrooke on Maginot Line: Alanbrooke, 37.

39 Roosevelt-Lindsay meeting: FO371/10659/A2378, PRO. See also David Reynolds, 204.

40 "Mr. Roosevelt is of course notoriously": FO371/21527/A8474, PRO.

40 Chamberlain on Hitler: Feiling, 367.

40 "Thousands, millions of young lives": Charlton diary, box 88/13/2, IWM.

40 Service chiefs' report: CAB27/627, PRO.

42 "From Podolian villages": Lukacs 1976, 24.

42 Bullitt was so impressed: Fromkin, 469.

43 "If your theory is that Britain": Morgenthau, 199.

45 Berle memo to Roosevelt: Berle, 183.

46 "The whole democratic world is oozing": speech, Jan. 30, 1939.

47 Roosevelt described Hitler: Langer and Gleason, 316.

48 On the evening of July 18 he convened: Hull, 649; McKenna, 362.

49 "My husband invited them": Eleanor Roosevelt, 200.

50 "He is easy to get to know": Wheeler-Bennett 1968, 385.

52 "This only means a free hand": Esnouf.
53 Roosevelt knew about these secret talks: Langer and Gleason, 160; Morgan, 280.
55 Berle diary entry: Berle and Jacobs, 195.
55 "Well, Bill, it's come at last": Manchester, 203.
55 Kennedy telephoned Roosevelt: Whalen, 264.
56 "crumbled, despondent and old": Alvar Liddell quoted in Aster, 389.
56 "I could tell by the dazed look": diary, Sept. 3, 1939, Last.
56 "The declaration of war made me feel": Charlton diary, box 88/13/1, IWM.

3. Phony War

58 "Do not make yourself conspicuous": Kee, 49.
60 "We were quite untrained": Hillary, 21.
60 uncertain about which side George Washington: Cooper, 77.
61 "The reason why I have been prepared": David Reynolds, 86.
62 As Oswald Garrison Villard wrote: New Republic, June 15, 1939.
64 "The further into the country one moved": Miller, 82.
66 Roosevelt . . . met with leading senators: Hull, 682; Langer and Gleason, 222.
68 "We are beaten 63–30": Vandenberg, 3.
68 "These foreign orders mean prosperity": Morgenthau, 118.
68 "The British and French Governments had to spend": Hancock and Gowing, 118.
68 Henry L. Stimson told a senator: Stettinius, 22.
71 Officials concluded that 600,000 people could be killed: Titmuss, 13, 20.
72 "Where public houses are to be used": Turner, 58.
72 "London left dark, childless, cinemaless": Muggeridge, 312.
72 "The mothers were trying to hold back": Inglis, 13.
73 The nine-year-old Michael Caine . . . One little girl: personal accounts to the author.
73 In one town a suspicious billeting officer: Evacuation Records, MOA.
73 "That's a bed for dead folk": Inglis, 41.
73 "We have been in luck": Last, 24.
74 The Treasury estimated that overseas reserves: P149(39), CAB24/28, PRO.
76 Admiral Karl Doenitz said later: Morison, 47.
77 "This was a vital condition of success": Dalton, 353.
78 "Their chief value was probably": Richards and Saunders, vol.1, p. 81.
78 Chamberlain wrote to Roosevelt: David Reynolds, 76.
79 "One thought has been constantly present": Esnouf.
79 Kennedy . . . told Roosevelt in a cable: PSF Diplomatic, box 37, FDRL.
79 "I quite agree that the skeletons": FO371, box 24251, PRO.
80 "The Maginot Line will narrow the gap": Steel, 381.
81 They even had plans to bomb: Reynaud, 264; Amery, 344; Langer and Gleason, 389.
81 "Roosevelt believes the Allies can't win": FO371, box 24238, PRO.
81 Welles . . . found Hitler impressive: PSF, 9, box 43, FDRL.
82 "Heaven knows, I don't want the Americans": David Reynolds, 78.

83 "an appeaser who failed to understand": Morgenthau diaries, roll 187, FDRL.

83 "There is the rising feeling here": FO371, box 24238, PRO.

84 "I always disliked him": diary entry, Kennedy, 411.

84 Roosevelt's first letter read: all quotations from Roosevelt's and Churchill's letters and cables to each other are from Kimball.

86 Some of the earlier Roosevelt's concerns were prophetic: Theodore Roosevelt quoted in Howard K. Beale, *Theodore Roosevelt and the Rise of American Power* (Baltimore: Johns Hopkins University Press), 136, 347, 131.

86 Whitelaw Reid hailed "the undivided": quoted in Hitchens, 125.

87 "We have no necessary interest": diary, June 28, 1939, Berle.

87 two or three years at Oxford: diary, Oct. 11, 1938, Moffat.

88 When Gallup pollsters asked Americans: *Public Opinion Quarterly*, July 1938.

89 General Edward Mackesy objected: Gilbert 1989, 56.

90 Chamberlain summoned Halifax, Churchill, and Margesson: Roberts 1991, 205. This differs slightly from the account Churchill gives in his history of the war, which is the one most often cited. It is based on Halifax's recollection the day after the event. Churchill appears to have forgotten that Margesson was present.

92 "The country had fallen into the hands": Colville quoted in Wheeler-Bennett 1968, 49.

92 Norman Brook recalled listening: Wheeler-Bennett 1968, 17.

4. Blitzkrieg

97 The French military attaché in Bern learned: Spears, 120.

97 Hans Oster told the Dutch military attaché: Horne, 247.

98 "It was almost as if they were retracing": Middleton quoted in Horne, 289.

99 "Quickly, the rearward artillery command": Horne, 343.

100 "On the whole the advantage is with us": Ironside, 303.

101 "I soon became accustomed to hearing it": Spears, 142.

101 Blanchard ... "sitting for an hour": Marc Bloch, 28.

102 Churchill told publisher Cecil King: King, 51.

104 Roosevelt ... appealed to Mussolini: Langer and Gleason, 451.

104 "We are beaten": Churchill vol. 2, p. 38.

106 Daily summaries of the war: PSF Diplomatic, box 38, FDRL.

106 "Where is the strategic reserve?": Churchill vol. 2, p. 40.

107 Baudouin describes Churchill: quoted in Horne, 461.

108 Dowding had presented a paper: WP(40)159, PRO.

108 "However many calls there might be": Richards and Saunders, 63.

109 "The disorder of this army": Horne, 442.

109 "Our fighter pilots were very tired": Terraine, 147.

110 "They were all haggard-looking": Alanbrooke, 67.

110 Mendès-France ... saw "strings of these wagons": quoted in Horne, 521.

111 There were episodes of heroism: Horne, 471.

111 Peter Vaux looked up a dispatch rider: Clayton and Craig, 173.

112 Gort complained to the War Office: CAB65/13, minute 14, PRO.
113 He was appalled by his meeting: Ironside, 303.
113 In a rage at one point: Horne, 572.
114 Anthony Eden sent a message: PREM3/204, PRO.
116 "We must be careful not to let the Americans": Churchill vol. 2, p. 128.
116 "Suppose Hitler offered Britain": diary, May 26, 1940, Ickes.
117 King wrote an account of this: Clayton and Craig, 69, 97-99.
118 Back in February, Marshall had suggested: Watson, 164.
119 "It is the general feeling of Congress": Watson, 170.
119 "It is a drop in the bucket": Morgenthau, 150.
120 "If we were required to mobilize": Watson, 312.
121 "Nuts on the army": Morgenthau, 155.
121 The senator was "in a towering rage": PSF, box 58, FDRL.
122 Kirk cabled the State Department: FRUS.
122 Army's War Plans Division memo: Watson, 125.
123 Roosevelt told the navy to draw up plans: Watson, 95.
123 "I am sure you will agree that if we acquiesce": Welles papers, box 150, folder 14, FDRL.
125 "If we help France and England to win": *Reader's Digest,* Nov. 1939.
125 "The rest of the world will do well to recognize": *New York Herald Tribune,* May 16, 1940.

5. Retreat and Deliverance

127 On May 25, the British chiefs of staff: WP(40)168, PRO.
128 "My advice to you": Austin, 186.
130 "It was all pretty bloody": letter courtesy of Mrs. Hazel Hucker.
130 Gort warned . . . Eden: PREM3/204, PRO.
130 they might get 30,000 men: Ironside, 331.
130 "Nothing but a miracle": Alanbrooke, 67.
133 Cudahy . . . wrote to Roosevelt: PP1193, FDRL.
133 "Al Capone will enter the war": Craig and Gilbert, 665.
134 Roosevelt . . . sent Mussolini: Langer and Gleason, 451.
134 "Their success presupposes a degree": FO111/67, May 17, PRO.
134 Churchill injected some harsh realism: CAB65/13, PRO.
135 Lloyd George . . . gave no encouragement: he told his private secretary, A. J. Sylvester, that he thought Churchill wanted him in the government so that if they were forced to make a compromise peace with Hitler, he would be the one to do it. Sylvester told the author this in a 1967 interview.
136 "The freedom of conversation": Gilbert 1989, 705.
137 meeting of the War Cabinet, the first of three: CAB65/13, WM(40), PRO.
138 "The cabinet are feverishly considering": diary, May 26, 1940, Colville.
139 The two correspondents of the *Chicago Daily News:* PSF Navy, box 62, FDRL.
139 When the War Cabinet met the next day: CAB65/13, WM(40)141, 142, PRO.
140 At the meeting the next day: CAB65/13, WM(40)145, PRO.
141 "He [Churchill] was quite magnificent": Dalton, 335.

142 "The PM dislikes any move towards Musso": quoted in Lukacs 2000, 120.

144 Ministry of Information summary: INF1, 264, PRO.

144 Mass Observation surveys bear out this picture: MO 246, 263, and others, MOA.

146 "Every road scouring the landscape": Austin, 184.

147 "The one thought in everybody's mind": Marc Bloch, 18.

147 Bridges was with a group of men: personal account by John Bridges.

148 "It is very difficult to write on paper": Blew-Jones's letter to his sister, lent to the author.

148 "Beg pardon, sir": Richard Collier, 119.

149 Lightoller, who had been an officer on the *Titanic:* Gelb 1980, 272; Richard Collier, 195.

149 Raphael de Sola . . . went across: *Daily Express,* London, June 3.

149 "I cannot see who you are": Richard Collier, 202.

150 In the Admiralty files: ADM334/83, PRO.

151 George Kimber, a civil servant: Shakespeare, 148.

152 "We landed at Dover": Marc Bloch, 20.

153 "The boys just back from Dunkirk": Schimanski and Treece, 72.

154 "Men swarmed into the hospital": Shephard, 171.

154 The theater director Basil Dean: Calder 1969, 109.

154 Suicide pill and "My darling, how infectious courage is": diary entries, May 28, May 31, Nicolson.

154 "I forgot that I was a middle-aged woman": diary, June 5, 1940, Last.

155 "The war has now for the first time become": diary, June 4, 1940, Colville.

157 "So profound were the effects": Basil Collier, 120.

6. The Great Debate

158 Jerome Green wrote to an old friend: FO24323, PRO.

160 When a writer . . . accused student anti-interventionists: *Atlantic Monthly,* Aug. and Sept., 1940.

160 Leaders of the American Youth Congress: Eleanor Roosevelt, 208; Lash 1971, 604.

160 MacLeish . . . had some apt words: speech reprinted in *New Republic,* June 10, 1940.

161 "There have been a number of fierce national quarrels": Schlesinger, 141.

162 "They have felt the wave of the future": quoted in Schoonmaker and Fielding's collection of arguments against intervention.

163 "I knew I had his private support": Johnson, 529.

163 Even the *Ladies' Home Journal* weighed in: issue of Nov. 1940.

164 "whether the war is on the up and up": Ingersoll, 52.

165 Reynaud cabled Churchill: Reynaud, 453.

165 Bullitt telephoned him from Paris: Langer and Gleason, 459; Lash, 515.

166 Roosevelt inserted into the script: Lash, 152; see also Morgan.

166 "This was it": Wheeler-Bennett 1975, 97.

168 "My correspondence is heaping up": Johnson, 545.

169 Roosevelt told Bullitt he should leave: Hull, 789; Bullitt, 466.

169 Churchill flew over for a meeting: CAB99, 4,5,6, PRO; Churchill, 136; Spears, 137–40; Ismay, 138.
171 Three days later he was back: CAB99, 4,5,6/141, PRO.
171 Behind Baudouin stood the Countess: Spears, 92; Horne, 223; Boothe, 98.
172 French soldiers apparently with nothing to do: Spears, 231.
173 Kennedy read him the message: Kennedy, 441.
173 Churchill told Reynaud in a message: CAB June 13, annex II, PRO.
174 "We could not send soldiers": diary entry, June 15, 1940, Ickes.
175 "The Prime Minister does not want you": Alanbrooke, 81.
176 He said in a cable to Lothian: PREM3/462,3,166, PRO.
178 The British government proposed to join: my account of the Anglo-French Union proposal is taken from British cabinet papers, PRO; and from Churchill, Colville, de Gaulle, Monnet, Reynaud, and Spears.
185 "At the end there was a roar": Middleton, 11.

7. The White Cliffs

188 "It is hard to explain what that means": *Atlantic Monthly*, Oct. 1940.
189 "At the station there was a queue": diary entry, June 24, 1940, Channon.
189 "Hitler may hurl hell at Britain": quoted on BBC radio program about 1940, June 4, 2000.
189 One reporter saw a seven-year-old girl: Shakespeare, 257. Geoffrey Shakespeare managed the overseas evacuation scheme.
190 The army did a tally: WP(40)339, Aug. 29, 1940, PRO.
190 He established a static defense line: Basil Collier, 129.
191 When Churchill visited beach defenses: Churchill vol. 2, p. 148.
191 "If the Germans ever attempt": Ironside, 346.
191 The Chiefs of Staff made this clear: Churchill vol. 2, p. 78.
192 "We have a machine gun and a rifle": Mayhew, 85.
192 There was one other anti-invasion tactic: Colville, 213; Alanbrooke, 94.
192 RAF bomber crews flew practice runs: personal accounts by participants in these exercises.
192 "You may rest assured": Gilbert 1991, 667.
193 "In view of past experience": Ismay quoted in Gelb 1985, 14.
195 "I pictured myself with my young baby": Longmate, 107.
195 Rebecca West fairly burned: *Time and Tide*, June 8, 1940.
196 "There were shepherds, farm hands": Graves, 27.
197 *Picture Post* carried a series: the story of the Home Guard school is told in Hopkinson, and in *Picture Post*, Sept. 21, 1940.
198 "I had never thought to spend": Sackville-West, 88.
198 "A charge of shot"; "I defy a dozen"; "My conclusion is": *Daily Telegraph*, May 31, June 2, June 3.
199 The secret resistance network: Lampe, 70; Peter Fleming.
200 "There had to be a cabinet decision": quoted in article by David Pryce-Jones, in Peter Fleming.
200 "There are moments when the whole nation": Orwell, *The Lion and the Unicorn* (London, 1941), 30.

201 "The British people had been": Hancock and Gowing, 209.
201 One firm making metal office equipment: *Tribune,* June 21, 1940.
202 "As I looked down on the sea": Cooper, 284.
202 "I have always loved England": diary entry, June 28, 1940, Nicolson.
202 "No wonder men, and women too": Brittain, 248. The poem she quotes is John Masefield, "August, 1914."
203 The American writer Clare Boothe: Boothe, 291.
205 "There's a slight ray of hope": Morgenthau, 161.
205 Roosevelt told Ickes that the ships: Ickes, 30.
206 "As you know, we are in urgent need": PSF Diplomatic, box 38, FDRL.
206 The French Caribbean island of Martinique: Morison; Hull.
208 The British cabinet discussed this: WP(40)176, June 2, PRO.
208 "When I don't know where to move": Langer and Gleason, 597.
209 Using Enigma, they were learning to decode: the Ultra story is told in Winterbotham and in Lewin.
210 plans for Operation Sea Lion: Peter Fleming, 53; Churchill vol. 2, p. 268.
211 He telephoned Halifax, entreating him: diary entry, July 22, 1940, Nicolson.
213 "One of the best reasons for choosing": Willis, 115.
214 "Where the speed of an enemy's advance": Basil Collier, 162.
217 Another German pilot shortly after: Banner, 27.
217 A local reporter recorded: Watt, 27.
219 "All our attack practice had been designed": Middleton, 92.
220 Captain Ben Kelsey wrote an assessment: file 2083-1644, box 871, NA.
221 "Sir, I'll eat my hat if that one": journal of Mrs. R. Rayner, box 89/10/1, IWM.
221 "It seemed rather indecent to stand lamely": Foster, 88.
222 "Rumors would sweep through the town": Lewis, 45.
222 Ben Robertson . . . came to Britain: Clayton and Craig, 233.
222 "High in the wind and the sun": Sheean, 196.
223 "This fortress built by nature for herself": Shakespeare, *Richard the Second,* act 2, scene 1.

8. Panzers in Philadelphia

224 Roosevelt argued that the announcement: Sherwood, 163.
226 the ideal American establishment figure: Galbraith quoted in Rovere, 5.
229 "I regard this as a semi-religious movement": *Time,* May 2, 1940.
230 "You're a member of a church council": Neal, 289.
231 "The fact that Willkie is running": Morgenthau, 163.
231 "I have never been more disgusted": Parmet and Hecht, 121.
231 "They would not have organized Willkie clubs": *Time,* July 8, 1940.
232 James Farley . . . called on Roosevelt: Thomas Fleming, 68.
235 Because they met at the Century Club: Chadwin, 44; see also Agar.
240 Hopkins . . . told Burns to be more ambitious: Sherwood, 197.
240 "You've got to bluff": Morgenthau, 112.
241 "like *Who's Who*": *American National Biography* (New York: Oxford University Press, 1969) 4: 930.

244 Roosevelt insisted that the fifth column: *New York Times,* June 6, 1940.

244 However, there was a fifth column: the story of British Security Coordination has come out bit by bit. Some of it was first told in Stevenson and in Hyde, which overemphasize Stephenson's admittedly important role. Then on Sept. 17, 1989, the *Washington Post* published excerpts of what it said was a secret official history of BSC, and its authenticity was not disputed. Thomas Mahl dug up some more for his book *Desperate Deception.* In 2000, St. Ermin's Press published without attribution what it said was the full official history, edited by Nigel West, who has written elsewhere about British intelligence with what appears to be special access.

246 Schlesinger gave some broadcast talks over WRUL: Schlesinger, 248.

248 "We must be sure that the contracts contain provisions": Morgenthau, 176.

248 A magazine editor cabled Vincent Sheean: Sheean, 187.

248 Westrick . . . organized a private dinner: Stevenson, 106; Hyde.

250 "The American Government is debating": Stevenson, 114.

252 An army technical specialist . . . told Stimson: Watson, 140.

252 "I do not see what we are going to get": PREM3 475/1, PRO.

253 David Gray tried to get some movement on the issue: Langer and Gleason, 248.

253 the British Government began secret negotiations with the Irish: PREM131/1, PRO.

254 "The British Empire is rendering its own fat": Grafton, 50.

255 "Unless when the time comes the Americans": P149(39) 168CAB, PRO.

255 "So long as the gold and other assets": FO371/31, June 30, PRO.

255 When Britain and France needed smokeless powder: Morgenthau, 114.

256 Sir Frederick told Morgenthau . . . did not fare much better when he saw Roosevelt: Morgenthau, 170.

256 Butler met the Swedish minister in London: the documentation on this meeting comes entirely from Swedish, German, and Italian sources. Part of the minutes of a British cabinet meeting on June 19, at which it was presumably discussed, has still not been declassified.

257 Churchill messaged the navy chief: Roskill, 253.

258 Cohen . . . produced a plan: PSF Diplomatic, box 62, FDRL.

259 Roosevelt . . . received three members of the Century Group: Langer and Gleason, 749; see also Wilz.

9. "The Most Critical Month"

261 "I missed the 'glorious twelfth'": Townsend, 311.

262 Alan Deere, a New Zealander: Gelb 1985, 92.

262 "One used to look down and see": Bungay, 116.

263 After watching operations: Ismay, 179.

263 Lydia Lopkova, the Russian-born ballerina: Skidelsky, 79.

265 "It was a complete panic take-off": Johnstone, 119.

266 "What they heard often distressed the girls": Gelb 1985, 185.

267 "One of the prettiest girls I'd seen": Page, 104.

267 "It was the general opinion": FDR personal letters vol. 2: 1050–51, FDRL.

269 White told Cordell Hull: Hull, 83.

270 Then they wrote it as a letter to the *New York Times:* Acheson, 109; Shogan, 190.

271 Acheson wanted him to see the letter immediately: Acheson, 113.

271 Roosevelt . . . tried to win over David Walsh: Langer and Gleason, 760.

271 A. V. Alexander was furious at this request: FO800/433, PRO.

272 He pointed out to Halifax in a memo: PREM475/1, PRO.

273 In his car on the way back from Parliament: Colville, 227.

274 "Anybody who knows anything about the German methods": Elliott Roosevelt, 330.

275 "All seemed to believe that England": diary, Aug. 17, 1940, Moffat.

276 As General Lee recorded his reactions: Lee, 42.

277 "It got worse and worse": Allingham, 230.

277 "A real tremor and shock goes through": MO file 313, 1940, MOA.

277 "I heard a bomb in the distance": Croall, 68.

277 People talked about it constantly: MO file 296, 1940, MOA.

278 "The air battles by day were a marvel": Sayers, 40.

278 "Then the planes arrive. They fly overhead": Sackville-West, 112.

279 "We are going to bed after the news": diary entry, Sept. 1, 1940, Last.

279 "But we held our fête on Saturday": the letter, though not written for publication, was published in the *New Statesman and Nation,* Aug. 31, 1940.

279 "I think I can claim to be the only person": Kingsley Martin, *New Statesman and Nation,* Sept. 7, 1940.

280 "It is the most delightful incident": Mayhew, 66.

280 "Considered reports from U.S. consuls": file no. 2060-1234, box 795, NA.

281 The Hungarian-born writer: Koestler tells this story in the second volume of his autobiography, *The Invisible Writing* (New York: Macmillan, 1954), 517.

281 "My reason tells me that it will be": diary, June 15, 1940, Nicolson.

282 The Ministry of Information had another source: CAB 21/493, Aug. 30, PRO.

284 Advertisements such as these appeared daily: *Times,* Aug. 26 and 28, 1940.

284 "London lives well": diary, Sept. 1, 1940, Channon.

284 "The ladies left and conversation turned": diary, June 10, Spears.

284 "If you ration four or five foods": Anthony Hern, *Tribune,* Aug. 16, 1940.

285 Sir Kingsley Wood circulated: WM(40)324, CAB66/11, PRO.

286 The cabinet discussed this report: WM(40) minute 1, Aug. 22, PRO.

10. The Biggest Target

288 "To help you in England": Longmate, 110.

289 "We listen to the radio constantly": box 220, IWM.

289 Drew Middleton . . . was amazed at the attitude: Cull, 109.

289 Asked whether the United States: American Institute of Public Opinion poll, Sept. 22, 1940.

290 "The U.S. press has never been": FO, A3769, PRO.

290 "We would get hold of some commando": quoted in Cull, 86.
291 "Can we afford to indulge in half-measures": *San Francisco Chronicle*, Sept. 3, 1940.
292 Churchill . . . sent a memo to Beaverbrook: diary, July 8, 1940, Colville.
292 "Young man, you did a very fine thing": Niven tells the story in his autobiography, *The Moon's a Balloon* (New York: Dell, 1972), 217.
293 Churchill once told her that every citizen: Sally Bedell Smith, *Reflected Glory: The Life of Pamela Churchill Harriman* (New York: Simon and Schuster, 1996).
293 "Normally as frightened as anyone": Townsend, 344.
293 Squadron Leader Pat Hughes: Willis, 135.
294 Park reported on Sept. 5: Townsend, 381.
294 On Sept. 7, Dowding called a meeting: Terraine, 150.
296 "Far more important to us": Churchill, 291.
297 Lothian warned the British government: PREM 3/462/2/3, Aug. 28, PRO.
298 "There was of course no comparison": Churchill vol. 2, p. 357.
298 "Congress will probably raise hell": Langer and Gleason, 776.
301 "Second only to the Battle of Britain": Neal, viii.
302 "We warmongers knew that the enemy": Agar, 150.
302 "To judge from the many cables": Hull, 842.
304 "With the conquest of France": Richards and Saunders.
305 Alan Rook was with a searchlight unit: Schimanski and Treece, 82.
305 "I'd never seen so many aircraft": Gelb 1985, 230.
305 Ada pointed to the sky: Clayton and Craig, 291.
306 "I was not let down lightly": Dixon, 24.
307 "Inside the cathedral the light": quoted in Fitzgibbon, 61.
307 "See the fire chaps last night?": Schimanski and Treece, 82.
308 "Warning went at 5 p.m.": Masel's notes, Blitz files, MOA.
308 "Imagine a ground floor flat": Kops, 63.
309 "It was possible to get too tired": Richardson, 121.
309 "He looked invincible": Perry, 121.
311 "Had an invasion developed": Alanbrooke (rev. ed.), 96 (note).
312 to issue the code message Cromwell: Basil Collier, 120; Alanbrooke, 97.
313 "Don't let anybody in, lovey": Longmate, 140.
313 "So the bastards are coming": Johnstone, 41.
313 Cooper was holding a weekend house party: Wheeler-Bennett 1968, 110.
313 Whitelaw Reid was spending the weekend: Clayton and Craig, 296.
314 Churchill . . . memoed Halifax: PREM3 463/1, PRO.
314 Stimson said that the only thing to do: Stimson and Bundy, 190; Goodhart, 191.
315 Lothian assured Churchill that he was active: PREM3 463/1, Sept. 21, 1940, PRO.
316 The American officers were frank: Abbazia, 100; Goodhart, 195.
316 "This was easily corrected": Goodhart, 195.
316 The British were in a hurry: ADM 109, 167, PRO.
316 "Any destroyer that could steam": Goodhart, 237.

11. Odds Long, Stakes Infinite

319 "I must support whatever is necessary": Bertrand Russell, *Autobiography* (London: Routledge, 1967).

319 Esmond Romilly, a British: His story is told in Jessica Mitford's memoir, *Hons and Rebels* (London, 1960).

319 Francis Cammaerts: personal communication.

319 David Dawson, a streetwise cockney: David Dawson (not his real name) is the subject of a short story by Gordon Childs, who knew him and vouches for the truth of it.

320 "If Hitler wins this war": *Tribune*, Sept. 13, 1940.

320 "If only the Germans had had the sense": Attlee, 114.

321 "At the beginning": Fremlin, Blitz, MOA.

322 "An extraordinary mood of exaltation": Anderson, 109.

322 "When you take a girl out": Woon, 172.

322 Joan Wyndham was an art student: BBC radio, *Woman's Hour*, Jan. 3, 2002.

323 The director of the London Zoo: Ziegler, 123.

323 "Servicemen had priority": Croall, 68.

323 "I'm glad we've been bombed": Wheeler-Bennett 1965, 470.

325 "At this time I was not the only one": Astley, 63.

325 "This morning on duty": Croall, 113.

326 "I went downtown to get some warm boots": Cotton journal, box 93/3/1, IWM.

327 "It was terribly depressing": Woon, 64.

327 "A neat row of cots": Ingersoll, 120.

329 When the Murphy home was hit: Lewis, 52; see also Fitzgibbon.

329 One fireman who understood: Richardson, 122.

330 "The Government tells me to hate Hitler": Strachey, 29.

331 "It was a strange life": Astley, 82.

332 The comedian Spike Milligan: he recalls this in *Adolf Hitler: My Part in His Downfall* (London: Penguin, 1971), an account of his army career.

332 "We can at present reasonably believe": *Times*, Sept. 15, 1940.

332 "Britain must keep her hands clean": *Times*, Sept. 17.

333 "Some people seeking an outlet": INF1, 264, Sept. 9, 1940, PRO.

333 One woman explained: Allingham, 236.

334 Vincent Sheean came out with: Woon, 145.

334 "Considering what they have been through": MO observer Jack Atkins, MOA, *The Blitz*.

335 "I went to work as usual": Hunt and Marshall, 30.

336 "Events showed that most people": Titmuss, 350.

337 "I should almost have enjoyed": Brittain 1941, 240.

337 A group of psychiatrists warned: Titmuss, 10.

337 But when they were given a cup of tea: T. A. Ross, quoted in Shephard, 181.

337 "The proximity of death": Titmuss, 347.

340 "This is total war": *New York Times Magazine*, Sept. 22, 1940.

340 "Everywhere there were craters": Ben Robertson, 115.

340 "In this crisis, the friendly courage": *Life*, Sept. 23, 1940.

340 "London fights down her fears": quoted in Cloud and Olsen, 98.
343 "If 15th Aug. showed": Basil Collier, 222.
345 "I was struck by the extraordinary change": Winterbotham, 59.

12. After the Summer

349 Churchill likened the American attitude: PREM 3/469, PRO.
350 some of the more enthusiastic advocates of strategic bombing: for example, General Henry L. Arnold, chief of staff, U.S. Air Force, said in 1942: "By air power alone we might bring Germany so completely to its knees that it might [be] unnecessary [for] ground forces to make a landing."
351 With much of the American fleet in ruins: Churchill vol. 3, p. 540.
352 American academics . . . were cautioned: Winks, 266.
355 "Among their fellow prisoners": R.M.D. Stewart, *The Struggle for Crete* (1966), quoted in Lukacs 1976, 210.

SELECT BIBLIOGRAPHY

Much of the material for this book comes from official archives in America and Britain, and some from official histories (noted below with an asterisk). Several diarists near the center of events in Washington and London provided source material, as did Churchill in his history of the war and Cordell Hull in his memoirs. The Roosevelt-Churchill correspondence is from the collection edited by Warren Kimball, which is to all intents and purposes the official record.

For British people's experience of war, I have drawn mostly on contemporary accounts and local histories, and also on two excellent repositories. One is the files of Mass Observation at the University of Sussex, with its records of people's talk and behavior; for an explanation of Mass Observation, see Chapter 5. The other is the collection of diaries and letters in the Imperial War Museum in London.

Abbazia, Patrick. *Mr. Roosevelt's Navy: The Private War of the U.S. Atlantic Fleet, 1939–1942.* Annapolis, Md.: Naval Institute Press, 1971.

Acheson, Dean. *Morning and Noon.* London: Hamish Hamilton, 1967.

Adler, Selig. *The Isolationist Impulse: Its Twentieth-Century Reaction.* New York: Abelard-Schuman, 1956.

Agar, Herbert. *The Darkest Hour: Britain Alone, June 1940–June 1941.* New York: Doubleday, 1973.

Alanbrooke, Field Marshal Lord. *War Diaries 1939–1945.* London: Weidenfeld and Nicolson, 2001.

Allingham, Margery. *The Oaken Heart.* London: Michael Joseph, 1941.

Amery, L. S. *My Political Life*, vol. 3. London: Hutchinson, 1955.

Anderson, Verily. *Spam Tomorrow*. London: Rupert Hart-Davis, 1956.

Aster, Sidney. *1939: The Making of the Second World War*. London: André Deutsch, 1974.

Astley, Joan Bright. *The Inner Circle: A View of War at the Top*. London: Hutchinson, 1971.

Austin, John (Gun Buster). *Return Via Dunkirk*. London: Hodder and Stoughton, 1940.

Banner, Hubert. *Kentish Fire: Wartime Life in Kent and Sussex*. London: Hurst and Blackett, 1944.

Barnes, Joseph S. *Willkie: The Events He Was Part Of, the Ideas He Fought For.* New York: Simon & Schuster, 1952.

Barnett, Corelli. *The Collapse of British Power*. London: Eyre Methuen, 1972.

Beard, Charles A. *American Foreign Policy in the Making, 1932–1940*. New Haven: Yale University Press, 1946.

Benoist-Méchin, J. *Sixty Days That Shook the West*. Trans. Peter Wiles. London: Jonathan Cape, 1963.

Berle, Adolf. *Navigating the Rapids 1918–1971: From the Papers of Adolf A. Berle.* Ed. Beatrice Bishop Berle and Travis Beal Jacobs. New York: Harcourt, Brace Jovanovich, 1973.

Bloch, Marc. *Strange Defeat*. Trans. Gerard Hopkins. Oxford: Oxford University Press, 1949.

Bloch, Michael. *Ribbentrop*. London: Bantam Books, 1992.

Boothe, Clare. *Europe in the Spring*. New York: Alfred A. Knopf, 1940.

Brendon, Piers. *The Dark Valley: A Panorama of the 1930s*. New York: Alfred A. Knopf, 2000.

Brittain, Vera. *England's Hour*. London: Macmillan, 1941.

———. *Testament of Experience*. London: Gollancz, 1957.

Bullock, Alan. *Hitler: A Study in Tyranny*. London: Odhams Press, 1952.

Bungay, Stephen. *The Most Dangerous Enemy: A History of the Battle of Britain.* London: Aurum Press, 2000.

*Butler, J. R. M. *Grand Strategy*. London: Her Majesty's Stationery Office, 1950.

———. *Lord Lothian (Philip Kerr)*. London: Macmillan, 1956.

Cadogan, Sir Alexander. *The Diaries of Sir Alexander Cadogan*. Ed. David Dilks. New York: Putnam, 1971.

Calder, Angus. *The People's War: Britain 1939–1945*. London: Jonathan Cape, 1969.

———. *The Myth of the Blitz*. London: Jonathan Cape, 1991.

Calvacoressi, Peter, and Guy Wint. *Total War*. London: Allen Lane, Penguin Press, 1972.

Carr, E. H. *The Twenty Years' Crisis 1919–1939*. London: Macmillan, 1942.

"Cato." *Guilty Men*. London: Gollancz, 1940.

Chadwin, Mark Lincoln. *The Hawks of World War II*. Chapel Hill: University of North Carolina Press, 1968.

Channon, Sir Henry. *Chips: The Diaries of Sir Henry Channon*. Ed. Robert Rhodes James. London: Weidenfeld and Nicolson, 1967.

Churchill, Winston. *The Second World War*, vols. 1 and 2. London: Cassell, 1949.

Cloud, Stanley, and Lynne Olsen. *The Murrow Boys*. Boston: Houghton Mifflin, 1996.

* Collier, Basil. *The Defence of the United Kingdom*. London: HMSO, 1957.

Collier, Richard. *The Sands of Dunkirk*. London: Collins, 1961.

Colville, John. *The Fringes of Power: Downing Street Diaries*, vol. 1. London: Hodder and Stoughton, 1985.

Cooper, Alfred Duff. *Old Men Forget*. London: Rupert Hart-Davis, 1953.

Cooper, Matthew. *The German Air Force 1943–1945: An Anatomy of Failure*. London: Jane's, 1972.

Craig, Gordon, and Felix Gilbert, eds. *The Diplomats 1919–1939*. Princeton, N.J.: Princeton University Press, 1953.

Croall, Jonathan. *Don't You Know There's a War On?* London: Hutchinson, 1986.

Cull, Jonathan. *Selling War: The British Propaganda Campaign Against American Neutrality in World War Two*. Oxford: Oxford University Press, 1996.

Dalton, Hugh. *The Fateful Years: Memoirs 1931–45*. London: Frederick Muller, 1953.

Davis, Kenneth S. *The Hero: Charles A. Lindbergh: The Man and the Legend*. New York: Doubleday, 1959.

de Courcy, Anne. *1939: The Last Season*. London: Thames and Hudson, 1981.

de Gaulle, Charles. *War Memoirs*, vol. 1: *The Call to Honour*. Trans. Jonathan Griffin. London: Collins, 1955.

Deighton, Len. *Fighter: The Story of the Battle of Britain*. London: Jonathan Cape, 1977.

Divine, David. *The Nine Days of Dunkirk*. London: Faber & Faber, 1959.

Divine, Robert A. *The Reluctant Belligerent: American Entry into World War Two*. New York: John Wiley & Son, 1965.

Douglas-Hamilton, James. *Motive for a Mission*. London: Macmillan, 1971.

Ericco, Charles Joseph. "Foreign Affairs and the Presidential Election of 1940." Ph.D. dissertation, University of Maryland, 1973.

Esnouf, Guy Nicholas. "British Government War Aims and Attitudes Towards a Negotiated Peace, September 1939 to July 1940." Ph.D. dissertation, King's College, London University.

Feiling, Keith. *Neville Chamberlain*. London: Macmillan, 1946.

FitzGibbon, Constantine. *The Blitz*. London: Allen Wingate, 1957.

Fleming, Peter. *Operation Sea Lion*. New York: Simon and Schuster, 1957.

Fleming, Thomas. *The New Dealers' War: F.D.R. and the War Within World War II*. New York: Basic Books, 2001.

Foster, Reginald. *Dover Front*. London: Secker and Warburg, 1941.

Fromkin, David. *In the Time of the Americans*. New York: Alfred A. Knopf, 1995.

Gabler, Neal. *Walter Winchell: Gossip, Power and the Cult of Celebrity*. New York: Alfred A. Knopf, 1994.

Gannon, Franklin Reid. *The British Press and Germany 1936–1939*. Oxford: Clarendon Press, 1971.

Gelb, Norman. *Dunkirk: The First Step in the Defeat of Hitler*. New York: William Morrow, 1980.

———. *Scramble: A Narrative Account of the Battle of Britain*. San Diego: Harcourt Brace Jovanovich, 1985.

Gilbert, Martin. *Churchill's Political Philosophy: Three Lectures.* Oxford: Oxford University Press, 1981.

———. *The Second World War.* London: Weidenfeld & Nicolson, 1989.

———. *Churchill: A Life.* London: Heinemann, 1991.

Gilbert, Martin, and Richard Gott. *The Appeasers.* London: Weidenfeld & Nicolson, 1963.

Goldberg, Alfred. *A History of the United States Air Force, 1907 to 1957.* Princeton, N.J.: Van Nostrand, 1957.

Goodhart, Philip. *Fifty Ships That Saved the World.* London: Heinemann, 1965.

Graves, Charles. *The Home Guard of Britain.* London: Hutchinson, 1943.

* Hall, Duncan. *North American Supply.* London: HMSO, 1955.

* Hancock, W. K., and M. M. Gowing. *British War Economy.* London: HMSO, 1949.

Harman, Nicholas. *Dunkirk: The Necessary Myth.* London: Hodder and Stoughton, 1980.

Herzstein, Robert. *Roosevelt and Hitler.* New York: Paragon, 1989.

Hillary, Richard. *Falling Through Space.* London: Macmillan, 1942.

Hitchens, Christopher. *Blood, Class, and Nostalgia: Anglo-American Ironies.* New York: Farrar, Straus and Giroux, 1990.

Hitler, Adolf. *Mein Kampf.* Trans. James Murphy. London: Hurst & Blackett, 1939.

Hopkinson, Tom. *Of This Our Time: A Journalist's Story.* London: Hutchinson, 1982.

Horne, Alastair. *To Lose a Battle: France 1940.* London: Macmillan, 1969.

Hull, Cordell. *The Memoirs of Cordell Hull.* New York: Macmillan, 1948.

Hunt, Valerie, and Leslie Marshall. *Wartime Camden.* London: Borough of Camden, 1983.

Hyde, H. Montgomery. *The Quiet Canadian: The Secret Service Story of Sir William Stephenson.* London: Constable, 1989.

Ickes, Harold. *The Secret Diaries of Harold Ickes.* New York: Simon & Schuster, 1964.

Ingersoll, Ralph. *Report on England.* New York: Simon and Schuster, 1940.

Inglis, Ruth. *The Children's War: Evacuees 1939–1945.* London: William Collins Sons, 1989.

Ironside, General Sir Edmund. *The Ironside Diaries 1937–1940.* Ed. Roderick Macleod and Denis Kelly. London: Constable, 1962.

Ismay, Hastings. *The Memoirs of Lord Ismay.* London: Heinemann, 1960

Johnson, Walter. *William Allen White's America.* New York: Henry Holt, 1947.

Johnstone, J. E. *Wing Leader.* London: Chatto & Windus, 1956.

Kee, Robert. *The World We Left Behind: A Chronicle of the Year 1939.* London: Weidenfeld & Nicolson, 1984.

Keegan, John. *The Second World War.* London: Hutchinson, 1969.

Kennedy, Joseph. *Hostages to Fortune: The Letters of Joseph P. Kennedy.* Ed. Amanda Smith. New York: Viking, 2000.

Ketchum, Richard M. *The Borrowed Years, 1938–1941.* New York: Random House, 1989.

Kimball, Warren F., ed. *Churchill and Roosevelt: The Complete Correspondence*. Princeton, N.J.: Princeton University Press, 1984.

King, Cecil. *With Malice Towards None: The War Diaries of Cecil H. King*. Ed. William Armstrong. London: Sidgwick and Jackson, 1970.

Kops, Bernard. *The World Is a Wedding*. London: MacGibbon & Kee, 1963.

Lamberton, John. *American Visions of Europe*. Cambridge: Cambridge University Press, 1994.

Lampe, David. *The Last Ditch*. London: Cassell, 1968.

Langer, William L., and S. Everett Gleason. *The Challenge to Isolation 1937–1940*. New York: Harper & Row, 1952.

Lash, Joseph. *Eleanor and Franklin: The Story of Their Relationship*. New York: W. W. Norton, 1971.

———. *Roosevelt and Churchill 1939–1941: The Partnership That Saved the West*. New York: W. W. Norton, 1976.

Last, Nella. *Nella Last's War: A Mother's Diary*. Ed. Richard Broad and Suzie Fleming. London: Falling Walls Press, 1981.

Lee, Raymond. *The London Journal of General Raymond E. Lee, 1940–1941*. London: Hutchinson, 1972.

Leigh, Michael. *Mobilizing Consent: Public Opinion and American Foreign Policy, 1937-1947*. Westport, Conn.: Greenwood Press, 1976.

Lewin, Ronald. *Ultra Goes to War*. London: Hutchinson, 1978.

Lewis, Peter. *A People's War*. London: Methuen, 1986.

Loewenheim, Francis L., Harold D. Langley, and Manfred Jonas, eds. *Roosevelt and Churchill: Their Secret Wartime Correspondence*. New York: Saturday Review Press, 1975.

Longmate, Norman. *The Real Dad's Army: The Story of the Home Guard*. London: Hutchinson, 1974.

Lubell, Samuel. *The Future of American Politics*. New York: Harper Brothers, 1952.

Lukacs, John. *The Last European War, September 1939/December 1941*. London: Routledge & Kegan Paul, 1976.

———. *Five Days in London, May 1940*. New Haven: Yale University Press, 2000.

Mahl, Thomas A. *Desperate Deception: British Covert Operations in the United States 1939–44*. Washington, D.C.: Brassey's, 1998.

Manchester, William. *The Glory and the Dream: A Narrative History of America 1932–72*. London: Michael Joseph, 1975.

Marcus, Sheldon. *Father Coughlin: The Tumultuous Life of the Priest of the Little Flower*. Boston: Little, Brown, 1973.

Mayhew, Patrick, ed. *One Family's War*. London: Hutchinson, 1985.

McDonough, Frank. *Neville Chamberlain: Appeasement and the British Road to War*. Manchester: Manchester University Press, 1992.

McKenna, Marian C. *Borah*. Ann Arbor: University of Michigan Press, 1961.

Middleton, Drew. *The Sky Suspended*. New York: Longman, Green, 1960.

Miller, Arthur. *Timebends: A Life*. New York: Penguin, 1995.

Milligan, Spike. *Adolf Hitler: My Part in His Downfall*. London: Michael Joseph, 1971.

Moffat, Jay Pierrepont. *The Moffat Papers: Selections from the Diplomatic Papers of J. Pierrepont Moffat 1919–1943.* Cambridge, Mass.: Harvard University Press, 1956.

Monnet, Jean. *Memoirs.* Trans. Richard Mayne. London: Collins, 1978.

Morgan, Ted. *FDR: A Biography.* New York: Simon and Schuster, 1995.

Morgenthau, Henry Jr. *Years of Urgency, 1938–1941.* Ed. John Morton Blum. Boston: Houghton Mifflin, 1965.

* Morison, Samuel Eliot. *History of U.S. Naval Operations in World War II,* vol. 1: *The Battle of the Atlantic, September 1939–May 1943.* Washington, D.C.: U.S. Navy.

Muggeridge, Malcolm. *The Thirties: 1930–40 in Great Britain.* London: Collins, 1967.

Neal, Steve. *Dark Horse: A Biography of Wendell Willkie.* Lawrence: University of Kansas Press, 1984.

Nel, Elizabeth. *Mr. Churchill's Secretary.* London: Hodder & Stoughton, 1958.

Nicolson, Harold. *Diaries and Letters 1940–1945.* London: Weidenfeld & Nicolson, 1966.

Niven, David. *The Moon's a Balloon.* New York: Putnam, 1971.

Nixon, Barbara. *Raiders Overhead.* London: Lindsay Drummond, 1943.

Osgood, Robert Endicott. *Ideals and Self-Interest in American Foreign Relations.* Chicago: University of Chicago Press, 1953.

Page, Geoffrey. *Tale of a Guinea Pig.* London: Pelham, 1981.

Parmet, Herbert S., and Marie B. Hecht. *Never Again: A President Runs for a Third Term.* New York: Macmillan, 1968.

Pelling, Henry. *Winston Churchill.* London: Macmillan, 1974.

Perry, Colin. *A Boy in the Blitz: A 1940 Diary.* London: Corgi, 1974.

Pogue, Forrest G. *George C. Marshall: Ordeal and Hope.* New York: Viking Press, 1963.

Reynaud, Paul. *In the Thick of the Fight.* Trans. James Lambert. London: Cassell, 1955.

Reynolds, David. *The Creation of the Anglo-American Alliance, 1937–1941.* London: Europa, 1981.

Reynolds, Quentin. *By Quentin Reynolds: An Autobiography.* New York: McGraw-Hill, 1963.

* Richards, Denis, and Hilary Saunders. *The Royal Air Force 1939–1945.* London: HMSO, 1974.

Richardson, Maurice. *London's Burning.* London: Robert Hall, 1941.

Roberts, Andrew. *The Holy Fox: A Biography of Lord Halifax.* London: Weidenfeld & Nicolson, 1991.

————. *Eminent Churchillians.* London: Weidenfeld & Nicolson, 1994.

Robertson, Ben. *I Saw England.* New York: Alfred A. Knopf, 1941.

Robertson, Esmonde M., ed. *The Origins of the Second World War.* London: Macmillan, 1961.

Roosevelt, Eleanor. *This I Remember.* Westport, Conn.: Greenwood Press, 1975.

Roosevelt, Elliott, ed. *The Personal Letters of Franklin D. Roosevelt,* vol. 3: *1928–1945.* New York: Duell, Sloan and Pearce, 1947.

* Roskill, Stephen. *The War at Sea,* vol. 2: *Battle of the Atlantic.* London: HMSO, 1954.

Rovere, Richard. *The American Establishment and Other Reports.* New York: Harcourt, Brace & World, 1946.

Sackville-West, Vita. *Country Notes in Wartime.* London: Hogarth Press, 1940.

Sayers, W. C. Berwick. *Croydon in the Second World War.* Croydon, Surrey: Croydon Corporation, 1950.

Schimanski, Stefan, and Henry Treece, eds. *Leaves in the Storm: A Book of Diaries.* London: Lindsay Drummond, 1947.

Schlesinger, Arthur Jr. *A Life in the Twentieth Century.* Boston: Houghton Mifflin, 2001.

Schneider, James C. *Should America Go to War: The Debate over Foreign Policy in Chicago, 1939–1941.* Chapel Hill: University of North Carolina Press, 1989.

Schoonmaker, Nancy, and Doris Fielding. *We Testify.* New York: Reid, Smith, and Dunnell, 1941.

Shakespeare, Geoffrey. *Let Candles Be Brought.* London: Macdonald, 1949.

Sheean, Vincent. *Between the Thunder and the Sun.* New York: Random House, 1943.

Shephard, Ben. *A War of Nerves: Soldiers and Psychiatrists 1914–1994.* London: Jonathan Cape, 2000.

Sherwood, Robert. *Roosevelt and Hopkins: An Intimate History.* New York: Harper Brothers, 1948.

Shirer, William. *The Rise and Fall of the Third Reich.* London: Secker and Warburg, 1960.

Shogan, Robert. *Hard Bargain.* New York: Scribners, 1995.

Skidelsky, Robert. *John Maynard Keynes,* vol. 3: *Fighting for Britain 1937–1946.* London: Macmillan, 2000.

Spears, Major-General Edward. *Assignment to Catastrophe.* London: Heinemann, 1954.

Steel, Ronald. *Walter Lippmann and the American Century.* New York: Vintage Books, 1981.

Stettinius, Edward R. *Lend Lease: Weapon of Victory.* New York: Macmillan, 1944.

Stevenson, William. *A Man Called Intrepid: The Secret War.* London: Macmillan, 1976.

Stimson, Henry L., and McGeorge Bundy. *On Active Service in Peace and War.* New York: Harper & Brothers, 1947.

Strachey, John. *Post D: Some Experiences of an Air Raid Warden.* London: Gollancz, 1941.

Taylor, A. J. P. *The Origins of the Second World War.* London: Hamish Hamilton, 1961.

Terraine, John. *The Right of the Line: The Royal Air Force in the European War.* London: Hodder and Stoughton, 1985.

* Titmuss, Richard M. *Problems of Social Policy.* London: HMSO, 1950.

Tomas, Manfred. *Isolationism in America.* Ithaca, N.Y.: Cornell University Press, 1965.

Tomkins, David. *Senator Arthur H. Vandenberg: The Evolution of a Modern Republican*. East Lansing: Michigan State University Press, 1970.

Townsend, Peter. *Duel of Eagles*. London: Weidenfeld & Nicolson, 1970.

Turner, E. S. *The Phony War on the Home Front*. London: Michael Joseph, 1961.

Vandenberg, Arthur. *The Private Papers of Senator Vandenberg*. Ed. Arthur Vandenberg Jr. Boston: Houghton Mifflin, 1952.

* Watson, Mark Skinner. *The United States Army in World War Two: Chief of Staff: Prewar Plans and Preparations*. Washington, D.C.: Department of the Army, 1949.

Watt, Peter. *Hitler vs. Havering*. Aneley, Essex: Carlton Armitage Press, 1974.

West, Nigel, ed. *British Security Coordination: The Secret History of British Intelligence in the Americas 1940–1945*. London: St. Ermin's Press, 1998.

Whalen, Richard. *The Founding Father: The Story of Joseph P. Kennedy*. London: Hutchinson, 1965.

Wheeler-Bennett, John. *King George VI*. London: Macmillan, 1965.

———. *Special Relations: America in Peace and War*. London: Macmillan, 1975.

Wheeler-Bennett, John, ed. *Action This Day: Working with Churchill*. London: Macmillan, 1968.

Willis, John. *Churchill's Few: The Battle of Britain Remembered*. London: Michael Joseph, 1975.

Wilz, John E. *From Isolation to War 1931–41*. New York: Crowell, 1968.

Winks, Robin W. *Cloak and Gown: Scholars in the Secret War, 1939–61*. New Haven: Yale University Press, 1957.

Winterbotham, Frederick. *The Ultra Secret*. London: Weidenfeld and Nicolson, 1941.

Woon, Basil. *Hell Came to London*. London: Peter Davies, 1941.

Ziegler, Philip. *London at War 1939–1945*. London: Sinclair-Stevenson, 1995.

INDEX